NICHO

WATERWAYS GUIDE 4

Four Counties & the Welsh Canals

Collins

Also available:

Collins NICHOLSON

Waterways guides and map

1 **Grand Union, Oxford & the South East**

2 **Severn, Avon & Birmingham**

3 **Birmingham & the Heart of England**

5 **North West & the Pennines**

6 **Nottingham, York & the North East**

7 **River Thames & the Southern Waterways**

Inland Waterways Map of Great Britain

Published by Nicholson
An imprint of HarperCollins*Publishers*
Unit 4, Manchester Park, Tewkesbury Road,
Cheltenham, Gloucestershire GL51 9EJ

www.harpercollins.co.uk
www.bartholomewmaps.com

River Thames Guide first published by Nicholson 1969
Waterways guides 1 South, 2 Midlands and 3 North first published by Nicholson 1971
This edition first published by Nicholson and Ordnance Survey 1997
New edition published by Nicholson 2000, 2003, 2006, 2009
Reprinted 2006, 2007

Wildlife text from *Collins Complete Guide to British Wildlife* and *Collins Wild Guide*.

Researched and written by Jonathan Mosse, Judith Pile and David Lobban.
Designed by Bob Vickers.

The publishers gratefully acknowledge the assistance given by British Waterways and
their staff in the preparation of this guide.

Grateful thanks is also due to the Environment Agency
and members of the Inland Waterways Association.

All photographs reproduced by kind permission of Derek Pratt Photography, apart from:
Paul Huggins p122, p170; Shutterstock/ David Hughes p24, p43–60, NatalieJean (Wood sorrel) p96,
Gala_Kan (Knapweed) p96, Dave McAleavy p127, Christian Musat (Speckled wood butterfly) p152,
Steve McWilliam (Large skipper butterfly) p152, Robert Hardholt (Holly blue butterfly) p156, Jens Stolt (Orange-tip
butterfly) p156, Karel Gallas p167, Iurii Konoval (Reed warbler) p170, Marcin Perkowski (Tree sparrow) p170,
Michael Woodruff (Teasel) p170, Rainbow (Buddleia) p170, David Hughes p171–181.

Printed in China.

ISBN 978-0-00-728164-0

Wending their quiet way through town and country, the inland navigations of Britain offer boaters, walkers and cyclists a unique insight into a fascinating, but once almost lost, world. When built this was the province of the boatmen and their families, who lived a mainly itinerant lifestyle: often colourful, to our eyes picturesque but, for them, remarkably harsh. Transporting the nation's goods during the late 1700s and early 1800s, negotiating locks, traversing aqueducts and passing through long narrow tunnels, canals were the arteries of trade during the initial part of the industrial revolution.

Then the railways came: the waterways were eclipsed in a remarkably short time by a faster and more flexible transport system, and a steady decline began. In a desperate fight for survival canal tolls were cut, crews toiled for longer hours and worked the boats with their whole family living aboard. Canal companies merged, totally uneconomic waterways were abandoned, some were modernised but it was all to no avail. Large scale commercial carrying on inland waterways had reached the finale of its short life.

At the end of World War II a few enthusiasts roamed this hidden world and harboured a vision of what it could become: a living transport museum which stretched the length and breadth of the country; a place where people could spend their leisure time and, on just a few of the wider waterways, a still modestly viable transport system.

The restoration struggle began and, from modest beginnings, Britain's inland waterways are now seen as an irreplaceable part of the fabric of the nation. Long abandoned waterways, once seen as an eyesore and a danger, are recognised for the valuable contribution they make to our quality of life, and restoration schemes are integrating them back into the network. Let us hope that the country's network of inland waterways continues to be cherished and well-used, maintained and developed as we move through the 21st century.

If you would like to comment on any aspect of the guides, please write to Nicholson Waterways Guides, HarperCollins Publishers, Unit 4, Manchester Park, Tewkesbury Road, Cheltenham, Gloucestershire GL51 9EJ or email nicholson@harpercollins.co.uk.

CONTENTS

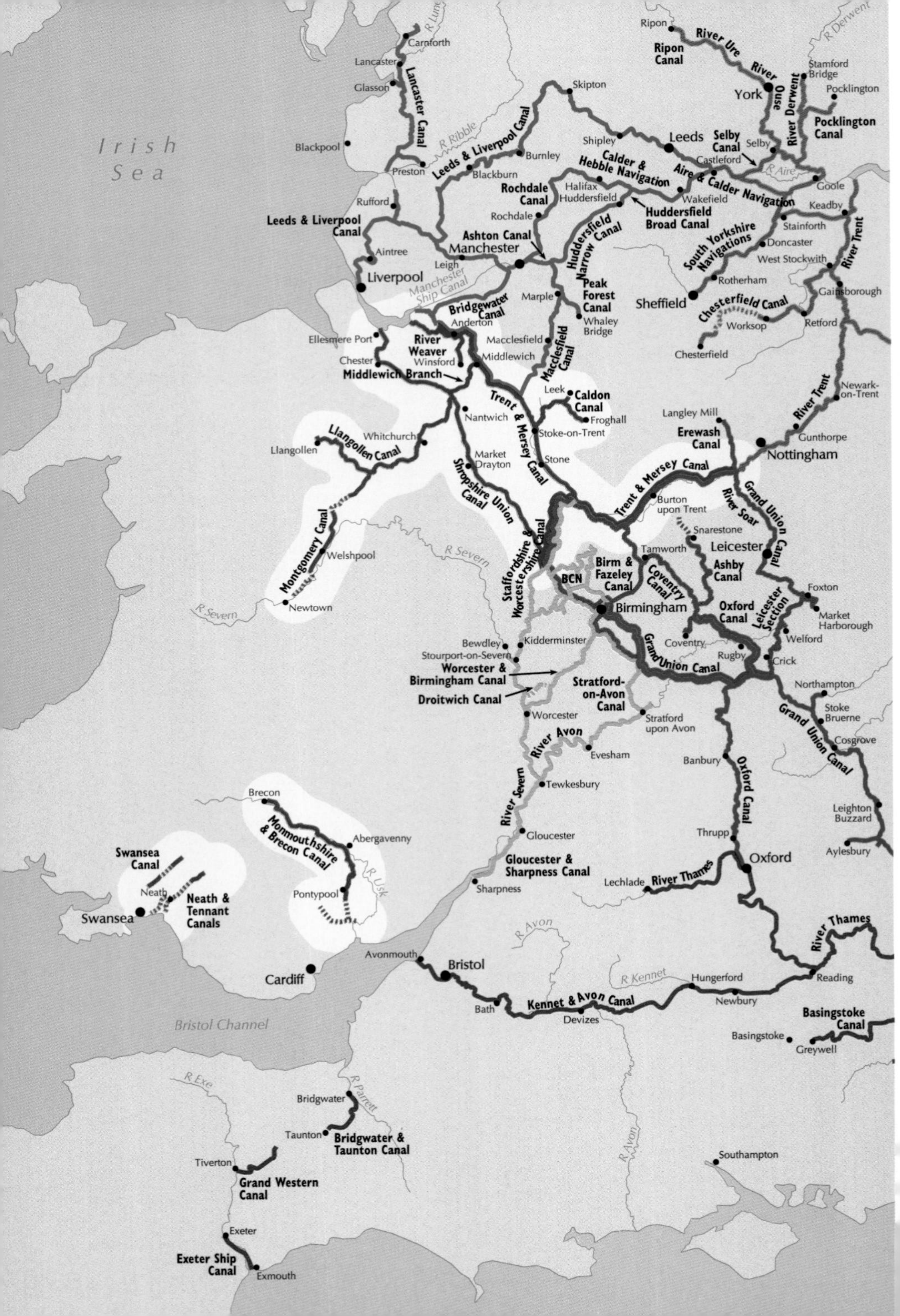

Irish Sea
Bristol Channel
Ripon
Ripon Canal
River Ure
River Ouse
York
R Derwent
River Derwent
Stamford Bridge
Pocklington
Pocklington Canal
Carnforth
R Lune
Lancaster
Glasson
Lancaster Canal
Blackpool
Preston
R Ribble
Skipton
Shipley
Leeds
Selby Canal
Selby
Castleford
R Aire
Goole
Leeds & Liverpool Canal
Burnley
Blackburn
Calder & Hebble Navigation
Aire & Calder Navigation
Rochdale Canal
Halifax
Huddersfield
Wakefield
Rochdale
Huddersfield Broad Canal
Huddersfield Narrow Canal
Keadby
Rufford
Stainforth
South Yorkshire Navigations
Doncaster
West Stockwith
River Trent
Ashton Canal
Manchester
Aintree
Leigh
Liverpool
Manchester Ship Canal
Rotherham
Gainsborough
Sheffield
Peak Forest Canal
Marple
Whaley Bridge
Bridgewater Canal
Anderton
Chesterfield Canal
Worksop
Retford
Chesterfield
Ellesmere Port
River Weaver
Winsford
Macclesfield
Macclesfield Canal
Chester
Middlewich
Middlewich Branch
Trent & Mersey Canal
Leek
Caldon Canal
Froghall
Newark-on-Trent
Nantwich
Stoke-on-Trent
Langley Mill
Erewash Canal
Gunthorpe
Nottingham
Whitchurch
Llangollen Canal
Llangollen
Market Drayton
Stone
Shropshire Union Canal
Burton upon Trent
River Soar
Grand Union Canal
Snarestone
Montgomery Canal
Welshpool
R Severn
Staffordshire & Worcestershire Canal
Tamworth
Leicester
Birm & Fazeley Canal
Coventry Canal
Ashby Canal
BCN
Newtown
Birmingham
Oxford Canal
Leicester Section
Foxton
Market Harborough
Bewdley
Kidderminster
Coventry
Welford
Stourport-on-Severn
Rugby
Crick
Worcester & Birmingham Canal
Droitwich Canal
Stratford-on-Avon Canal
Northampton
Worcester
Stratford upon Avon
Stoke Bruerne
River Avon
Evesham
Banbury
Cosgrove
Tewkesbury
River Severn
Brecon
Monmouthshire & Brecon Canal
Abergavenny
Leighton Buzzard
Gloucester
Thrupp
Aylesbury
Swansea Canal
Oxford
Gloucester & Sharpness Canal
R Usk
Neath
Neath & Tennant Canals
Pontypool
Lechlade
River Thames
Sharpness
Swansea
R Avon
Avonmouth
Bristol
Cardiff
R Kennet
Hungerford
Reading
Bath
Kennet & Avon Canal
Newbury
Devizes
Basingstoke Canal
Basingstoke
Greywell
R Exe
R Parrett
Bridgwater
Taunton
Bridgwater & Taunton Canal
Southampton
Tiverton
Grand Western Canal
Exeter
Exeter Ship Canal
Exmouth

The Waterways of Britain

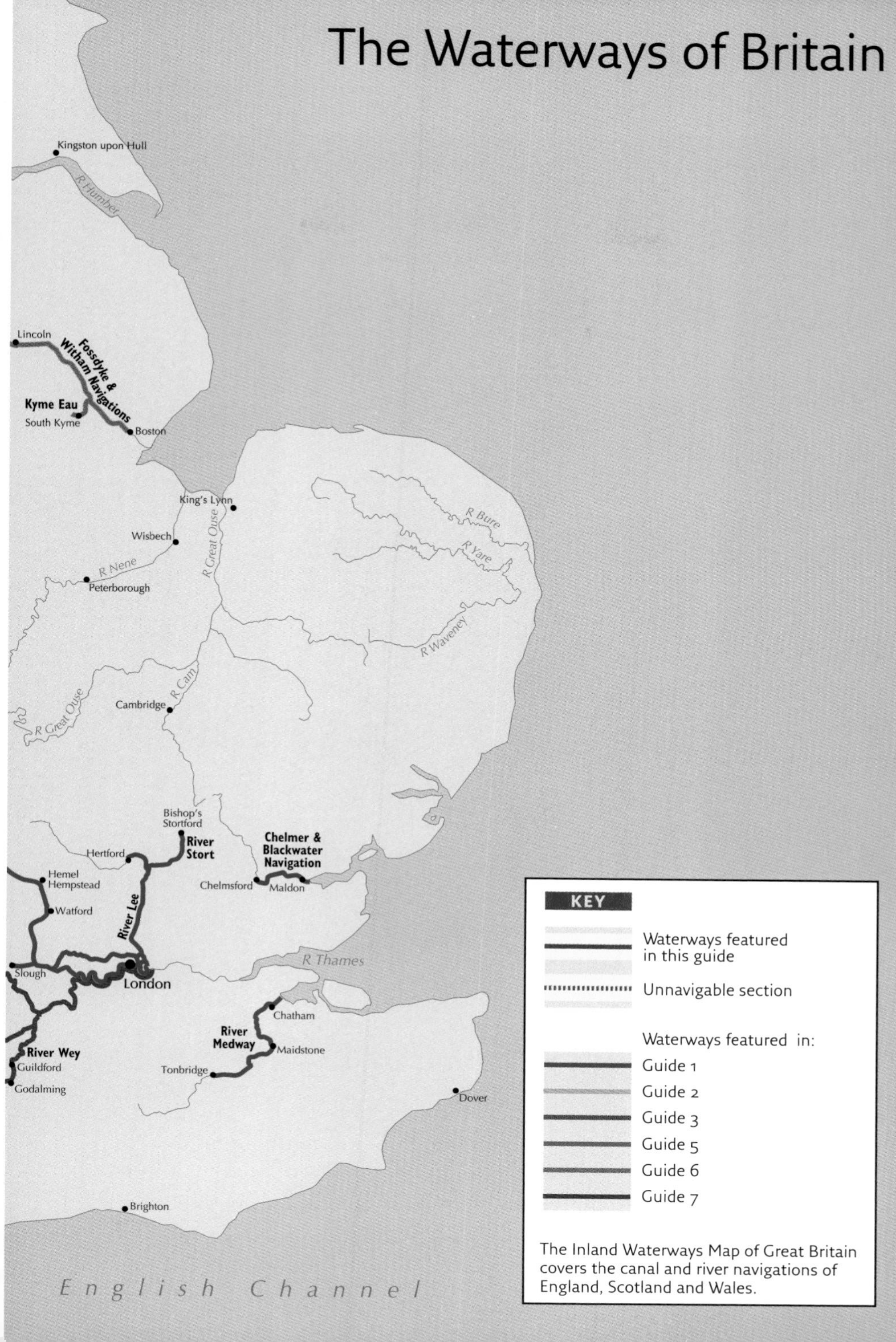

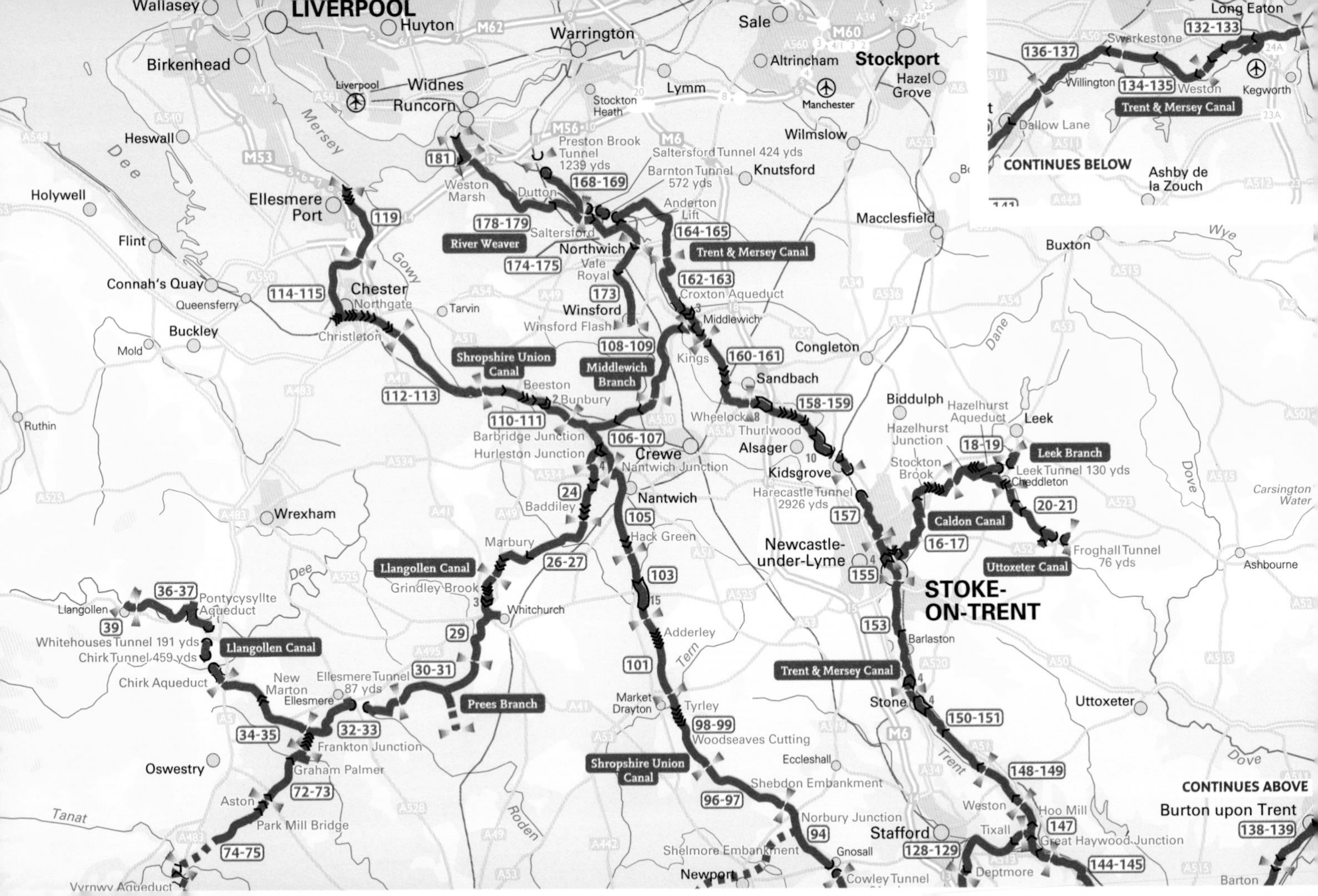

LIVERPOOL
Wallasey
Huyton
Birkenhead
Widnes
Runcorn
Warrington
Sale
Altrincham
Stockport
Hazel Grove
Manchester
Lymm
Stockton Heath
Wilmslow
Knutsford
Macclesfield
Heswall
Mersey
Dee
Holywell
Ellesmere Port
Flint
Connah's Quay
Queensferry
Buckley
Mold
Ruthin
Chester
Northgate
Christleton
Gowy
Tarvin
181
Weston Marsh
Preston Brook Tunnel 1239 yds
168-169
Dutton
178-179
River Weaver
Saltersford
Northwich
174-175
Vale Royal
173
Winsford
Winsford Flash
Saltersford Tunnel 424 yds
Barnton Tunnel 572 yds
Anderton Lift
164-165
Trent & Mersey Canal
162-163
Croxton Aqueduct
Middlewich
108-109
Middlewich Branch
Kings
160-161
Congleton
Sandbach
158-159
119
114-115
Shropshire Union Canal
112-113
Beeston
Bunbury
110-111
Barbridge Junction
Hurleston Junction
106-107
Crewe
Nantwich Junction
Wheelock
Thurlwood
Alsager
Kidsgrove
Harecastle Tunnel 2926 yds
157
Newcastle-under-Lyme
155
STOKE-ON-TRENT
Biddulph
Hazelhurst Aqueduct
Hazelhurst Junction
Leek
18-19
Leek Branch
Leek Tunnel 130 yds
Cheddleton
Stockton Brook
20-21
Caldon Canal
16-17
Uttoxeter Canal
Froghall Tunnel 76 yds
Buxton
Wye
Dane
Dove
Carsington Water
Ashbourne
Wrexham
24
Baddiley
Nantwich
105
Hack Green
Marbury
26-27
Llangollen Canal
Grindley Brook
Whitchurch
103
Adderley
Tern
101
Market Drayton
Tyrley
98-99
Woodseaves Cutting
Eccleshall
Shropshire Union Canal
96-97
Shebdon Embankment
Norbury Junction
94
Shelmore Embankment
Newport
Gnosall
Cowley Tunnel
153
Barlaston
Trent & Mersey Canal
Stone
150-151
Uttoxeter
Trent
148-149
Weston
Hoo Mill
147
Tixall
Great Haywood Junction
Stafford
128-129
Deptmore
144-145
Barton
Burton upon Trent
138-139
CONTINUES ABOVE
36-37
Llangollen
39
Pontycysyllte Aqueduct
Whitehouses Tunnel 191 yds
Chirk Tunnel 459 yds
Llangollen Canal
Chirk Aqueduct
New Marton
Ellesmere
Ellesmere Tunnel 87 yds
29
30-31
Prees Branch
32-33
34-35
Frankton Junction
Oswestry
Graham Palmer
72-73
Aston
Park Mill Bridge
74-75
Tanat
Roden
Vyrnwy Aqueduct
Long Eaton
132-133
136-137
Swarkestone
Willington
134-135
Weston
Kegworth
Trent & Mersey Canal
Dallow Lane
CONTINUES BELOW
Ashby de la Zouch

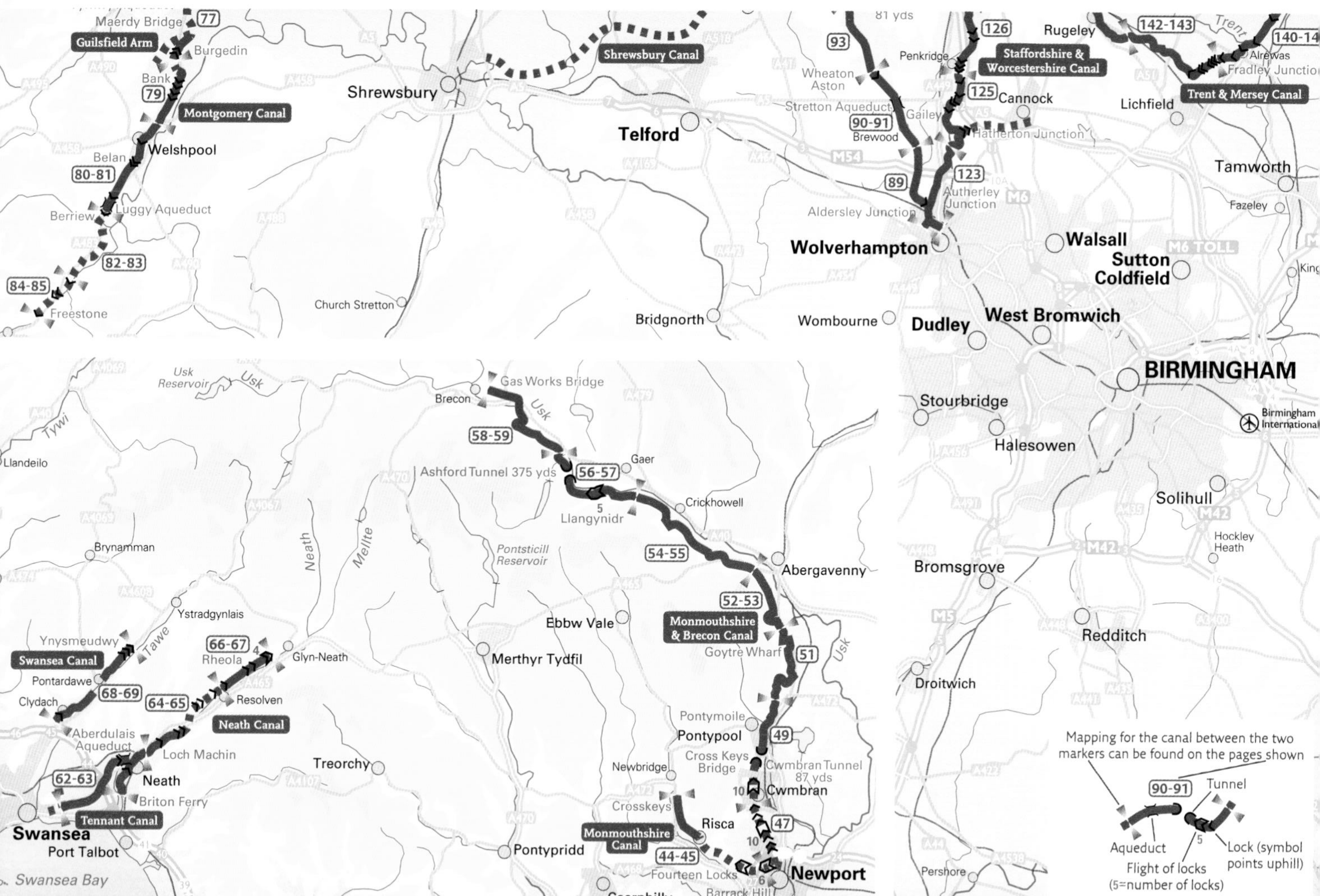

Maerdy Bridge
77
Guilsfield Arm
Burgedin
Bank
79
Montgomery Canal
Welshpool
Belan
80-81
Luggy Aqueduct
Berriew
82-83
84-85
Freestone
Shrewsbury
Shrewsbury Canal
Telford
Church Stretton
Bridgnorth
93
Wheaton Aston
Stretton Aqueduct
90-91
Brewood
Penkridge
126
Staffordshire & Worcestershire Canal
125
Cannock
Gailey
Hatherton Junction
123
89
Autherley Junction
Aldersley Junction
Wolverhampton
Wombourne
Rugeley
142-143
Trent
140-14
Alrewas
Fradley Junctio
Trent & Mersey Canal
Lichfield
Tamworth
Fazeley
Walsall
Sutton Coldfield
M6 TOLL
Dudley
West Bromwich
BIRMINGHAM
Stourbridge
Halesowen
Birmingham International
Solihull
Hockley Heath
Bromsgrove
Redditch
Droitwich
Pershore
Usk Reservoir
Usk
Tywi
Llandeilo
Brecon
Gas Works Bridge
58-59
Ashford Tunnel 375 yds
56-57
Gaer
Crickhowell
5
Llangynidr
Brynamman
Neath
Mellte
Pontsticill Reservoir
54-55
Abergavenny
52-53
Monmouthshire & Brecon Canal
Goytre Wharf
51
Ystradgynlais
Ebbw Vale
Ynysmeudwy
Tawe
Swansea Canal
66-67
Rheola
4
Glyn-Neath
Merthyr Tydfil
Pontardawe
68-69
Clydach
64-65
Resolven
Neath Canal
Aberdulais Aqueduct
Loch Machin
Treorchy
62-63
Neath
Briton Ferry
Tennant Canal
Swansea
Port Talbot
Swansea Bay
Pontypridd
Pontymoile
Pontypool
49
Cross Keys Bridge
Cwmbran Tunnel 87 yds
Newbridge
10
Cwmbran
Crosskeys
Risca
47
Monmouthshire Canal
10
44-45
Fourteen Locks
6
Newport
Caerphilly
Barrack Hill
Mapping for the canal between the two markers can be found on the pages shown
90-91
Tunnel
Aqueduct
5
Lock (symbol points uphill)
Flight of locks (5=number of locks)

GENERAL INFORMATION FOR WATERWAYS USERS

INTRODUCTION

Boaters, walkers, fishermen, cyclists and gongoozlers (on-lookers) all share in the enjoyment of our quite amazing waterway heritage. British Waterways and the Environment Agency, along with other navigation authorities, are empowered to develop, maintain and control this resource. It is to this end that a series of guides, codes, and regulations have come into existence over the years, evolving to match a burgeoning - and occasionally conflicting - demand. Set out in this section are key points as they relate to everyone wishing to enjoy the waterways.

The *Boater's Handbook* is available from all navigation authorities and can be downloaded from www.aina.org.uk. It contains a complete range of safety information, boat-handling know-how, warning symbols and illustrations.

BRITISH WATERWAYS

British Waterways (BW) cares for 2,200 miles of the country's canals and rivers. *The Waterways Code* gives advice and guidance to visitors on how to enjoy the inland waterways safely. It, and the *Boater's Handbook*, are available from the Customer Service Centre or from www.waterscape.com/downloads. BW Customer Service Centre is staffed Mon–Fri, 08.00–18.00, Sat 09.00–13.00. The helpful staff will answer general enquiries and provide information about boat licensing, boating holidays and activities on the waterways. They can be contacted on 0845 6715530; enquiries@britishwaterways.co.uk; British Waterways Customer Service Centre, 64 Clarendon Road, Watford WD17 1DA. Visit www.waterscape.com for up-to-date information on almost every aspect of the inland waterways, from news and events to moorings.

Emergency Helpline Available from BW outside normal office hours on weekdays and throughout weekends. For emergency help, or to report something dangerous, such as serious damage to structures or water escaping, call 0800 47 999 47.

ENVIRONMENT AGENCY

The Environment Agency (EA) manages around 600 miles of the country's rivers. For general enquiries or to obtain a copy of the *Boater's Handbook*, contact EA Customer Services on 08708 506 506; enquiries@environment-agency.gov.uk. To find out about their work nationally (or to download a copy of the *Handbook)* and for lots of other useful information, visit www.environment-agency.gov.uk.

Incident Hotline The EA maintain an Incident Hotline. To report damage or danger to the natural environment, damage to structures or water escaping, telephone 0800 80 70 60.

LICENSING - BOATS

The majority of the navigations covered in the Nicholson guides are controlled by BW and are managed on a day-to-day basis by local Waterway Offices (you will find details of these in the introductions to each waterway). All craft using the inland waterways must be licenced and charges are based on the dimensions of the craft. In a few cases, these include reciprocal agreements with other waterway authorities (as indicated in the text). BW and the EA offer an optional Gold Licence which covers unlimited navigation on the waterways of both authorities. Permits for permanent mooring on BW waterways are issued by BW.

Contact the BW Boat Licensing Team on 0845 6715530; www.britishwaterways.co.uk/licenseit; British Waterways Boat Licensing, PO Box 162, Leeds LS9 1AX.

BOAT SAFETY SCHEME

BW and the EA operate the Boat Safety Scheme – boat construction standards and regular tests required by all licence holders on BW and EA waterways. A Boat Safety Certificate (for new boats, a Declaration of Conformity), is necessary to obtain a craft licence. BW also requires proof of insurance for Third Party Liability for a minimum of £1,000,000 for powered boats. The scheme is gradually being adopted by other waterway authorities. Contact details are: 01923 201278; www.boatsafetyscheme.com; Boat Safety

Scheme, 64 Clarendon Road, Watford, Herts WD17 1DA. The website offers useful advice on preventing fires and avoiding carbon monoxide poisoning.

TRAINING

The Royal Yachting Association (RYA) runs one and two day courses leading to the Inland Waters Helmsman's Certificate, specifically designed for novices and experienced boaters wishing to cruise the inland waterways. For details of RYA schools, telephone 0845 345 0384 or visit www.rya.org.uk. The practical course notes are available to buy. Contact your local boat clubs, too. The National Community Boats Association (NCBA) run courses on boat-handling and safety on the water. Telephone 0845 0510649 or visit www.national-cba.co.uk.

LICENSING - CYCLISTS

Not all towpaths are open to cyclists. Maps on www.waterscape.com show the stretches of towpath open to cyclists, and local offices can supply more information. A cycle permit is usually required. For further information and to obtain a permit, contact BW Customer Services or visit www.waterscape.com.

TOWPATHS

Few, if any, artificial cuts or canals in this country are without an intact towpath accessible to the walker at least and the Thames is the only river in the country with a designated National Trail along its path from source to sea. However, on some other river navigations, towpaths have on occasion fallen into disuse or, sometimes, been lost to erosion. The indication of a towpath in this guide does not necessarily imply a public right of way or mean that a right to cycle along it exists. Horse riding and motorcycling are forbidden on all towpaths.

INDIVIDUAL WATERWAY GUIDES

No national guide can cover the minutiae of detail concerning every waterway, and some BW Waterway Managers produce guides to specific navigations under their charge. Copies of individual guides (where available) can be obtained from the relevant BW Waterway Office or downloaded from www.waterscape.com/boatersguides. Please note that times - such as operating times of bridges and locks - do change year by year and from winter to summer.

STOPPAGES

BW and the EA both publish winter stoppage programmes which are sent out to all licence holders, boatyards and hire companies. Inevitably, emergencies occur necessitating the unexpected closure of a waterway, perhaps during the peak season. You can check for stoppages on individual waterways between specific dates on www.waterscape.com/stoppages, lockside noticeboards or by telephoning 01923 201401; for stoppages and river conditions on EA waters, visit www.environment-agency.gov.uk.

NAVIGATION AUTHORITIES AND WATERWAYS SOCIETIES

Most inland navigations are managed by BW or the EA, but there are several other navigation authorities. For details of these, contact the Association of Inland Navigation Authorities on 0113 243 3125 or visit www.aina.org.uk. The boater, conditioned perhaps by the uniformity of our national road network, should be sensitive to the need to observe different codes and operating practices.

BW is a public corporation, responsible to the Department for Environment, Food and Rural Affairs in England and Wales, and is linked with an ombudsman. BW has a comprehensive complaints procedure and a free explanatory leaflet is available from Customer Services. Problems and complaints should be addressed to the local Waterway Manager in the first instance. For more information, visit their website.

The EA is the national body, sponsored by the Department for Environment, Food and Rural Affairs, to manage the quality of air, land and water in England and Wales. For more information, visit its website.

The Inland Waterways Association (IWA) campaigns for the use, maintenance and restoration of Britain's inland waterways, through branches all over the country. For more information, contact them on 01494 783453; iwa@waterways.org.uk; www.waterways.org.uk; The Inland Waterways Association, Island House, Moor Road, Chesham HP5 1WA. Their website has a huge amount of information of interest to boaters, including comprehensive details of the many and varied waterways societies.

STARTING OUT

Extensive information and advice on booking a boating holiday is available from the Inland Waterways Association, www.visitthames.co.uk and www.waterscape.com. Please book a waterway holiday from a licensed operator – only in this way can you be sure that you have proper insurance cover, service and support during your holiday. It is illegal for private boat owners to hire out their craft. If you are hiring a holiday craft for the first time, the boatyard will brief you thoroughly. Take notes, follow their instructions and don't be afraid to ask if there is anything you do not understand. BW have produced a short DVD giving basic information on using a boat safely. Copies are available from BW Customer Services (charge).

PLACES TO VISIT ALONG THE WAY

This guide contains a wealth of information, not just about the canals and rivers and navigating on them, but also on the visitor attractions and places to eat and drink close to the waterways. Opening and closing times, and other details often change; establishments close and new ones open. If you are making special plans to eat in a particular pub, or visit a certain museum it is always advisable to check in advance.

MORE INFORMATION

An internet search will reveal many websites on the inland waterways. Those listed below are just a small sample:

National Community Boats Association is a national charity and training provider, supporting community boat projects and encouraging more people to access the inland waterways. Telephone 0845 0510649; www.national-cba.co.uk.

National Association of Boat Owners is dedicated to promoting the interests of private boaters on Britain's canals and rivers. Visit www.nabo.org.uk.

www.canalplan.org.uk is an online journey-planner and gazetteer for the inland waterways.

www.canals.com is a valuable source of information on anything related to cruising the canals, with loads of links to canal and waterways related websites.

www.saveourwaterways.org is the website of Save Our Waterways, a campaign which embraces all waterways users and is dedicated to securing the long-term future of the inland waterways.

www.ukcanals.net lists services and useful information for all waterways users.

GENERAL CRUISING NOTES

Most canals and rivers are saucer shaped, being deepest at the middle. Few canals have more than 3-4ft of water and many have much less. Keep to the centre of the channel except on bends, where the deepest water is on the outside of the bend. When you meet another boat, keep to the right, slow down and aim to miss the approaching craft by a couple of yards. If you meet a loaded commercial boat keep right out of the way and be prepared to follow his instructions. Do not assume that you should pass on the right. If you meet a boat being towed from the bank, pass it on the outside. When overtaking, keep the other boat on your right side.

Some BW and EA facilities are operated by pre-paid cards, obtainable from BW and EA regional and local waterways offices, lock keepers and boatyards. Weekend visitors should purchase cards in advance. A handcuff/anti-vandal key is commonly used on locks where vandalism is a problem. A watermate/sanitary key opens sanitary stations, waterpoints and some bridges and locks. Both keys and pre-paid cards can be obtained via BW Customer Service Centre.

Safety

Boating is a safe pastime. However, it makes sense to take simple safety precautions, particularly if you have children aboard.

- Never drink and drive a boat – it may travel slowly, but it weighs many tons.
- Be careful with naked flames and never leave the boat with the hob or oven lit. Familiarise yourself and your crew with the location and operation of the fire extinguishers.
- Never block ventilation grills. Boats are enclosed spaces and levels of carbon monoxide can build up from faulty appliances or just from using the cooker.

- Be careful along the bank and around locks. Slipping from the bank might only give you a cold-water soaking, but falling from the side of, or into a lock is more dangerous. Beware of slippery or rough ground.
- Remember that fingers and toes are precious! If a major collision is imminent, never try to fend off with your hands or feet; and always keep hands and arms inside the boat.
- Weil's disease is a particularly dangerous infection present in water which can attack the central nervous system and major organs. It is caused by bacteria entering the bloodstream through cuts and broken skin, and the eyes, nose and mouth. The flu-like symptoms occur two-four weeks after exposure. Always wash your hands thoroughly after contact with the water. Visit www.leptospirosis.org for details.

Speed

There is a general speed limit of 4 mph on most BW canals. There is no need to go any faster - the faster you go, the bigger a wave the boat creates: if your wash is breaking against the bank, causing large waves or throwing moored boats around, slow down. Slow down also when passing engineering works and anglers; when there is a lot of floating rubbish on the water (try to drift over obvious obstructions in neutral); when approaching blind corners, narrow bridges and junctions.

Mooring

Generally you may moor where you wish on BW property, as long as you are *not causing an obstruction*. Do not moor in a winding hole or junction, the approaches to a lock or tunnel, or at a water point or sanitary station. Your boat should carry metal mooring stakes, and these should be driven firmly into the ground with a mallet if there are no mooring rings. Do not stretch mooring lines across the towpath and take account of anyone who may walk past. Always consider the security of your boat when there is no one aboard. On tideways and commercial waterways it is advisable to moor only at recognised sites, and allow for any rise or fall of the tide.

Bridges

On narrow canals slow down well in advance and aim to miss one side (usually the towpath side) by about 9 inches. *Keep everyone inboard when passing under bridges and ensure there is nothing on the roof of the boat that will hit the bridge.* If a boat is coming the other way, that nearest to the bridge has priority. Take special care with moveable structures - the crew member operating the bridge should be strong and heavy enough to hold it steady as the boat passes through.

Going aground

You can sometimes go aground if the water level on a canal has dropped or you are on a particularly shallow stretch. If it does happen, try reversing *gently*, or pushing off with the boat hook. Another method is to get your crew to rock the boat from side to side using the boat hook, or move all crew to the end opposite to that which is aground. Or, have all crew leave the boat, except the helmsman, and it will often float off quite easily.

Tunnels

Again, ensure that everyone is inboard. Make sure the tunnel is clear before you enter, and use your headlight. Follow any instructions given on notice boards by the entrance.

Fuel

Hire craft usually carry fuel sufficient for the rental period.

Water

It is advisable to top up daily.

Lavatories

Hire craft usually have pump out toilets. Have these emptied *before* things become critical. Keep the receipt and your boatyard will usually reimburse you. The Green Blue, an organisation providing environmental advice for boating and watersports, has produced a series of maps locating pump out facilities within the UK. Visit www.thegreenblue.org.uk/youandyourboat for these and other advice.

Boatyards

Hire fleets are usually turned around on a Saturday, making this a bad time to call in for services.

VHF Radio

The IWA recommends that all pleasure craft navigating the larger waterways used by freight carrying vessels, or any tidal navigation, should carry marine-band VHF radio and have a qualified radio operator on board. In some cases the navigation authority requires craft to carry radio and maintain a listening watch. Two examples of this are for boats on the tidal River Ouse wishing to enter Goole Docks and the Aire & Calder Navigation, and for boats on the tidal Thames, over 45ft, navigating between Teddington Lock and Limehouse Basin. VHF radio users must have a current operator's certificate. The training is not expensive and will present no problem to the average inland waterways boater. Contact the RYA (see Training) for details.

PLANNING A CRUISE

Don't try to go too far too fast. Go slowly, don't be too ambitious, and enjoy the experience. Mileages indicated on the maps are for guidance only. A *rough* calculation of time taken to cover the ground is the lock-miles system:

Add the number of *miles* to the number of *locks* on your proposed journey, and divide the resulting figure by three. This will give you an approximate guide to the number of *hours* your travel will take.

TIDAL WATERWAYS

The typical steel narrow boat found on the inland waterways is totally unsuitable for cruising on tidal estuaries. However, the adventurous will inevitably wish to add additional 'ring cruises' to the more predictable circuits of inland Britain. Passage is possible in most estuaries if careful consideration is given to the key factors of weather conditions, tides, crew experience, the condition of the boat and its equipment and, perhaps of overriding importance, the need to take expert advice. In many cases it will be prudent to employ the skilled services of a local pilot. Within the text, where inland navigations connect with a tidal waterway, details are given of sources of advice and pilotage. It is also essential to inform your insurance company of your intention to navigate on tidal waterways as they may very well have special requirements or wish to levy an additional premium. This guide is to the inland waterways of Britain and therefore recognizes that tideways – and especially estuaries – require a different approach and many additional skills. We do not hesitate to draw the boater's attention to the appropriate source material.

LOCKS AND THEIR USE

A lock is a simple and ingenious device for transporting your craft from one water level to another. When both sets of gates are closed it may be filled or emptied using gates, or ground paddles, at the top or bottom of the lock. These are operated with a windlass.

If a lock is empty, or 'set' for you, the crew open the gates and you drive the boat in. If the lock is full of water, the crew should check first to see if any boat is waiting or coming in the other direction. If a boat is in sight, you must let them through first: do not empty or 'turn' the lock against them. This is not only discourteous, and against the rules, but wastes precious water.

In the diagrams the *plan* shows how the gates point uphill, the water pressure forcing them together. Water is flooding into the lock through the underground culverts that are operated by the ground paddles: when the lock is 'full', the top gates (on the left of the drawing) can be opened. One may imagine a boat entering, the crew closing the gates and paddles after it.

In the *elevation*, the bottom paddles have been raised (opened) so that the lock empties. A boat will, of course, float down with the water. When the lock is 'empty' the bottom gates can be opened and the descending boat can leave.

Remember that when going *up* a lock, a boat should be tied up to prevent it being thrown about by the the rush of incoming water; but when going *down* a lock, a boat should never be tied up or it will be left high and dry.

- Make safety your prime concern. *Keep a close eye on young children*.
- Always take your time, and do not leap about.
- Never open the paddles at one end without ensuring those at the other end are closed.
- Keep to the landward side of the balance beam when opening and closing gates.

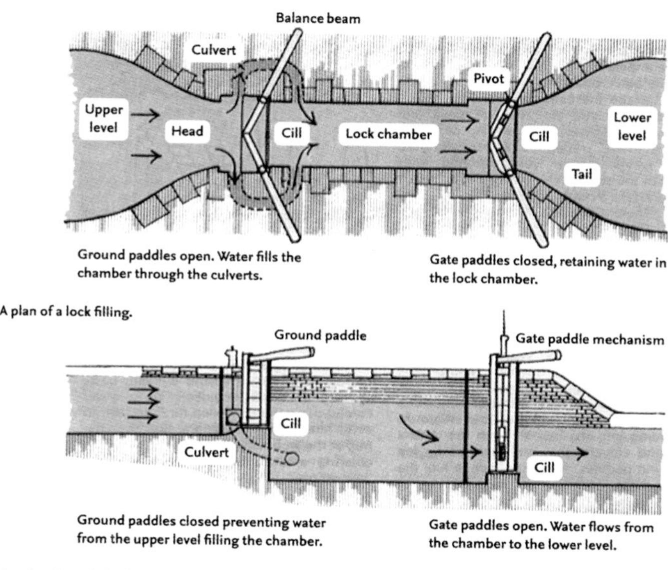

A plan of a lock filling.

An elevation of a lock emptying.

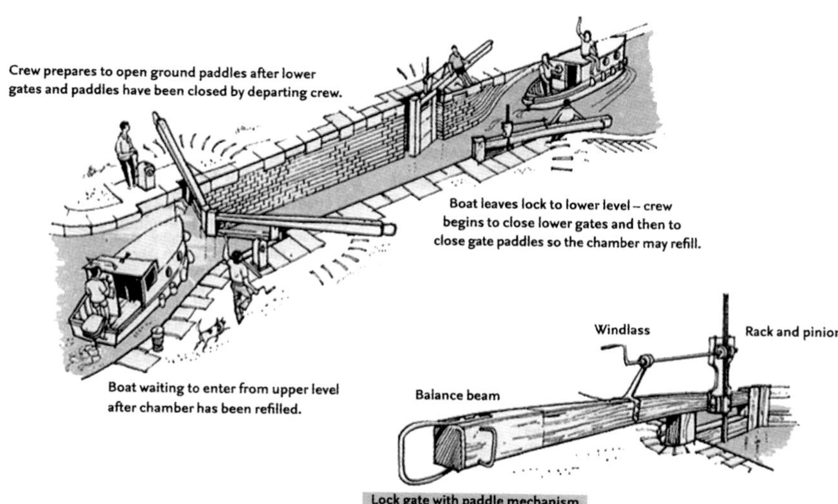

Lock gate with paddle mechanism.

- Never leave your windlass slotted onto the paddle spindle – it will be dangerous should anything slip.
- Keep your boat away from the top and bottom gates to prevent it getting caught on the gate or the lock cill.
- Never drop the paddles – always wind them down.
- Be wary of fierce *top gate* paddles, especially in wide locks. Operate them slowly, and close them if there is *any* adverse effect.
- Always follow the navigation authority's instructions, where given on notices or by their staff.

Milepost on the Shropshire Union Canal (see *page 86*)

CALDON CANAL

MAXIMUM DIMENSIONS

to Consall Forge
Length: 72'
Beam: 7'
Headroom: 6' 8"

through Froghall Tunnel
Length: 72'
Beam: 6' 6"
Headroom: 4' 9"

WATERWAY UNIT MANAGER

01606 723800
enquiries.walesandbordercounties@
britishwaterways.co.uk

MILEAGE

ETRURIA TOP LOCK
(Trent & Mersey Canal) *to:*
Hanley: 2 miles
Foxley: 4½ miles
Stockton Brook Summit: 7 miles
Hazelhurst Junction (Leek Branch): 9½ miles
LEEK TERMINUS: 12¼ miles
Cheddleton Flint Mill: 11½ miles
FROGHALL TERMINUS: 17 miles

Locks: 17

The Caldon Canal – or, more correctly, the Caldon Branch of the Trent & Mersey Canal – was designed as an outlet on to the canal system for the Caldon limestone quarries near Froghall. It was opened as a single branch to Froghall in 1779, tramways being constructed to bring the vast quantities of limestone down from Caldon Low quarries a couple of miles to the east. Froghall soon became a very busy terminus. Eighteen years later the Caldon's owners, the Trent & Mersey Canal Company, decided to build a secondary branch from the Caldon Canal to Leek, the main purpose of the extension being to use the line as a feeder from their new reservoir at Rudyard. The fact that the feeders from Rudyard had to enter the summit level of the canal, and the later advent of the railway, brought about significant changes in the layout of the canal between Endon and Hazelhurst, and resulted in the fascinating cross-over junction that exists at Denford today. In 1811 yet another branch was completed from Froghall down the Churnet Valley for 13 miles to Uttoxeter. This branch had a short life, and in 1845 a railway line was built, much of the track using the canal bed. However the first lock and the basin at Froghall have now, remarkably, been restored.

The limestone from Froghall remained the chief commodity carried on the Caldon Canal for years. With its 17 locks and roundabout route the Caldon must have been an obvious target for railway competitors. However, the canal, with the rest of the Trent & Mersey, was owned by the North Staffordshire Railway from the 1840s onward, so presumably the NSR saw no point in competing against itself. But at the beginning of the 20th C a new railway line was eventually opened and inevitably canal traffic slumped badly. The canal then gradually deteriorated until it became more or less unnavigable in the early 1960s. The Caldon Canal Society led the struggle to re-open the route; public interest grew and local authorities recognised the great recreational potential of this beautiful waterway for the thousands of people living in the nearby Potteries. Much was achieved in the way of essential works by the British Waterways Board (now BW) and volunteer efforts. The canal was finally fully reopened to navigation in 1974, representing a splendid addition to the cruising network, and a much-needed linear park for the Potteries.

Hanley

The Caldon Branch of the Trent & Mersey Canal leaves the main line at Etruria Top Lock, and soon passes a statue of James Brindley, builder of the Trent & Mersey. The first two locks up are combined in a staircase – the only one in north Staffordshire. Planet Lock is soon reached, with shops and pubs close by: this is followed by Hanley Park, where there are good moorings. There is a grocery store a short distance west of Milton bridge. Engine Lock follows, so called because a huge beam engine used to be housed nearby to pump water from mine workings. By bridge 21 the unnavigable feeder from Knypersley Reservoir joins the waterway. Five locks at Stockton Brook raise the canal up to the summit level 484ft above the sea.

Hanley
Staffs. All services (laundrette 1/4 mile N of bridge 4). Hanley is one of the six towns that were amalgamated in 1910 to form the present Stoke-on-Trent.
The Potteries Walk north from bridge 8 along Lichfield Street. Ahead is The Potteries Shopping Centre: to the left, off Potteries Way, you will find:
The Potteries Museum & Art Gallery Bethesda Street, Hanley ST1 3DW (01782 232323; www.stoke.gov.uk), where the history of the area is brought to life. There is also a fine ceramics collection. *Open Mar–Oct, Mon–Sat 10.00–17.00, Sun 14.00–17.00; Nov–Feb, Mon–Sat 10.00–16.00, Sun 13.00–16.00.* Free.
Bridgewater Factory Shop Lichfield Street, Hanley ST1 3EJ (01782 201328; www.emmabridgewater.co.uk). Just north of bridge 8. Earthenware, textiles and gifts. *Open Mon–Sat 09.30–17.30, Sun 11.00–16.00.*
Etruria Industrial Museum Lower Bedford Street, Etruria, Hanley ST4 7AF (01782 233144; www.stoke.gov.uk). At the junction with the Trent & Mersey. This is a Victorian steam-powered potter's miller's works, built in 1857 and which ground bone, flint and stone for the pottery industry, until closure in 1972. It has now been restored as part of an industrial

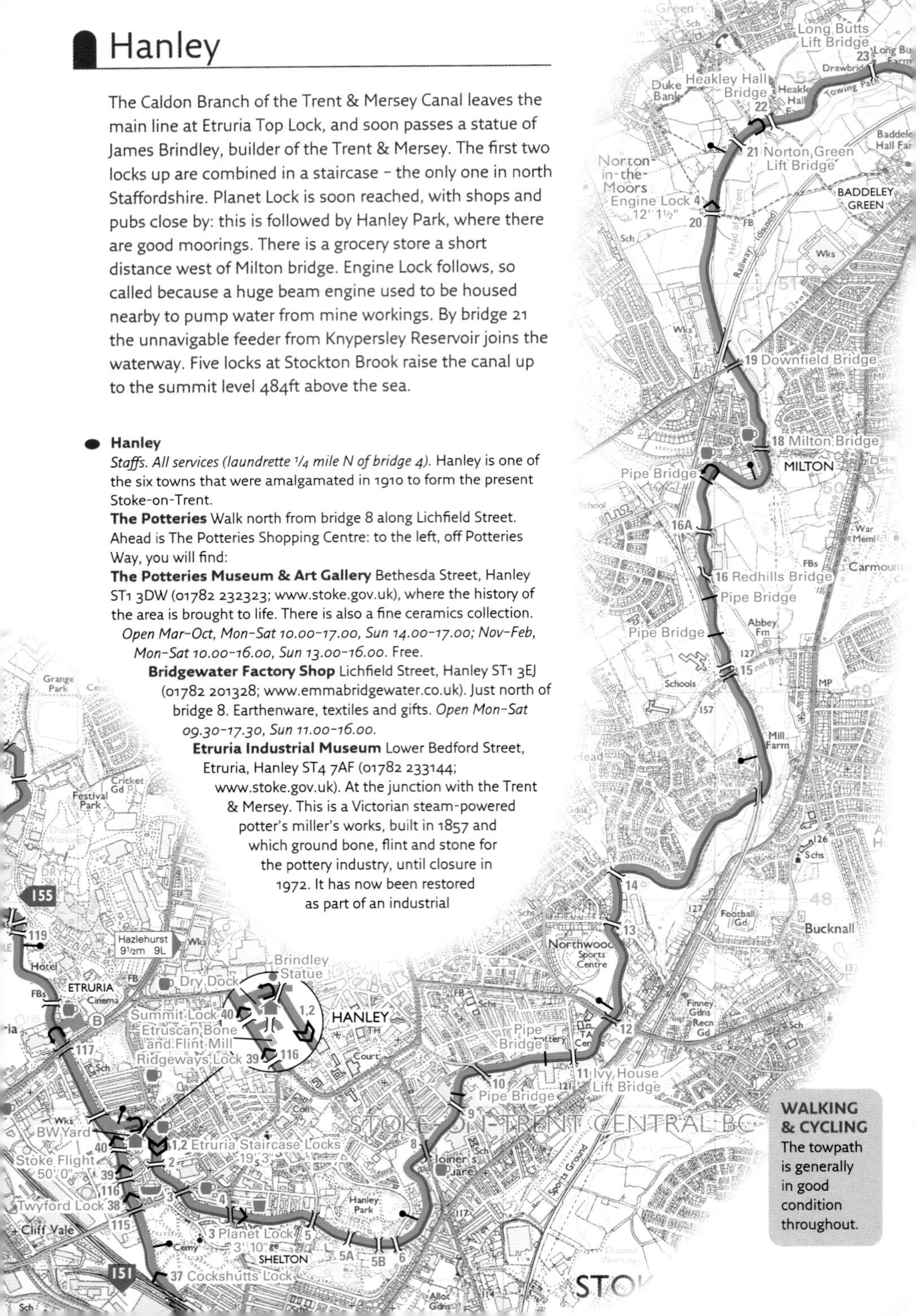

WALKING & CYCLING
The towpath is generally in good condition throughout.

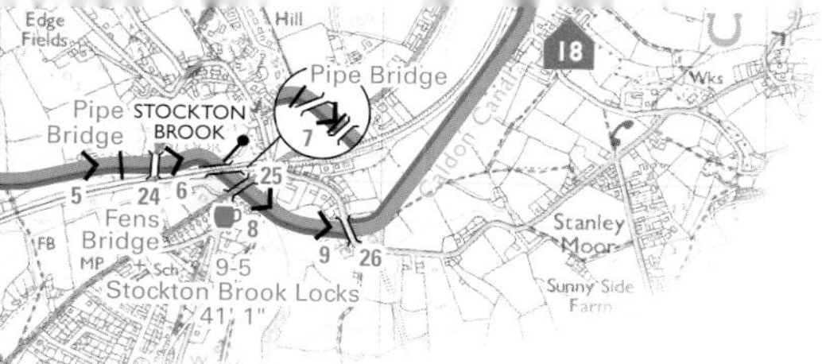

NAVIGATIONAL NOTES

1 Some of the bridges on this section are very low.
2 Your BW key will be required for Ivy House Lift Bridge, 11.
3 You will need a windlass to operate bridges 21 and 23.

complex incorporating a blacksmith's shop with working steam-powered machinery. Originally the raw materials and ground products were transported by canal, and present-day canal travellers will find plenty of moorings available. *Open Wed-Sun 12.00–16.30, but telephone to check.* Guided tours. Also operate special steam days *first weekend each month Apr–Dec*, telephone 01782 287557 for details. Voluntary charge. Tearoom and shop.

Tourist Information Centre Potteries Shopping Centre, Quadrant Road, Hanley ST1 1RZ (01782 236000; www.visitstoke.co.uk). The visitor map of the Potteries, available here, gives full details of factory visits.

- **Milton**
Staffs. PO, tel, stores, fish & chips. A little village on the side of a hill, forming an agreeable background to the canal.

- **Knypersley Reservoir**
3½ miles north of Milton. This feeds water to the Trent & Mersey summit level via the Caldon Canal. Surrounded by woodland, the reservoir is a delightful setting for picnicking and rambling.

- **Stockton Brook**
Staffs. PO, tel, stores. A pleasant and useful place. The five locks have a charming position, with views back down the headwaters of the River Trent. There is a splendid Victorian waterworks at the bottom of the flight, and pubs and shops near the middle.

Boatyards

Ⓑ **BW Etruria Yard** at junction with Trent & Mersey Canal (01606 723800). Pump out, toilet, showers (including facilities for disabled people).

Pubs and Restaurants

The Bird in Hand 79 Etruria Vale Road, Etruria, Hanley ST1 4BP (01782 205048). A canal enthusiasts' pub serving real ale. Bar meals and snacks are served *L and E*. Children welcome, and there is a garden.

Baillies Bar 46 Shelton New Road, Shelton ST1 4PG (01782 283097). Real ale is served, and food is available *L and E*. Children welcome *until 18.00*.

The Old Corner Cupboard 198 Caldon Road, opposite Hanley Park, Shelton ST4 2DY (01782 418911). Real ale and bar meals available *L and E*. Children welcome *until 19.00*.

The Norfolk Norfolk Street, overlooking Planet Lock, Shelton ST1 4PB (01782 214577). Real ale. Meals available *L Mon–Fri*. Children welcome *until 20.00*. Mooring above and below the lock.

Oggy's 227 Lichfield Street, Hanley ST1 3EJ (01782 281271). South of bridge 8. There is still an air-raid shelter under this pub. Real ales. Food available *L and E*. Children welcome *until 18.00*. Garden. Regular entertainment at *weekends*.

The Miners Arms 125 Millrise Road, Milton ST2 7DW (01782 545510). By bridge 18. Real ale is served, and children are welcome. Garden.

The Millrace 21 Maunders Road, Milton ST2 7DU (01782 543338). By bridge 18. A handsome and friendly pub with coal fires and a traditional bar area. Real ales and bar snacks *L Fri, Sat and Sun*. Children welcome, and there is a garden. Karaoke, quizzes. *Shops nearby.*

The Foaming Quart 5 Frobisher Street, Norton Green ST6 8PD (01782 538321). Real ale and bar food *L and E*. Children welcome, and there is outside seating where dogs are welcome.

The Foxley Foxley Lane, Stockton Brook ST2 7DU (01782 545525). Canalside at the junction with the former Foxley Arm, this is a traditional red-brick real ale pub. Bar meals served *L and E*. Children welcome. Garden.

The Hollybush Harvester Stanley Road, Stockton Brook ST9 9NL (01782 502116). Real ale. Restaurant and bar meals available *L and E*. Children welcome, and there is outside seating.

The Rose & Crown Stanley Road, Stockton Brook ST9 9LL (01782 503893). Real ale and food *L and E*. Children welcome at mealtimes. Garden.

The Sportsman 1074 New Leek Road, Stockton Brook ST9 9NT (01782 504536). Close to Railway Lock. Cosy traditional pub, where skittles are played. Children welcome. Real ale. There is a patio.

Greenway Hall Golf Club Stanley Road, Stockton Brook ST9 9LJ 01782 503158. Food *daily L and E (not Mon E)*.

Hazelhurst Locks

The canal passes to the east of Endon, negotiates the bend after Doles Bridge and approaches Hazelhurst, where it divides. The Fine Feathers farm shop near bridge 28 is a friendly place, offering coffee and teas, some supplies, and rare breeds. There are shops 250yds north west of bridge 28, and the Spar here sells BW swipe cards, needed for the facilities at Park Lane Bridge (there are showers, pump out and a laundrette here). At the junction the main line falls through three locks before turning east and then south to accompany the River Churnet, while the Leek Branch bears right along the hillside, then crosses the main line on a large aqueduct. The railway and Endon Brook are also traversed by aqueducts and eventually the Leek Branch reaches the north side of this narrow valley. Just north of bridge 6 there is a tiny post office/store. A lagoon provides an opportunity to wind just before the 130yd Leek Tunnel. Beyond the tunnel, only a short stretch of canal remains, ending on a fine stone aqueduct over the River Churnet. The last half-mile beyond the Churnet Aqueduct and straight along to Leek Basin has been filled in.
The main line to Froghall drops through three attractive and isolated locks and passes under the Leek Branch. The canal and the River Churnet now run side by side for the next 7 miles. Cheddleton Flint Mill makes a fascinating stop, with *nb Vienna* moored at the wharf.

Stanley
Staffs. Tel, stores. A stiff climb southwards from bridge 28 leads to this brown-stone hill village. There are fine views across the valley to Endon.

Endon
Staffs. Tel, stores, garage, bank. The real village is up the hill just north of the main road and is attractive, especially during its traditional well-dressing ceremony. Endon Basin, built in 1917, and once a canal/railway interchange basin, is now used as the Stoke-on-Trent Boat Club's base.

Leek
Staffs. All services. A silk town, which also gained a reputation for its dyeing and embroidery: the Leek School of Embroidery was founded here in the 1870s by Lady Wardle, and it was about this time that William Morris, founder of the Arts & Crafts Movement, worked here. James Brindley, the canal engineer, started in business as a millwright in Leek. The parish church of St Edward (ST13 6AB) is 14th-C, but was restored in 1856, and the chancel rebuilt in 1867.

Brindley Mill Macclesfield Road, Leek ST13 8HA (01538 483741; www.brindleymill.net). Turn right along the A53 from the canal feeder, and then follow signs to Macclesfield. The mill will be seen about 2 miles from the canal terminus, by the A523. It is a working corn mill built in 1752 by James Brindley, the canal engineer, when he worked as a millwright in Leek. Milling display, Brindley's notebook and theodolite. *Open Easter–Sept, weekends and B Hols, also Jul–Aug, Mon–Wed 14.00–17.00.* Modest charge.

Tourist Information Centre 1 Market Place, Leek ST13 5HH (01538 483741; www.staffsmoorlands.gov.uk).

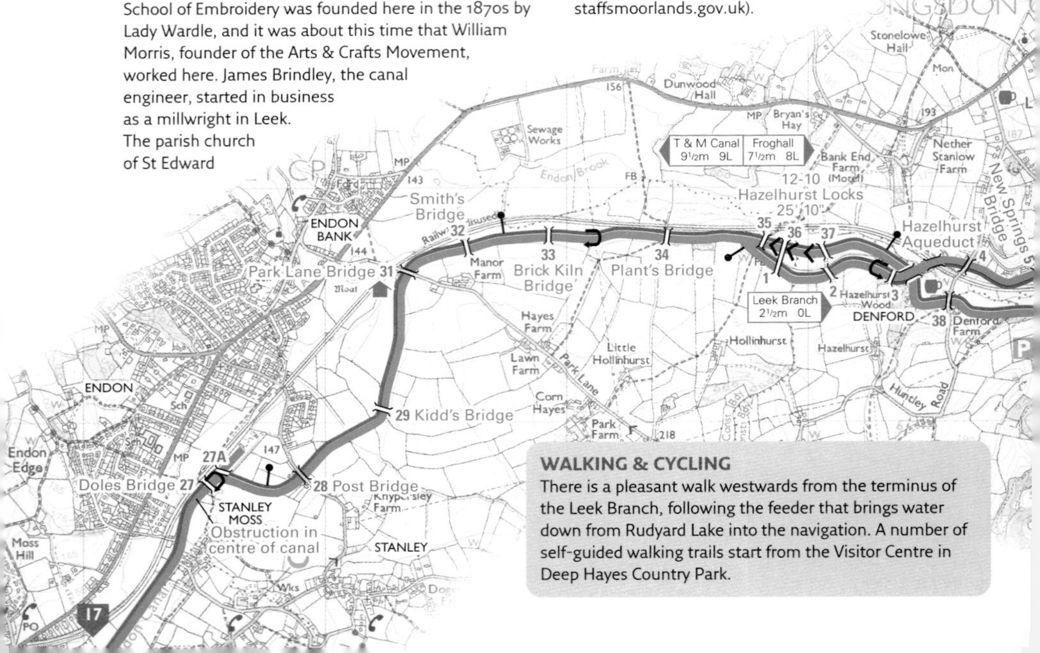

WALKING & CYCLING

There is a pleasant walk westwards from the terminus of the Leek Branch, following the feeder that brings water down from Rudyard Lake into the navigation. A number of self-guided walking trails start from the Visitor Centre in Deep Hayes Country Park.

Deep Hayes Country Park Park Lane, near Cheddleton, Leek ST9 9QD (www.staffordshire.gov.uk). South east of Denford. This was once an industrial area, where coal and clay were extracted, iron was smelted and bricks were made. The pools were built in 1848 by the Potteries Waterworks Company to compensate for water taken from the River Churnet. Now it is a delightful mixture of woods and meadows. The Visitor Centre is *open summer Sat 11.00–17.00, Sun 11.00–18.00; winter weekdays 14.00–16.00 (booked only).*

● **Cheddleton**

Staffs. PO, tel, stores, garage nearby. A main road rumbles through the village, but away from this is the charming Flint Mill, by the canal. The village is grouped around the ancient stone church of St Edward the Confessor. Little of the original building remains, but some 14th-C work is worth a look.

Cheddleton Flint Mill Cheddleton ST13 7HL (01782 502907; www.people.exeter.ac.uk) superbly restored mill where you can watch two water wheels driving the flint grinding pans, in a charming and picturesque setting. Machinery collection includes a 100hp Robey steam engine and a 1770 haystack boiler. For group visits please telephone in advance. *Open Sat and Sun 10.00–16.00 and most weekdays 13.00–16.00, but telephone to check.* Free but donations welcome. The beautifully preserved *nb Vienna* is usually moored at the wharf.

Pubs and Restaurants

The Travellers Rest Tompkin Road, Stanley ST9 9LX (01782 502580). A choice of real ale, with bar meals served *L and E.* Children welcome.

The Black Horse Inn 381 Leek Road, Endon ST9 9BA (01782 502239). A friendly pub serving real ale and light snacks *L and E.* Children welcome, and there is a patio at the front.

Toby Carvery Leek Road, Endon ST9 9BE (01782 502115). Real ale, along with meals *all day.* Children welcome, and there are some seats outside.

The Holly Bush Denford Road, Denford ST13 7JT (01538 371819). Near bridge 38. Traditional 17th-C canalside pub with an open fire set in 3 acres of grounds, with children's play area. Choice of real ale, and food is available *all day, every day.* Children welcome. There is live music *every Thu,* and their Tug 'o War team have been world champions. Mooring on the main (lower) line, although access from the Leek Branch is easy enough.

The Red Lion 37 Cheadle Road, Cheddleton ST13 7HN (01538 360935). Near bridge 43. Real ale, and meals available *L and E.* Children welcome, garden with play area.

The Wheel Inn Leek Road, Longsdon ST9 9DF (01538 385012). A country pub serving real ale. Home-made meals available *L and E,* including traditional *Sun* lunch. Children welcome. Garden with large play area.

The Black Lion. Hollow Lane, Cheddleton ST13 7HP (01538 361647). Up the hill by the church south of bridge 42. Fine traditional and welcoming old country pub with log fires, next to the 13th-C church. Real ales. Food available *L and E (not Sun E).* Children are welcome *until 21.00.* The licensees are narrowboat owners.

Castro's Restaurant By the bridge, Cheddleton ST13 7HN (01538 361500) Mexican food. *Open Tue-Sun 18.00 till late.*

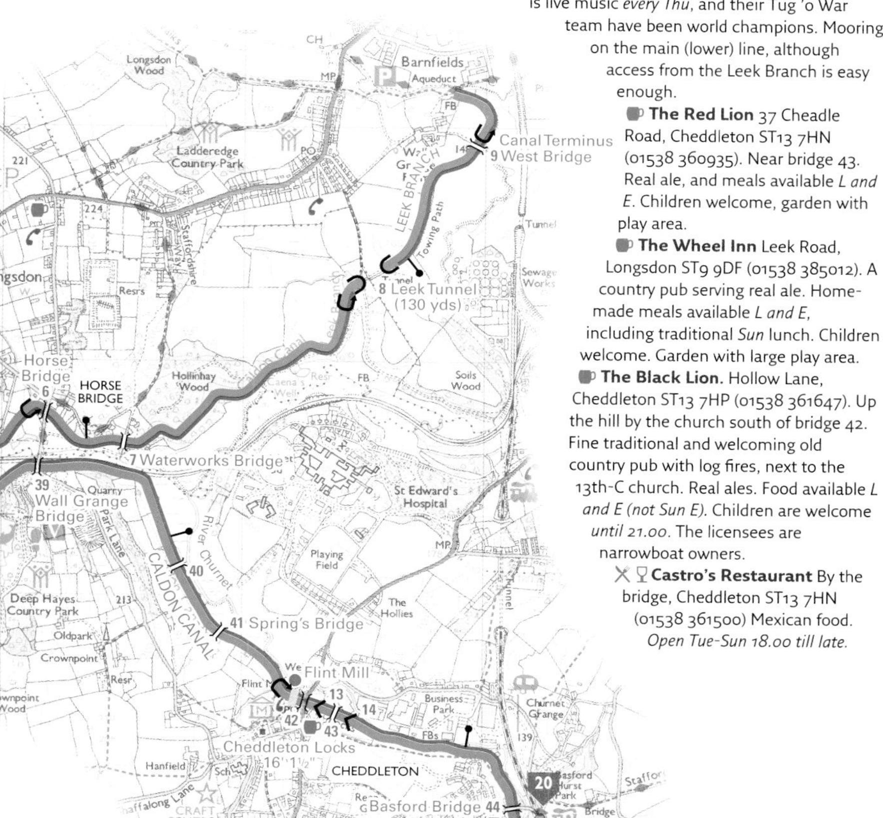

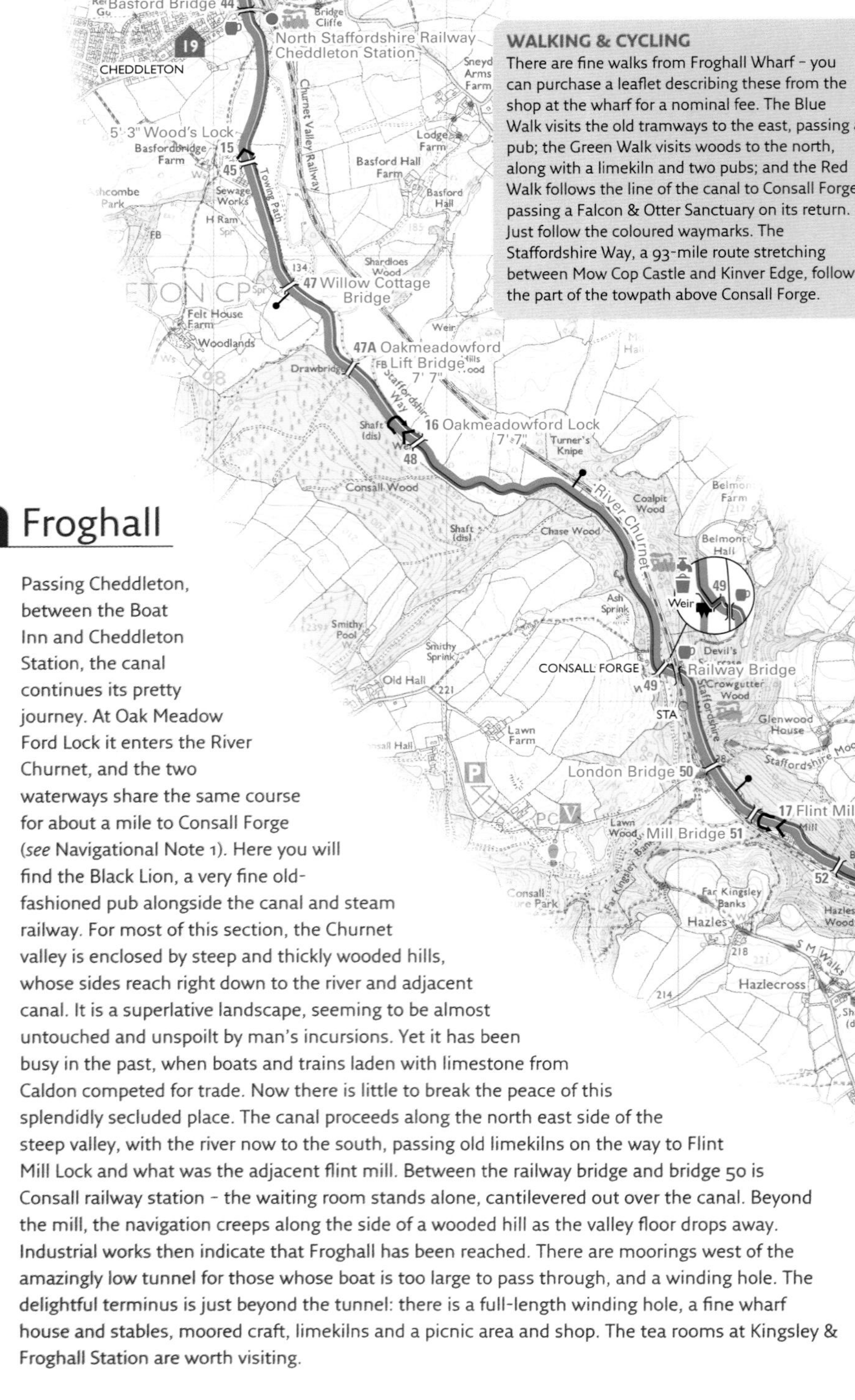

WALKING & CYCLING

There are fine walks from Froghall Wharf – you can purchase a leaflet describing these from the shop at the wharf for a nominal fee. The Blue Walk visits the old tramways to the east, passing a pub; the Green Walk visits woods to the north, along with a limekiln and two pubs; and the Red Walk follows the line of the canal to Consall Forge, passing a Falcon & Otter Sanctuary on its return. Just follow the coloured waymarks. The Staffordshire Way, a 93-mile route stretching between Mow Cop Castle and Kinver Edge, follows the part of the towpath above Consall Forge.

Froghall

Passing Cheddleton, between the Boat Inn and Cheddleton Station, the canal continues its pretty journey. At Oak Meadow Ford Lock it enters the River Churnet, and the two waterways share the same course for about a mile to Consall Forge (*see* Navigational Note 1). Here you will find the Black Lion, a very fine old-fashioned pub alongside the canal and steam railway. For most of this section, the Churnet valley is enclosed by steep and thickly wooded hills, whose sides reach right down to the river and adjacent canal. It is a superlative landscape, seeming to be almost untouched and unspoilt by man's incursions. Yet it has been busy in the past, when boats and trains laden with limestone from Caldon competed for trade. Now there is little to break the peace of this splendidly secluded place. The canal proceeds along the north east side of the steep valley, with the river now to the south, passing old limekilns on the way to Flint Mill Lock and what was the adjacent flint mill. Between the railway bridge and bridge 50 is Consall railway station – the waiting room stands alone, cantilevered out over the canal. Beyond the mill, the navigation creeps along the side of a wooded hill as the valley floor drops away. Industrial works then indicate that Froghall has been reached. There are moorings west of the amazingly low tunnel for those whose boat is too large to pass through, and a winding hole. The delightful terminus is just beyond the tunnel: there is a full-length winding hole, a fine wharf house and stables, moored craft, limekilns and a picnic area and shop. The tea rooms at Kingsley & Froghall Station are worth visiting.

NAVIGATIONAL NOTES

1 The canal and river share a common course between Oak Meadow Ford Lock and Consall Forge, and care should be exercised along here.
2 Boats which cannot pass through Froghall Tunnel can wind just before it. Maximum dimensions for the tunnel are 4ft 4in high and 5ft 6in wide at the cabin-top.
3 The last mile or so of canal is very narrow – in places two boats cannot pass.

Consall Forge Pottery Mill Cottages, Consall Forge, Wetley Rocks ST9 0AJ (01538 266625; www.4ateapot.co.uk). Hand-thrown craft pottery and ceramics, especially teapots. *Open daily 10.00– 17.00 but telephone to confirm before visiting.*

Churnet Valley Railway Cheddleton Station ST13 7EE (01538 360522; www.churnetvalleyrailway.co.uk). Near bridge 44. Opened by the North Staffordshire Railway in 1849 between North Rode and Macclesfield, the last stretch of this line closed in 1988. Purchased by enthusiasts, a steam-operated passenger train first ran again in August 1996. This superb line, which retains a 1950s ambience, is open from Leekbrook Junction through Cheddleton and Consall to Kingsley & Froghall, and there is a buffet service on every train. They also run 'Steam & Canal Trips'. *Steam trains Easter–Sep, Sun; also Aug, Wed and all B Hol Mons. Diesels Jul–Aug, Sat.* Plus other special events.

● **Froghall**
Staffs. PO, tel. Tucked away in the heart of unspoilt Staffordshire, Froghall has been an outpost of industry ever since the advent of the canal fostered the growth of the Caldon lime quarries a few miles east. The limestone was carted down the hills by a plate tramway, built originally in 1758 and the first to use iron rails. This was re-aligned in 1785, and finally re-built in 1800. A cable railway replaced the whole lot in 1849. The limestone was transhipped into waiting canal boats at Froghall Basin, serviced by the locomotives *Frog, Toad* and *Bobs*. Production ceased in 1920, with much of the trade being lost to the railways. Just west of the final bridge by the basin was the junction with the old canal arm to Uttoxeter (explaining the distances on the milestones): this locked down to the Churnet valley. The branch was closed in 1847 and the railway now occupies most of the canal's course, although much of the canal bed can still be traced. Froghall these days comprises almost entirely of factories and dwellings associated with Thomas Bolton's copper works.

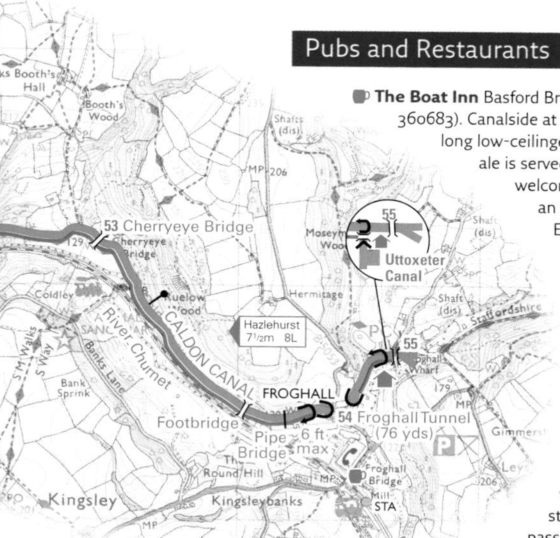

Pubs and Restaurants

The Boat Inn Basford Bridge Lane, Cheddleton ST13 7EQ (01538 360683). Canalside at bridge 44. Handsome stone-built pub, with long low-ceilinged bar decorated with plates and jugs. Real ale is served, bar meals are available *L and E*. Children welcome. Outside seating on the patio. There is an old bridge across the River Churnet nearby. Entertainment some weekends, *telephone for details*.

The Black Lion Consall Forge, Wetley Rocks ST9 0AJ (01782 550294). A splendid canalside pub of outstanding isolation, in a beautiful setting and with a fine garden. Although the interior is quite straightforward, there is an open fire and real ale to enjoy, along with meals *L and E (not Thu Oct–Mar)* which include specials. B & B. A popular place in summer, when it is busy with boaters, back packers and families. The steam trains of the Churnet Valley Railway pass within 20yds of the front door.

The Railway Inn Froghall ST10 2DN (01538 754782). Handy for the steam railway. Real ale. Bar meals *L and E*. Garden. B & B.

BOAT TRIPS

Froghall Wharf Boat Trips Froghall Wharf, Foxton Road, Froghall ST10 2HJ (01538 266486). Operate public trips in *nb Birdswood* from *May B Hol–Sep, Thu 10.30 and Sun 11.30 and 15.00*. Also private charter.

ZANTE
MAGNOLIA
A&M.FRANCIS
WEM

LLANGOLLEN CANAL

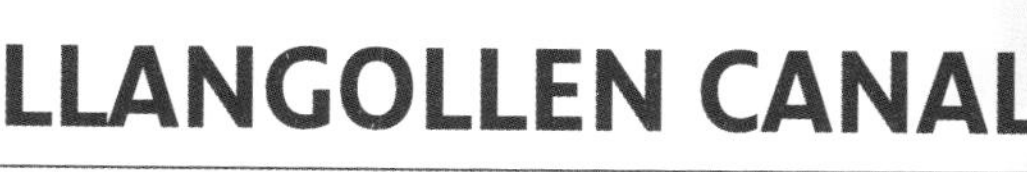

MAXIMUM DIMENSIONS

Length: 72'
Beam: 6' 10"
Headroom: 7'
Draught:
Hurleston to Pontcysyllte: 2' 3"
Pontcysyllte to Llangollen: 2'

WATERWAY UNIT MANAGER

01606 723800
enquiries.walesandbordercounties@britishwaterways.co.uk

MILEAGE

HURLESTON JUNCTION (Shropshire Union) *to:*
Frankton Junction: 29 miles
Pontcysyllte Aqueduct: 40 miles
LLANGOLLEN: 44½ miles
Llantysilio: 46 miles

Locks: 21

In 1791 a plan was published for a canal from the Mersey to the Severn, to pass through Chester, and the iron and coal fields around Ruabon, Ellesmere and Shrewsbury. There were to be branches to the limestone quarries at Llanymynech, and to the Chester Canal via Whitchurch. The new terminus on the Mersey was to be at the little fishing village of Netherpool, known after 1796 as Ellesmere Port. After extensive arguments about routes, the company received its Act in 1793. William Jessop was appointed engineer, and work began. By 1796 the Wirral line from Chester to Ellesmere Port was open, and was immediately successful, carrying goods and passengers (in express flyboats) to Liverpool. The same year, the Llanymynech Branch was completed. The company continued to expand and build inwards, but failed to make the vital connections with the Dee and the Severn; the line south to Shrewsbury never got further than Weston, and the line northwards to Chester stopped at Pontcysyllte. By 1806 the Ellesmere company had opened 68 miles of canal, which included lines from Hurleston on the Chester Canal to Plas Kynaston via Frankton, and from Chester to Ellesmere Port; there were branches to Llanymynech, Whitchurch, Prees and Ellesmere, and a navigable feeder to Llangollen; the two great aqueducts at Chirk and Pontcysyllte were complete. However, it was a totally self-contained system, its only outlet being via the old Chester Canal at Hurleston. Despite this, the Ellesmere Canal was profitable; it serviced a widespread local network, and gave an outlet to Liverpool (via the River Mersey) for the ironworks and the coalfields that were grouped at the centre of the system. This profitability was dependent upon good relations with the Chester Canal Company. An attempted take over in 1804 failed, but in 1813 the inevitable merger took place, and the Ellesmere & Chester Canal Company was formed. Today the Llangollen Canal is quite justly one of the most popular canals in the country, with fascinating architecture, spectacular aqueducts and splendid scenery. As a result it can become crowded during the summer months. Those who cruise out of the peak season, or avoid the mid-week rush to Llangollen, will have a more relaxing time. And of course you can always divert along the initial navigable section of the Montgomery Canal from Frankton Junction.

Whixall Marina (see *page 31*)

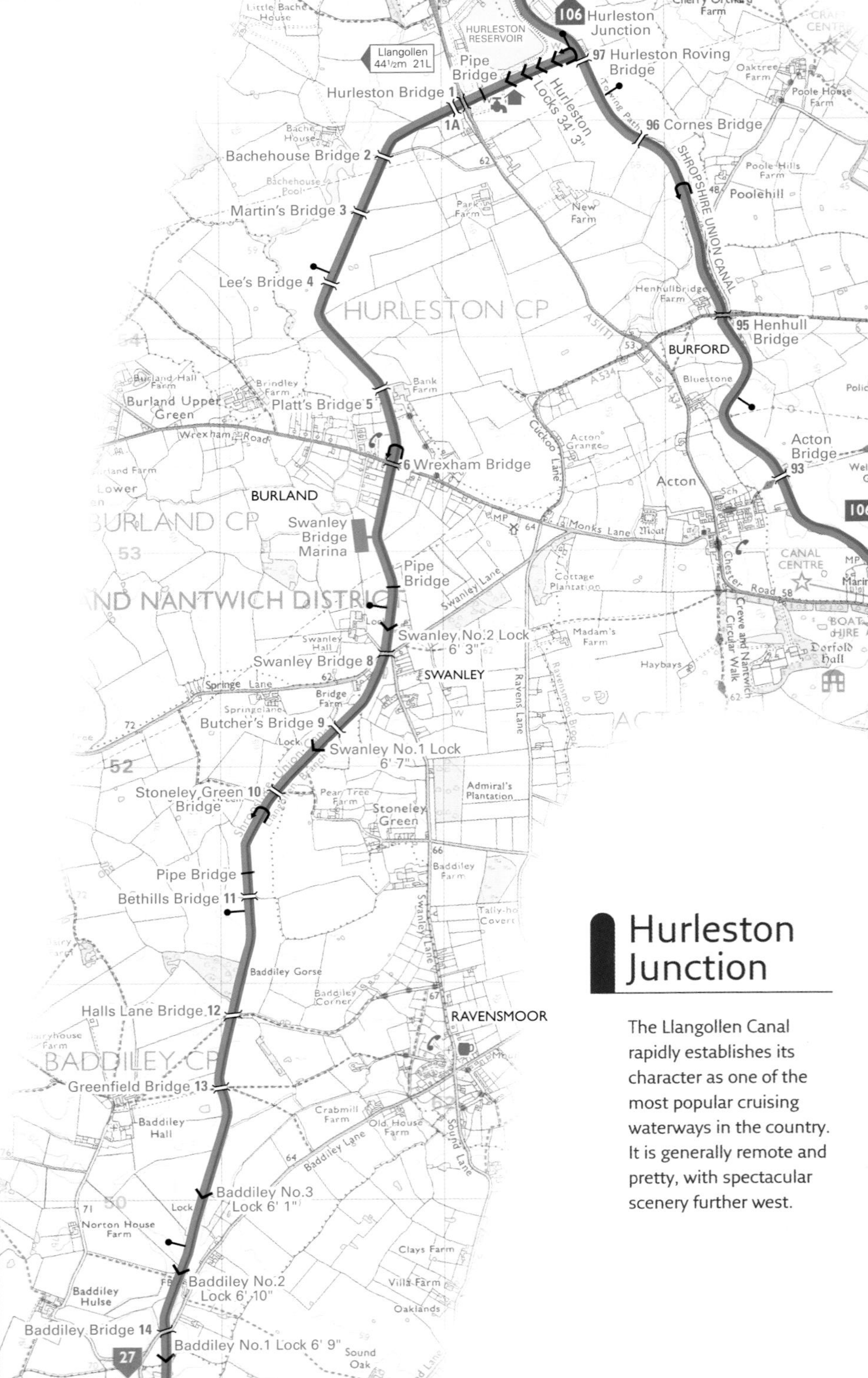

Hurleston Junction

The Llangollen Canal rapidly establishes its character as one of the most popular cruising waterways in the country. It is generally remote and pretty, with spectacular scenery further west.

Leaving Hurleston Junction, the canal immediately climbs the four tidy Hurleston Locks (note the unusual ground paddle gear on the third lock up) before running through a very shallow valley to reach Swanley Locks. A few houses, some with attractive canalside gardens, are passed before the canal enters flat, rich farmland. The next three locks encountered are at Baddiley; the tall Georgian house surrounded by trees to the west of the bottom lock is Baddiley Hall.

Pubs and Restaurants

Farmers Arms Marsh Lane, Ravensmoor CW5 8PN (01270 623522). Welcoming creeper-clad inn serving real ale and meals *L and E*. Children welcome if you are dining. Large garden. Barbecues when the weather is fine. Best access is probably from bridge 12.

NAVIGATIONAL NOTES

Water is fed into the Llangollen Canal by the River Dee at Llantysilio, so there is a noticeable flow of water from west to east, slowing your journey to Llangollen. The flow can be particularly strong at the lock tails where bypass weirs discharge – this can make the approach from below difficult unless an allowance is made.

Hurleston Reservoir CW5 6AS. With a capacity of 85,000,000 gallons, Hurleston Reservoir receives its supply, via the Llangollen Canal, from the River Dee at Llantysilio. It is used both as drinking water, and as a supply for the Shropshire Union Canal.

WALKING & CYCLING

The towpath is passable *for walkers* throughout most of its length, although there is a diversion between bridges 42 and 43. Cyclists will not find the towpath easy going, in spite of a few smooth stretches. The towpath is closed between bridges 63 and 69 due to erosion.

Boatyards

Ⓑ **Swanley Bridge Marina** Springe Lane, Swanley CW5 8NR (01270 524571; www.swanleybridgemarina.com). South of Bridge 6. **D** Pump out, overnight mooring, gas, dry dock, marine engineering, DIY facilities, coal, logs, toilets, showers, laundry, chandlery, coal and logs, frozen food for sale.

In the Brecon Beacons National Park (see *page 60*)

Wrenbury

The canal passes Wrenbury Hall, which is north west of bridge 17, and soon the first of many delightful lift bridges is encountered. Their scale seems entirely sympathetic with that of the canal and, whilst most are generally left open, those that require operation provide added interest. Wrenbury Wharf is a splendid place where there is a fine restored warehouse converted into a pub, a former mill now occupied by a boatyard, and another pub, all grouped around the push-button lift bridge. Beyond the wharf, the soft green Cheshire countryside leads to Marbury Lock: the village is a short walk to the south, along School Lane, and is well worth visiting. The tall obelisk visible to the south east is in distant Combermere Park. Leaving Marbury the waterway again enters remote and peaceful countryside before reaching Quoisley Lock, where the road briefly intrudes, and then continues towards Willeymoor Lock.

NAVIGATIONAL NOTES

A BW key is required for the lift bridge at Wrenbury.

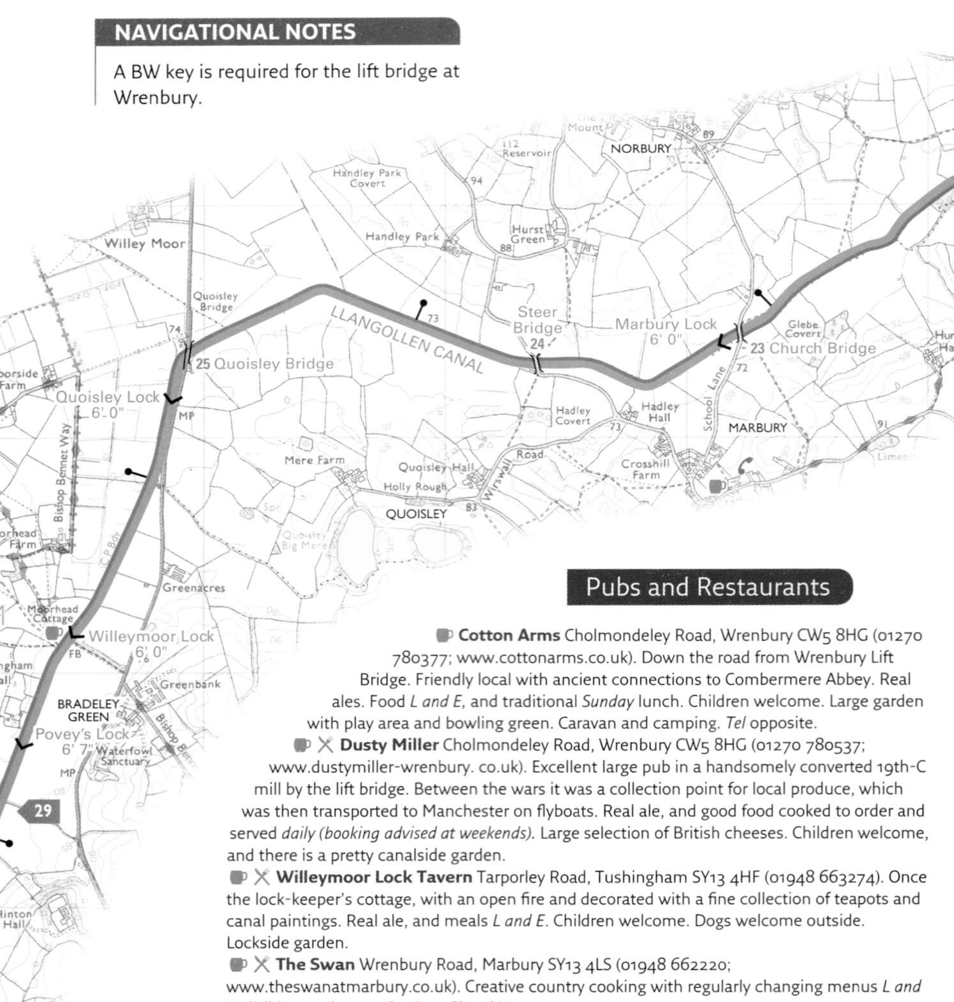

Pubs and Restaurants

Cotton Arms Cholmondeley Road, Wrenbury CW5 8HG (01270 780377; www.cottonarms.co.uk). Down the road from Wrenbury Lift Bridge. Friendly local with ancient connections to Combermere Abbey. Real ales. Food *L and E*, and traditional *Sunday* lunch. Children welcome. Large garden with play area and bowling green. Caravan and camping. *Tel* opposite.

Dusty Miller Cholmondeley Road, Wrenbury CW5 8HG (01270 780537; www.dustymiller-wrenbury. co.uk). Excellent large pub in a handsomely converted 19th-C mill by the lift bridge. Between the wars it was a collection point for local produce, which was then transported to Manchester on flyboats. Real ale, and good food cooked to order and served *daily (booking advised at weekends)*. Large selection of British cheeses. Children welcome, and there is a pretty canalside garden.

Willeymoor Lock Tavern Tarporley Road, Tushingham SY13 4HF (01948 663274). Once the lock-keeper's cottage, with an open fire and decorated with a fine collection of teapots and canal paintings. Real ale, and meals *L and E*. Children welcome. Dogs welcome outside. Lockside garden.

The Swan Wrenbury Road, Marbury SY13 4LS (01948 662220; www.theswanatmarbury.co.uk). Creative country cooking with regularly changing menus *L and E*. Children welcome. Garden. *Closed Mon.*

Boatyards

Ⓑ **Alvechurch Boat Centre** Wrenbury CW5 8HG (01270 780544; www.alvechurch.co.uk). In the old mill by bridge 20. D Pump out, gas, narrowboat hire, overnight mooring, crane, boat sales, boat and engine repairs, toilets, showers, gifts, public telephone nearby.

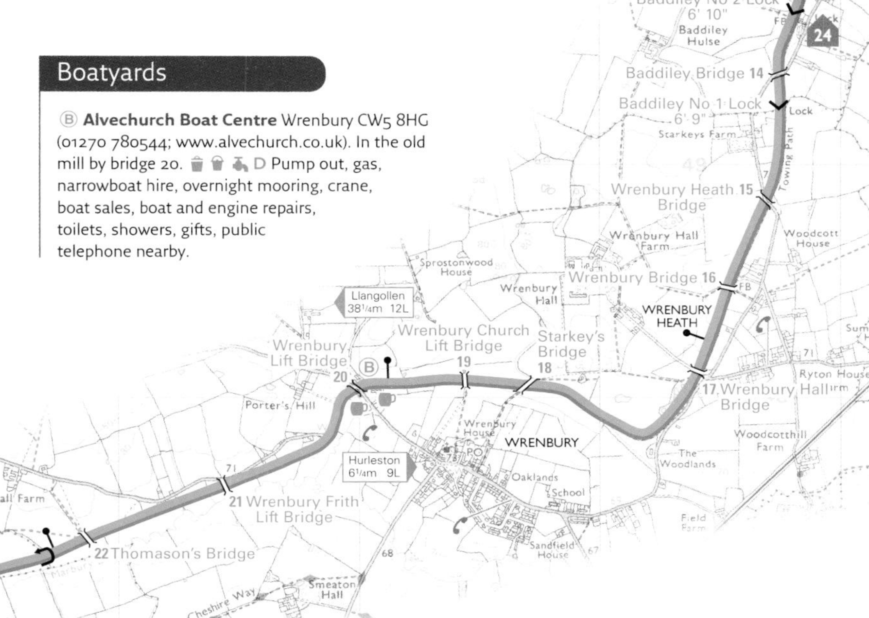

extent that an arbitrator, in 1748, allocated the south side of the church to the Cottons and the north to the Starkeys, in an effort to resolve matters. Next to the door is 'the dog-whipper's pew'. The job of the dog-whipper, later known as Beadle, was to throw out unruly dogs, and to keep dozing parishioners awake during particularly tedious sermons. The last holder of this esteemed position, Thomas Vaughan, died in 1879 and is buried by the door. Have a look in the churchyard for the most unusual cast iron grave plaques, dating from the early 1800s. These were an expression, in their time, of the very latest technology.

Wrenbury

Ches. PO, tel, stores, station, cash machine. About ¼ mile from the wharf - access can be made from the footpath by bridge 19. A quiet village recorded in the Domesday Book as Warenberie. Two miles to the south east are the remains of Combermere Abbey, established by Cistercian monks in 1133 who, in 1180, took the village church as a daughter chapel. By the church gates is the schoolmaster's cottage: this stood next door to one of the earliest parish schools in Cheshire, founded in 1605. There are some thatched magpie cottages around the green and, remarkably, the railway station still operates. It is a further ¼ mile to the south east. The line goes from Crewe to Shrewsbury.

St Margaret's Church CW5 8EY Overlooking Wrenbury village green, this large, battlemented 14th-C church is built from red Cheshire sandstone, with a late 15th-C west tower and an early 17th-C chancel and pulpit. The interior is very light and airy and contains a number of fine monuments. You will also notice the visible manifestation of an enduring dispute between two important local families: the Cottons of Combermere Abbey, and the Starkeys of Wrenbury Hall. They challenged each other's ownership of land and rights to church pews for over 400 years, to such an

Marbury

Ches. Tel. An enchanting village ½ mile south of Marbury Lock. Centred on an ancient farm, the village boasts several other fine old and timbered buildings. 'Marbury Merry Days' are held in May, and the village wakes (holidays) once featured dancing bears, and puddings.

St Michael's Church SY13 4LN This is a gem, and its setting is unrivalled: it stands on top of a small hill overlooking the beautiful Little Mere. The church was first mentioned in 1299: what remains today dates from the 15th C. When you walk around the building look out for the many gargoyles: monkeys and grotesque faces expressing both pleasure and pain. The pulpit is the second oldest in Cheshire and, dating from the 15th C, is in excellent condition. The grounds contain not just a graveyard but a charming garden: from here you will be able to see that the tower has developed an alarming tilt.

Grindley Brook

The canal continues to rise through a series of isolated locks as the valley begins to close in. At the end of a straight stretch a massive railway embankment precedes a sharp bend to the bottom of the six locks at Grindley Brook; care should be exercised on the approach to these locks, and any boats stopping should remain below the railway embankment. The first three locks are followed at the A41 bridge by three staircase locks. Anyone requiring assistance or advice should look for the friendly lock keeper, who will be there to help *Apr–Oct daily 08.30–18.30*. The canal now approaches Whitchurch: a lift bridge marks the entrance to the Whitchurch Arm, where you can moor to take the ½ mile walk to visit the town centre. After passing under the busy road bridge, and by the boatyard, the canal once again enters typically quiet and pretty countryside.

Grindley Brook
Shropshire. The famous staircase locks have made this a canal monument.
Lockside Stores Grindley Brook, Whitchurch SY13 4QH (01948 663385). Farm-cured bacon, locally produced cheese, free-range eggs, pies, pasties and a very wide range of other food and supplies. Licensed. Tea, coffee and snacks served in the **@29 Café** where there is internet access and laundry facilities. Open *Easter–Oct 08.30–18.00 Mon–Fri (09.00 weekends & B. Hols).*

Whitchurch
Shropshire. PO, tel, stores, garage, bank, station, laundrette, swimming pool. A fine town with some beautiful old houses of all periods in the centre. The streets are narrow and there is much to discover. It has its origins in Roman times as Mediolanum, 'the place in the middle of the plain', a stop on the route from Chester to Wroxeter. It was recorded in the Domesday Book as Westune, but was later to become White Church, or Whitchurch, for obvious reasons. There are lots of splendid pubs in the town, but unfortunately none near the canal. J. B. Joyce & Co was established here in 1690, and continues to make very fine tower clocks. Sir Edward German was born in St Mary's Street in 1862 – he composed *Tom Jones* and *Merrie England*. If you visit on *Friday*, look out for farmhouse Cheshire cheese in the market.

St Alkmund's Church SY13 1LB This striking church on the hill was built in 1713 by William and Richard Smith as the replacement for a late 14th-C building which 'fell ye 31 of July 1711'. This in turn had been built to succeed the Norman White Church which was attributed to William de Warren, one of William the Conqueror's lieutenants, who died in 1089. In 1862 the old pews were removed, and many human bones were found beneath them. These were re-buried and a new floor was laid. Under the porch is buried the heart of John Talbot, who was killed in 1453 at the Battle of Castille, the last of the Hundred Years Wars. He was Earl of Shrewsbury and a principal character in Shakespeare's *Henry VI*. The rector here in 1779 was Francis Henry Egerton, 8th and last Earl of Bridgewater and a successor to the third Duke, who built the Bridgewater Canal. Those who know the Oxford Canal will recognise the present church's similarity to the magnificent church of the same vintage at Banbury. It has very large windows and a stunning interior. Indeed the whole church is on a grand scale and is well worth a visit. *Open daily.*
Heritage & Tourist Information Centre 12 St Mary's Street, Whitchurch SY13 1QY (01948 664577; www.shropshiretourism.co.uk). A fascinating centre, with displays of Whitchurch clocks, plus the illustrations of Randolph Caldecott.

Pubs and Restaurants

Horse and Jockey Grindley Brook, Whitchurch SY13 4QJ (01948 662723). Large, friendly, family-run pub near the bottom lock, with a cosy woodburning stove in the lounge, and a resident ghost. Real ale. Meals available *L and E*. Play area and garden. Moorings nearby.

The Greyhound 20 Bargates, Whitchurch SY13 1LL (01948 663269). A 15th-C inn, with a resident 17th-C ghost called Freddie. Real ale, and home-cooked food *L and E*. Children welcome. B & B.

Black Bear High Street, Whitchurch SY13 1AR (01948 663624). Real ale and meals *L and E*. Friendly staff. Children welcome and there is a garden. Pool and darts.

Red Lyon 46 High Street, Whitchurch SY13 1BB (01948 667846). Wetherspoons pub serving real ale and food *all day*. Children welcome in the family lounge if you are eating. Garden. Pool table and large-screen TVs.

Old Town Hall Vaults St Mary's Street, Whitchurch SY13 1QU (01948 662251). Birthplace of Sir Edward German (1862–1936), composer of *Merrie England* and *Tom Jones*. Real ale. Home-made meals available *L and E*. Children welcome. No dogs. Patio with hop and grape vines.

White Bear 10 High Street, Whitchurch SY13 1AR (01948 662638). Attractive former coaching inn with pretty courtyard. Real ale and food available *L and E, all day in summer*. Children welcome. No dogs.

Star Hotel Watergate Street, Whitchurch SY13 1DW (01948 665879). Traditional locals' pub. Outside seating. Children and dogs welcome.

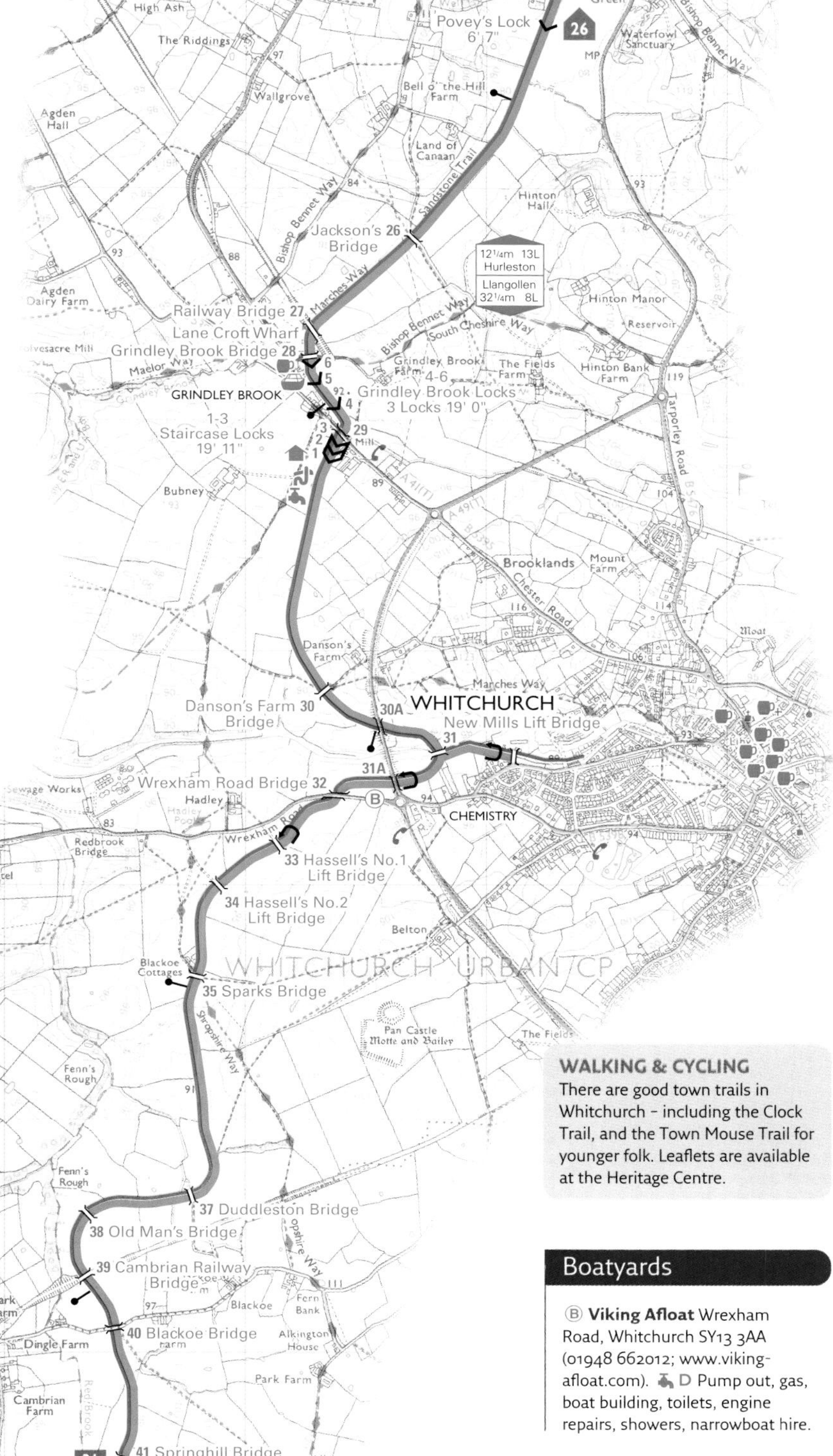

WALKING & CYCLING

There are good town trails in Whitchurch - including the Clock Trail, and the Town Mouse Trail for younger folk. Leaflets are available at the Heritage Centre.

Boatyards

Ⓑ **Viking Afloat** Wrexham Road, Whitchurch SY13 3AA (01948 662012; www.viking-afloat.com). D Pump out, gas, boat building, toilets, engine repairs, showers, narrowboat hire.

Whixall Moss

The canal now begins to traverse a very remote and underpopulated area, passing no villages for miles. At Platt Lane the navigation straightens out and is carried on an embankment across the uncharacteristically flat area of Whixall Moss. A solitary lift bridge interrupts the long straight, then there is a junction with the Prees Branch, which leads to a marina and a nature reserve. Bridge 1 on the branch is grade II listed, and has been restored (*see* Navigational Note). The main line veers off to the north west along another straight embankment, this time accompanied by woodlands, crossing the border between England and Wales. Leaving Whixall Moss, the canal passes Bettisfield and begins to wind this way and that, passing into Wales and then out again.

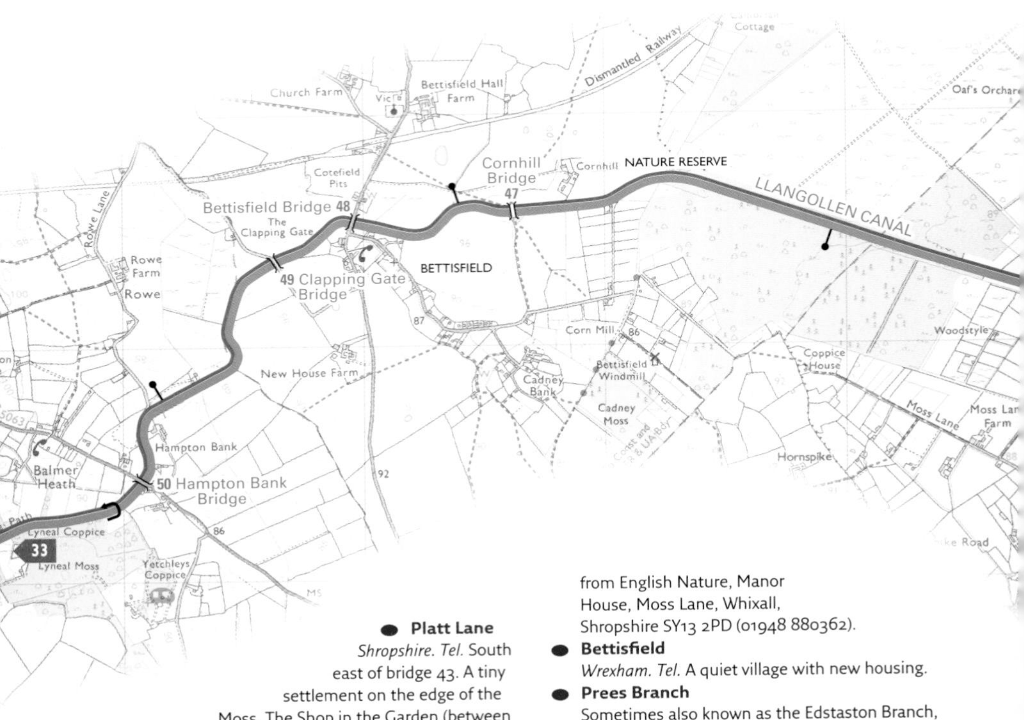

● **Platt Lane**
Shropshire. Tel. South east of bridge 43. A tiny settlement on the edge of the Moss. The Shop in the Garden (between bridges 43 and 44) sells fresh bread, cakes and a range of pies to take away.

● **Whixall Moss**
A raised bog rich in flora and insect fauna – including mosquitoes! Like other meres and bogs in the area, Whixall Moss came into existence at the end of the Ice Age, as huge blocks of ice were left behind when the remainder of the ice cap melted and drained off into what is now the Severn valley. The peat surface remains, in spite of the past cutting of the peat for garden use, and is now a SSSI, and an important site for rare insect and plant life which survive on this delicate habitat. Details from English Nature, Manor House, Moss Lane, Whixall, Shropshire SY13 2PD (01948 880362).

● **Bettisfield**
Wrexham. Tel. A quiet village with new housing.

● **Prees Branch**
Sometimes also known as the Edstaston Branch, this arm curved round to Quina Brook – it never did reach Prees. Its principal value in recent years lay in the clay pits just over a mile from the junction: the clay from here was used until a few years ago for repairing the 'puddle' in local canals. The arm had been disused for some years, but now the first ½ mile gives access to a marina constructed in the old pit. It is all very pleasant, and the canal arm has two lift bridges – one of which is a rare skewed example. Interesting plant communities exist along the unrestored section of the branch: enquiries may be made to English Nature at the number given above if you wish to explore.

WALKING & CYCLING

The Mosses Trails can be followed over Whixall Moss. Pick up a leaflet from the dispensers at bridges 44 and 45 and at the entrance to the reserve.

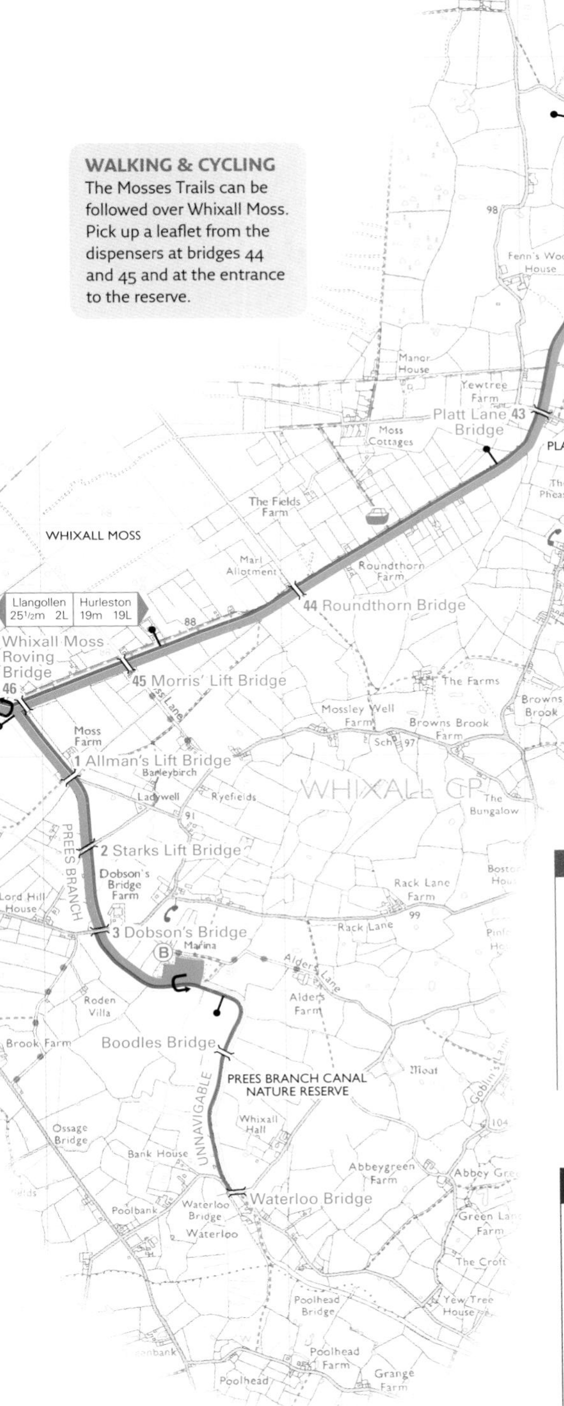

NAVIGATIONAL NOTES

Bridge 1 on the Prees Branch, having been rebuilt, now requires considerable strength to open and close, *so take great care and keep children well clear when it is up*. Leave the bridge down once you have passed through.

Boatyards

Ⓑ **Whixall Marina** Alders Lane, Whixall SY13 2QS (01948 880420; www.bwml.co.uk). At the end of the Prees Branch. D E Pump out, gas, long-term mooring, slipway, boat sales, boat and engine repairs, public telephone, toilets, showers, launderette, chandlery, groceries. *Closed Sun–Mon* in winter.

Ellesmere

Soon the open countryside gives way to the hilly wooded landscape that lies to the east of Ellesmere and contains several beautiful meres. The canal skirts first Cole Mere, which is below and mostly hidden from it by tall trees; there is a delightful timbered cottage at the west end. Then the navigation runs right beside Blake Mere: this is a charming little lake, surrounded by steep and thickly wooded hills. The canal enters the 87yd Ellesmere Tunnel and emerges into open parkland beyond. You will notice many oak trees alongside the canal around here – this is said to be the legacy of the Shropshire Union's policy of planting trees to provide the raw materials to replace their carrying fleet. Leaving Blake Mere and the tunnel, Ellesmere is soon reached, and access is via a short arm. A fine old warehouse and a small canalside crane testify to the canal trading that used to be carried on from here. The main line of the canal to Llangollen bears round sharply to the south west at the junction: the buildings here house the BW office and maintenance yard, with facilities for pleasure boats. Beech House was once the canal company's office. Beyond the yard, the country once again becomes quiet and entirely rural, while the canal's course becomes very winding. At Frankton Junction the Montgomery Canal branches south towards Newtown: it is currently navigable to Gronwyn Wharf, just beyond Maesbry Marsh, and further restoration continues.

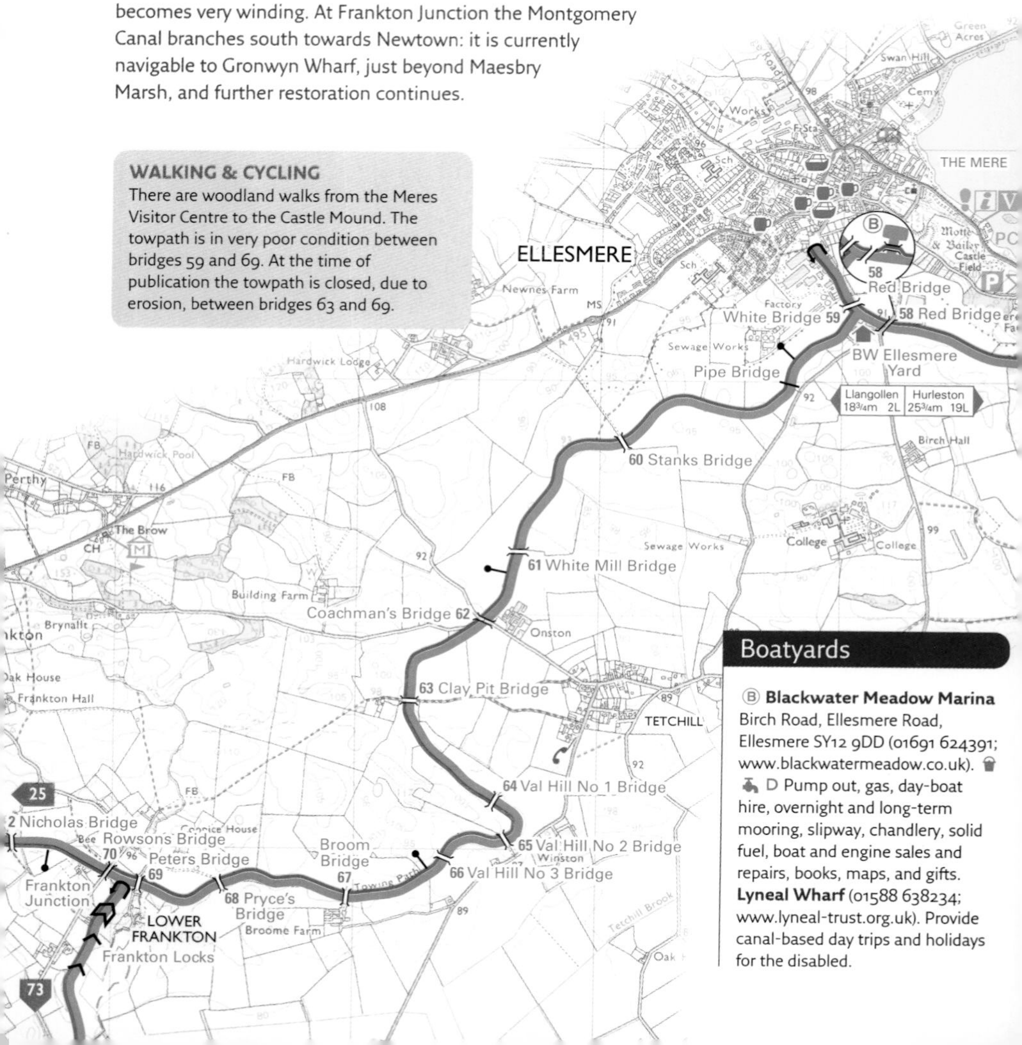

WALKING & CYCLING

There are woodland walks from the Meres Visitor Centre to the Castle Mound. The towpath is in very poor condition between bridges 59 and 69. At the time of publication the towpath is closed, due to erosion, between bridges 63 and 69.

Llangollen	Hurleston
18¾m 2L	25¾m 19L

25

73

Boatyards

Ⓑ **Blackwater Meadow Marina** Birch Road, Ellesmere Road, Ellesmere SY12 9DD (01691 624391; www.blackwatermeadow.co.uk). D Pump out, gas, day-boat hire, overnight and long-term mooring, slipway, chandlery, solid fuel, boat and engine sales and repairs, books, maps, and gifts.

Lyneal Wharf (01588 638234; www.lyneal-trust.org.uk). Provide canal-based day trips and holidays for the disabled.

- **Welshampton**
  Shropshire. Garage, pub. 1 mile west of bridge 50.
- **Tetchill**
  Shropshire. A small farming village, quiet and unpretentious.
- **Ellesmere**
  Shropshire. PO, tel, stores (excellent greengrocer with local produce), garage, laundrette, bank. This handsome and busy 18th-C market town, with its narrow winding streets, is an attractive place to visit, with good access from the canal basin. There are many tall red-brick houses and several terraces of old cottages. It takes its name from the large and beautiful mere beside it. The Meres Visitor Centre, next to the Mere, has well presented information and organised activities. *Open Easter-Oct* (01692 622981).
  St Mary's Church SY12 9EG Standing on a hill overlooking the mere, the general appearance of this large red-stone church is Victorian, belying its medieval origins. It contains a medieval chest hewn out of a solid block of oak, many fine effigies and a beautiful 15th-C font.
  Tourist Information Centre Wharf Road, Ellesmere SY12 0EJ (01691 624488) *Open 10.00-16.00; Sat 10.00-12.00 (closed Thu & Sun).*

NAVIGATIONAL NOTES

Frankton Locks on the Montgomery Canal are *open Mon-Fri 09.30-10.30 & 14.30-15.30, Sat 10.00-12.00, Sun 14.00-16.00, when the lock-keeper will assist you. Don't arrive late!*

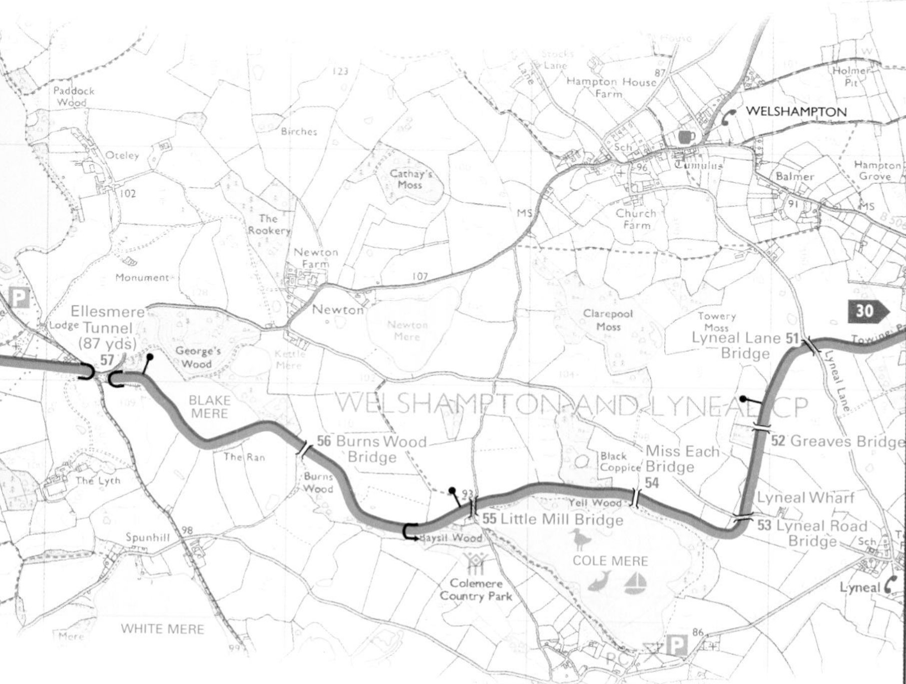

Pubs and Restaurants

The Sun Hill Bottom, Welshampton SY12 0PH (01948 710637). A quiet local serving real ale. Bar meals available *L and E.* Garden and children's play area. Caravan site.

The Black Lion Scotland Street, Ellesmere S712 0EG (01691 622418). Smart pub with a Tudor bar and beams. Restaurant and bar meals – steaks, seafood and steak & kidney pudding *L and E.* Outside seating. B & B.

The Ellesmere Hotel The High Street, Ellesmere SY12 0ES (01691 622055). Friendly town pub serving real ale along with food *L and E.* Children welcome, outside seating. B & B.

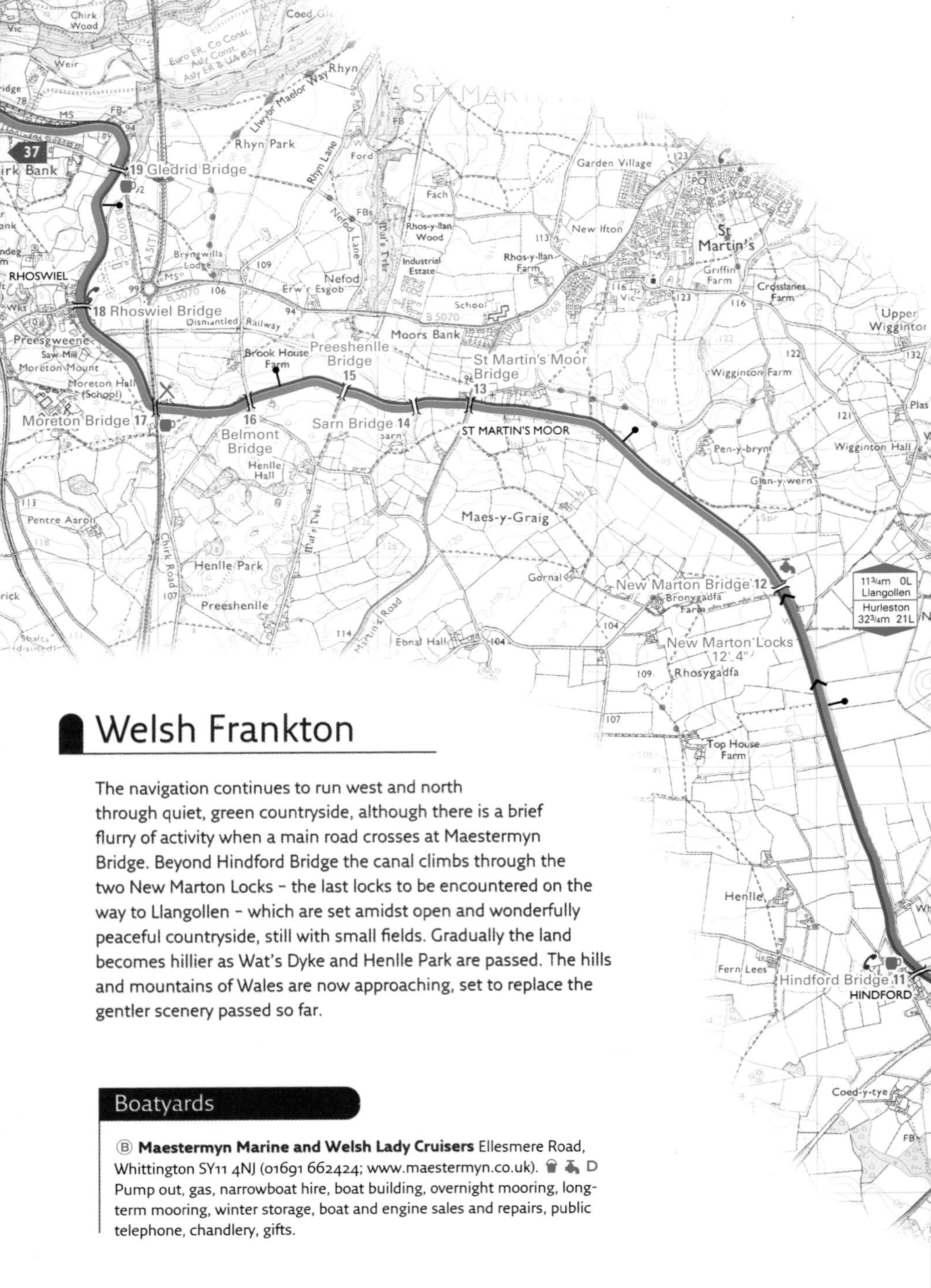

Welsh Frankton

The navigation continues to run west and north through quiet, green countryside, although there is a brief flurry of activity when a main road crosses at Maestermyn Bridge. Beyond Hindford Bridge the canal climbs through the two New Marton Locks – the last locks to be encountered on the way to Llangollen – which are set amidst open and wonderfully peaceful countryside, still with small fields. Gradually the land becomes hillier as Wat's Dyke and Henlle Park are passed. The hills and mountains of Wales are now approaching, set to replace the gentler scenery passed so far.

Boatyards

Ⓑ **Maestermyn Marine and Welsh Lady Cruisers** Ellesmere Road, Whittington SY11 4NJ (01691 662424; www.maestermyn.co.uk). D Pump out, gas, narrowboat hire, boat building, overnight mooring, long-term mooring, winter storage, boat and engine sales and repairs, public telephone, chandlery, gifts.

Rhoswiel

Shropshire. Tel, stores. A tiny village on the Welsh border; the canal runs through it in a slight cutting.

Pubs and Restaurants

Narrowboat Inn Ellesmere Road, Whittington SY11 4DJ (01691 661051). Friendly pub with a nautical theme, situated in the old Canal Office. Real ale. Meals *L and E.* Children's menu. Canalside garden and moorings.

Lion Quays Hotel Moreton, nr Weston Rhyn SY11 3EN (01691 684300; www.lionquays.co.uk). By bridge 17. Waterside bar, restaurant, hotel, country club and spa. Food served daily. Children welcome. Outside seating. Regular entertainment, *telephone or visit website for details.*

Jack Mytton Inn and Restaurant Hindford SY11 4NL (01691 679861; www.jack-mytton.co.uk). Cosy country pub in attractive hamlet. Real ale. Wide range of bar meals and à la carte available *L and E.* Children welcome. Extensive grounds, with a bar and servery, and moorings.

Poachers Pocket Gledrid, Chirk LL14 5DG (01691 773250). Popular and friendly pub serving real ale. Good value, home-cooked meals *daily.* Garden and outdoor play area. Moorings.

Shell garage at bridge 17 The garage has a canalside café serving breakfasts and lunches.

WALKING & CYCLING

The towpath is in very poor condition between bridge 9 and Frankton Junction.

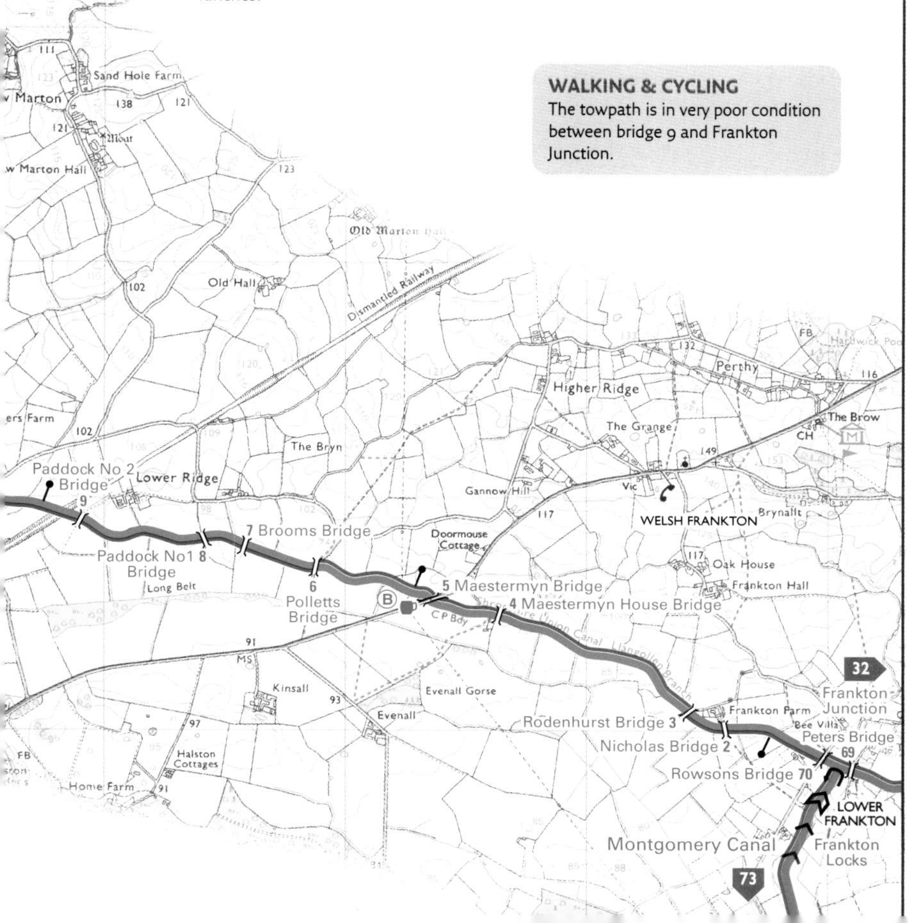

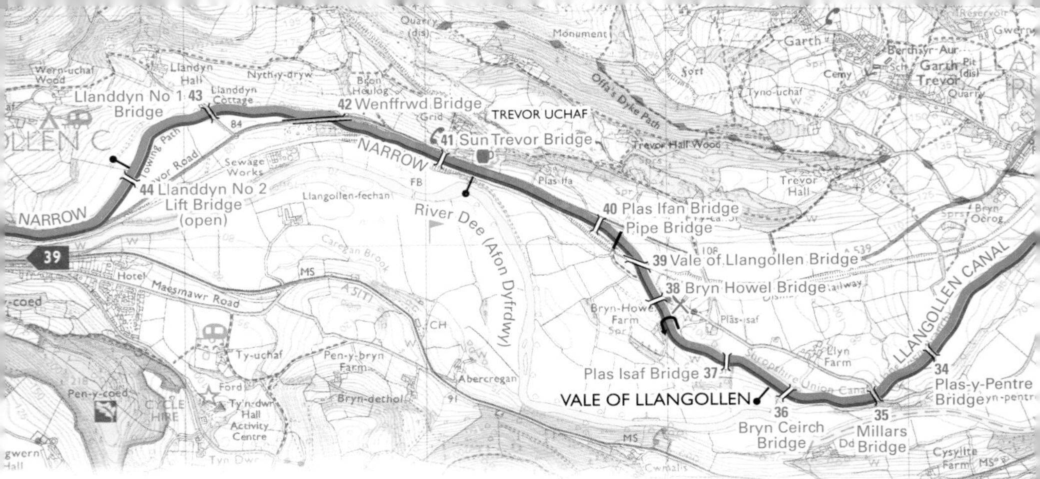

Chirk and Pontcysyllte

As Chirk Bank is reached, the approaching Welsh mountains drive the navigation into a side cutting half-way up the side of a hill. The canal then rounds a corner and suddenly Chirk Aqueduct appears – an impressive structure by any canal enthusiast's standards, and accompanied by a very fine railway viaduct alongside. At the end of the aqueduct the canal immediately enters a tunnel, with Chirk Station nearby. A long wooded cutting follows, and then the railway reappears alongside. Another, shorter, tunnel at Whitehouses is negotiated before the canal meets the valley of the River Dee. Here the railway charges off to the north on a magnificent viaduct, while the canal clings to the hillside. Now the scenery really is superb and the views over and along the valley of the River Dee are excellent. Passing the village of Froncysyllte, the canal launches out into this deep valley on a massive embankment, then crosses the River Dee on the breathtaking Pontcysyllte Aqueduct. At the north end of the aqueduct there is a fascinating short arm with a boatyard straight ahead, but to continue to Llangollen it is necessary to make a tricky left turn. The short arm towards Ruabon was originally projected as the canal's main line towards Chester and the Mersey, and the dry dock at Trevor Junction dates from this time. The line from Trevor to Llantysilio was envisaged purely as a navigable feeder. However the idea of a direct line to Chester was soon dropped and a connection made instead with the Chester Canal at Hurleston Junction. There are good moorings at the north end of Chirk Tunnel, and moorings and a turning place in the restored basins beyond the boatyard at Trevor. The canal, now generally quite narrow, continues in a westerly direction towards Llangollen, clinging spectacularly to the side of the valley above the Dee.

WALKING & CYCLING

The alternative route of Offa's Dyke Path crosses the aqueduct. On the north side of the aqueduct three walks are indicated on a board. Cyclists must dismount when crossing the Pontcysyllte Aqueduct. There is an excellent walk from the aqueduct along the towpath to bridge 27. Turn left to Newbridge then return through Ty Mawr Country Park along a path beside the River Dee.

NAVIGATIONAL NOTES

1. Do not enter the Pontcysyllte Aqueduct if a boat is approaching from the opposite direction. Wait until it is clear.
2. From Trevor to Llangollen the canal is very shallow, accentuating the flow downstream. It is not recommended for boats drawing more than 21 inches. It is also, in places, very narrow. Just go slowly and keep a sharp watch for approaching boats.

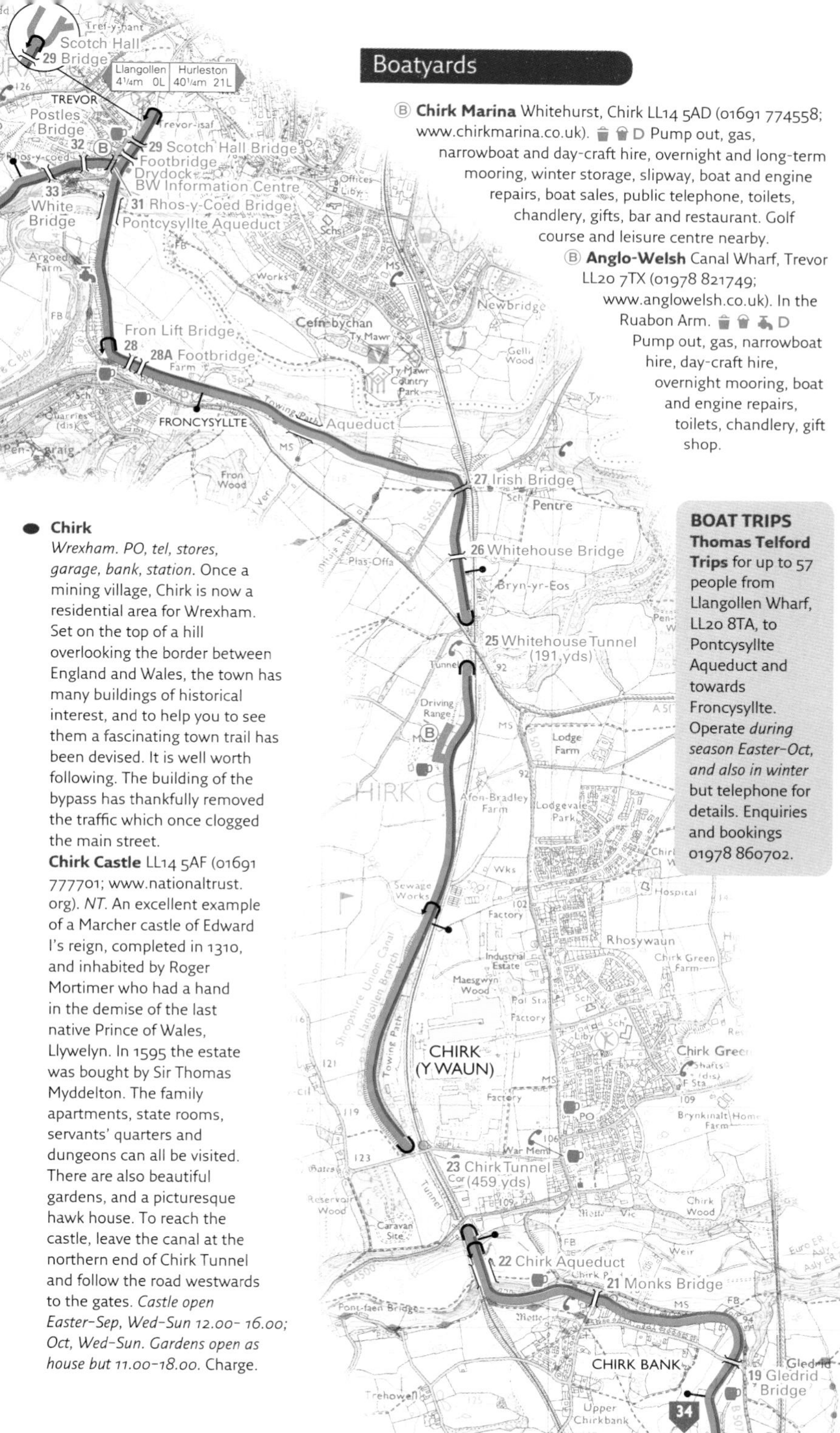

Boatyards

Ⓑ **Chirk Marina** Whitehurst, Chirk LL14 5AD (01691 774558; www.chirkmarina.co.uk). D Pump out, gas, narrowboat and day-craft hire, overnight and long-term mooring, winter storage, slipway, boat and engine repairs, boat sales, public telephone, toilets, chandlery, gifts, bar and restaurant. Golf course and leisure centre nearby.

Ⓑ **Anglo-Welsh** Canal Wharf, Trevor LL20 7TX (01978 821749; www.anglowelsh.co.uk). In the Ruabon Arm. D Pump out, gas, narrowboat hire, day-craft hire, overnight mooring, boat and engine repairs, toilets, chandlery, gift shop.

BOAT TRIPS

Thomas Telford Trips for up to 57 people from Llangollen Wharf, LL20 8TA, to Pontcysyllte Aqueduct and towards Froncysyllte. Operate *during season Easter–Oct, and also in winter* but telephone for details. Enquiries and bookings 01978 860702.

● **Chirk**

Wrexham. PO, tel, stores, garage, bank, station. Once a mining village, Chirk is now a residential area for Wrexham. Set on the top of a hill overlooking the border between England and Wales, the town has many buildings of historical interest, and to help you to see them a fascinating town trail has been devised. It is well worth following. The building of the bypass has thankfully removed the traffic which once clogged the main street.

Chirk Castle LL14 5AF (01691 777701; www.nationaltrust.org). *NT.* An excellent example of a Marcher castle of Edward I's reign, completed in 1310, and inhabited by Roger Mortimer who had a hand in the demise of the last native Prince of Wales, Llywelyn. In 1595 the estate was bought by Sir Thomas Myddelton. The family apartments, state rooms, servants' quarters and dungeons can all be visited. There are also beautiful gardens, and a picturesque hawk house. To reach the castle, leave the canal at the northern end of Chirk Tunnel and follow the road westwards to the gates. *Castle open Easter–Sep, Wed–Sun 12.00–16.00; Oct, Wed–Sun. Gardens open as house but 11.00–18.00.* Charge.

Chirk and Whitehouses Tunnels Neither of these tunnels is wide enough for two boats to pass, although each tunnel has a towpath running through it. Chirk Tunnel is 459yds long. Whitehouses Tunnel is 191yds long.

Chirk Aqueduct
Opened in 1801, this is a splendidly massive brick and stone aqueduct carrying the canal in a narrow cast iron trough from England into Wales. The River Ceiriog flows 70ft below, and the great railway viaduct is beside and a little higher than the aqueduct.

Froncysyllte
Wrexham. PO, tel, stores. A village distinguished by its superb position on the side of the valley.

Pontcysyllte Aqueduct
Easily the most famous and most spectacular feature on the whole canal system, this aqueduct cannot fail to astonish visitors. Apart from its great height of 126ft above the River Dee and its length of 1007ft, the excitement to be derived from crossing this structure by boat is partly due to the fact that, while the towpath side is fenced off with, albeit widely spaced, iron railings, the offside is completely unprotected from about 12in above the water level *so the only way for children to enjoy the voyage across this great aqueduct is from inside the boat.* It is generally considered to have been built by Thomas Telford and, if so, is reckoned to be one of his most brilliant and successful works. The concept of laying a cast iron trough along the top of a row of stone piers was entirely new, and entirely Telford's: he realised that such a high crossing of the Dee valley was inevitable if time- and water-wasting locks were to be avoided, and it was obvious to the canal company that a conventional brick or stone aqueduct would be quite unsuitable. His plan for the aqueduct was greeted at first with derision; but the work went ahead, was completed in ten years and opened in 1805 at an estimated cost of £47,018. One can hardly imagine the utter amazement felt by people of that time as they witnessed boats moving easily across this tall, beautiful and unique structure. Today, the aqueduct remains as built, apart from renewals of balustrading and the towpath structure. The masonry is apparently in prime condition (note the very thin masonry joints, which were bonded by a mortar made from a mixture of lime and ox blood), and the dove-tailed joints in the iron trough, sealed with a combination of Welsh flannel and lead dipped in boiling sugar, hardly leak at all. The cast iron side plates of the trough are all wedge shaped, like the stones in a masonry arch. It is, without doubt, a masterpiece and, as we go to press, likely to become the centrepiece of a World Heritage Site.

Pubs and Restaurants

Poachers Pocket Gledrid, Chirk LL14 5DG (01691 773250). Popular and friendly pub serving real ale. Restaurant meals *all day, every day.* Children welcome. Moorings.

The Bridge Inn Chirk Bank, Chirk 01691 773213 (01691 773213). The 'last pub in England', with a fine view of Chirk Aqueduct. Cosy welcoming bar with an open fire. Real ale. Meals *all day, every day.* Children welcome. Patio and marvellous views. B & B.

✕ **The Hand Hotel** Church Street, Chirk LL14 5EY (01691 773472; www.thehandhotelchirk.co.uk). Smart hotel, with resident ghosts, serving real ale. Food available in the Castle Room and Regency Restaurant *L and E.* Children welcome. Garden with play area. Large-screen TV in public bar. B & B.

Stanton House Inn Church Street, Chirk LL14 5NA (01691 774150). Traditional locals' pub serving real ale and food *L and E, daily.* Children welcome. No dogs. Quiz and bingo. B & B.

✕ **Chirk Golf Course** Chirk LL14 5AD (01691 774407). By Chirk Marina. Food *L and E.* Children welcome. Outside seating. Eighteen- and nine-hole golf courses and driving range available to all, includes equipment.

The Aqueduct Inn Holyhead Road, Froncysyllte LL20 7PY (01691 772481). Old coaching inn above bridge 28, with an excellent view over the aqueduct. Real ale. Meals *L and E.* Children welcome. Patio and garden. Traditional pub games. B & B.

✕ **The Telford Inn** Station Road, Trevor LL20 7TT. Next to Anglo-Welsh (01978 820469). Busy pub with canalside seating. Real ale in the holiday season. Food *L and E.* Children welcome.

✕ **Sun Trevor** Sun Bank, Llangollen LL20 8EG (01978 860651; www.suntrevor.co.uk). Above bridge 41. Beautifully situated pub with exceptional views of the valley, river and canal. Brasses, beams and a fine inglenook with a cosy curved settle are there to enjoy in a haunted building, which has its origins in the 14th C. Real ales. Food, using local ingredients, *L and E.* Garden with children's play area. Children welcome. B & B. Moorings.

✕ **Bryn Howel Hotel and Restaurant** Trevor, Llangollen LL20 7UW (01978 860331; www.brynhowel.com). Canalside at bridge 38. Family-owned hotel with award-winning restaurant.

Llangollen

This is another stretch of very great beauty, with the waterway's route through Llangollen being made in an often very narrow channel on the side of tree-covered mountains, with views down into the Vale of Llangollen. The canal passes high above the town, flowing through picturesque white bridges and passing the backs of charming and modestly eccentric houses. But it doesn't stop there: the tiny channel continues beyond the new mooring basin and winding hole as a feeder to weave up the valley to Llantysilio, passing a country hotel and a chain bridge over the nearby River Dee, while steam trains on the restored railway complete an utterly charming scene. At Horseshoe Falls a large semicircular weir across the Dee, built by Telford, provides the water which is constantly passed into the canal. Then it flows past Llangollen and the aqueducts, right back down to Hurleston Reservoir – to the tune of 12 million gallons a day.

NAVIGATIONAL NOTES

1. There is **no** turning point west of the mooring marina at Llangollen, so boats longer than about 10ft must not venture up the feeder. However, the towpath is in excellent shape and makes a very enjoyable walk.
2. The new mooring marina west of bridge 45 provides 33 excellent moorings, or you can moor east of bridge 45. Tickets for moorings must be obtained from the hut by bridge 45. A *48 hour restriction* applies to both the marina and canalside moorings in combination (i.e. *you can't moor for 48 hours at one and then 48 hours at the other*).

Llangollen

Denbighshire. PO, tel, stores, garage, bank, bike hire. Founded in the 7th C by St Collen, the town has become established as one of North Wales' major tourist venues, especially during the month of July, when the International Musical Eisteddfod attracts performers and visitors from all around the world. Its superb setting in the upper Dee Valley has made it a great centre for outdoor pursuits, including pony trekking, climbing, walking and canoeing. For the less energetic there are canal trips, steam railway rides, the wonderful house of Plas Newydd, a Victorian School Museum and a Motor Museum. Visitors to the surrounding hills can explore Castell Dinas Bran, Valle Crucius Abbey and Elisegs Pillar, as well as enjoying superb walks. It was the construction of Telford's A5 road from London to Holyhead in 1815 which firmly placed Llangollen on the tourist map, but another 60 years were to pass before the streets of the town were to exchange their earthen surface for stone, quarried from Trevor Rocks. The town was a staging post on a drover's road, the routes used to move livestock to the distant markets of eastern England. In 1854 George Borrow recorded a meeting with a massive pig being driven along the road near Llangollen in his book *Wild Wales*. He noted that it weighed 'eighteen score of pounds' and 'walked with considerable difficulty'. At this time a pig would change hands at between 18 and 20 shillings – 'dire was the screaming of the porkers, yet the purchaser invariably seemed to know how to manage his bargain'. At the centre of the town is the parish church of St Collen, who was thought to be the first abbot of Valle Crucius Abbey. The 15th-C carved oak roof and stained glass window of St Collen are well worth seeing. The Ladies of Llangollen (*see* below) are buried in the churchyard.

International Musical Eisteddfod Eisteddfod Office, 1st Floor, Royal International Pavilion, Abbey Road, Llangollen LL20 8SW (01978 862001; www.eisteddfod-ryngwladol.co.uk). For *one week every July* the town attracts singers, dancers and musicians from all over the world, who perform both in organised concerts, and impromptu street events. The gallery displays local and national touring exhibitions, and local craft work is displayed in the Craft Showcase, where items can be purchased. There are concerts, festivals and other events all year round at the Pavilion (01978 860111; www.royal-pavilion.co.uk).

Church of St Collen This church was probably founded by St Collen, who was the first abbot of nearby Vale Crucis Abbey, and its establishment dates from the 7th century. The present building is of Norman origin, with many later additions and alterations. It has a beautifully carved oak roof, dating from the 15th C, and the stained glass window dedicated to St Collen is worth locating. In the churchyard is the tomb of the Ladies of Llangollen (*see* Plas Newydd across) and Mary Carryll, their maid.

The Llangollen Railway Llangollen Station LL20 8SN (01978 860979 for enquiries, or 01978 860951 for a talking timetable; www.llangollen-railway.co.uk). The original Llangollen station was called Whitehurst Halt, and was situated close to Froncysyllte, from where the hotels in the town ran a taxi service to fetch the visitors. The building of the line was completed in 1862 after many delays, since the work, supervised by the chief engineer Henry Robertson, took much longer than anticipated. Vast numbers of navvies were employed, but in spite of their working on Sundays (to the disgust of the locals), the bad winter if 1860–1 brought their work to a halt. The first passenger train finally arrived on 2nd June 1862. The line was later extended to Corwen, when the present station was opened in 1865, and subsequently as far as Dolgellau. Soon trips to the coast at Barmouth were to become very popular amongst the locals. The line closed to passenger traffic in 1965, and to goods in 1968, and the station and tracks were left to fall into a ruinous state. Fortunately local enthusiasts came to its rescue, and they now operate steam and heritage diesel trains to Carrog (LL21 9BD) on over 8 miles of track in the direction of Corwen. They also operate a canal/rail service (01691 690322), special dining trains and a vintage bus service (*Sat and Sun in summer*).

Victorian School of the 3 Rs Parade Street, Llangollen LL20 8RB (01978 860794; secretary@victorianschool.co.uk). Take a one-hour lesson subjected to the rigours of a Victorian school headmaster, while dressed as a pupil – it's a far cry from the schooling of today! Next door is a museum, with exhibits demonstrating a Victorian school-childs' daily life, from boots and shoes to 'never absent, never late' medals. Education cost a penny a week, and for an extra penny a week in the winter you could sit near the fire. *Telephone for opening times.*

Motor Museum and Canal Exhibition Pentrefelin, Llangollen LL20 8EE (01978 860324; www.llangollenmotormuseum.co.uk) Near bridge 48. Housed in a building dating from the 1830s which was once a slate dressing works, this museum successfully recreates the atmosphere of a working 1950s garage, with tools and other motoring items lying around, and complete with living quarters. Cars, motorcycles, toys and memorabilia dating from the early part of the 20th C until the 1970s can be seen, and there is usually some restoration work under way. The Canal Exhibition explains, in pictures and words, how the canals were built and operated, their decline and their more recent revival. Working models of the Barton swing aqueduct, the Anderton boat lift, Worsley coal mine and how a lock is built and operated. *Open Mar–Oct, Tue–Sun 10.00–17.00; winter opening by arrangement.* Charge.

Tourist Information Centre Castle Street, Llangollen LL20 8NU (01978 860828). Good choice of guide books.

Plas Newydd Hill Street, Llangollen L20 8AW (01978 861314). On the southern outskirts of town. From 1779–1831 it was the home of the eccentric Lady Eleanor Butler and Miss Sarah Ponsonby, 'the two most celebrated virgins in Europe'. Their visitors, who included Browning, Tennyson, Walter Scott and Wordsworth, presented them with antique curios, which are now on display in the elaborately panelled

rooms. Part of the 12-acre grounds is a public park. *House open daily Apr-Oct, 10.00- 17.00.* Charge. Entry to the grounds is free, and these are *open all year round.*
Castell Dinas Bran 1/2 mile north of canal. The ruins of the castle built for Eliseg, Prince of Powys, can be seen from the waterway while approaching the town, and stand on a 1100ft mountain accessible to energetic walkers from various points along the canal, including bridge 45. A prince known as Bran is thought to have built the original fortification on this site, following a dispute with his brother Beli. Their mother was Corwena, who lived near what is now Corwen. The castle is thought to have had links with the legendary Holy Grail. The visible remains date from the late 13th C, and were built by the Princes of Powys.
Eliseg's Pillar 1/4 mile north of the abbey. Erected in the 18th C to commemorate Eliseg, who built the fortress on the top of Dinas Bran.
Eglwyseg Rocks To the north east of the town, this is an impressive and brilliantly white escarpment of carboniferous limestone laid down some 400 million years ago, when this area was covered by the sea. It is now very popular with fossil hunters.
Llantysilio
Denbighshire. Overlooking Horseshoe Falls. Parts of the interior of the church are taken from the nearby Valle Crucis Abbey.
Valle Crucis Abbey LL20 8EE (01978 860326). 1½ miles north west of the town. Finely preserved ruins of the Cistercian abbey founded in 1201 by Madoc, Prince of Powys, and rebuilt in more lavish style after a fire in 1250. The abbey fell into neglect following the dissolution of the monasteries in 1539. Its finest feature is the vaulted chapter house and screened library cupboard. There is also the only surviving monastic fish pond to be seen in Wales. Occasional theatrical and musical events are held in the grounds. *Open Apr-Sep, daily 10.00-17.00; Oct- Mar, daily 09.30-16.00.* Charge.

Pubs and Restaurants

There is a wide variety of friendly pubs and restaurants in Llangollen, including:
Ponsonby Arms Mill Street, Llangollen LL20 7RY (01978 861119). On the A539 east of bridge 45, overlooking the River Dee, and handy for the Llangollen moorings. Themed on The Ladies of Llangollen. Food served *L and E.* Children's play area in south-facing garden.
Bridge End Hotel Mill Street, Llangollen LL20 8RY (01978 860634) Below bridge 45. Large and comfortable pub serving real ale. Bar and restaurant meals *L and E.* Children welcome. Outside seating. B & B.
The Wharf Wharf Hill, Llangollen LL20 8TA (01978 860702; www.horsedrawnboats.co.uk). Friendly café right by original town wharf, complete with a crane. Food *L.* Children welcome. Canal giftware.
The Royal Hotel Bridge Street, Llangollen LL20 8PG (01978 860202). Traditional riverside hotel serving real ale in the small bar, and meals *L and E.* Restaurant *open E only.* Children welcome. *Weekend* disco.
The Corn Mill Dee Lane, Llangollen LL20 8PN (01978 869555; www.cornmill-llangollen.co.uk). A pub in converted Corn Mill, with terraces above the mill race and the river rapids, serving an interesting range of food and real ale *L and E.* Well-behaved children welcome but note that the location makes it less suitable for younger children. Views across the river to the restored Llangollen Station.
Chain Bridge Hotel Berwyn LL20 8BS (01978 860215; www.chainbridgehotel.com). In a splendid position overlooking the river and the chain bridge, where monks from Valle Crucis once crossed the river. Food *L and E.* Restaurant meals should be booked. Children welcome. Garden.

WALKING & CYCLING

Llangollen is a great centre for both activities. The Tourist Information Centre has a range of guides. From bridge 45 you can follow a path north to visit Castell Dinas Bran and Trevor Rocks; from bridge 48 you can take a circular walk to Valle Crucis Abbey, returning via bridge 48A, and visiting Horseshoe Falls and the canal's end. The towpath is good for cycling as far as Pontcysyllte, and after *walking* your bike over the aqueduct you can return to Llangollen along quiet lanes to the south of the A5 (avoid riding on this busy road!).

BOAT TRIPS

The Wharf Llangollen LL20 8TA (01978 860702; www.horsedrawnboats.co.uk). Horse-drawn trips have been available in Llangollen since 1884, visiting Pentrefelin and Berwyn. There are also trips on *nb Thomas Telford* over the Pontcysyllte Aqueduct. Gift shop and café.

Pontcysyllte Aqueduct (see *page 38*)

MONMOUTHSHIRE & BRECON CANALS

MAXIMUM DIMENSIONS

Length: 55'
Beam: 8' 6"
Headroom: 5' 11"
Draught: 2' 6"

WATERWAY UNIT MANAGER

Monmouthshire & Brecon Canal (Brecon to Solomons Bridge [47])
01606 723800
enquiries.walesandbordercounties@britishwaterways.co.uk

Monmouthshire Canal
This is currently managed by three separate councils:
Solomons Bridge to below Ash Tree Bridge (32): Torfaen: 01495 762200
Ash Tree Bridge to Barrack Hill Tunnel; Malpas to Harry Roberts Bridge (10): Newport: 01633 232814
Harry Roberts Bridge to Cwmcarn/Pontywaun: Caerphilly: 02920 888777

MILEAGE

Monmouthshire Canal
PONTYWAUN to:
Risca: 1¾ miles
Fourteen Locks: 5¼ miles
Malpas, junction with main line: 7 miles
CWMBRAN Five Locks: 13 miles
Pontymoile: 15½ miles

Navigable section
CWMBRAN Five Locks to:
Pontymoile : 2½ miles
Brecon & Abergavenny Canal:
Goytre Wharf: 8½ miles
Llanfoist: 14 miles
Gilwern: 17 miles
Llangattock Bridge: 20½ miles
Talybont: 29 miles
BRECON: 35¾ miles

Monmouthshire Canal
Locks: 50 (6 restored)
Brecon & Abergavenny Canal
Locks: 6

The Monmouthshire, Brecon and Abergavenny Canals Trust, 95 The Highway, New Inn, Pontypool NP4 0PN (01495 762823) is concerned with the whole Monmouthshire & Brecon canals and is actively concerned with their regeneration. The Islwyn Canal Association (01633 614257) is concerned with the Caerphilly section of the canal.

In 1792 the Act of Authorisation for the Monmouthshire Canal was passed. This gave permission for a canal to be cut from the estuary of the River Usk at Newport to Pontnewynydd, north of Pontypool. In addition to this Main Line, there was to be an 11-mile branch from Malpas to Crumlin. Thomas Dadford Jnr was appointed engineer, and the canal was opened in 1796. When the Act for the Brecknock & Abergavenny Canal was passed in 1793, the canal was originally planned to connect Brecon with the River Usk near Caerleon, but the directors of the Monmouthshire Canal persuaded the promoters to alter their plans to include a junction with their own canal. And so the Brecknock & Abergavenny Canal, with Thomas Dadford Jnr again as engineer, was cut from Brecon to Pontymoile Basin, where it joined the Monmouthshire Canal. The Brecknock & Abergavenny Canal was fully opened in 1799. For a while the two canals were profitable, because the iron and coal cargoes justified the use of both canal and tramway. However, the greater speed and efficiency of the railways soon became apparent, and by the 1850s there were several schemes to abandon the canal. In 1865 the Monmouthshire bought the Brecknock & Abergavenny Canal Company, but already it was too late for this to be effective. Bit by bit the original Monmouthshire Canal was closed, but the Brecon line was kept open as a water channel. In 1962 the network was formally abandoned, and parts were filled in. In 1964 the slow task of restoration was begun, and boats were once more able to cruise from Pontymoile to Talybont. The present limit of navigation is Five Locks, although plans to extend south to Newport and Pontywaun to reclaim the Monmouthshire Canal are now coming to fruition.

Fourteen Locks

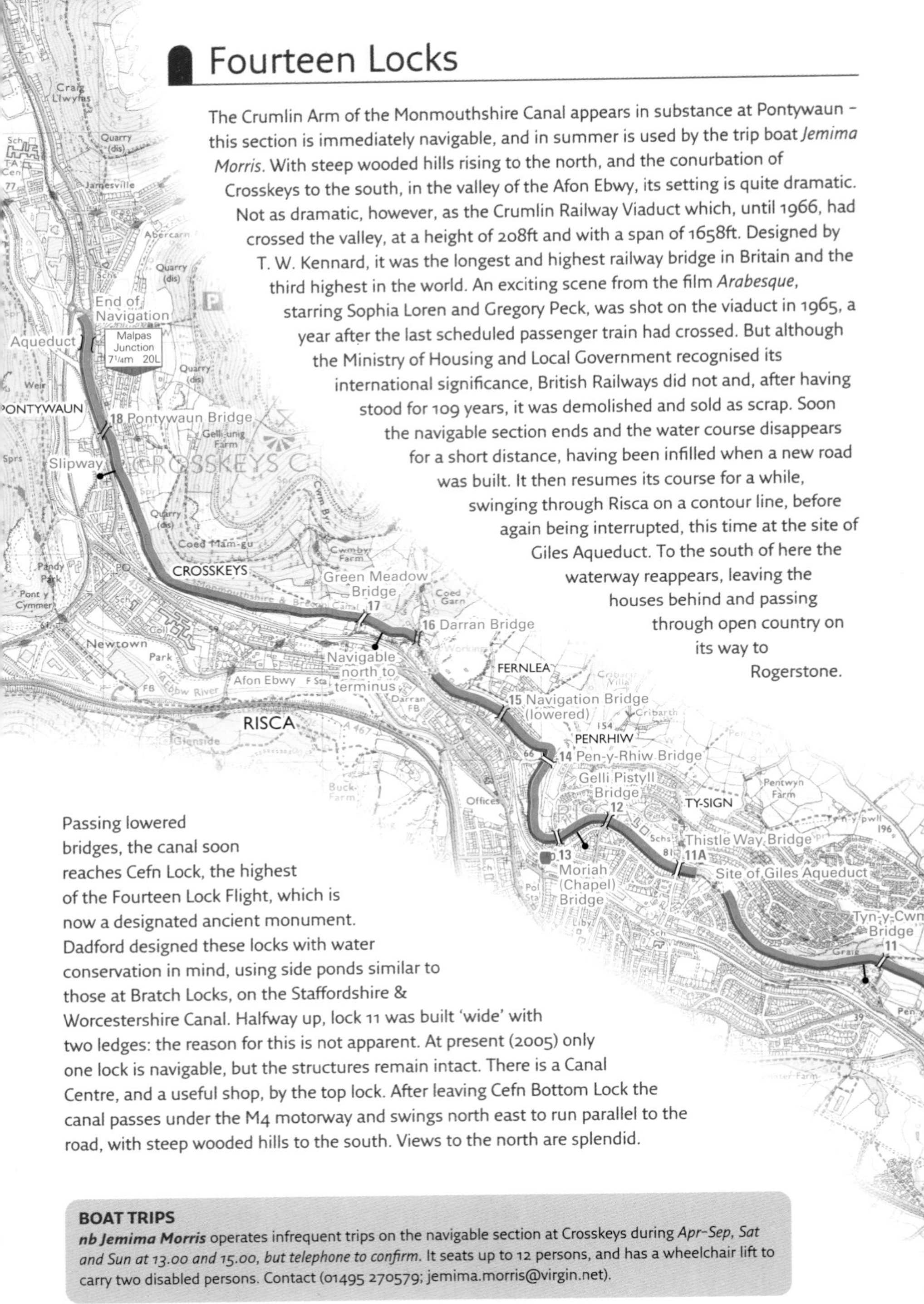

The Crumlin Arm of the Monmouthshire Canal appears in substance at Pontywaun – this section is immediately navigable, and in summer is used by the trip boat *Jemima Morris*. With steep wooded hills rising to the north, and the conurbation of Crosskeys to the south, in the valley of the Afon Ebwy, its setting is quite dramatic. Not as dramatic, however, as the Crumlin Railway Viaduct which, until 1966, had crossed the valley, at a height of 208ft and with a span of 1658ft. Designed by T. W. Kennard, it was the longest and highest railway bridge in Britain and the third highest in the world. An exciting scene from the film *Arabesque*, starring Sophia Loren and Gregory Peck, was shot on the viaduct in 1965, a year after the last scheduled passenger train had crossed. But although the Ministry of Housing and Local Government recognised its international significance, British Railways did not and, after having stood for 109 years, it was demolished and sold as scrap. Soon the navigable section ends and the water course disappears for a short distance, having been infilled when a new road was built. It then resumes its course for a while, swinging through Risca on a contour line, before again being interrupted, this time at the site of Giles Aqueduct. To the south of here the waterway reappears, leaving the houses behind and passing through open country on its way to Rogerstone.

Passing lowered bridges, the canal soon reaches Cefn Lock, the highest of the Fourteen Lock Flight, which is now a designated ancient monument. Dadford designed these locks with water conservation in mind, using side ponds similar to those at Bratch Locks, on the Staffordshire & Worcestershire Canal. Halfway up, lock 11 was built 'wide' with two ledges: the reason for this is not apparent. At present (2005) only one lock is navigable, but the structures remain intact. There is a Canal Centre, and a useful shop, by the top lock. After leaving Cefn Bottom Lock the canal passes under the M4 motorway and swings north east to run parallel to the road, with steep wooded hills to the south. Views to the north are splendid.

BOAT TRIPS

nb Jemima Morris operates infrequent trips on the navigable section at Crosskeys during *Apr-Sep, Sat and Sun at 13.00 and 15.00, but telephone to confirm*. It seats up to 12 persons, and has a wheelchair lift to carry two disabled persons. Contact (01495 270579; jemima.morris@virgin.net).

Cwmcarn Forest Drive & Visitor Centre
Nantcarn Road, Cwmcarn, Crosskeys NP11 7FA (01495 272001; www.forestry.gov.uk). Off the A467. A 7-mile drive, plus opportunities for mountain biking and walking. Superb views, sculpture exhibition. Visitor Centre *open Mon–Fri 09.00–17.00; Oct–Easter Fri 09.00–16.30*. Gift and coffee shop. Charge.

● **Crosskeys**
Caerphilly. A village at the confluence of the rivers Ebbw and Sirhowey, its setting in a wooded valley is superb.

● **Risca**
Caerphilly. PO, tel, stores. Lying in the valley below the canal, the town is making the transformation from the old economies of mining and, unusually, metal typesetting to newer, lighter industries. It was the scene, on 15 July 1880, of a dreadful mining accident, when a gas explosion killed 130 men and boys. It was though to have been caused by the use of the old Clanny lamp, which the miners preferred because it gave much better illumination than Sir Humphrey Davy's safety lamp. In 1892 there were 1050 men and 102 horses working in Risca colliery, and it was later one of the first to be lit by electricity, with underground traction using compressed air. It continued to grow, and by 1918, together with the nearby Blackvein Colliery, 2084 miners were employed. It closed in 1967 and the land is now an industrial estate.

● **Fourteen Locks Canal Centre and Museum**
High Cross, Newport NP10 9GN (01633 894802; www.fourteenlocks.co.uk). An interpretive centre which demonstrates how vital canal transport was during the early stages of the Industrial Revolution, and tells the story of the Monmouthshire Canal. This superb flight of 14 locks, completed in 1799 by Thomas Dadford Jnr, raises the canal 168ft in under half a mile, and has now been designated an ancient monument. The top lock was restored during the summer of 2002, and the section to bridge 6A is navigable for boats up to 23ft – a slipway has been built in the pond below lock 21. There is a waymarked walk. Visitor Centre and art gallery *open daily 09.30–16.30*. Tea room. Free. Occasional family-fun days and boat trips organised.

Pubs and Restaurants

The Castle Twyncarn Road, Pontywaun, Crosskeys NP11 7DU (01495 271232). Traditional pub serving real ale. Food *L and E (not Sun E)*. Children welcome, and there is a garden.

The Philanthropic Twyncarn Road, Pontywaun, Crosskeyes NP11 7DU (01495 271448). Real ale in a traditional pub, with bar snacks *always available*. Children welcome. Garden.

Prince of Wales Dixon Place, Risca NP11 6PY (01633 612780). Welcoming traditional pub with an unspoilt bar and a fine view over the town, and the rugby club, from the terrace. Real ale. Rolls available in *summer*. Children welcome. Garden. Darts teams thrive – men on *Mon*, women on *Tue*.

Rising Sun 1 Cefn Road, Rogerstone, Newport, NP10 9A (01633 895126). Just above the top lock, across the road from the canal. Family owned. Bar and restaurant with wide range of food on offer. Children's play area. B & B.

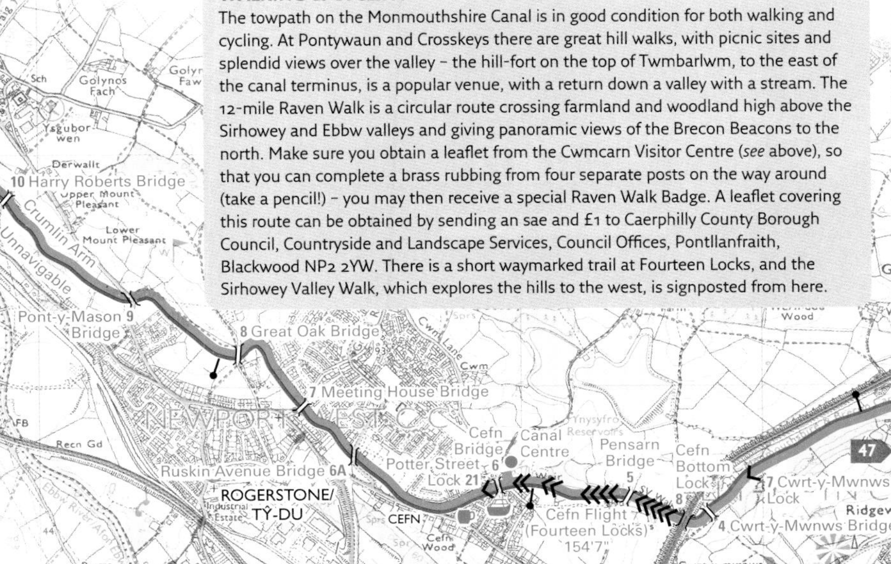

WALKING & CYCLING

The towpath on the Monmouthshire Canal is in good condition for both walking and cycling. At Pontywaun and Crosskeys there are great hill walks, with picnic sites and splendid views over the valley – the hill-fort on the top of Twmbarlwm, to the east of the canal terminus, is a popular venue, with a return down a valley with a stream. The 12-mile Raven Walk is a circular route crossing farmland and woodland high above the Sirhowey and Ebbw valleys and giving panoramic views of the Brecon Beacons to the north. Make sure you obtain a leaflet from the Cwmcarn Visitor Centre (*see* above), so that you can complete a brass rubbing from four separate posts on the way around (take a pencil!) – you may then receive a special Raven Walk Badge. A leaflet covering this route can be obtained by sending an sae and £1 to Caerphilly County Borough Council, Countryside and Landscape Services, Council Offices, Pontllanfraith, Blackwood NP2 2YW. There is a short waymarked trail at Fourteen Locks, and the Sirhowey Valley Walk, which explores the hills to the west, is signposted from here.

Barrack Hill

Six locks are passed to the south of the motorway before reaching the junction at Malpas, where the main line heads off to the north. The last of these, Gwastad, has been restored. Ahead, in under half a mile, and having passed Crindau Bridge, the line which once connected with the docks at Pillgwenlly in Newport ends at what was the entrance to Barrack Hill Tunnel, closed in the early 1930s. If you wish to visit Newport, you will have to complete the journey by road.
The main line heads north from Barrack Hill, crossing an aqueduct which, at one time, had a sundial built into the wall, to aid innumerate boatmen. The open expanse of Crindau Park lies to the west, with housing estates to the east, as Gwasted Lock, the first of many on the way to Cwmbran, is passed. At Bettws Lane Bridge there is a slipway, and you will also notice that a balance beam on the lock is hinged, a device to cope with a lack of space. You then pass some smarter gardens before gradually emerging into a stretch of open country, punctuated by a flurry of locks that continue the climb towards Cwmbran. All too soon houses reappear, the canal becomes shallow, and then piped, a short way beyond the Waterloo pub. There is then one very short section in water before the course of the waterway disappears altogether. Thankfully National Cycle Route 46 follows the canal, so if you keep to the waymarked trail, you won't get lost.

City of Newport
Gwent. All services. This is Wales' third-largest urban area, standing on the banks of the Severn, with the River Usk flowing through. Its original Welsh name was Casnewydd-ar-Wysg (pron: casneweth-ar-ooisg), meaning 'the new castle on the Usk', although there is now little to see of this 14th-C building, built by Hugh d'Audele or Ralph, Earl of Stafford, his son-in-law. Enlarged during the 15th C by the 1st Duke of Buckingham, it began to fall into disrepair when the 3rd Duke of Buckingham was beheaded. During the 19th C the Chartists rioted in Newport, led by Henry Vincent, who was arrested in May 1838 for making inflammatory statements and demanding greater rights for working people. His arrest brought 5000 marchers to the town who, upon hearing he was being held at the Westgate Hotel, went there and began chanting 'surrender our prisoners'. Soldiers stationed in the hotel opened fire: 20 marchers were killed and 50 wounded. The leaders were arrested and sentenced to be hung, drawn and quartered, although this was later reduced to transportation. The bullet holes can still be seen in the entrance pillars of the Westgate Hotel. A mosaic off John Frost Square commemorates the Chartists. City status was granted to Newport by the Queen, during her Golden Jubilee in 2002.
St Woolos Cathedral Stow Hill, Newport NP20 4EA (01633 263338; www.churchinwales.org.uk). There has been a church on this site since AD500. Left in ruins after being attacked by pirates, it was rebuilt c.1080 by the Normans, with the tower being added during the 15th C.
Newport Transporter Bridge 62–4 Cardiff Road, Newport NP20 2UA (01633 250322; www.newport.gov.uk). The first recorded permanent river crossing of the Usk in Newport was in 1158, when a wooden bridge was built. Rapid industrial development in the late 19th C made the need for a new bridge a matter of urgency, and something had to be designed to cope with the passage of high-masted ships on the river, and the second-greatest tidal range in the world. The borough engineer at the time, R. H. Haynes, had heard about an 'aerial ferry' built by Ferdinand Arnodin, and suggested he design a similar structure for Newport. This was agreed and work began in 1902, with completion in 1906 at a cost of £98,000. It was in constant use until 1985, when the structure was found to be in a dangerous condition. Saved from demolition, it was re-opened in 1996 after four years of restoration costing £3 million. The largest remaining example of a transporter bridge left in the world, it is a magnificent sight. Following a structural inspection in 2008, the bridge was closed on safety grounds, pending repairs.
Tourist Information Centre John Frost Square, Newport NP20 1PA (01633 842962; www.newport.gov.uk). The Newport Museum and Art Gallery is also within this building, depicting local history, natural sciences and archaeology. Of note is the John Wait teapot display. Free.

Cwmbran
Torfaen. All services. A 1950s new town which once paid little attention to the canal and, in places, completely covered it. Cwmbran now booms, with a population that numbers over 60,000. Apparently it has the biggest shopping centre in Wales.

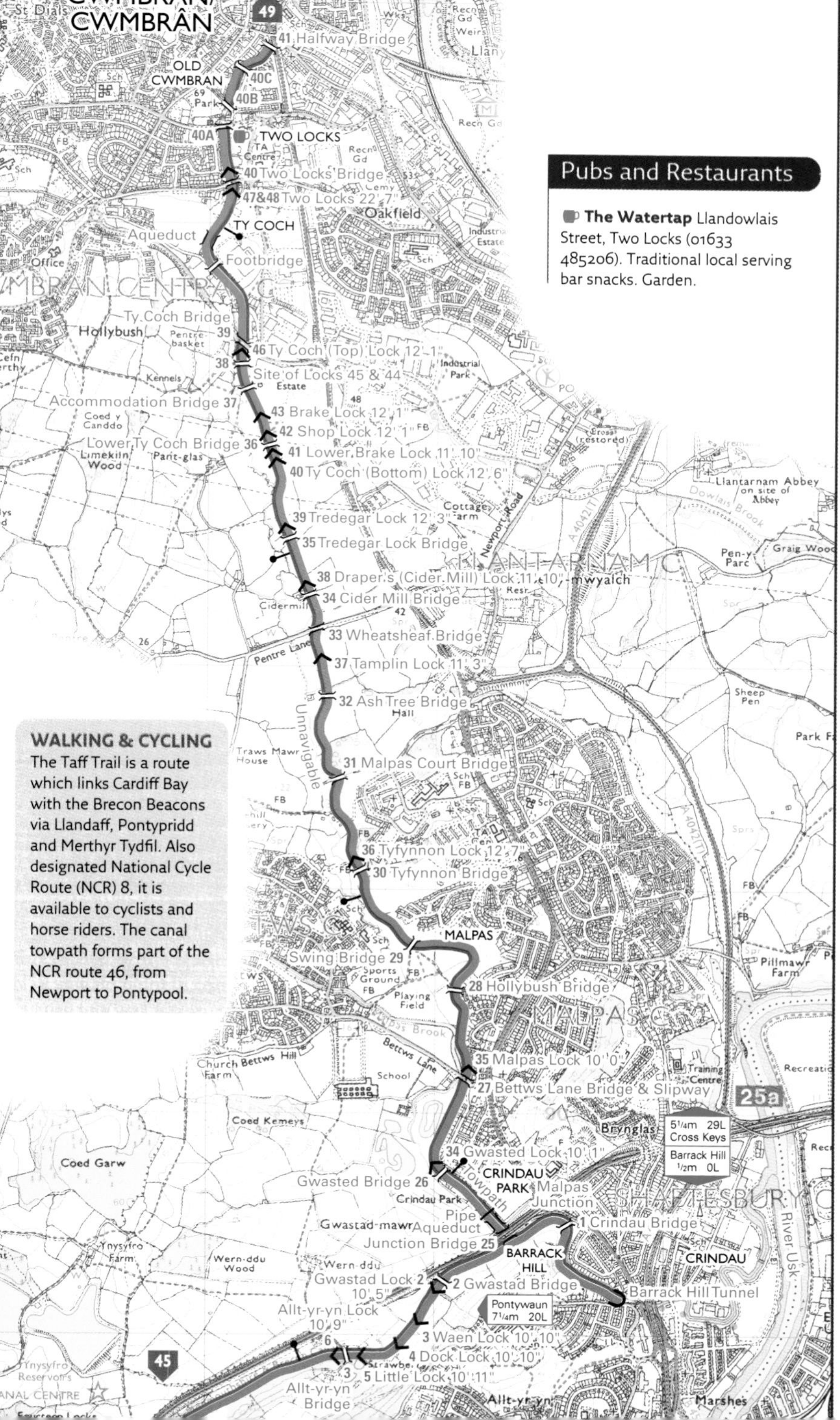

Pubs and Restaurants

The Watertap Llandowlais Street, Two Locks (01633 485206). Traditional local serving bar snacks. Garden.

WALKING & CYCLING

The Taff Trail is a route which links Cardiff Bay with the Brecon Beacons via Llandaff, Pontypridd and Merthyr Tydfil. Also designated National Cycle Route (NCR) 8, it is available to cyclists and horse riders. The canal towpath forms part of the NCR route 46, from Newport to Pontypool.

Pontypool

To the north of Cwmbran the Monmouthshire Canal reappears, climbing short flights of locks at the evocatively named Forge Hammer, plus Three Locks, Pontnewydd and finally Cross Keys where, to the north of the road, navigation towards the Brecon & Abergavenny Canal begins. This initial section, as far as Sebastopol, is under the care of Torfaen Borough Council. Overnight moorings are available at Five Locks Basin. Heading north towards Pontypool the canal, which is quite shallow here, enters the short Cwmbran Tunnel, constructed to cope with the watershed from the adjacent mountains. One of the old Monmouthshire Canal Company mileposts stands beside the towpath, a memento of when the navigation extended its full course. Emerging from the tunnel, the land designated as Five Locks Nature Reserve is on the west bank. At Crown Bridge *fish & chips* are available opposite the pub. At Pontymoile the town centre is about one mile to the north west, through the lovely Pontypool Park. The old toll cottage at Pontymoile Basin, now available for rent as a holiday cottage, marks the junction of the Brecon & Abergavenny Canal with the Monmouthshire Canal. The cottage was built in 1813 for the tollkeeper who gauged boats which were moving from one canal to the other by measuring the height of the hull above the water. The nearby Marina Tea Rooms is open for tea, coffee, breakfast and lunches, *February–November*. There is a shop and cash point at Upper Pontnewydd Bridge, number 44.

Pontypool
Torfaen. All services. Pontypool has been an industrial town since Roman times, concentrating on the production of iron. In 1720 tin plate was produced here for the first time in Britain and in the 19th C the town was a centre for japanning – the coating of objects with an extract of oils from coal, so producing a black varnish similar to Japanese lacquer. Japan ware remained popular well into the 19th C. Despite its industrial heritage, Pontypool has always remained a farming centre and so the hard industrial elements are softened by the traditions of a rural market town.
Pontypool Park Trosnant Street, Pontypool NP4 8AT. Originally the seat of the Hanburys, the famous iron and steel family, this Georgian mansion is now a school. The park is open to the public.
Pontypool Museum Park Road, Pontypool NP4 6JH (01495 752043; www.pontypoolmuseum.org.uk). Situated in the stable block of Pontypool Park House. Tells the story of the Torfaen valley and its people. *Open daily Mon–Fri 10.00–17.00, Sat and Sun 14.00–17.00. Closed Xmas.* Charge.
The Shell Grotto Pontypool Park, Trosnant Street, Pontypool NP4 8AT (01495 764688). Built by Capel Hanbury Leigh in the 1830s with internal decorations of shell, animal bones and crystals. *Open May–Sep, Sat, Sun and B Hols 14.00– 17.00, groups by appointment at other times.* Free.
The Folly Tower Trosnant Street, Pontypool NP4 8AT. Commanding views over Gwent. The tower was demolished in 1940 by order of the Ministry of Defence as there were fears that it might guide the Luftwaffe bombers to the Royal Ordnance factory at Glascoed. Rebuilt in 1992. Opening details as for the Shell Grotto (above).

Pubs and Restaurants

Cross Keys Inn 55 Five Locks Road, Lowlands, Pontnewydd NP44 1BT (01633 861545). Log fires warm you on chilly days in this friendly, family-run, canalside pub. Food is available, bar snacks *L* and full meals *E*, with special *Sunday* lunches. Children welcome, and there is a play area. Large garden. B & B. Moorings.

The New Bridge Inn Greenhill Road, Forge Hammer, Pontypool NP44 3DG (01633 484596). Known locally as 'The Bottom Bridge', this pub welcomes walkers and cyclists. Outside seating. Children welcome. Karaoke and disco on *Sat*, live band on *Sun*.

✕ **Open Hearth** Wern Road, Sebastopol Pontypool NP4 5DR (01495 763752). Canalside, between bridges 48 and 49, south of Pontymoile Basin. A fine collection of real ales await you at this friendly pub. An extensive collection of bottled beers decorates the lounge bar. An imaginative choice of food is available *all day* Garden. Children welcome. Mooring. Ask to see the original IWA 'boater's book'. Occasional entertainment, *telephone for details. Open all day.*

Masons Arms Station Road, Griffithstown, Pontypool NP4 5JL (01495 763819). South of bridge 50. A selection of real ales are served in this friendly (and haunted) canalside pub together with a range of home-cooked food *L and E (not Sun E).* Children welcome. Mooring and outside seating.

✕ **Horse & Jockey** Usk Road, Pontymoile, Pontypool NP4 8AF (01495 762721). On the A472, 100yds east of bridge 55. A picturesque, thatched pub, haunted by Martha the ghost, with a warm welcome and serving real ale. Reasonably priced bar food with daily specials on offer *L and E, every day.* Children welcome. Garden and children's play area.

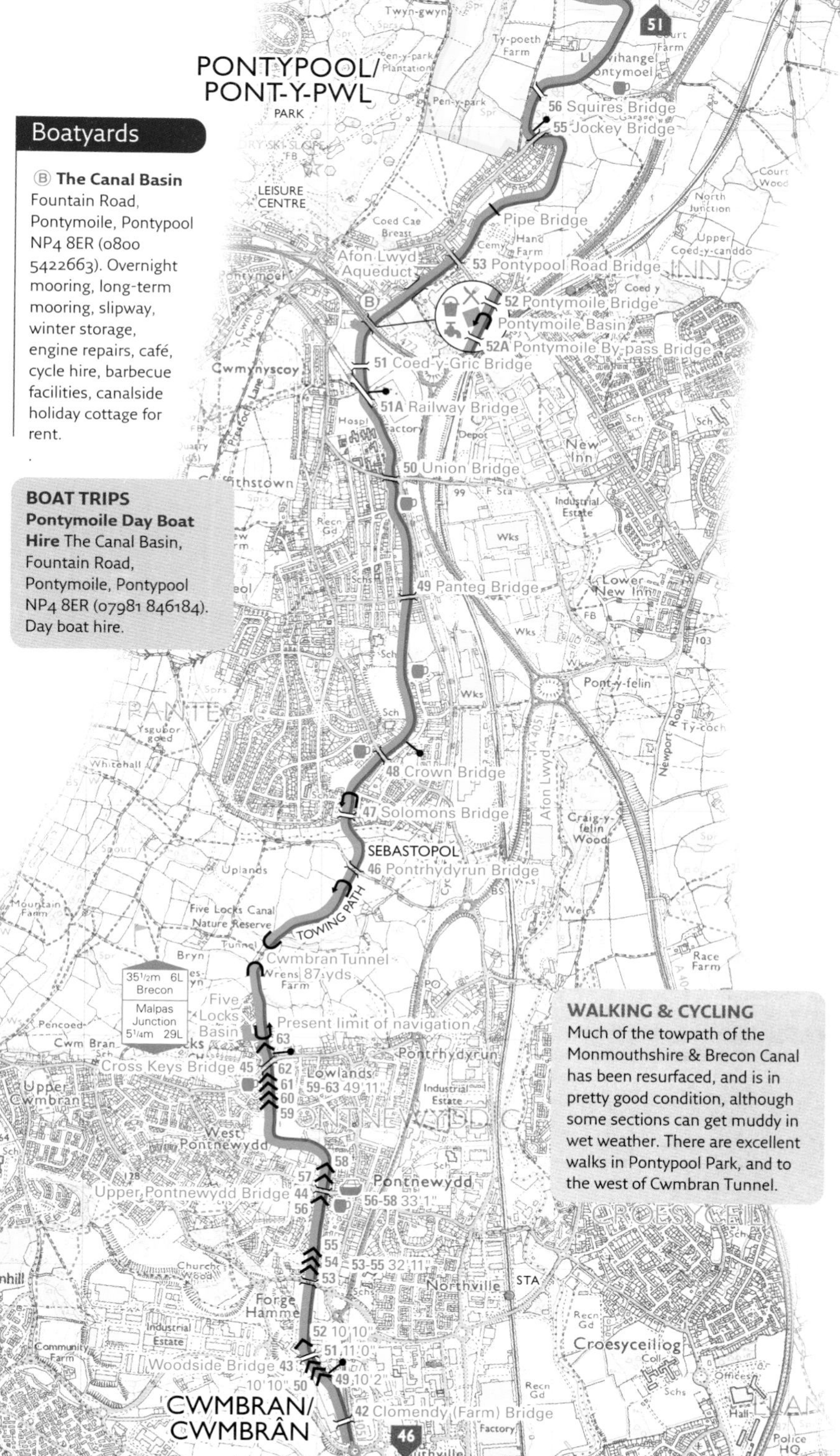

Boatyards

Ⓑ **The Canal Basin** Fountain Road, Pontymoile, Pontypool NP4 8ER (0800 5422663). Overnight mooring, long-term mooring, slipway, winter storage, engine repairs, café, cycle hire, barbecue facilities, canalside holiday cottage for rent.

BOAT TRIPS

Pontymoile Day Boat Hire The Canal Basin, Fountain Road, Pontymoile, Pontypool NP4 8ER (07981 846184). Day boat hire.

WALKING & CYCLING

Much of the towpath of the Monmouthshire & Brecon Canal has been resurfaced, and is in pretty good condition, although some sections can get muddy in wet weather. There are excellent walks in Pontypool Park, and to the west of Cwmbran Tunnel.

Goytre Wharf

As the canal leaves Pontypool it twists and turns, clinging to the hillside on the west, while to the east wide views open up across the rolling pastures and woods of the Usk valley. The winding course and the frequent stone bridges make the canal interesting, for every bend offers a different view of the steep hills to the west and the valley to the east, while the canal itself remains entirely quiet, rural and isolated. Navigators should look out for the GWR boundary posts on the non-towing path side. There are no villages by the canal in this section, but services and pubs are never more than a short walk away at Mamhilad and at Penperlleni where the *stores* are open daily. Main roads keep their distance, although they are generally clearly visible in the valley below the canal. After passing the long tunnel-like Saron's bridge, the seclusion is interrupted by long lines of moored boats, which are the prelude to Goytre Wharf – look out for Machine Cottage, where the weigh-bridge was once controlled, and the modelled figures in the lime-kilns. Just beyond the wharf the canal passes through a thick, wooded cutting before continuing its winding course with the open valley to the east.

Goytre Wharf Heritage, Activity & Study Centre Goytre Wharf, Llanover, Abergavenny NP7 9EW (01873 881069). Steeped in over 200 years of industrial history, Goytre Wharf occupies an 8-acre site and offers the visitor a rich diversity of walks, wildlife and the chance to absorb the feats of a bygone industrial era. Crafts and souvenirs, exhibitions and a natural amphitheatre, together with a tramroad exhibition, tourist information, children's play area and picnic area. Visitor moorings.

Mamhilad
Torfaen. Tel. A little hillside hamlet scattered around the church of St Illtyd. The pleasantly kept churchyard is overshadowed by massive yew trees, the largest of which reaches some 38ft in circumference. This suggests that the tree could well be between 2000–3000 years old and would have therefore been standing when missionaries from the monastery of St Illtyd at Llantwit Major first visited in the 6th C.

Penperlleni
Monmouth. PO, tel, stores (open 7 days), garage. Main road village useful for supplies. The estate here was bought in 1794 by Colonel Henry Bird, who is depicted on the pub sign.

Boatyards

Ⓑ **Red Line Boats** Goytre Wharf, Llanover, Abergavenny NP7 9EW (01873 880516; www.redlineboats.co.uk; www.goytrewharf.com). D Pump out, gas, narrowboat hire, day-hire craft (including canoes), overnight and long-term mooring, winter storage, slipway, boat and engine sales and repairs, telephone, toilets, showers, café, chandlery, books, maps and gifts. *Emergency call out.*

Pubs and Restaurants

The Goytre Arms Penperlleni, Llanover NP4 0AH (01873 880376). ¼ mile east of bridge 72. The unusual inn sign depicts Colonel Henry Bird returning from the American War in 1794 with his new Indian wife. Real ale is served in the bar which once specialised in the making of coffins! Food served *L and E (not Sun E)*. Children welcome. Garden. Moorings.

Waterside Rest Goytre Wharf, Llanover NP7 9EW (01873 881355). Restaurant and bar serving real ale *L and E in season (not Sun E)*. Children welcome. Moorings.

The Horseshoe Inn Mamhilad, Llanfoist NP4 8QZ (01873 880542). ¼ mile north of bridge 65 is a very scenic area. It is worth the short walk uphill to this pleasant little, possibly haunted, pub. A sign outside, referring to the view, reads, 'Relax, take in the view. God made this place when he finished his apprenticeship.' Real ale and meals *L and E, daily.* Outside seating. Children welcome. B & B.

The Star Folly Lane, Mamhilad, Llanfoist NP4 0JF (01495 785319). 200yds east of bridge 62. Cosy little pub serving a choice of real ale. Food available *L and E (not Sun E or Mon L)*. Children welcome, garden.

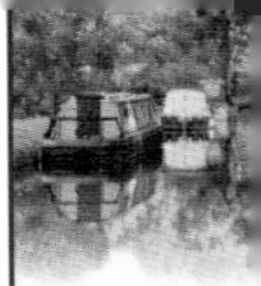

WALKING & CYCLING
A dense network of footpaths and minor lanes to the west of the canal give plenty of opportunities for circular rambles.

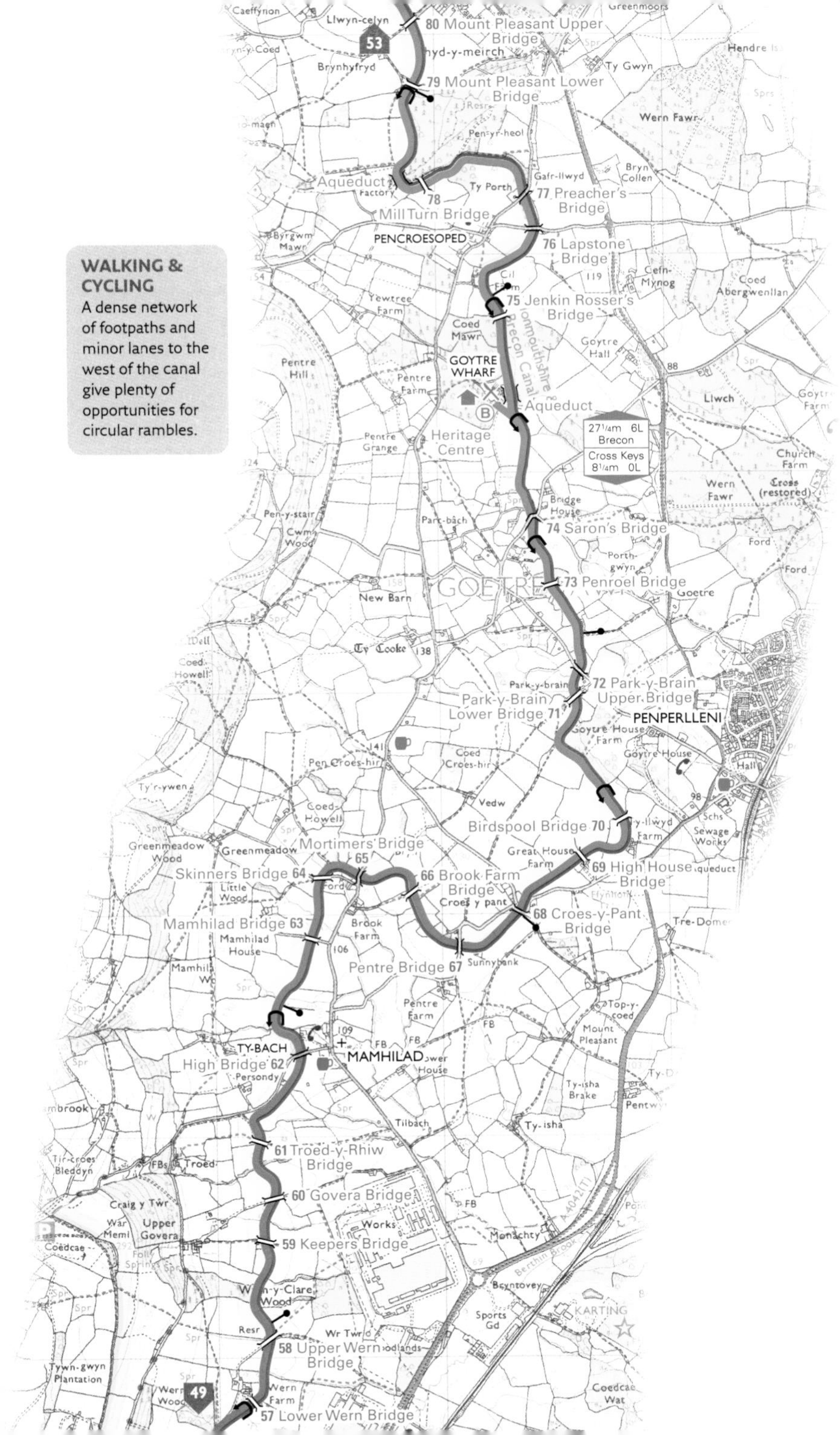

80 Mount Pleasant Upper Bridge
79 Mount Pleasant Lower Bridge
Aqueduct
78
77 Preacher's Bridge
Mill Turn Bridge
PENCROESOPED
76 Lapstone Bridge
75 Jenkin Rosser's Bridge
Monmouthshire & Brecon Canal
GOYTRE WHARF
Aqueduct
Heritage Centre
27¼m 6L Brecon
Cross Keys 8¼m 0L
74 Saron's Bridge
73 Penroel Bridge
GOETRE
72 Park-y-Brain Upper Bridge
Park-y-Brain Lower Bridge 71
PENPERLLENI
Birdspool Bridge 70
69 High House Bridge
68 Croes-y-Pant Bridge
Mortimers Bridge 65
Skinners Bridge 64
66 Brook Farm Bridge
Mamhilad Bridge 63
Pentre Bridge 67
TY-BACH
MAMHILAD
High Bridge 62
61 Troed-y-Rhiw Bridge
60 Govera Bridge
59 Keepers Bridge
58 Upper Wern Bridge
57 Lower Wern Bridge
53
49
KARTING

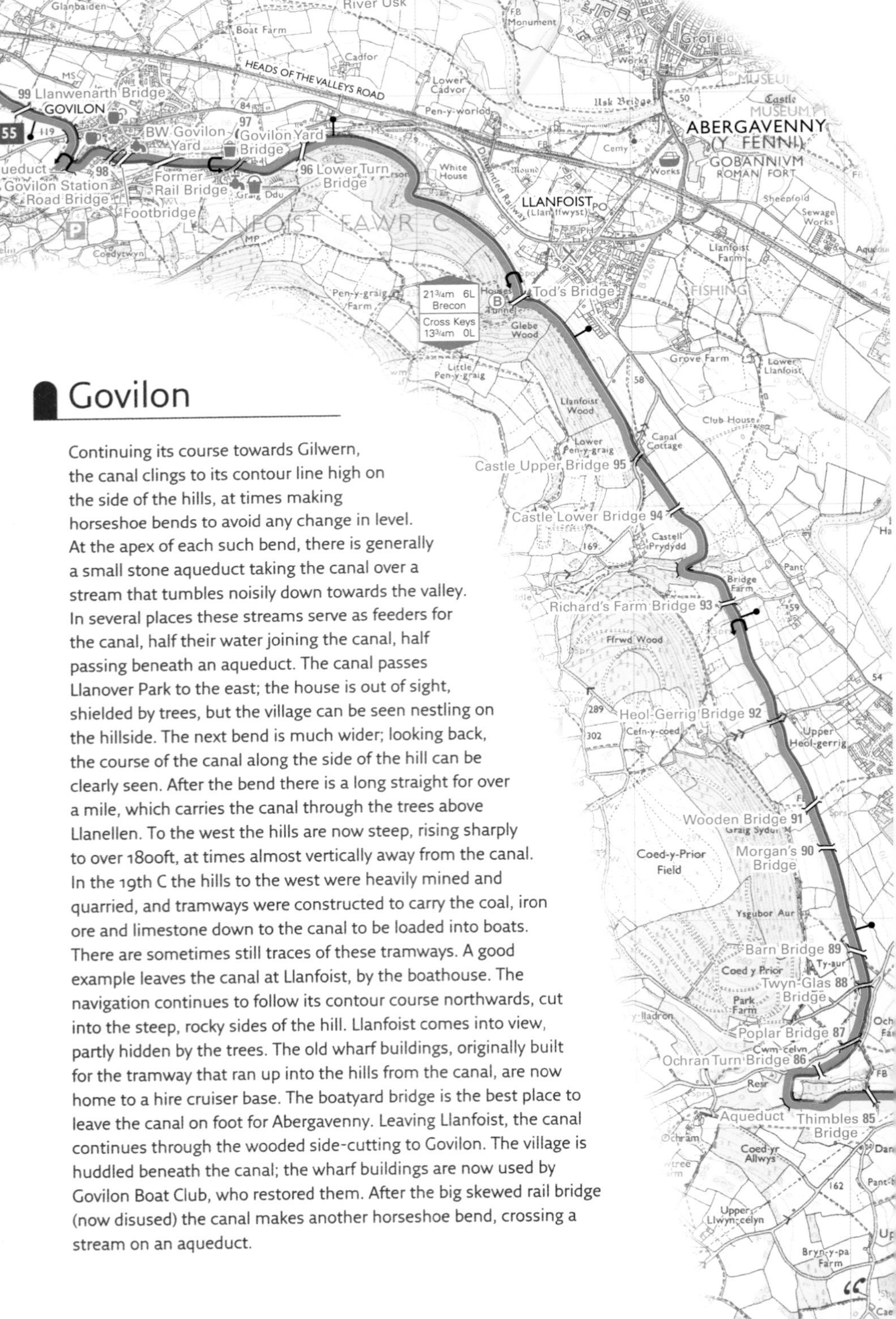

Govilon

Continuing its course towards Gilwern, the canal clings to its contour line high on the side of the hills, at times making horseshoe bends to avoid any change in level. At the apex of each such bend, there is generally a small stone aqueduct taking the canal over a stream that tumbles noisily down towards the valley. In several places these streams serve as feeders for the canal, half their water joining the canal, half passing beneath an aqueduct. The canal passes Llanover Park to the east; the house is out of sight, shielded by trees, but the village can be seen nestling on the hillside. The next bend is much wider; looking back, the course of the canal along the side of the hill can be clearly seen. After the bend there is a long straight for over a mile, which carries the canal through the trees above Llanellen. To the west the hills are now steep, rising sharply to over 1800ft, at times almost vertically away from the canal. In the 19th C the hills to the west were heavily mined and quarried, and tramways were constructed to carry the coal, iron ore and limestone down to the canal to be loaded into boats. There are sometimes still traces of these tramways. A good example leaves the canal at Llanfoist, by the boathouse. The navigation continues to follow its contour course northwards, cut into the steep, rocky sides of the hill. Llanfoist comes into view, partly hidden by the trees. The old wharf buildings, originally built for the tramway that ran up into the hills from the canal, are now home to a hire cruiser base. The boatyard bridge is the best place to leave the canal on foot for Abergavenny. Leaving Llanfoist, the canal continues through the wooded side-cutting to Govilon. The village is huddled beneath the canal; the wharf buildings are now used by Govilon Boat Club, who restored them. After the big skewed rail bridge (now disused) the canal makes another horseshoe bend, crossing a stream on an aqueduct.

Pubs and Restaurants

✕ 🍷 **Exotic East** Merthyr Road, Llanfoist NP7 9LP (01873 855553). Contemporary Indian restaurant. *Open 17.30–23.30 daily.*

The Bridgend Inn Church Lane, Govilon NP7 9RP (01873 830177). Below the aqueduct. A cosy, well-kept pub where you can enjoy real ale. Food available *L and E.* Children and dogs welcome. Patio. Often live music *Fri. Closed Mon L.*

The Lion Inn Merthyr Road, Govilon NP7 9PT (01873 830404). Real ales on offer and food is served *E Tue–Sun; Sat, Sun, all day.* Outside seating. Children and dogs welcome.

There are many pubs and restaurants in Abergavenny.

● **Llanover**
Monmouth. PO, tel, garage. The famous bell Big Ben in Westminster was named after the politician Benjamin Hall (Lord Llanover) who was responsible for the construction of the tower whilst Chief Commissioner of Works. He also initiated the tramway from Buckland House Wharf to Rhymney Ironworks, east of Talybont reservoir.

● **Llanellen**
Monmouth. PO, tel, stores. Although modern housing has greatly extended Llanellen into a suburb of Abergavenny, it is still an attractive village.

● **Llanfoist**
Monmouth. PO, tel, stores. The boatyard, housed in the old stone wharf buildings, has given this area of the waterway a new lease of life. There is a good walk from the boathouse into the mountains, following the course of the old tramway.

● **Abergavenny**
Monmouth. All services. Abergavenny lies beside the fast-flowing River Usk, surrounded on all sides by mountains and hills; the Sugar Loaf, Blorenge and the Skirrids overlook the town.

There is an annual event held at the end of March which involves the ascent of three peaks in one day.

Abergavenny Tourist Information Centre The Bus Station, Swan Meadow, Monmouth Road, Abergavenny NP7 5HH (01873 857588; www.abergavenny.co.uk).

Abergavenny Museum and Castle Castle Street, Abergavenny NP7 5EE (01873 854282; www.abergavennymuseum.co.uk). The mound of the castle dominates the town. Built in the 11th C, the castle now houses the museum which presents the story of the market town from prehistoric times to the present day. *Open Mar–Oct, Mon–Sat 11.00–13.00 and 14.00–17.00, Sun 14.00–17.00; Nov–Feb, closed at 16.00 and all day Sun.* Charge. Children free when accompanied by an adult.

St Mary's Church Monk Street, Abergavenny NP7 6EP (www.stmarys-priory.org). Originally the chapel of the Benedictine priory, the church was extensively rebuilt in the 14th C. It contains a fine carving of Jesse, hewn from a single oak trunk.

Abergavenny Leisure Centre Old Hereford Road, Abergavenny NP7 6EP (01873 735360; www.abergavenny.net). Swimming pool, squash courts and a sports hall amongst other facilities. *Open Mon–Fri 07.00–22.00, Sat 08.30–18.00, Sun 08.30–18.00.*

Sugar Loaf A conspicuous landmark 2 miles north west of Abergavenny, so named because of its shape. The National Trust owns 2130 acres, including the 1955ft summit.

● **Govilon**
Monmouth. PO, tel, stores, garage. Beside the aqueduct are steps leading down to Govilon, little of which can be seen from the canal.

WALKING & CYCLING
There is a 3-mile section of scenic railway path between Llanfoist and Govilon, which makes for an excellent cycle ride. The surface is fine gravel, and climbs are gentle. Start from The Cutting, by the Post Office in Llanfoist.

Boatyards

Ⓑ **Beacon Park Boats** The Boathouse, Llanfoist, Abergavenny NP7 9NG (01873 858277; www.beaconparkboats.com).
D Pump out, gas, narrowboat hire, day-hire craft, slipway, café.

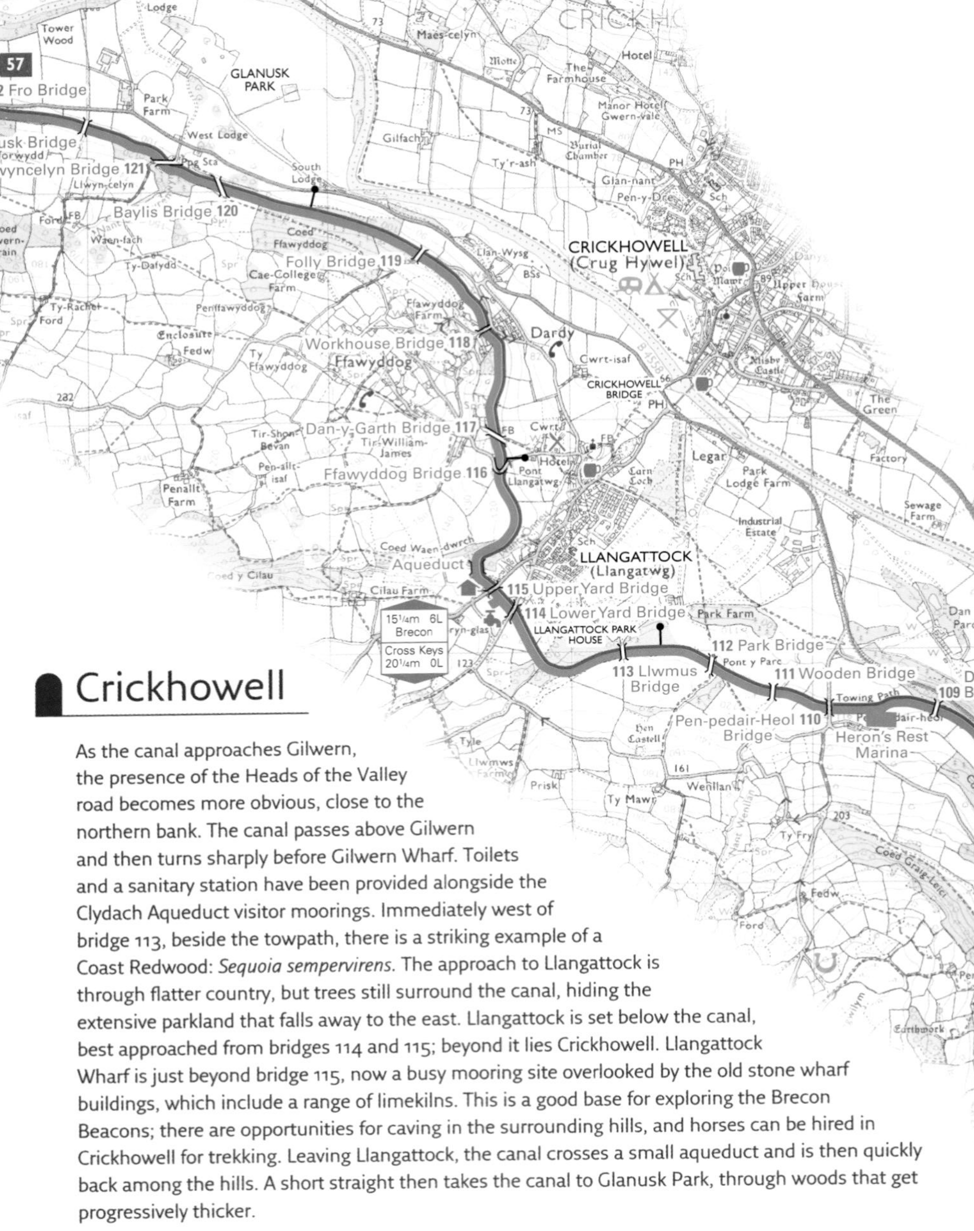

Crickhowell

As the canal approaches Gilwern, the presence of the Heads of the Valley road becomes more obvious, close to the northern bank. The canal passes above Gilwern and then turns sharply before Gilwern Wharf. Toilets and a sanitary station have been provided alongside the Clydach Aqueduct visitor moorings. Immediately west of bridge 113, beside the towpath, there is a striking example of a Coast Redwood: *Sequoia sempervirens.* The approach to Llangattock is through flatter country, but trees still surround the canal, hiding the extensive parkland that falls away to the east. Llangattock is set below the canal, best approached from bridges 114 and 115; beyond it lies Crickhowell. Llangattock Wharf is just beyond bridge 115, now a busy mooring site overlooked by the old stone wharf buildings, which include a range of limekilns. This is a good base for exploring the Brecon Beacons; there are opportunities for caving in the surrounding hills, and horses can be hired in Crickhowell for trekking. Leaving Llangattock, the canal crosses a small aqueduct and is then quickly back among the hills. A short straight then takes the canal to Glanusk Park, through woods that get progressively thicker.

Boatyards

Ⓑ **Castle Narrowboats** Church Road Wharf, Gilwern NP7 0EP (01873 830001; www.castlenarrowboats.co.uk). Pump out, narrowboat hire, day-boat hire, hoist, boat building, boat repairs, engine sales and repairs, chandlery, books, maps, and gifts. BW sanitary station opposite.

Ⓑ **Road House Narrowboats** 50 Main Road, Gilwern NP7 0AS (01873 830240; www.narrowboats-wales.co.uk). Pump out, gas, narrowboat hire, overnight mooring, engine repairs.

- **Gilwern**
Monmouth. PO, tel, stores. The village is built along one main street which falls steeply away from the canal. There is a useful, well-stocked, gift shop across the road at bridge 103.
- **Llangattock**
Powys. This little village, just down the lane from bridge 116, was once famous for its weaving and its limekilns. It also has a 12th-C church, founded in the 6th C. The hills behind the village are riddled with limestone caves and quarries.
- **Crickhowell**
Powys. PO, tel, stores, butcher, garage, bank, fish & chips. The road down through Llangattock leads to the 13-arch medieval stone bridge over the Usk. In the centre of the town are the scant remains of the Norman castle. Apart from hill walking, there are opportunities for fishing and pony trekking. **Tourist Information Centre** Beaufort Chambers, Beaufort Street, Crickhowell NP8 IAA (01873 812105; www.crickhowellinfo.org.uk). *Open Apr–Oct, 10.00–17.00.*

Pubs and Restaurants

The Beaufort Arms Main Road, Gilwern NP7 0AU (01873 832235). Downhill from bridge 103. Real ale is served, along with food *L and E (not Sun E)*. Children welcome.

The Bridgend Inn 49 Main Road, Gilwern NP8 1AR (01873 830939). Canalside at bridge 103. Reai ale and home-cooked food *L and E*. Children welcome. Patio.

The Corn Exchange Crickhowell Road, Gilwern NP7 0DG (01873 830337). A homely pub with some original features in the restaurant, where corn was once exchanged for goods. Real ale, and food *L and E*. Children welcome, outside seating. Mooring.

The Bridgend Inn Bridge Street, Crickhowell NP8 1AR (01873 810338). Well worth the 1-mile walk from either bridge 114 or 116 to visit this fine pub. Real ale and good food *L and E*. Children welcome. Riverside garden.

The Bear Hotel Crickhowell NP8 1BW (01873 810408; www.bearhotel.co.uk). The Bear has won many awards for its excellent food. Real ale. Meals served in both bar and restaurant *L and E (not Mon E or Sun E for restaurant)*. Children welcome, garden. B & B

The Horseshoe Inn Beaufort Road, Llangattock, Crickhowell NP8 1PA (01873 810393). East of Bridge 116. Beside a stream and surrounded by trees, this pub serves real ale, along with food *L and E (not Mon)*. Children welcome, garden.

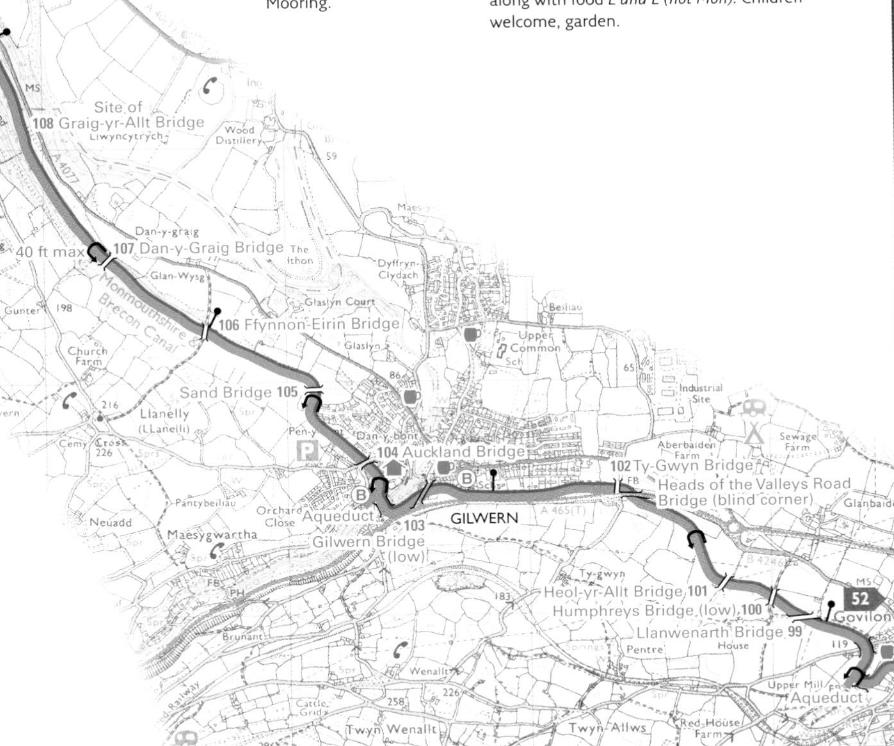

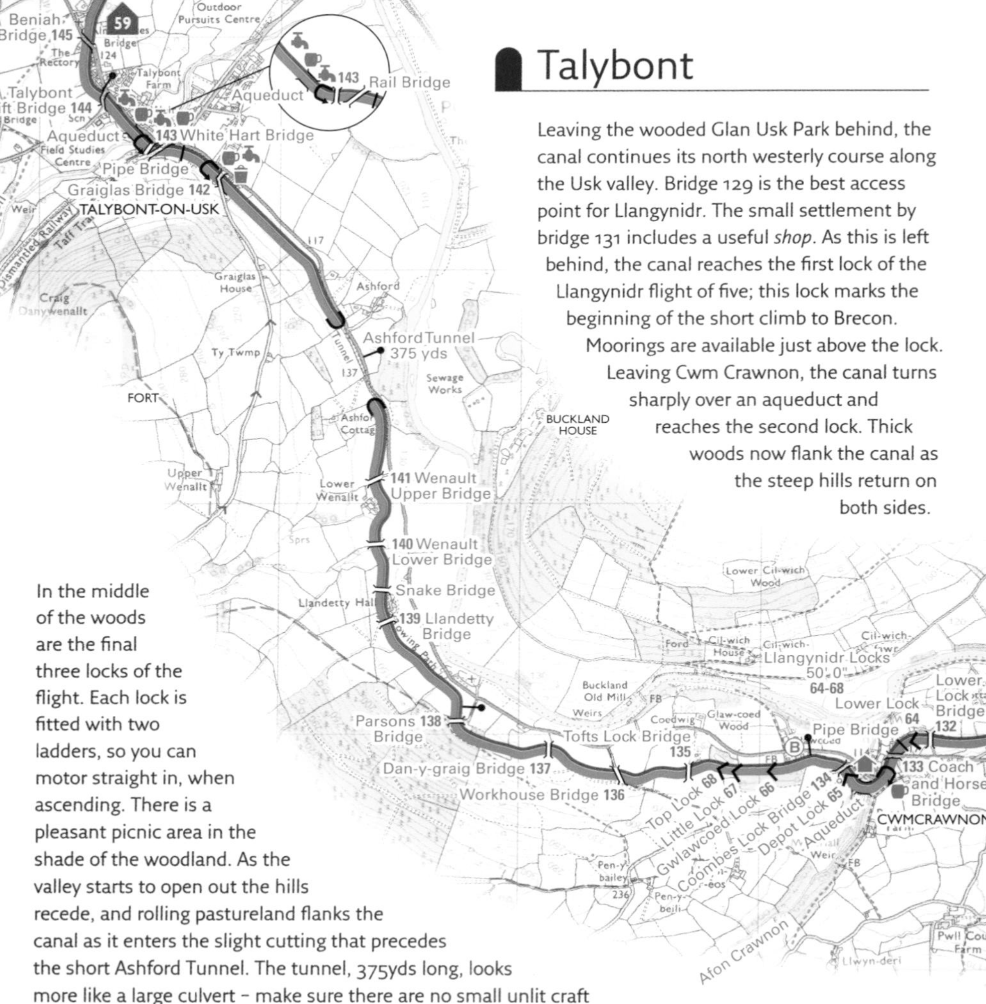

Talybont

Leaving the wooded Glan Usk Park behind, the canal continues its north westerly course along the Usk valley. Bridge 129 is the best access point for Llangynidr. The small settlement by bridge 131 includes a useful *shop*. As this is left behind, the canal reaches the first lock of the Llangynidr flight of five; this lock marks the beginning of the short climb to Brecon. Moorings are available just above the lock. Leaving Cwm Crawnon, the canal turns sharply over an aqueduct and reaches the second lock. Thick woods now flank the canal as the steep hills return on both sides.

In the middle of the woods are the final three locks of the flight. Each lock is fitted with two ladders, so you can motor straight in, when ascending. There is a pleasant picnic area in the shade of the woodland. As the valley starts to open out the hills recede, and rolling pastureland flanks the canal as it enters the slight cutting that precedes the short Ashford Tunnel. The tunnel, 375yds long, looks more like a large culvert – make sure there are no small unlit craft using it before you enter. The canal goes straight to Talybont through a low cutting then passes through the village on an embankment, crossing the fast-flowing Caerfanell river on an aqueduct. At the end of the village is a lift bridge. It is electrically operated and instructions are clearly posted. Leaving the village, pasturelands roll steeply away to the west, but to the east there are wide flat lands; the canal is carried on a low embankment which continues irregularly for the next 3 miles. There are three lift bridges on this section which are sometimes fixed in the open position to stop livestock crossing the canal; navigators should always leave them as they find them.

Boatyards

Ⓑ **Country Craft Narrowboats** Cwm Crawnon Warehouse, Llangynidr NP8 1ND (01874 730850; www.countrycraftnarrowboats.co.uk). Pump out, narrowboat hire, overnight mooring, toilets, showers.

Ⓑ **Brecon Boats** Travellers' Rest, Talybont-on-Usk LD3 7YP (01874 676401; www.travellersrestinn.com). Day boats with cabins seating up to five. Booking advised.

NAVIGATIONAL NOTES

Locks on this canal should be left empty with the bottom gates open.

- **Llangynidr**
  Powys. PO, tel, stores. Housing now sprawls up the hillside, linking the upper and lower parts of the village. There is a splendid stone bridge c.1600, which spans the Usk, and a pretty 19th-C church.
- **Cwm Crawnon**
  Powys. Clustered round the canal as it climbs the Llangynidr locks, this hamlet is famous for the Coach & Horses, an attractive pub and restaurant.
- **Talybont-on-Usk**
  Powys. PO, tel, stores. When the railway and canal were both operating commercially, Talybont must have been a busy village. Today it is a quiet holiday centre with facilities for fishing, pony trekking, mountain biking and hill walking, details of which can be obtained at the Talybont Venture Centre in the village. There is a useful stores and PO at bridge 144, selling groceries and gas, which also serves as an off-licence. The village also has an impressive line-up of three pubs. The leat to the old mill brought water from Afon Caerfanell which falls rapidly from Talybont reservoir in the hills to the south to join the Usk. The large wharf overlooks the village, which is clustered round the Caerfanell Aqueduct.

WALKING & CYCLING

The Taff Trail is part of the Sustrans Welsh National Cycle Route, which stretches between Cardiff and Brecon, and it follows a section of the towpath to Brecon. There is an excellent circular walk taking in the towpath between Cwmcrawnon and Aberhowy Bridge (126) with the return made along the path by the Usk.

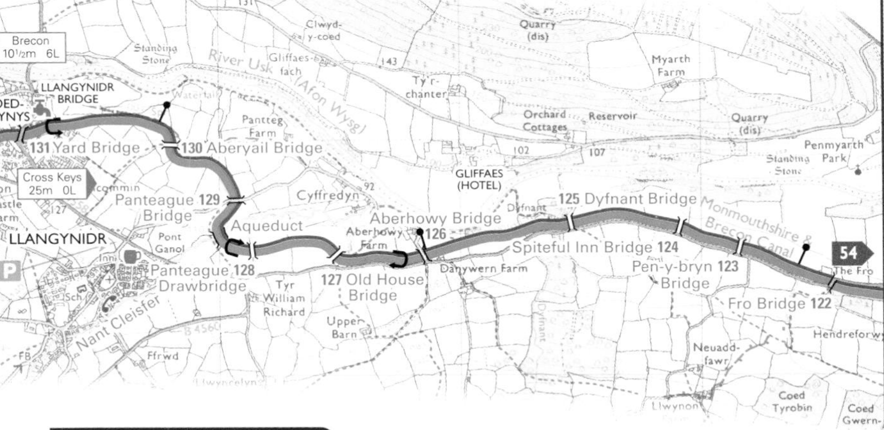

Pubs and Restaurants

The Red Lion Duffryn Road, Llangynidr NP8 1NT (01874 730223). Country village pub with plenty of ghosts and local characters. Real ale. Home-made food *L and E (not Mon L).* Children welcome. Garden. Occasional live music at *weekends.*

The Coach & Horses Cwm Crawnon, Llangynidr NP8 1LS (01874 730245). Canalside at bridge 133. Real ale, along with an interesting and well-priced menu, available *L and E.* Children welcome, garden. B & B.

The Travellers Rest Talybont-on-Usk LD3 7YP (01874 676233; www.travellersrestinn.com). Canalside pub at bridge 142 offering real ale and a good choice of bar food *L (in summer) and E.* Children welcome, garden. Camping and B & B. Moorings.

The White Hart Inn Talybont-on-Usk LD3 7JD (01874 676227). Canalside at bridge 143, and on the Taff Trail, this sociable pub serves real ale. Food, including curries and home-made pies, is served in bar and dining room *L and E.* Children welcome. Canalside seating. Karaoke *Sat E.* Moorings.

The Star Inn Talybont-on-Usk LD3 7YX (01874 676635). Traditional village inn by the aqueduct. A choice of real ale and good pub food *L and E.* Children welcome. Riverside garden. Live music *Wed during season.* B & B. *Open all day Sat and Sun, and on school holidays.*

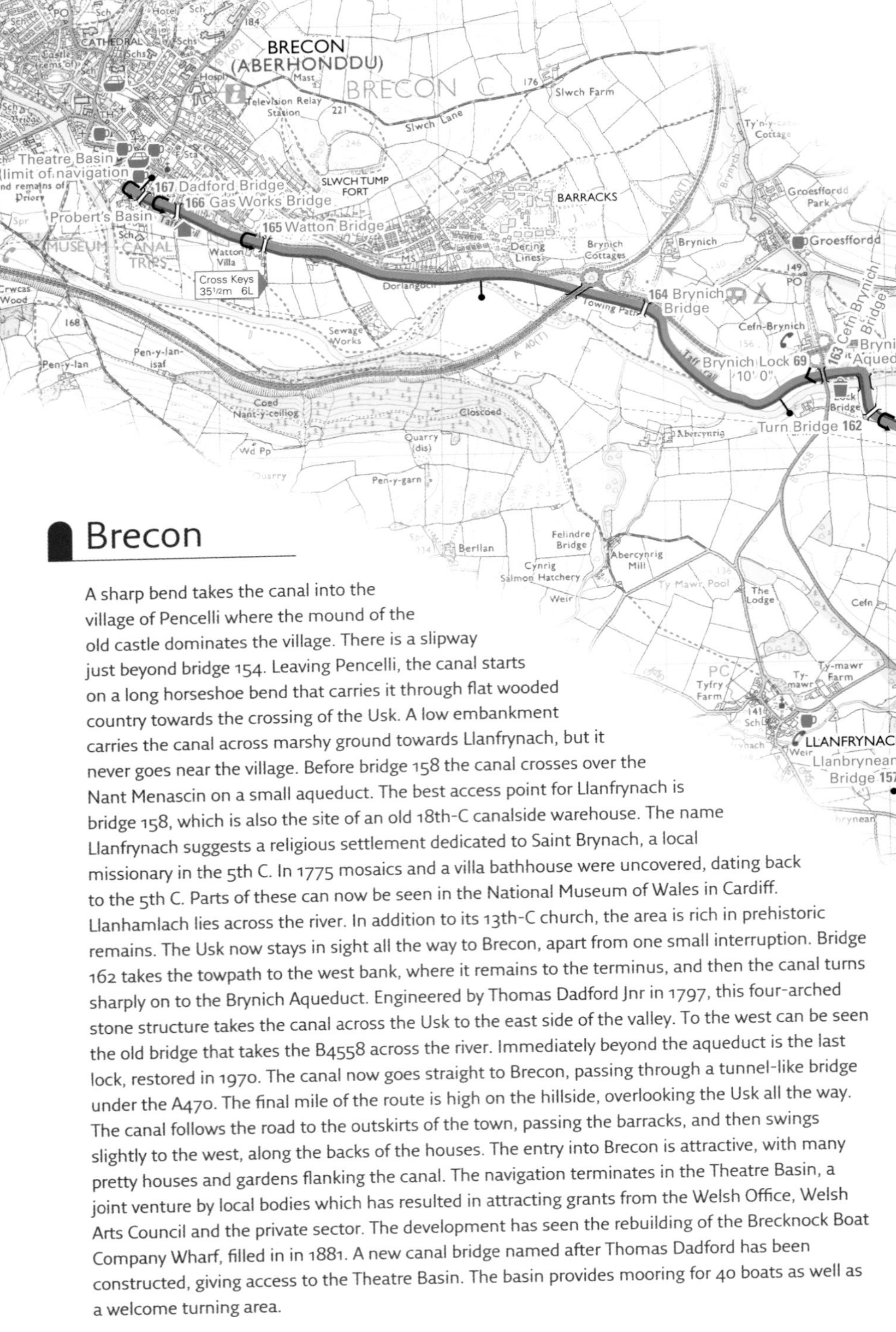

Brecon

A sharp bend takes the canal into the village of Pencelli where the mound of the old castle dominates the village. There is a slipway just beyond bridge 154. Leaving Pencelli, the canal starts on a long horseshoe bend that carries it through flat wooded country towards the crossing of the Usk. A low embankment carries the canal across marshy ground towards Llanfrynach, but it never goes near the village. Before bridge 158 the canal crosses over the Nant Menascin on a small aqueduct. The best access point for Llanfrynach is bridge 158, which is also the site of an old 18th-C canalside warehouse. The name Llanfrynach suggests a religious settlement dedicated to Saint Brynach, a local missionary in the 5th C. In 1775 mosaics and a villa bathhouse were uncovered, dating back to the 5th C. Parts of these can now be seen in the National Museum of Wales in Cardiff. Llanhamlach lies across the river. In addition to its 13th-C church, the area is rich in prehistoric remains. The Usk now stays in sight all the way to Brecon, apart from one small interruption. Bridge 162 takes the towpath to the west bank, where it remains to the terminus, and then the canal turns sharply on to the Brynich Aqueduct. Engineered by Thomas Dadford Jnr in 1797, this four-arched stone structure takes the canal across the Usk to the east side of the valley. To the west can be seen the old bridge that takes the B4558 across the river. Immediately beyond the aqueduct is the last lock, restored in 1970. The canal now goes straight to Brecon, passing through a tunnel-like bridge under the A470. The final mile of the route is high on the hillside, overlooking the Usk all the way. The canal follows the road to the outskirts of the town, passing the barracks, and then swings slightly to the west, along the backs of the houses. The entry into Brecon is attractive, with many pretty houses and gardens flanking the canal. The navigation terminates in the Theatre Basin, a joint venture by local bodies which has resulted in attracting grants from the Welsh Office, Welsh Arts Council and the private sector. The development has seen the rebuilding of the Brecknock Boat Company Wharf, filled in in 1881. A new canal bridge named after Thomas Dadford has been constructed, giving access to the Theatre Basin. The basin provides mooring for 40 boats as well as a welcome turning area.

Pubs and Restaurants

White Swan Llanfrynach LD3 7BZ (01874 665276; www.the-white-swan.com). A well-kept pub dating back some 300 years. Real ale is served along with well-priced, imaginative food *L and E (not Mon or Tue, except B Hols)*. Children welcome, large garden.

Royal Oak Pencelli LD3 7LX (01874 665396). Canalside at bridge 153. Traditional village local serving real ale. Home-cooked food available *L and E*. Children welcome, garden. *Closed L in winter*. Moorings.

Three Horseshoes Groesffordd LD3 7SN (01874 665672; www.threehorseshoesgroesffordd.co.uk). North of bridge 163. Inviting pub offering real ales and home made food serve *daily L and E*. Outside seating in garden. Children welcome and play equipment available.

There are many pubs and restaurants in Brecon, including:

George Hotel George Street, Brecon LD3 7LD (01874 623421; www.george-hotel.com). Welcoming family-run hotel serving real ale from its 17th-C bars. Good food, using fresh local produce, is served *all day until 22.00*. Children welcome. Paved courtyard.

Wellington Hotel The Bulwark, Brecon LD3 7AD (01874 625225). Old established, comfortable central Hotel serving food *L and E*. B & B.

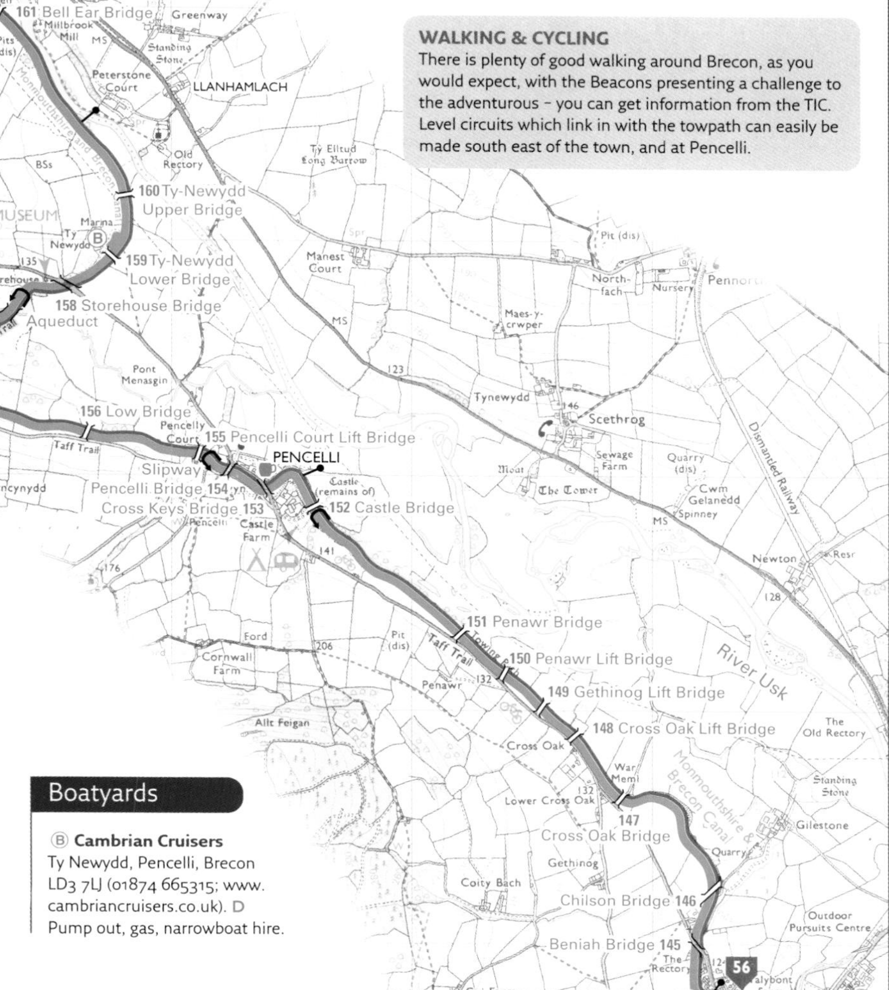

WALKING & CYCLING
There is plenty of good walking around Brecon, as you would expect, with the Beacons presenting a challenge to the adventurous - you can get information from the TIC. Level circuits which link in with the towpath can easily be made south east of the town, and at Pencelli.

Boatyards

Ⓑ **Cambrian Cruisers**
Ty Newydd, Pencelli, Brecon LD3 7LJ (01874 665315; www.cambriancruisers.co.uk). D Pump out, gas, narrowboat hire.

Pencelli

Powys. This little village was at one time the head of a medieval lordship, but the only indication of this today is the castle mound. The castle farm occupies the site of the old castle which can now only be recognised by the footings of some of the walls laid down in the 13th C. The castle is not open to the public.

Llanfrynach

Powys. An attractive village built in a square round the pretty church. Nearby is the site of a Roman bathhouse.

Brecon

Powys. PO, tel, stores, garage, bank, cinema, swimming pool. Built at the confluence of the Usk and Honddu rivers, Brecon has long been the administrative centre and market town for the Breconshire uplands. It dates back to the Roman period, and although little remains, the narrow streets that surround the castle give an idea of medieval Brecon. Today the town is famous as a touring centre and for its annual Jazz Festival which takes the town by storm *every August*. The cathedral and generous 18th-C architecture make it seem more English than Welsh. The Usk waterfront is especially attractive, dominated by the old stone bridge. Sarah Siddons and her brother Charles Kemble lived in the High Street.

Brecon Cathedral Cathedral Close, Brecon LD3 9DP. Originally the Priory Church of St John, founded by Bernard Newmarch, it was given cathedral status in 1923. Most of the building is 13th-C, although the nave is a century later. There is some fine glass, and side chapels dedicated to various medieval guilds.

Brecon Cathedral New Heritage Centre (01874 625222; www.breconcathedral.co.uk). Situated in the beautiful Cathedral Close the centre houses an exhibition on cathedral life alongside a restored 16th-C tithe barn. *Open Mon-Sat 10.30-16.00, also Sun in summer 12.30-15.30.* Charge. Restaurant serving coffee, lunches and teas *open 10.00-17.00.*

Brecon Castle Most of the remains of the 11th-C castle now stand in the grounds of the Brecon Hotel and permission to view must be obtained from the hotel. A large motte and bailey, parts of the walls and two towers survive. The destruction of the castle during the Civil War was hastened by the inhabitants of Brecon, who did not want either side to occupy it.

Brecknock Museum & Art Gallery Captain's Walk, Brecon LD3 7DW (01874 624121; www.powys.gov.uk). The collections include local history, natural history and a large archaeology section, from pre-Roman to medieval times. The museum also houses a fine collection of Welsh lovespoons. *Open Apr-Sep, Mon-Fri 10.00- 17.00, Sat 10.00-13.00 and 14.00-17.00, Sun 12.00-17.00.* Modest entry charge.

South Wales Borderers Museum The Barracks, Brecon LD3 7EB (01874 613310; www.rrw.org.uk/museums). History of two famous regiments over 280 years. *Open Mon-Fri 09.00-1700, Apr-Sep also open Sat, Sun, 10.00-16.00. Last admission 16.15.* Charge.

Theatre Brycheiniog Canal Wharf, Brecon LD3 7EW (01874 611622; www.theatrbrycheiniog.co.uk). Host to a rich diversity of touring drama and music, overlooking the canal terminus. Also café, bar and ice creams.

Tourist Information Centre Market Car Park, Brecon LD3 9DA (01874 622485).

BOAT TRIPS

Dragonfly Cruises Canal Wharf, Brecon LD3 7EW (07831 685222; www.dragonfly-cruises.co.uk). 2½ hour canal trip including a lock and an aqueduct on this 53-seater boat. *Easter-Oct, Sat, Sun and Wed; Jul also Thu; Aug also Tue, Thu and Fri. Telephone for times.*

BRECON BEACONS NATIONAL PARK

7 Glamorgan Street, Brecon (01874 624437; www.breconbeacons.org). The park covers 519 square miles of mountain and hill country, embracing parts of the old counties of Herefordshire, Monmouthshire, Breconshire and Carmarthenshire. It includes three nature reserves, a forest reserve, opportunities for fishing, caving, pony trekking, sailing and boating, and several towns of interest to tourists, notably Brecon, Crickhowell, Talgarth and Hay-on-Wye. Virtually all the canal is within the park - a factor that greatly strengthened the case for its restoration and reopening. The canal is an excellent introduction to the park, crossing it roughly from south east to north west; in several places there are foot and bridle paths leading away into the mountains from the towpath. A good place to start any exploration is the Mountain Centre (LD3 8ER; 01874 623366), 1000ft up on Mynydd Illtud, above the village of Libanus, 5 miles south west of Brecon. There are rest and refreshment rooms, car parks and picnic sites overlooking the Brecon Beacons.

NEATH & TENNANT CANALS SWANSEA CANAL

NEATH & TENNANT CANALS

Neath Canal (general)
Manager: R. Minty
01639 635282
neathcanalnav@btconnect.com

Neath Canal (North Resolven)
Colin Powell, Parks & Cemeteries Manager
Neath Port Talbot County Borough Council
01639 686176

Tennant Canal
Manager: D. Williams
01792 644699

MAXIMUM DIMENSIONS
Length: 60'
Beam: 9'
Headroom: 6'

MILEAGE
Tennant Canal
Junction with Glan-Y-Wern Canal *to:*
Neath Abbey: 3¼ miles
ABERDULAIS JUNCTION: 6½ miles

Neath Canal
BRITON FERRY to:
Croft Bridge: 3 miles
Aberdulais Junction: 5 miles
Resolven: 8¾ miles
YSGWRFA: 11¼ miles

Locks:
Tennant Canal: 1
Neath Canal: 14

SWANSEA CANAL
Manager:
01606 871471
enquiries.walesandbordercounties
@britishwaterways.co.uk

MAXIMUM DIMENSIONS
Length: 69'
Beam: 7' 6"
Headroom: 7'

Navigation has been extended 5.5 miles between Neath town centre and Abergarwed on the Neath Canal, but remains very limited on the Tennant and Swansea Canals.

THE NEATH & TENNANT CANALS
The Neath Canal received Royal Assent in 1791 and work started immediately, initially with Thomas Dadford as engineer, who was soon followed by the less capable Thomas Sheasby. The navigation opened in 1795, and was extended to Giant's Grave in 1799, eventually reaching Briton Ferry in 1842. Fed by numerous branch canals and tramways it prospered, in spite of railway competition, due to its position on the west side of the Neath Valley and its denial of the right to build railway or tramway bridges over it. This finally all changed in 1875 and the canal then went into decline. It is currently beautifully restored beyond Resolven. The section between Abergarwed and Bridge Street in Neath town centre has been completely restored for navigation, including the construction of the longest single span aqueduct in the UK across the River Neath at Ynysbwllog. Although a canal or drainage ditch may have been dug between the rivers Neath and Tawe in the Middle Ages, the Tennant Canal has its origins in a navigation planned by Richard Jenkins, who wished to transport coal from his colliery at Glan-y-Wern to the River Neath. Acquired by George Tennant in 1817, remarkably it is still in the ownership of his descendants, the Coombe-Tennant family.

THE SWANSEA CANAL
With the growth of collieries in the Tawe Valley, the expansion of the Ynysgedwyn Iron Works, increased copper smelting, improvements to Swansea harbour and the lack of a turnpike road, the demand for a canal in the Tawe Valley became irresistible. An Act was passed in 1794 sanctioning the building of such a waterway, and work began with initially Charles Roberts, and later Thomas Sheasby, as engineer. The canal between Swansea and Henneuadd opened fully in 1798. Success was, however, short-lived, and soon tolls were being cut in the face of railway competition, although the reduction in demand for iron also played its part in the canal's eventual demise. Carrying finally ceased in 1931 although its use as a water channel continued.

Neath

When navigation on the Tennant Canal is permitted, it will begin at its junction with the Glan-y-Wern Canal, which crosses Crymlyn Bog, an SSSI. The mile or so of the main line to the basin at Port Tennant remains heavily overgrown. Heading east the waterway soon reaches Jersey Marine, where there is a useful *PO* and *stores*. Passing under railway bridges the canal enters a post-industrial landscape, overshadowed by the M4 motorway. Bridge names give a clue to its busy past: Quarry, Gas Works, Abbey Wharf, Crown Copperworks and Skewen Tramroad are all passed on the approach to Neath. To the east the Afon Nedd brings tidal water inland, while gulls wheel overhead. Again the canal heads east, now passing the substantial remains of Neath Abbey. It then crosses the Clydach Aqueduct before being totally overshadowed by a web of roads and roundabouts.

The Neath Canal has completely lost its connection with the river at Briton Ferry, and is first revealed in the shadow of the A48 High Level Viaduct. Passing some old warehouses and light industry it soon loops past Giant's Grave and sets off beside football pitches towards Neath, passing the new Giant's Grave Lift Bridge, a sign, were it needed, that boats will one day again use this navigation. Shadowing the course of the river, the waterway heads east, passing the ruined walls of Neath Castle.

- **Jersey Marine**

Rhondda, Cynon, Taff. PO, tel, stores. By the Tower Hotel you can see a tall camera obscura, built 150 years ago, with what was a handsome 'fives' court below.

- **Neath**

Rhondda, Cynon, Taff. All services. Busy, bustling and friendly. A rich industrial past is revealed at Neath Abbey Ironworks, on the banks of the Afon Clydach. Owned by the Quaker families of Fox, Price and Tregelles, it dates from 1792 and produced about 80 tons of pig iron a week, which was then shipped to their Cornish foundry. Later the company was to become internationally renowned for its steam engines, locomotives and iron ships. The works closed in the 1880s.

Neath Abbey Baron Richard de Granville, a Norman, founded the abbey in 1130. A colourful history has included its use as a copper works, following the Dissolution. It is in the care of Cadw. *Open 10.00–16.00 daily.* Free.

Neath Castle First recorded in 1185, when the Welsh attacked it, the present structure probably dates from 1243–95, when the rest of the town was being built.

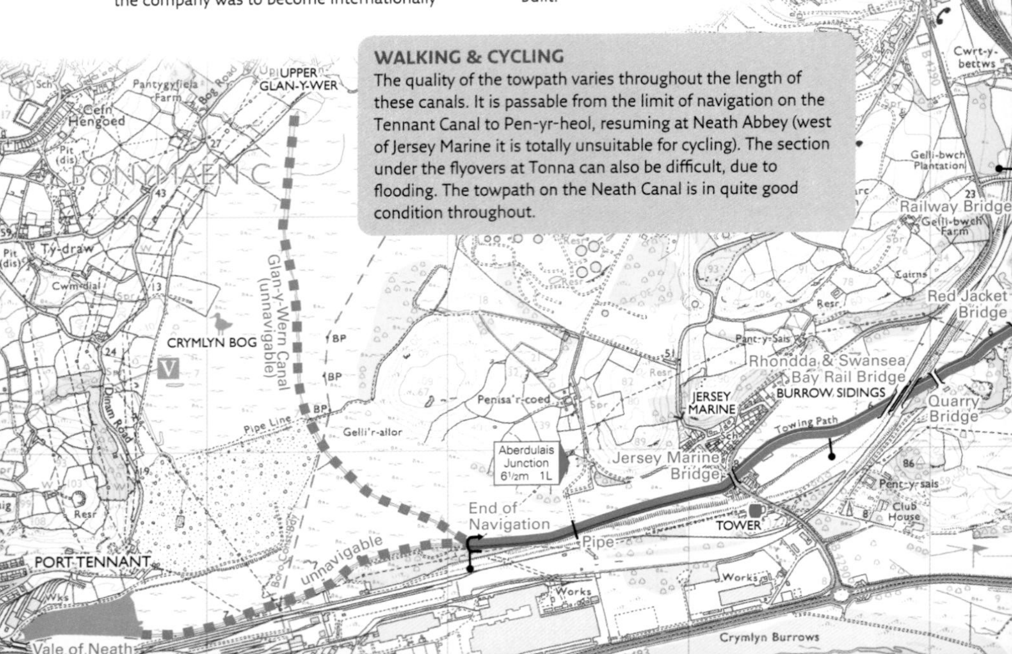

WALKING & CYCLING

The quality of the towpath varies throughout the length of these canals. It is passable from the limit of navigation on the Tennant Canal to Pen-yr-heol, resuming at Neath Abbey (west of Jersey Marine it is totally unsuitable for cycling). The section under the flyovers at Tonna can also be difficult, due to flooding. The towpath on the Neath Canal is in quite good condition throughout.

Society of Friends Meeting House Built in 1799 within the castle grounds on land donated by Lady Mackworth, it served the needs of the many Quaker entrepreneurs who were attracted by the area's industrial potential. Restored by the old Neath Borough Council, it is used for meetings and functions.

Tourist Information Centre Waterfalls Centre, Pontneathvaughan Road, Pontneddfechan, nr Glynneath SA11 5NR (01639 721795; www.breconbeacons.org).

BOAT TRIPS

The Neath & Tennant Canal Society runs the ***Thomas Dadford*** trip boat from the landing stage in the town centre (between B&Q and Morrisons) *Easter–Oct, Sat, and daily during school holidays, 11.00, 12.30 and 14.30.* Telephone 01792 426449 for details. Also available for private charter.

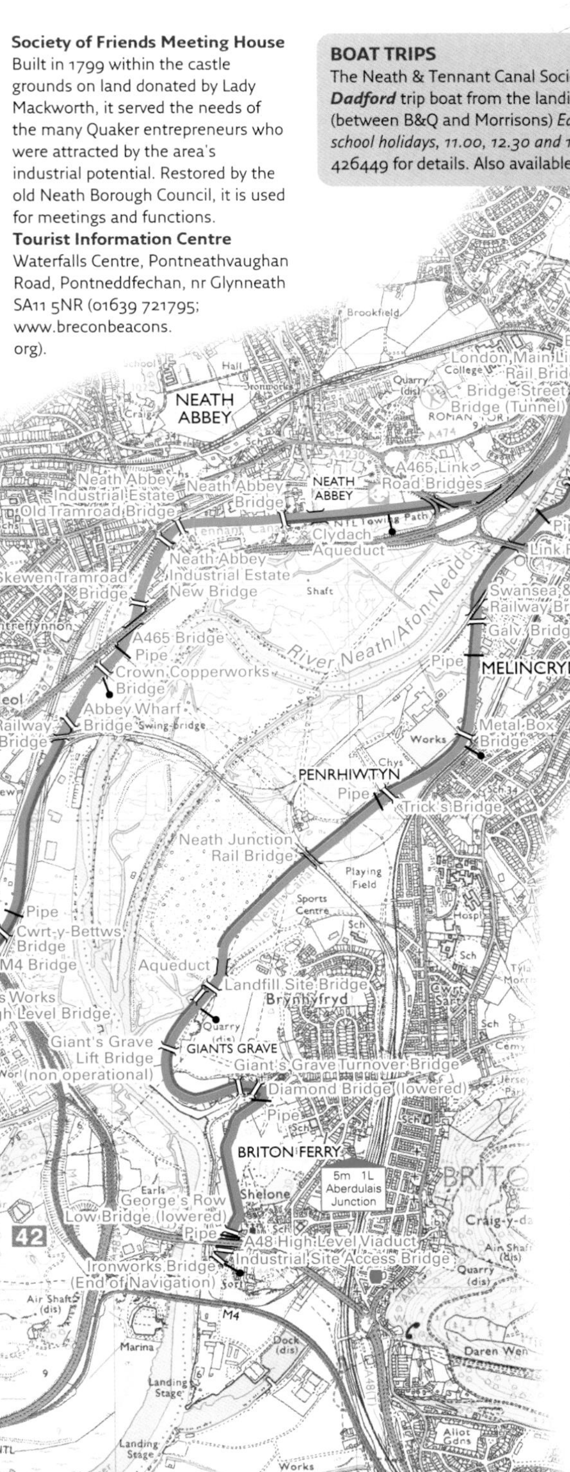

Pubs and Restaurants

Hooker Dyers Fabian's Way, Port Tennant, Swansea SA1 8PA (01782 538360). Friendly local, named after the owner's father. Children welcome in the lounge.

Towers Hotel Jersey Marine, Swansea Bay SA10 6JL (01792 818024; www.thetowersswanseabay.com). Smart hotel and spa set in attractive landscaped gardens, next to the camera obscura. Food, including locally caught fresh fish, is served *L and E daily.* Patio area. Children welcome.

Crown & Sceptre Main Road, Cadoxton, Neath SA10 8AP (01639 642145; www.crownandsceptreinn.co.uk). Lively village bar and restaurant, serving food *L and E (not Sun E)*, with *daily* specials. Children welcome. French windows open onto a patio. Quiz on *Sun.*

Hope & Anchor New Road, Neath Abbey, Neath SA10 7NG (01792 324731). Food, *Sun lunch only.* Beer garden. Children welcome until 21.00.

Aberdulais

The Tennant Canal continues towards Aberdulais, initially hemmed-in by roads and finally diving under a tangle of fly-overs, slip roads and roundabouts, to emerge at Aberdulais Lock and the squat and purposeful aqueduct, which carries the waterway to its junction with the Neath Canal at Aberdulais Basin.

The Neath Canal keeps close to the south bank of the Afon Nedd, passing within 10ft of St Illtyd's Church, all in a pretty, wooded, setting. The restored Tyn-yr-Heol Lock north to the junction at Aberdulais. The conurbation is then finally left behind as the canal makes its way along the Vale of Neath, accompanied by the river and a busy road which, surprisingly, does little to intrude upon the waterway's quiet progress. Locks now appear at fairly regular intervals, raising the canal to the point where it can finally cross the river at Ynysbwllog through the impressive new aqueduct which was completed in March 2008. From there the canal passes under the main A465 using the new basins and under the well restored Ynysbwllog Bridge. The Canal towpaths between Abergarwed and Neath now form part of the national cycle network. Beyond Resolven Lock and Ynysbiban Aqueduct the canal's course is abruptly interrupted by Commercial Road. Cross this and you are confronted with a vision of how splendid this navigation will one day be. With a fine pub nearby, a basin, a slipway and a lock, the whole canal from here to the terminus is beautifully restored, providing a fitting finale to your journey.

Pubs and Restaurants

Dulais Rock Aberdulais Neath SA10 8EY (01639 644611; www.dulaisrock.co.uk). Cromwell once stayed at this excellent coaching inn, which is now a family-friendly pub. Meals are served *L and E daily*. Patio. Live music *Fri*.

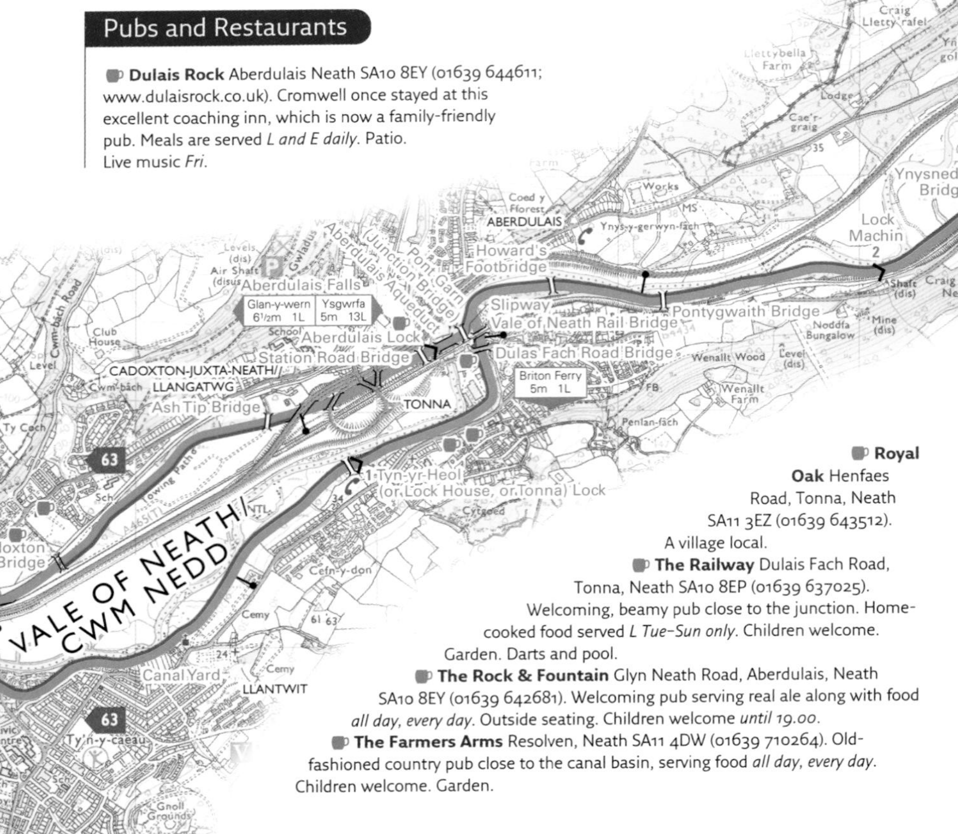

Royal Oak Henfaes Road, Tonna, Neath SA11 3EZ (01639 643512). A village local.

The Railway Dulais Fach Road, Tonna, Neath SA10 8EP (01639 637025). Welcoming, beamy pub close to the junction. Home-cooked food served *L Tue–Sun only*. Children welcome. Garden. Darts and pool.

The Rock & Fountain Glyn Neath Road, Aberdulais, Neath SA10 8EY (01639 642681). Welcoming pub serving real ale along with food *all day, every day*. Outside seating. Children welcome *until 19.00*.

The Farmers Arms Resolven, Neath SA11 4DW (01639 710264). Old-fashioned country pub close to the canal basin, serving food *all day, every day*. Children welcome. Garden.

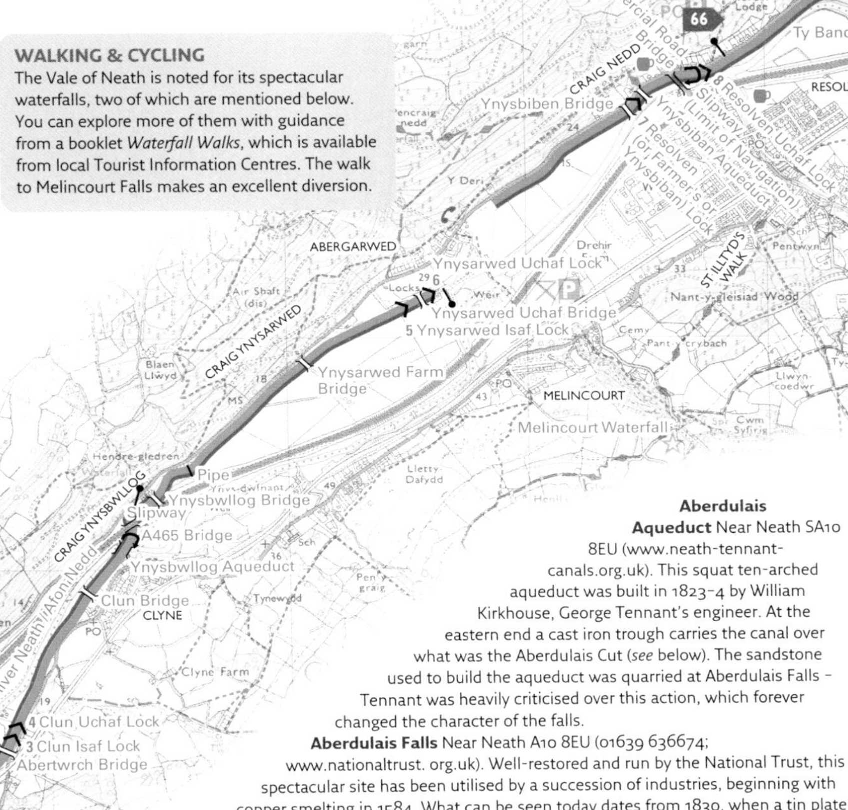

WALKING & CYCLING
The Vale of Neath is noted for its spectacular waterfalls, two of which are mentioned below. You can explore more of them with guidance from a booklet *Waterfall Walks*, which is available from local Tourist Information Centres. The walk to Melincourt Falls makes an excellent diversion.

Aberdulais Aqueduct Near Neath SA10 8EU (www.neath-tennant-canals.org.uk). This squat ten-arched aqueduct was built in 1823–4 by William Kirkhouse, George Tennant's engineer. At the eastern end a cast iron trough carries the canal over what was the Aberdulais Cut (*see* below). The sandstone used to build the aqueduct was quarried at Aberdulais Falls – Tennant was heavily criticised over this action, which forever changed the character of the falls.

Aberdulais Falls Near Neath A10 8EU (01639 636674; www.nationaltrust. org.uk). Well-restored and run by the National Trust, this spectacular site has been utilised by a succession of industries, beginning with copper smelting in 1584. What can be seen today dates from 1830, when a tin plate works operated here. The artist J. M. W. Turner visited in 1796. The water from the falls, which once powered these industries, now turns a water wheel (a replica of that which turned in the 19th C and now the largest in Europe generating electricity), and a modern turbine, which generates 200kw and provides enough to supply 20 houses. *Open Mar, Fri–Sun, 11.00–16.00; Apr– Oct, Mon-Fri, 10.00–17.00, Sat,Sun, 11.00–16.00; and Nov-mid Dec, Fri–Sun 11.00–16.00.* Charge. Shop.

Aberdulais Cut Near Neath SA10 8EU (www.neath-tennant-canals.org.uk). Built in 1751, this was one of the earliest canals in Wales, and ran for 600yds transporting materials between Dylais Forge and Ynysygerwn tin plate works. It passed under one of the railway arches by The Railway pub. Its use as a navigation was superseded by the canal.

St Illtyd's Church Canalside at Llantwit. Before the Dissolution of the monasteries by Henry VIII, this was the parish church of Neath. It was established on the site of a hermit's cell dating from the 6th C, with the present building dating from 1859. The area in front of the church, on the canal bank, was once a coal wharf, served by tramway from the Gnoll Estate.

Tonna Workshops Located by Tyn-yr-heol Lock, this was once the canal company's registered office, clerk's residence and maintenance yard, with a forge and a carpenter's shop. There was at one time a loading dock opposite where stone, quarried above Tonna, was brought down by tramroad and transhipped onto barges, which then took it into Neath.

Ynysbwllog Aqueduct Construction of the canal reached Ynysbwllog in 1792, at which point the engineer Thomas Dadford handed over to Thomas Sheasby, who supervised the work until he was arrested for 'irregularities' in 1794. The canal to Abernant was finally completed in 1795. In 1813 it was reported that Sheasby's work on this aqueduct was substandard, and rebuilding of the five-arch structure took place. Remaining in less than perfect condition, it was washed away by floodwater in 1979, although the towpath crossing has now been reinstated.

Melincourt Falls The falls can be reached by following the path which heads south east from above Ynysarwed Uchaf Lock. Beyond the road your route follows a tree-lined gorge, with the ruins of the old Melincourt Furnace hidden by trees above you on the opposite bank. Michael Faraday visited the falls in July 1819, and estimated their height to be some 70ft. He was taken there by a little 'welch damsel', and he paid her one shilling for guiding him.

● **Resolven**
Neath, Port Talbot. PO, tel, stores. Two useful pubs, but little else of note.

Rheola

Beyond Ty Banc the canal continues its steady climb towards Ysgwrfa Bridge. It is highly unlikely that restoration will proceed beyond this point, although there are those who think what is left of the watercourse could be reinstated. Beyond Crugiau Bridge two locks are climbed before you pass under Rheola Iron Aqueduct, which once carried the stream that now passes under the canal at Rheola Aqueduct. To the north is Rheola House, which was converted for use as a training centre by the British Aluminium Company and thus survived, while many other such houses were pulled down. Rheola Pond, where herons nest, lies to the north east. You then continue, closely accompanied by the busy main road, along the centre of the Vale of Neath, with fine views of the Rheola Forest on either side. It is easy to understand why this restored section won a highly acclaimed Civic Trust Award in 1992. At Maesgwyn a 19th C limekiln stands hidden amongst trees beside the lock – a demonstration that farming, as well as industry, was once well served by the canal. It is then just a short distance to Ysgwrfa Lock, which was at one time known as Pwllfa'r onn Lock, taking that name from a nearby colliery owned by the Neath Abbey Ironworks. Coal was loaded at a wharf below the lock, for transport to Neath. You are now at the end of the navigation, although this waterway originally climbed another five locks – Granary; Cae-dan-y-cwmwl (the field under the cloud); Pentremalwed; Lamb & Flag and Maesmarchog – before reaching its terminus at Glynneath. Part of this section can be followed, although the channel has been narrowed to accommodate a road.

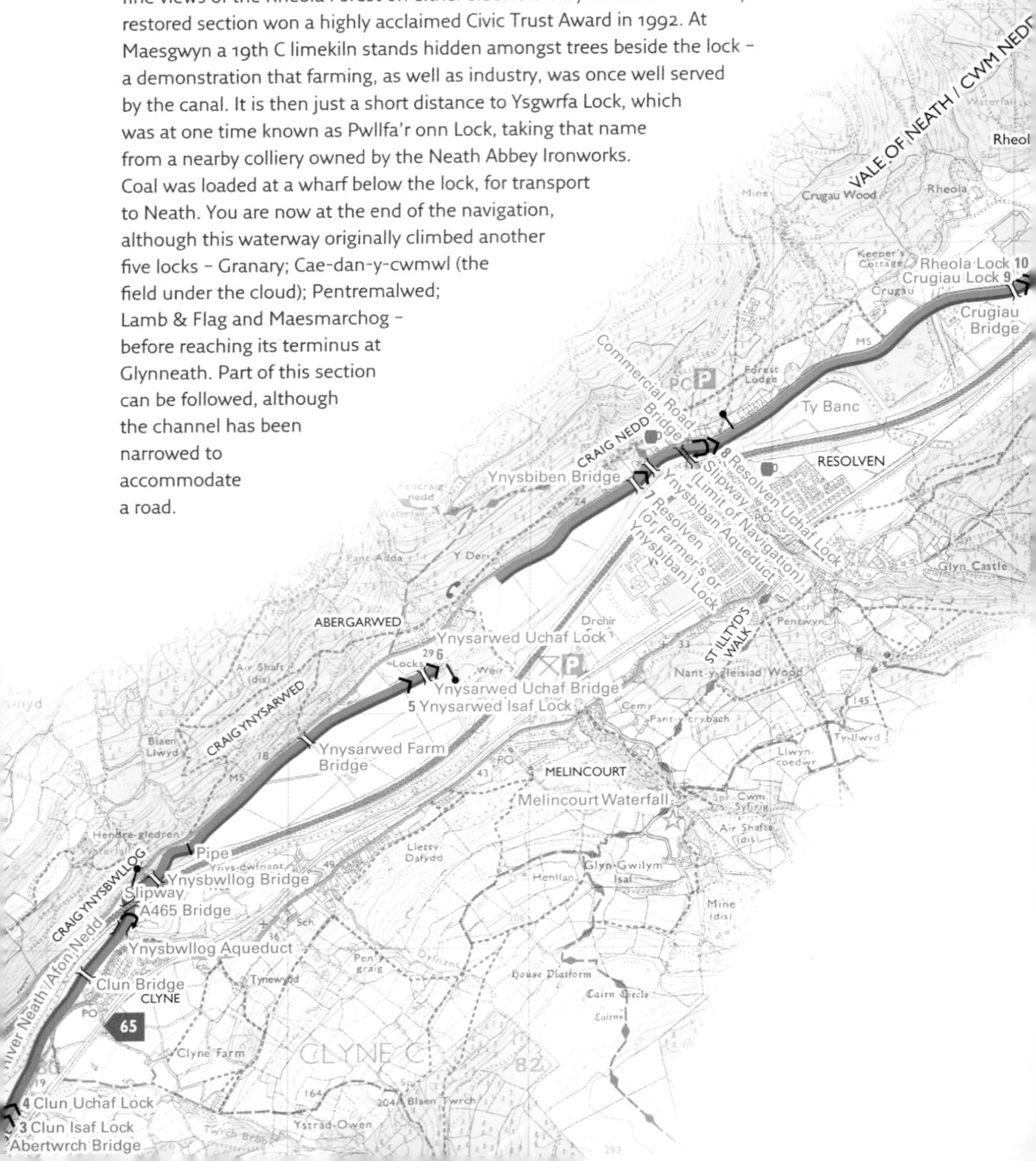

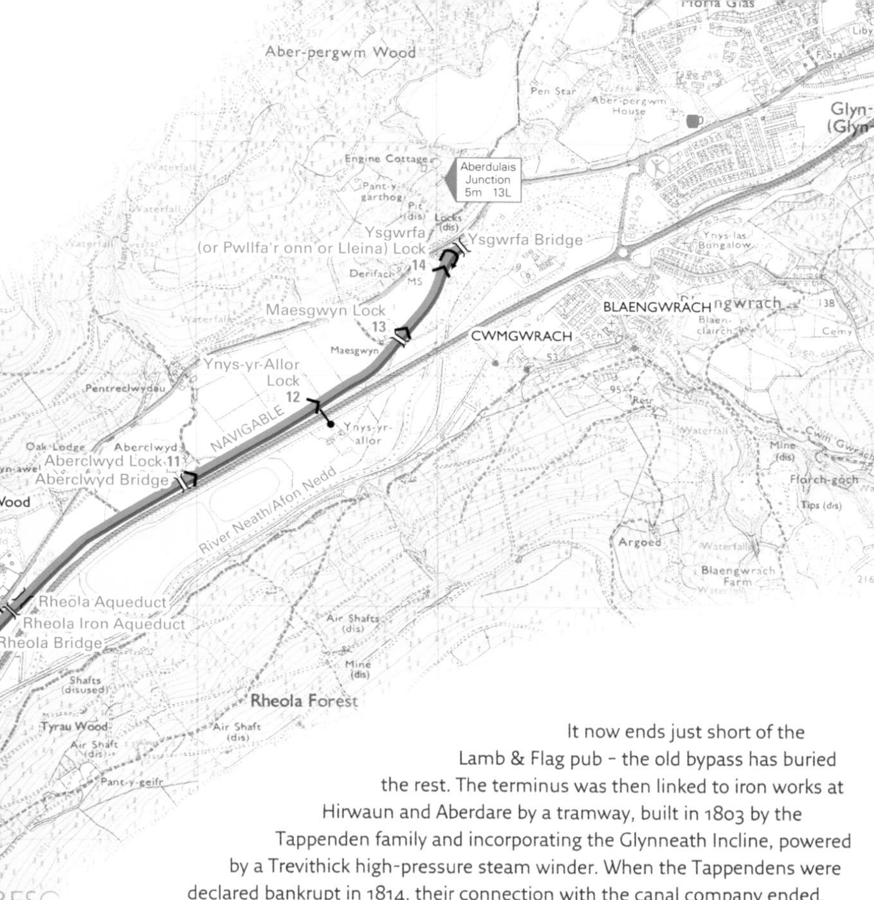

It now ends just short of the Lamb & Flag pub – the old bypass has buried the rest. The terminus was then linked to iron works at Hirwaun and Aberdare by a tramway, built in 1803 by the Tappenden family and incorporating the Glynneath Incline, powered by a Trevithick high-pressure steam winder. When the Tappendens were declared bankrupt in 1814, their connection with the canal company ended.

WALKING & CYCLING

In the Rheola Forest, north of Blaengwrach, keen mountain bikers will be excited to find the route used for the Dragon Downhill Course. It is about half a mile of single-track, and was classified as Extreme. Visit www.dragondownhill.co.uk for more details, and do not take your motor vehicle into the forest. There is also a low-level walking route between Resolven and Blaengwrach, on the southern side.

Pubs and Restaurants

The Lamb and Flag Blaengwrach, Glynneath, Neath SA11 5EP (01639 720227). Friendly and welcoming pub. Restaurant serving meals *L and E, daily (not Mon)*. Real ale. Children welcome *until 18.00* unless eating. Garden.

● **Rheola Forest**
This large forest has been used for two stages of the Network Q Rally of Great Britain, with Resolven as a base. Also excellent for mountain biking, it has recently been surveyed for the presence of red squirrels.

Pontardawe

Although the *Nicholson guides* usually cover waterways in a linear fashion, most visitors to the Swansea Canal will arrive at Pontardawe, which is the perfect access point for the two separate sections seen here.

Exploring this canal to the north east, the initial section has been well restored, with an excellent towpath overlooked by the exceptionally tall spire of St Peter's Church on the opposite bank. Soon you round a corner to reach a lowered bridge – cross the road and you are now on the navigable section, which heads out of town beside an industrial estate, separating the canal from the Afon Tawe at this point. Now the conurbation is left behind as you skirt water meadows on your way to Ynysmeudwy Lock, which has yet to be restored and thus marks the limit of navigation. However the surroundings are splendid, and at the road bridge you can leave the canal for a visit to the Ynysmeudwy Arms. Ynysmeudwy Bridge was once known as Pottery Bridge, since in 1850 there was a pottery here making Victorian table ware and jugs. Only 112 people were employed, but a wide variety of items were made, all now eminently collectable! It is then well worth crossing the road to continue to the limit of the canal, since you will pass several abandoned locks and a canal which appears almost river-like, flowing in places little more than 6 inches deep over the overgrown bed of the waterway. Finally you reach the end, just south east of Godre'r graig, at a road.

Travelling south west from Herbert Street Bridge, in the centre of Pontardawe, again the waterway seems secure, but this is short-lived, and the canal disappears underground just before a new road. To follow its course you should go through the underpass and turn right onto a tarmac path, which passes a large store, a school, a leisure centre and playing fields before the clear water of the canal manifests itself again, and immediately carries on as if nothing had happened! Now the Afon Tawe meanders right beside the towpath, as you pass the atypical back gardens of canal-side houses. Just before Pont Coed Gwilym, beside Coedgwilym Park, a memorial tells of this section of the canal's restoration, beside a slipway where small craft can be launched. Beyond the bridge there is just a short section before the canal is again piped. The towpath is easily followed and soon you are amongst herons and ducks and passing the buildings of the imposing INCO nickel refinery. The Tawe then dives in to meet the canal, which crosses

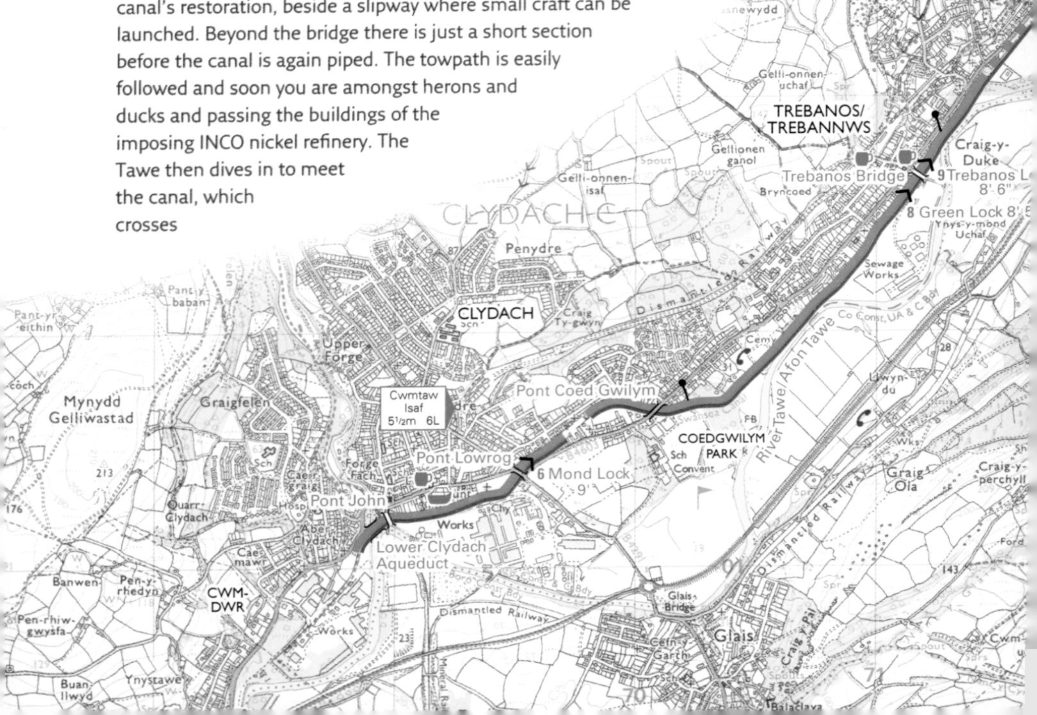

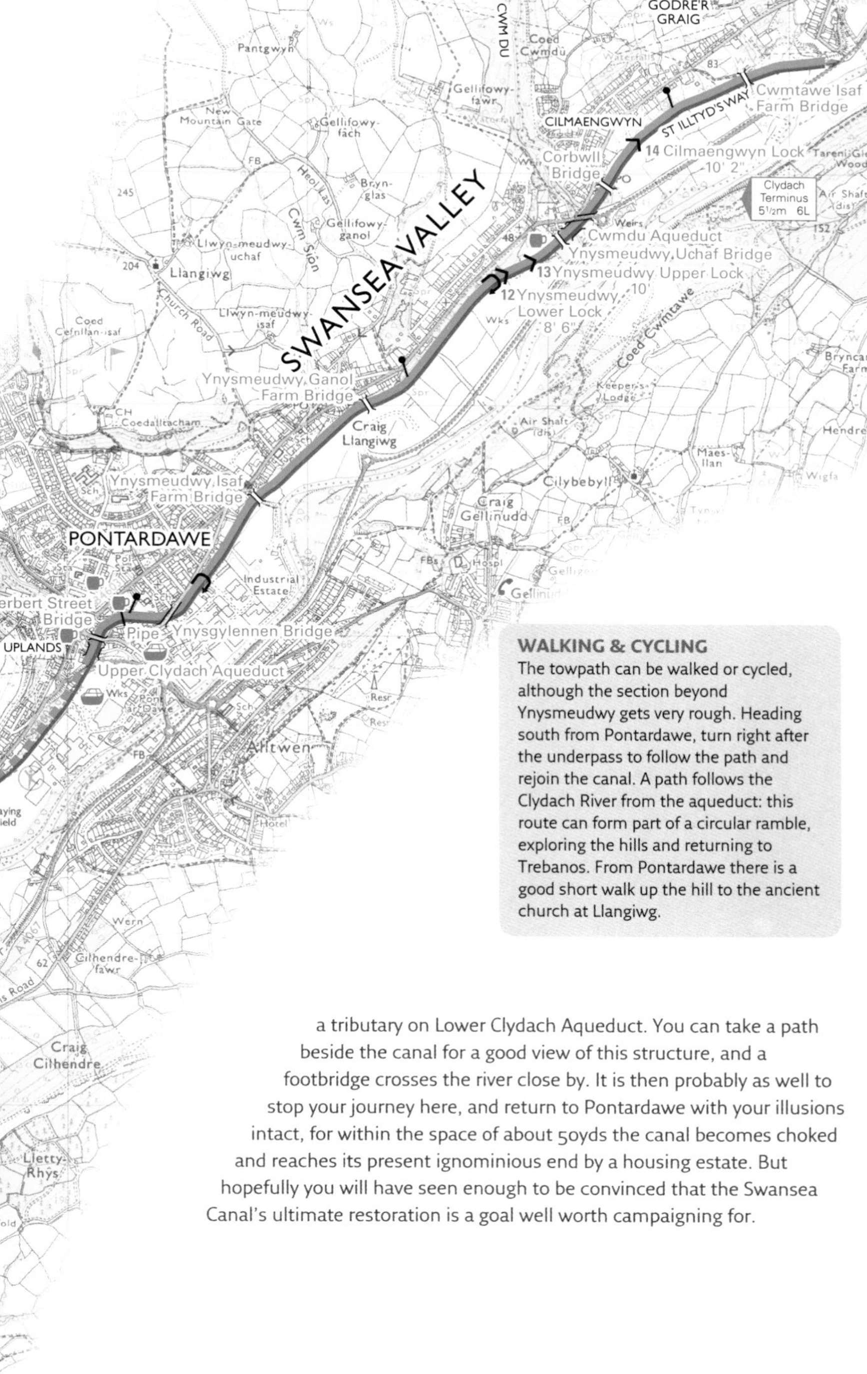

WALKING & CYCLING

The towpath can be walked or cycled, although the section beyond Ynysmeudwy gets very rough. Heading south from Pontardawe, turn right after the underpass to follow the path and rejoin the canal. A path follows the Clydach River from the aqueduct: this route can form part of a circular ramble, exploring the hills and returning to Trebanos. From Pontardawe there is a good short walk up the hill to the ancient church at Llangiwg.

a tributary on Lower Clydach Aqueduct. You can take a path beside the canal for a good view of this structure, and a footbridge crosses the river close by. It is then probably as well to stop your journey here, and return to Pontardawe with your illusions intact, for within the space of about 50yds the canal becomes choked and reaches its present ignominious end by a housing estate. But hopefully you will have seen enough to be convinced that the Swansea Canal's ultimate restoration is a goal well worth campaigning for.

Pontardawe

Neath, Port Talbot. PO, tel, stores. The 180ft-tall spire of St Peter's Church, erected in 1862, overlooks what was once an industrial town, where the Gilbertson's tin plate works and the chemical works of Jacob Lewis brought prosperity. But these are now gone, and the town provides a pleasant home for workers in nearby industries, while the surrounding countryside slowly recovers from the exposure to the highly toxic fumes these processes once produced. The main street, to the east of the canal bridge, is a lively place, with shops, pubs and restaurants around a fine new Arts Centre. The town's name means 'The bridge over the River Tawe', and it is this river which defines the valley: exploited for its mineral wealth and then abandoned when these resources were no longer needed, or were more cheaply obtained elsewhere. The channel of the Swansea Canal continues uninterrupted for a few miles to the north east; to the south west it ends abruptly by a new road. Beyond lie supermarkets, a school and a leisure centre.

Pontardawe Leisure Centre Parc Ynysderw, Pontardawe SA8 4EG (01792 830111; www.celticleisure.org). Swimming pool, fitness suite, squash courts. *Contact for opening times.*

The Arts Centre Herbert Street, Pontardawe SA8 4ED (01792 863722). A wide range of excellent entertainment, featuring jazz, folk, rock, storytelling, comedy, dance, drama and film.

Clydach

Swansea. PO, tel, stores. Currently marking the southern limit of recognisable canal, the town is indistinguishable from its neighbour Trebanos, and is dominated by the nickel refinery.

INCO Nickel Refinery This historic production facility, which stands right beside the canal, has produced high purity nickel pellets by the nickel carbonyl process for over 100 years on this site. It was an accidental discovery in a stable that led to one of the most elegant processes for refining metal. Ludwig Mond, born 1839 and a shrewd businessman and respected industrialist, pioneered this work in St John's Wood, London. Whilst conducting experiments with bleach, he stumbled upon a process for producing pure nickel, along with a previously unknown compound, which Mond named nickel carbonyl. After many teething troubles a pilot plant was built in Birmingham and began producing 3000 pounds of nickel a week. After unsuccessfully trying to sell his process, he set up this plant in Clydach in 1900, since here it could easily be supplied with anthracite fuel, had a good water supply, good transport links with the port of Swansea and a reliable labour force. Nickel ore was brought in from Canada and deliveries of 99.95 pure pellets were produced in 1902. The company later merged with the International Nickel Company of Canada, and production continues to this day.

Cwm Clydach

Ty'n y Berllan Craig Cefn Parc, Clydach (029 2035 3000; www.rspb.org.uk). 2 miles north of Clydach at the New Inn, on the B4291. This RSPB mixed woodland reserve is home to redstarts, breeding pied flycatchers and buzzards. There are two nature trails.

Tourism South and West Wales Chestnut House, Tawe Business Village, Enterprise Park, Swansea SA7 9LA (08708 300 306; www.southwestwales.info).

Pubs and Restaurants

There are plenty of pubs to choose from in Pontardawe.

Dillwyn Arms Herbert Street, Pontardawe SA8 4EB (01792 863310; www.thedillwynarms.co.uk). A community pub and restaurant, serving real ale, and food *L and E.* Outside seating. Children welcome. B & B.

Dynevor Arms Dynevor Terrace, Pontardawe SA8 4HX (01792 863750). A pub for the youngsters, which *opens evenings only.* Outside seating.

Castle Hotel High Street, Pontardawe SA8 4HU (01792 865491). Old-fashioned pub, which does not serve food. Outside seating. Children welcome until 19.00. Live music *Sun.*

Pink Geranium Hotel 31 Herbert Street, Pontardawe SA8 4EB (01792 862255). This pub is for the over 25s, and has live music *Fri and Sat.* B & B.

Carpenters Arms High Street, Clydach SA6 5LN (01792 843333/845715). With a landlord who is 'seriously into' real ale and canals, this pub has much to recommend it. Food served *L and E, daily.* Children welcome in the restaurant. Regular live music.

Colliers Arms Swansea Road, Trebanws SA8 4BU (01792 864847). Friendly family pub, where children are welcome. Bands, karaoke or discos *Sat.* Outside seating.

Ynysmeundwy Arms Ynysmeundwy Road, Pontardawe SA8 4QJ (01792 869542). Sociable family-run pub, serving food *L.* Children welcome *until 21.30.* Large garden.

MONTGOMERY CANAL

MAXIMUM DIMENSIONS

Length: 72'
Beam: 6' 10"
Headroom: 7'
Draught: 2'

MANAGER

01606 723800
enquiries.walesandbordercounties@
britishwaterways.co.uk

MILEAGE

FRANKTON JUNCTION to:
Carreghofa: 11½ miles
Welshpool: 21½ miles
Garthmyl: 27¾ miles
ABERBECHAN: 32½ miles

Locks: 25 (to Freestone Lock)

RESTORATION

The future of the Montgomery Canal as a navigable waterway now thankfully seems secure, although there are concerns about the preservation of rare flora and fauna on some sections. The restored sections are as follows:

From Frankton Junction to Gronwyn Bridge (82).

From Ardd-lin (bridge 103) to just south of Berriew (bridge 129) is navigable.

As we go to press, the section of the canal between bridges 82 and 85 is under restoration.

The Montgomery Canal has much to offer walkers and boaters alike, with its characteristic rurality and peacefulness. It is both rich in wildlife and in reminders of its industrial past. The villages dotted along the canal are mostly quiet and picturesque self-contained communities with pleasant country pubs, in which boaters and walkers can relax and explore. Welshpool is a good shopping centre and, of course, the impressive Powis Castle is well worth visiting.
The initial development of this canal was sparked by the publication of the plans for the Ellesmere Canal, which inspired a separate company to plan a canal from Newtown northwards to join the Llanymynech branch of the Ellesmere Canal at Carreghofa. The canal was authorised in 1793, and by 1797 the line was open from Carreghofa to Garthmyl. The Montgomery Canal was mainly agricultural; apart from the limestone, it existed to serve the farms and villages through which it passed, and so was never really profitable. The lack of capital and income greatly delayed the completion of the western extension to Newtown, which was not finally opened until 1821, having been financed by a separate company. So what eventually became known as the Montgomery Canal was in fact built by three separate companies over a period of 30 years. The downfall of the canal became inevitable with World War I when a pattern of regular and heavy losses started, from which the company was never able to recover. In 1921 the company gave up canal carrying and sold most of its boats to private operators. Locks began to close at weekends and standards of maintenance began to slip. From 1922 onwards many changes in the company ownership of the Shropshire Union Canal system began and, although the network remained open despite these changes, trade declined rapidly. Many traders were driven away by the lack of maintenance, which meant that most boats could only operate half full. In 1936 the breach of the Montgomery Canal at the Perry Aqueduct, just one mile south of Frankton Junction, precipitated the eventual closure of the line. Although the company set out to repair the damage they changed their minds, and with trade at a standstill there were no complaints. In 1944 an Act was passed making the closure official. The situation remained this way for many years, and with many road bridges lowered, it was thought that the waterway would fade away gracefully. But today the canal is dotted with restoration works, and considerable lengths are once again open to navigation. Look out for the distinctive paddle gear found on most locks, fitted by George Buck.

Frankton Junction

At Welsh Frankton, what was the original main line of the canal heads south towards Newtown, while the Llangollen Canal continues to the west (*see* page 35). Leaving the junction at Lower Frankton, the canal descends the four Frankton Locks: a staircase of two, and then two singles. Fresh eggs and salad vegetables are sold by the bottom lock, and the whole setting is impeccable. At Lockgate Bridge (71) there is a parking area and picnic tables which encourage walkers to visit the area, and moorings and a sanitary station are provided in a short remnant of the Weston Branch; the remainder is now a linear nature reserve. The canal then falls through Graham Palmer Lock and curves through open fields to Perry Aqueduct. During February 1936, a 40yd breach occurred in the east bank, north of the aqueduct. This was a major factor in the closure of the canal and resulted in its eventual demise in 1944. The canal passes the unnavigable Rednal Basin, which you can explore on foot and Heath Houses, where there is a fine restored warehouse by the canal. Open arable farmland and woods surround the navigation as it approaches Queen's Head, where there is a winding hole, moorings and a welcoming pub. The three Aston Locks, adjacent to Aston Nature Reserve, lower the canal as it approaches Llanymynech.

Heath Houses
Shropshire. A beautiful red-brick and timber warehouse stands by the elegant turn-over bridge, which takes the towpath to the east bank, where it remains until Newtown. To the north a short unnavigable arm leads to the completely intact Rednal Basin. On 7 June 1865 a railway disaster occurred 600yds north of the canal on the Great Western line, which crossed over just east of bridge 74. A way gang was lifting the line and, as a warning to any oncoming trains, placed a green flag on top of a pole. A large excursion train consisting of 32 coaches and two brake vans hauled by two engines, failed to see this crude warning. The train speeded on until the working men were seen, but by this time it was too late to shut off steam. Four coaches were destroyed, 11 damaged and 12 people were killed.

Queen's Head
Shropshire. Tel. An expanding canalside settlement intersected by the old main road and the busy A5. The pub is a focal point for canal visitors, with the village spreading south eastwards from the bridge.

WALKING & CYCLING

Although the canal is not yet fully open to navigation, the towpath makes a fascinating walk. You will, however, have to cross main roads here and there, and make one or two short diversions, until the waterway is completely restored.

Pubs and Restaurants

The Queen's Head Queen's Head, Oswestry SY11 4EB (01691 610255; www.thequeensheadoswestry.co.uk). A smart canalside pub with a conservatory eating area, popular with motorists. Real ale is served, and there are home-cooked bar and restaurant meals *L and E (all day Easter–Sep)*. Garden. Children are welcome. Moorings.

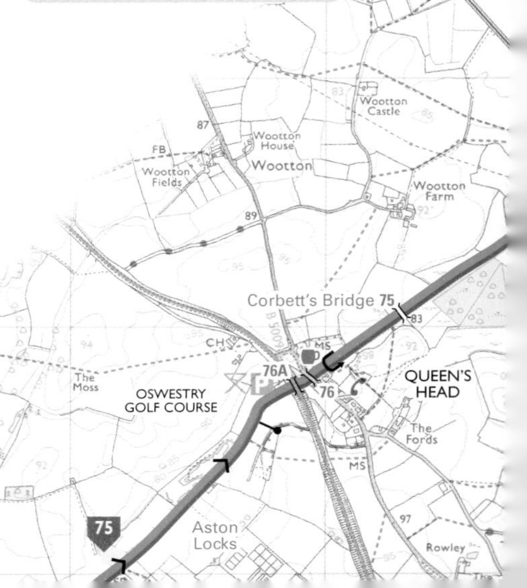

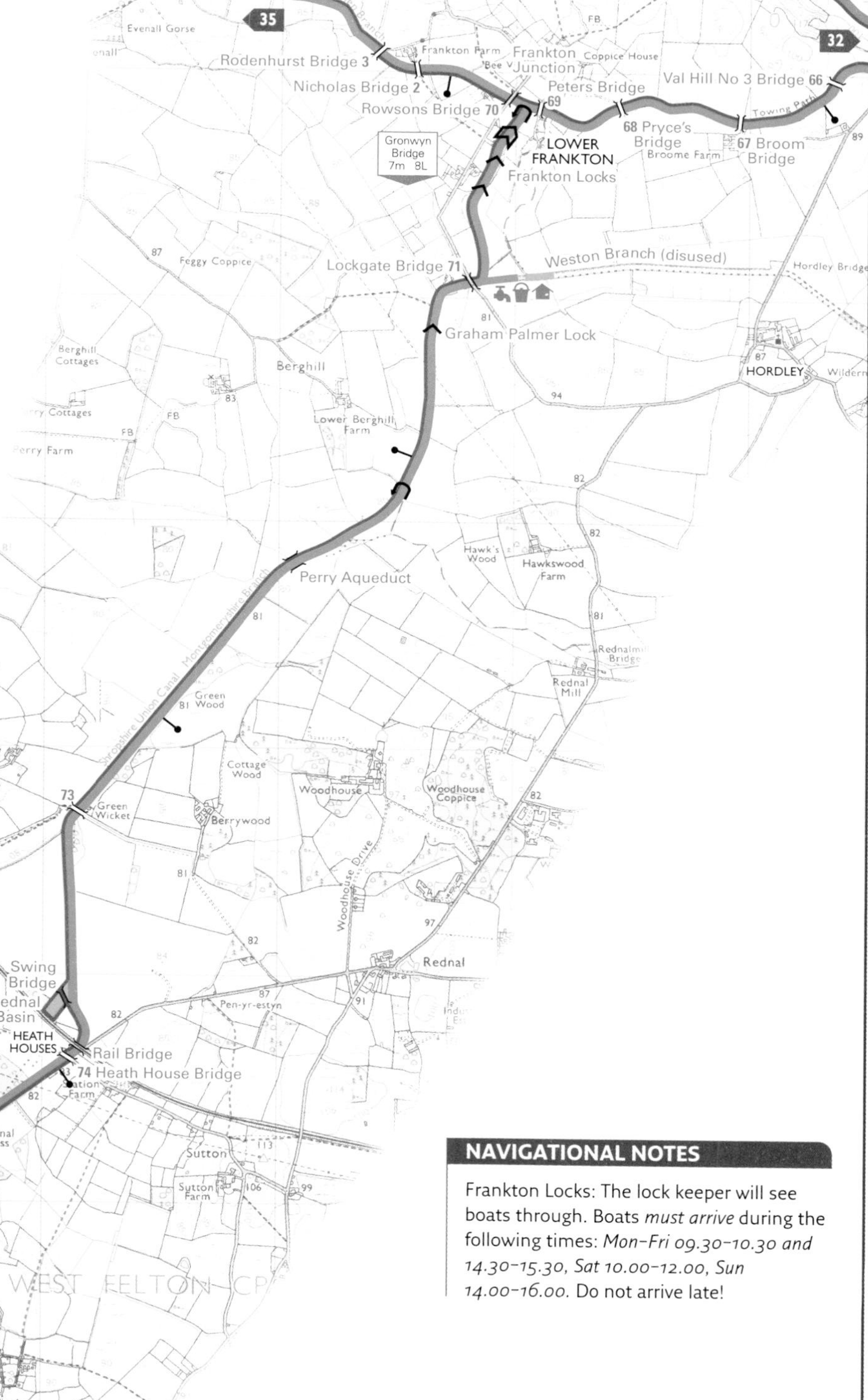

NAVIGATIONAL NOTES

Frankton Locks: The lock keeper will see boats through. Boats *must arrive* during the following times: *Mon–Fri 09.30–10.30 and 14.30–15.30, Sat 10.00–12.00, Sun 14.00–16.00.* Do not arrive late!

Llanymynech

The canal continues southwards. After the three Aston Locks the level remains constant for a while, crossing fields on low embankments or through shallow cuttings. At Maesbury Marsh a fine crane, built by Ormerod & Crierson of Manchester and thought to be the only surviving example of such a 15cwt crane, stands opposite the pub and marks the wharf, restored and used as a sanitary station. Beyond here, at Gronwyn Bridge, the remains of the old tramway from Morda can be seen. Note the fine limekilns by bridge 91, and the prominent chimney to the north, as the canal approaches Llanymynech. This marks the remains of a Warner Kiln, built in 1890 and which finally brought a virtual end to canal traffic. The waterway then begins to meander as it approaches Pant.

NAVIGATIONAL NOTES

A windlass is required to operate bridge 81.

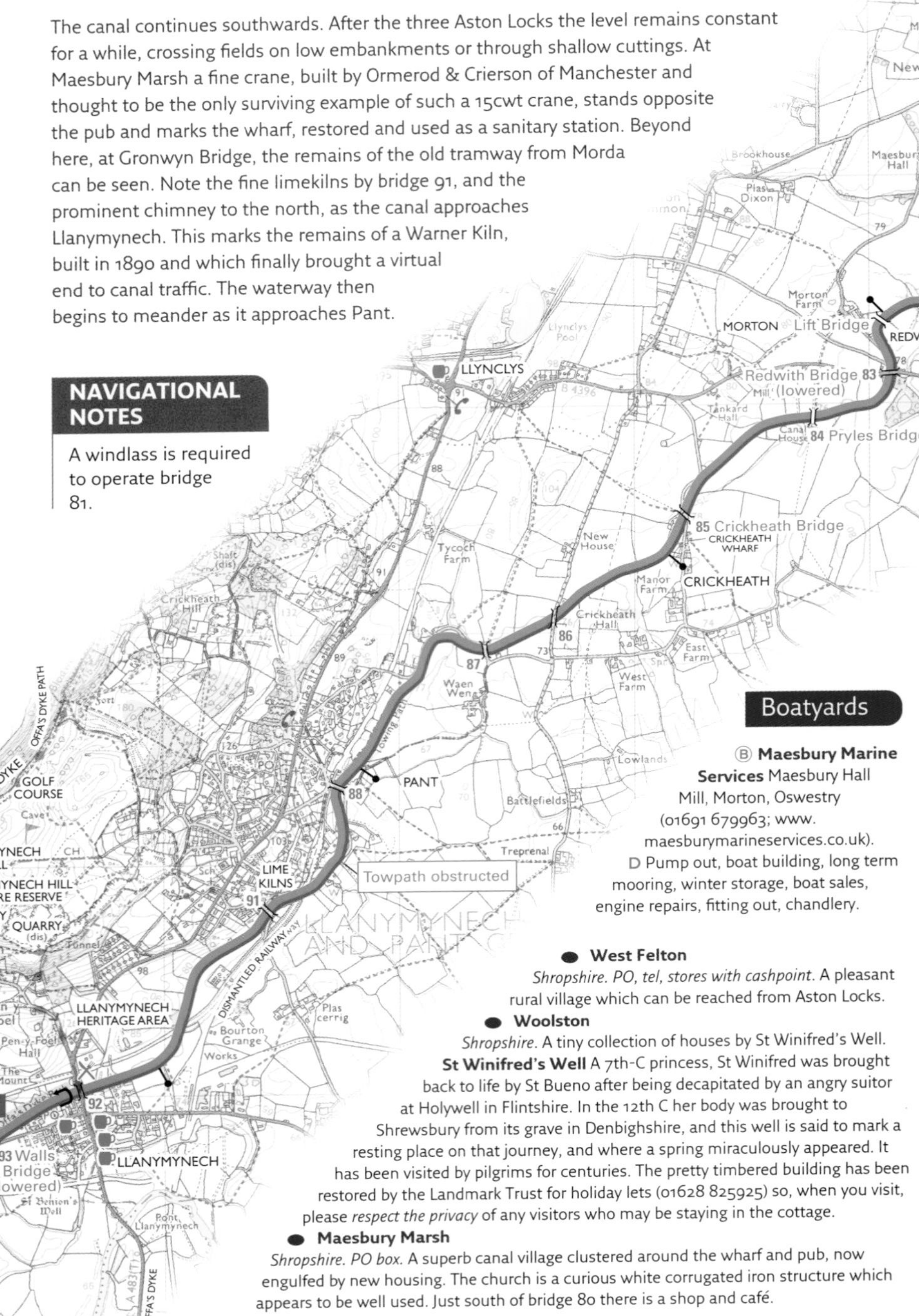

Boatyards

Ⓑ **Maesbury Marine Services** Maesbury Hall Mill, Morton, Oswestry (01691 679963; www.maesburymarineservices.co.uk). D Pump out, boat building, long term mooring, winter storage, boat sales, engine repairs, fitting out, chandlery.

● **West Felton**
Shropshire. PO, tel, stores with cashpoint. A pleasant rural village which can be reached from Aston Locks.

● **Woolston**
Shropshire. A tiny collection of houses by St Winifred's Well.

St Winifred's Well A 7th-C princess, St Winifred was brought back to life by St Bueno after being decapitated by an angry suitor at Holywell in Flintshire. In the 12th C her body was brought to Shrewsbury from its grave in Denbighshire, and this well is said to mark a resting place on that journey, and where a spring miraculously appeared. It has been visited by pilgrims for centuries. The pretty timbered building has been restored by the Landmark Trust for holiday lets (01628 825925) so, when you visit, please *respect the privacy* of any visitors who may be staying in the cottage.

● **Maesbury Marsh**
Shropshire. PO box. A superb canal village clustered around the wharf and pub, now engulfed by new housing. The church is a curious white corrugated iron structure which appears to be well used. Just south of bridge 80 there is a shop and café.

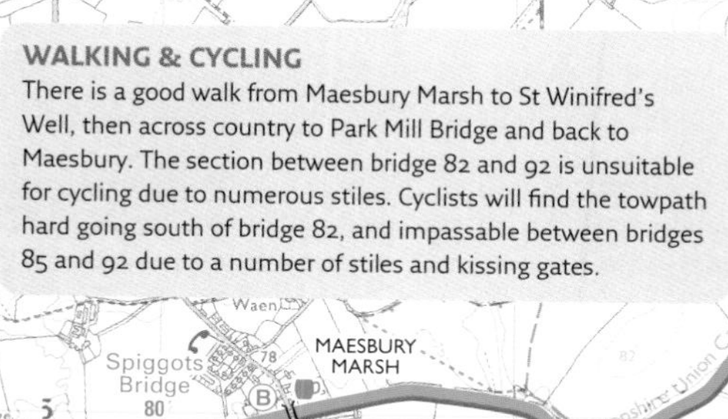

WALKING & CYCLING

There is a good walk from Maesbury Marsh to St Winifred's Well, then across country to Park Mill Bridge and back to Maesbury. The section between bridge 82 and 92 is unsuitable for cycling due to numerous stiles. Cyclists will find the towpath hard going south of bridge 82, and impassable between bridges 85 and 92 due to a number of stiles and kissing gates.

Llynclys

Shropshire. Tel. This village is drowned out by traffic on the A483, but the pub is just about close enough for those who leave the canal at Crickheath Wharf (bridge 85) and follow the footpath to the north west across farmland.

Pant

Shropshire. PO, tel, stores, garage. Pant grew up around the limestone quarries, one of the main reasons for the existence of the canal. The limekiln bank on the offside of the canal before bridge 91 has been excellently restored and is probably among the best examples to be seen along the Montgomery Canal.

Llanymynech

Powys. PO, tel, stores, garage, fish & chips. Offa's Dyke and the Anglo-Welsh border run through the village, their line actually passing through the bar of the Lion Hotel; it is possible to drink with one foot in each country. The church, St Agatha's, is very interesting, a 19th-C French-style Norman building with a lateral bell tower and huge clock face. Such Norman revival buildings were rare in the 19th C.

Llanymynech Heritage Area (www.shropshire.gov.uk) A short walk from the village along the towpath, this intriguing area is reached. It gives an insight to the industrial history and significance of Llanymynech in the production of limestone. There are some fine old kilns to be explored here. The Visitor Centre (01691 830506), with café, is *open Suns & B Hols 14.00–16.30*.

Llanymynech Rocks Nature Reserve The limestone cliffs reach 500ft, and the abandoned limestone quarry is now part of the nature reserve.

Pubs and Restaurants

The Punch Bowl Inn The Cross, West Felton, Oswestry SY11 4EH (01691 610201). A brisk walk from the towpath along the footpath which leaves Aston Locks to the south east. Real ale, and food is available *L and E Wed–Sun*. Children welcome. There is a garden with a play area. Barbecues during the *summer*.

The Navigation Inn and Warehouse Restaurant Maesbury Marsh, Oswestry SY10 8JB (01691 672958; www.thenavigation.co.uk). Warm and friendly 18th-C canalside inn incorporating a listed canal warehouse, dating from around 1785. Meals *L (Wed–Sun 12.00–14.00) and E (Tue–Fri 18.00–20.30, Sat 18.00–21.00)*, and snacks *L in summer*. Real ale. Children welcome. Quiz nights *third Sun of month*; dominoes tournament *second Fri of month*. Pub games. Canalside seating. Moorings.

The White Lion Inn Llynclys SY10 8LJ (01691 839019). Situated at the A438/B4396 crossroads. Real ale. Meals served *L and E Wed–Sat, and L Sun–Tue*. Children welcome and there is a garden.

The Dolphin Inn Llanymynech SY22 6ER (01691 831078). Reached by crossing the stile past bridge 92 and walking through the car park to the street. Friendly and sociable pub. Meals *L and E (not Wed E)*. Children welcome. Garden. B & B.

Cross Keys North Road, Llanymynech SY22 6EA (01691 831585; www.crosskeyshotel.info). Real ale and food served *L and E (not Mon L)*. Children welcome. Live music *Fri*. B & B.

Canal Central Café Spiggots Bridge, Maesbury Marsh SY10 8JG (01691 652168; www.canalcentral.co.uk). Breakfast, lunch and homemade cakes and pasties. Self-catering accommodation with balcony overlooking the canal. Well-stocked shop, post office and IT centre.

The Bradford Arms Hotel & Restaurant Llanymynech SY22 6EJ (01691 830582; www.bradfordarmshotel.com). Comfortable hotel with luxury accommodation and well-priced, innovative food, all prepared on the premises, *L and E (not Mon, and check Jan and Sep)*. Real ale. Children welcome. *Closed Mon*. B & B.

Ardd-lin

The two locks at Carreghofa, in a beautiful setting, continue the descent, while the line of the old Tanat feeder, which used to join the canal between the locks, can still be seen to the west of the road bridge. The lock cottage here is inhabited. The toll house, built in 1825, has also been restored by volunteers and this makes a good resting place for walkers of the towpath and of Offa's Dyke, which follows the canal to the east here, after crossing at Llanymynech. South of the Vyrnwy Aqueduct a wooden crane stands beside a sturdy stone wharf building; the canal follows the course of the hills to the west, often running through woods in an embanked side-cutting. It then continues south through rolling countryside on the western side of the Severn and dominated by hills to the west. Before the two pretty Burgedin Locks lower the canal further, the disused Guilsfield Arm can be seen running away to the west. From the locks there are superb views of the Breidden Hills to the east, and the Long Mountain, which reaches a height of 1338ft. Henry Tudor camped here in 1485, gathering strength for his battle against Richard III at Bosworth, in which Henry was victorious and took the English throne.

- **Vyrnwy Aqueduct**
Opened in 1796, the stone aqueduct across the river Vyrnwy is one of the canal's original features. Its building was fraught with problems; one arch collapsed during construction, and after completion subsidence distorted the whole structure, necessitating the addition of iron braces in 1823. The distortion also caused continual leakage problems; in 1971 repairs were undertaken to try yet again to stop the leaks, and further restoration has subsequently been carried out. To the north a long embankment precedes the aqueduct, partly of earth and partly of brick arches, which makes it altogether a much longer structure than it appears at first sight.
- **Offa's Dyke**
Offa's Dyke, which runs from Chepstow to Prestatyn, passes near the canal at several points in the area. Although the dyke is at times only fragmentary, its 168-mile course has been designated a long-distance public footpath. The dyke was constructed by Offa, King of Mercia, between AD750 and AD800 to mark the boundary of Wales. The impressive structure consisted of a long mound of earth with a ditch on one side, though in parts it is hardly recognisable as such.
- **Four Crosses**
Powys. PO, tel, stores, garage. A main road village comprising old and new housing, and built around Offa's Dyke.
- **Guilsfield Arm**
This 2-mile arm runs close to the village of Guilsfield and is reached by crossing the road just before bridge 104. It is now a nature reserve, providing a haven for wildlife.
- **Ardd-lin**
Powys. A small settlement to the west of the canal.

Pubs and Restaurants

The Horseshoe Inn Ardd-lin SY22 6PU (01938 590318). Small and friendly village pub offering real ale. Meals *L and E*, prepared with fresh vegetables. Children welcome, and there is a large secure play area with swings. B & B.

Golden Lion Hotel Four Crosses SY22 6RB (01691 830295). A short walk from the canal, this family-run pub serves real ale, along with bar meals *L and E*. Children welcome, and there is a garden. B & B and self-contained accommodation.

Four Crosses Four Crosses SY22 6RE. Accessible from road bridge 100. Friendly country pub serving real ale and meals.

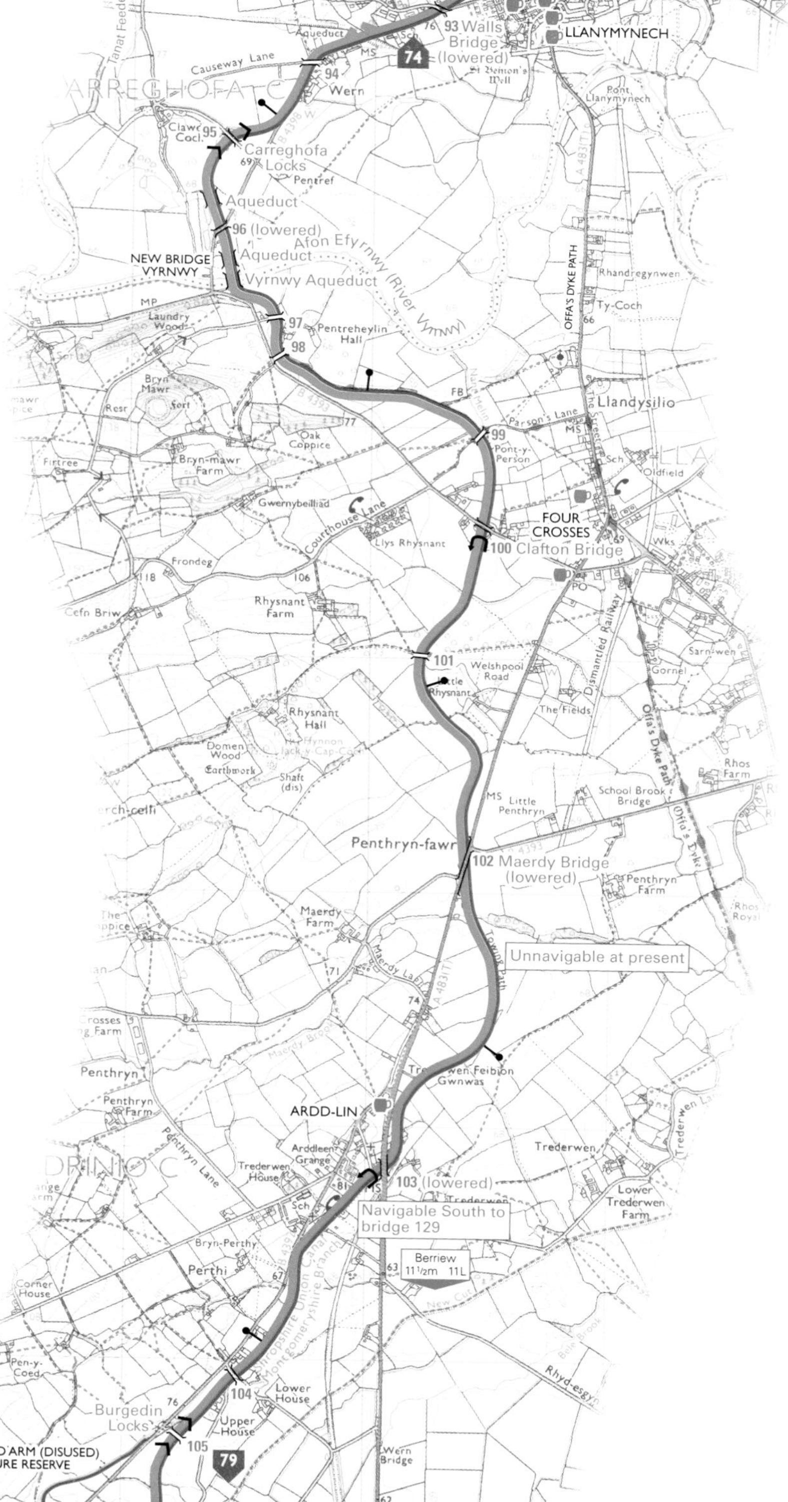
LLANYMYNECH
93 Walls Bridge (lowered)
74
Aqueduct
Causeway Lane
94
Wern
Clawdd Coch
95
Carreghofa Locks
Pentref
Aqueduct
96 (lowered)
Afon Efyrnwy (River Vyrnwy)
NEW BRIDGE VYRNWY
Aqueduct
Vyrnwy Aqueduct
Laundry Wood
97
Pentreheylin Hall
98
Bryn Mawr Fort
Oak Coppice
Bryn-mawr Farm
Firtree
Gwernybeilliad
Courthouse Lane
Llys Rhysnant
Frondeg
Rhysnant Farm
Cefn Briw
99
Pont-y-Person
Llandysilio
Parson's Lane
Rhandregynwen
Ty-Coch
OFFA'S DYKE PATH
Oldfield
FOUR CROSSES
100 Clafton Bridge
PO
Wks
101
Little Rhysnant
Welshpool Road
Dismantled Railway
Sarn-wen
Gornel
The Fields
Offa's Dyke Path
Rhysnant Hall
Domen Wood
Earthwork
Shaft (dis)
Little Penthryn
School Brook Bridge
Rhos Farm
Penthryn-fawr
102 Maerdy Bridge (lowered)
Penthryn Farm
Offa's Dyke
Maerdy Farm
Maerdy Lane
Towing Path
Unnavigable at present
Crosses Farm
Penthryn
Penthryn Farm
Trederwen Feibion Gwnwas
ARDD-LIN
Penthryn Lane
Arddleen Grange
Trederwen House
Trederwen
103 (lowered)
Lower Trederwen Farm
Navigable South to bridge 129
Sch
Bryn-Perthy
Perthi
Berriew 11½m 11L
Shropshire Union Canal Montgomeryshire Branch
New Cut
Corner House
Pen-y-Coed
104
Lower House
Upper House
Burgedin Locks
105
79
GUILSFIELD ARM (DISUSED) NATURE RESERVE
Wern Bridge

Pool Quay

Continuing south the canal clings to the steep hills to the west of the Severn Valley, often in a wooded side-cutting. There is a car park and picnic tables at bridge 106. Four locks around the Pool Quay area and one in the centre of Welshpool begin the canal's rise towards Newtown. The stretch of canal between Pool Quay and Welshpool is known as the Prince of Wales length, restored by the Prince of Wales Trust and the Shropshire Union Canal Society. There are many reminders of the industrial history of the canal along here, especially at Pool Quay, once the highest navigable point on the Severn, and later a transhipment point between river and canal. The Wern corn mill remains, and the clay pit is now a nature reserve. Information boards interpret the former uses of the site. Between the lock south of bridge 111 and Abbey Bridge (112) Offa's Dyke long-distance footpath follows the towpath. There is a cast iron milepost half-way along this stretch, similar to the one south of bridge 110. These were placed by the Montgomery Waterway Restoration Trust in 1983 and 1984 respectively. Before Welshpool there are two draw bridges, Abbey Bridge (112) and Moors Farm Bridge (114).

The Wern
At the Red Bridge (106) there is parking and a picnic site. The water from the lock overflow and bypass weir once powered the corn mill here, an ingenious use of the otherwise wasted 25,000 gallons of water released each time the lock operated. The sump level (or bottom level) of the canal is at The Wern, and this meant that the water-powered mill was in an excellent position for receiving the surplus water. Only the foundations of the mill remain with a small pool and sluice visible. The information boards here show what the mill would have looked like. Today the overflow weir provides water for the small but pleasant nature reserve created on the site of The Wern clay pits. This was the major source of puddling clay used to line the canal.

Pool Quay
Powys. Tel. This was a former river port at the limit of viable merchant transport up the River Severn from Bristol. Travelling northwards toward Welshpool the white-washed lock keeper's house, dating from 1820, is one of several interesting buildings here. Further along are the relics of buildings serving the grinding mills and maltings that were based in the village. The Powis Arms pub is well worth visiting – the beam in the bar was marked by navigators stranded here when the River Severn was in drought. An 18th-C red-brick warehouse once stood nearby, now replaced with new houses. Across the road is a now overgrown area beside the river, once known as Swan Wharf. This was a transhipment point where, amongst many other goods, fine oaks, for which the area was once famous, were stored prior to being loaded for carriage downstream to the naval dockyards at Bristol.

Buttington
Powys. ½ mile east of bridge 115. The church is a medieval building, restored in 1876. The village has twice suffered from attempted invasions – in AD894 by the Danish army which was evicted from here by King Alfred the Great, and in 1916 by a presumptuous German Zeppelin, whose crew mistakenly believed that the Welsh would offer less resistance than the English. Today the only air traffic floating overhead are the hot air balloons that regularly pass this area at sunset from Oswestry.

Buttington Wharf Just to the north of Buttington Bridge (115). A former kiln-bank, now a picnic site. The charging holes of the three kilns are still visible. The moorings here are good.

Breidden Hills
East of Buttington are the three impressive peaks of the Breidden Hills which dominate the flat landscape of the Shropshire Plain. The Breidden Crag (1324ft), increasingly defaced by quarrying, is best climbed from Criggion. An 18th-C pillar on the summit commemorates Admiral Rodney, who defeated a French fleet off Cape St Vincent, Dominica, in 1782. The excellent view from the summit across the Shropshire Plain highlights the meandering nature of the River Severn, particularly around the village of Melverley, which is constantly under threat of flood waters.

WALKING & CYCLING
There are circular walks from Red Bridge (106) around the nature reserve at The Wern clay pits, which was created in 1987. Offa's Dyke long-distance footpath, which stretches 180 miles between Chepstow and Prestatyn, follows the towpath between bridges 111 and 112. If you follow the lane west from Bank Lock, then turn left across country at Coppice East Farm, you will return to the canal at Abbey Lift Bridge. You can complete the circuit along the towpath, stopping for a pint at the Powis Arms (The Quay).

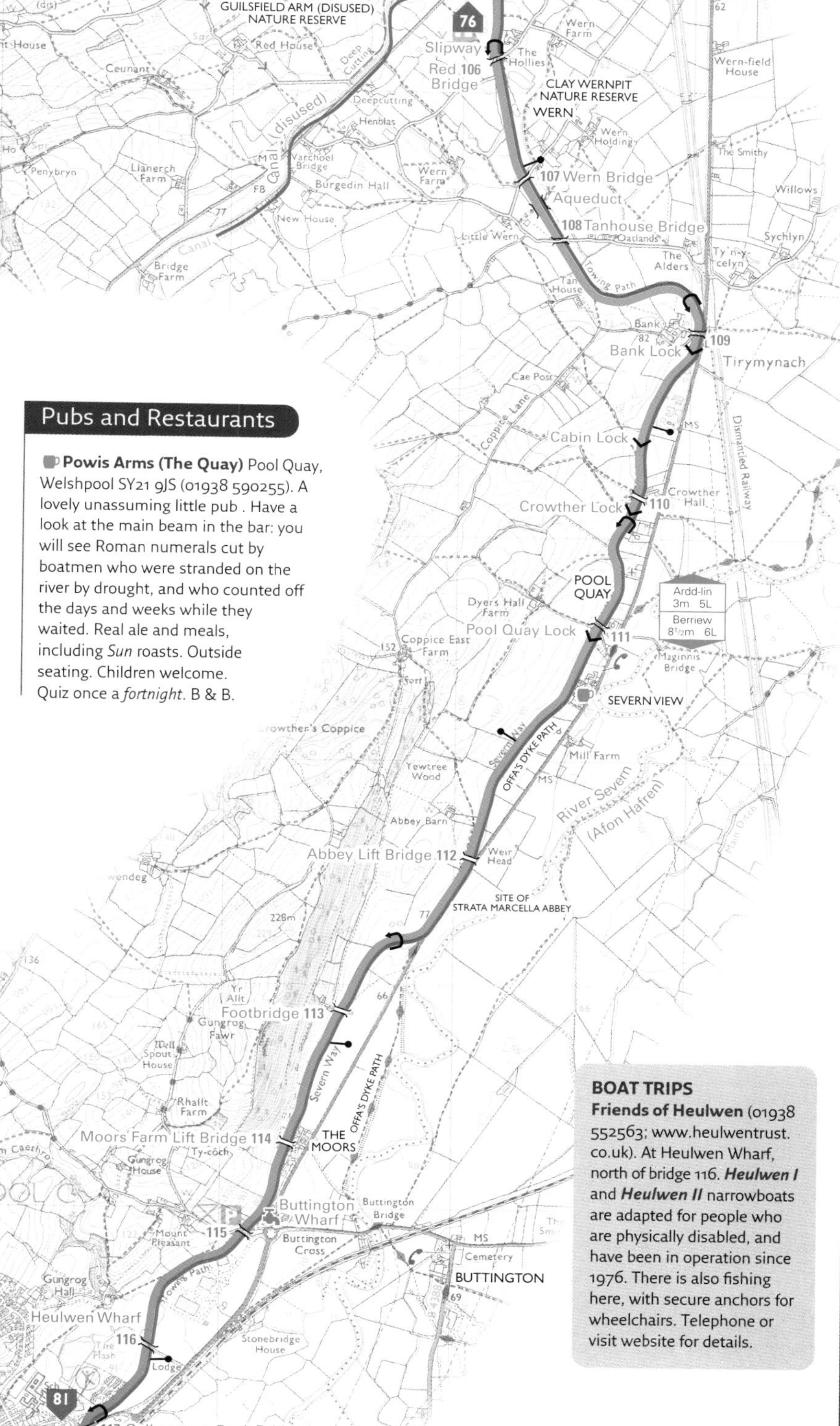

Pubs and Restaurants

Powis Arms (The Quay) Pool Quay, Welshpool SY21 9JS (01938 590255). A lovely unassuming little pub . Have a look at the main beam in the bar: you will see Roman numerals cut by boatmen who were stranded on the river by drought, and who counted off the days and weeks while they waited. Real ale and meals, including *Sun* roasts. Outside seating. Children welcome. Quiz once a *fortnight*. B & B.

BOAT TRIPS

Friends of Heulwen (01938 552563; www.heulwentrust.co.uk). At Heulwen Wharf, north of bridge 116. ***Heulwen I*** and ***Heulwen II*** narrowboats are adapted for people who are physically disabled, and have been in operation since 1976. There is also fishing here, with secure anchors for wheelchairs. Telephone or visit website for details.

Welshpool

As you enter Welshpool, there are few remains which give a hint of the importance of the canal to the town, for there were once limekilns, dry docks and wharfs, a gas works and factories. The metal bridge, 118, was built to carry the Welshpool & Llanfair Light Railway on its way through the town. Note the old Canal Agent's office by the museum – often the door is open and you can speak to the man at the desk. The town is a useful stop for boaters, with moorings and typical town centre facilities. By the side of the lock is a waterwheel pit and the last remains of the wheel bearings – unusually this canal usually had surplus water, which could be used to power mills. The canal runs at the foot of the landscaped grounds of Powis Castle, flanked by the A483, and then dives under the new Whitehouse Bridge, edging away from the River Severn for a few miles. Four locks continue the rise towards Newtown, with two at Belan, recently restored, and then two singles north of Berriew. The stretch towards Brithdir is an excellent area for bird watchers, with sightings of a broad range of species from kingfishers to herons and, high in the sky, buzzards, which can be seen circling the hilltops. At Brithdir there is a nature reserve adjacent to the lock. Beyond this, the antiquated Luggy Aqueduct carries the canal towards Berriew.

Welshpool
Powys. PO, tel, stores, garage, bank, station, cinema. The canal runs through the east of the town, passing attractive gardens and a traditional wharf and warehouse c.1880, now housing a museum *(see* below*)*. There are excellent moorings here with three jetties and a slipway, south of bridge 118. The town stretches away to the west – look out for the restored octagonal cockpit just off the main street, thought to be the only one in Wales which survives on its original site.

Powysland Museum and Montgomery Canal Centre The Canal Wharf, Welshpool, SY21 7AQ (01938 554656). Illustrates the archaeology, history and literature of the local area, and includes a canal exhibition and a display featuring the Montgomeryshire Yeomanry Cavalry. *Open summer, Mon–Tue and Thu–Fri 11.00–13.00 and 14.00–17.00, Sat 11.00–14.00; Sun during season all day.* Free.

Powis Castle *NT.* Access from High Street, Welshpool *SY21 8RF* (information line 01938 551944; www.nationaltrust.org.uk). The seat of the Earl of Powis, this impressive building has been continuously inhabited for over 500 years. It is a restored medieval castle with late 16th-C plasterwork and panelling, and has on display fine paintings, tapestries, early Georgian furniture and relics of Clive of India. The castle is in the centre of beautiful 18th-C terraced gardens and a park. Programme of events, fine plant shop, excellent tearooms. *Castle and museum open Thu–Mon; April 13.00–16.00; May–Aug 13.00–17.00; Sep–Oct 13.00–16.00; also B Hols during season. Garden open same days as museum 11.00–17.00.* Charge.

The Flash Leisure Centre Salop Road, Welshpool SY21 7DH (01938 555952). Swimming pool with a flume, bowls hall, fitness suite, sauna and sports hall. Café.

Tourist Information Centre Vicarage Gardens, Church Street, Welshpoo SY21 7DDl (01938 552043; www.virtual-shropshire.co.uk).

Welshpool & Llanfair Light Railway
The Station, Llanfair Caereinion, Welshpool SY21 0SF (01938 810441; www.wllr.org.uk). This delightful narrow-gauge railway originally opened in 1903, and is now restored and run by enthusiasts. Telephone or visit website for timetable.

Brithdir
Powys. A small main road settlement on the busy A483 with an isolated pub and scattered houses and farms. To the south is the Luggy Aqueduct, a small iron trough carrying the canal over the fast-flowing Luggy Brook, built in 1819 by George Buck, who was also responsible for the distinctive paddle gear found at the majority of locks.

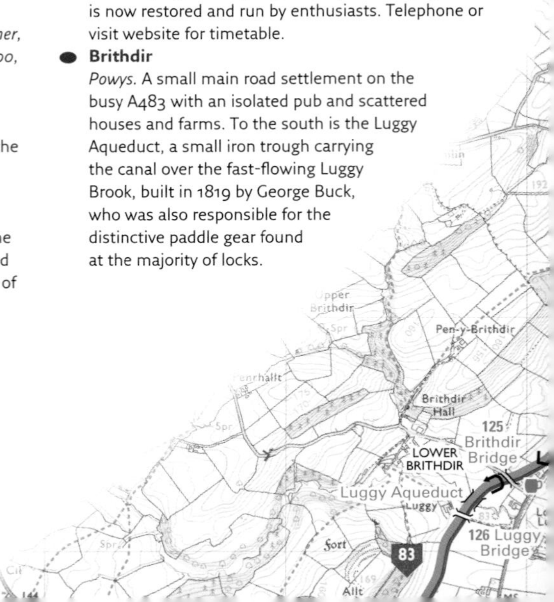

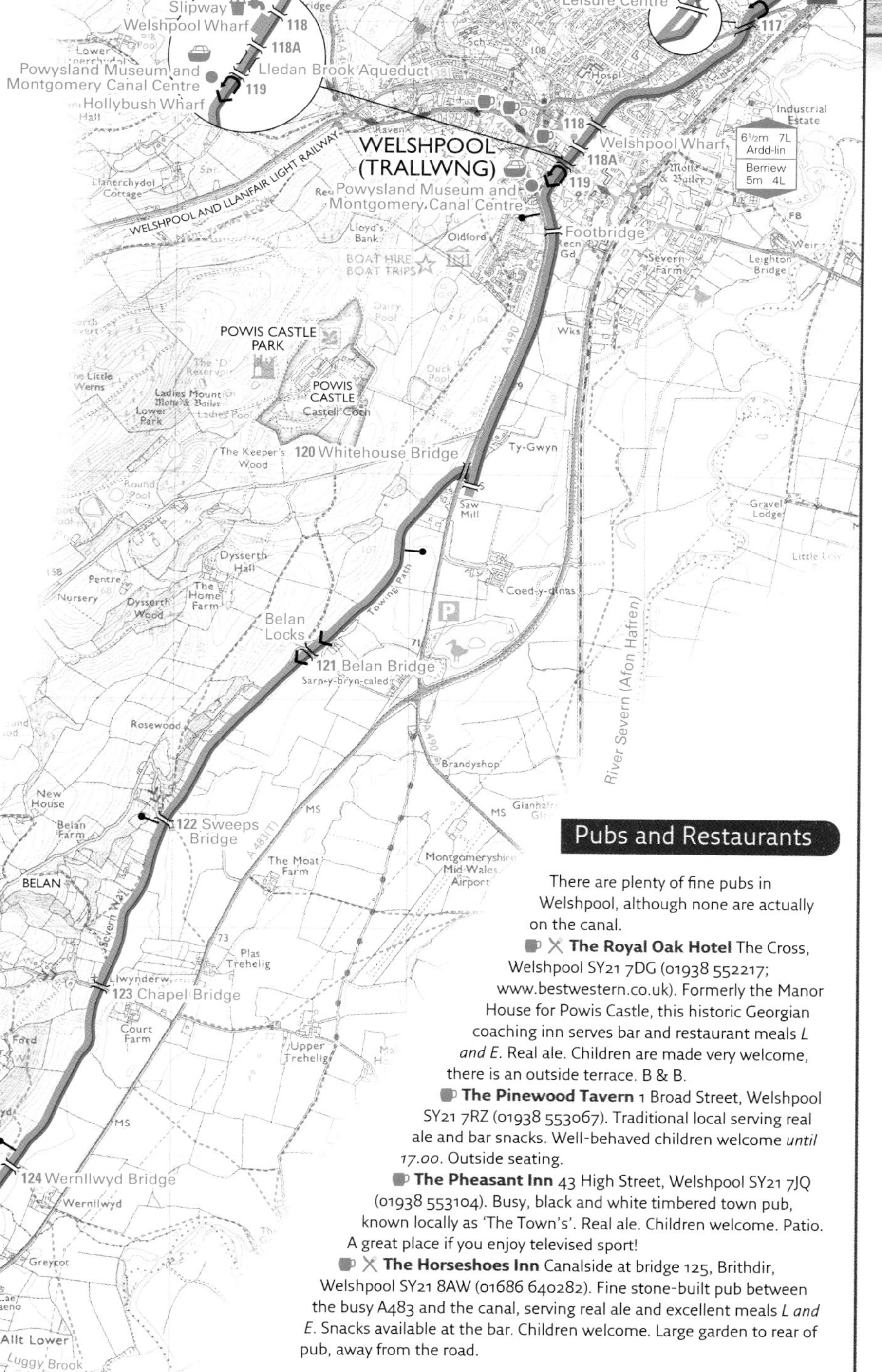

Pubs and Restaurants

There are plenty of fine pubs in Welshpool, although none are actually on the canal.

The Royal Oak Hotel The Cross, Welshpool SY21 7DG (01938 552217; www.bestwestern.co.uk). Formerly the Manor House for Powis Castle, this historic Georgian coaching inn serves bar and restaurant meals *L and E*. Real ale. Children are made very welcome, there is an outside terrace. B & B.

The Pinewood Tavern 1 Broad Street, Welshpool SY21 7RZ (01938 553067). Traditional local serving real ale and bar snacks. Well-behaved children welcome *until 17.00*. Outside seating.

The Pheasant Inn 43 High Street, Welshpool SY21 7JQ (01938 553104). Busy, black and white timbered town pub, known locally as 'The Town's'. Real ale. Children welcome. Patio. A great place if you enjoy televised sport!

The Horseshoes Inn Canalside at bridge 125, Brithdir, Welshpool SY21 8AW (01686 640282). Fine stone-built pub between the busy A483 and the canal, serving real ale and excellent meals *L and E*. Snacks available at the bar. Children welcome. Large garden to rear of pub, away from the road.

Berriew

Continuing south west, the canal passes Berriew on an aqueduct and then swings back towards the River Severn, as the valley is narrowed by the hills sweeping in from the east. The A483 follows the canal very closely. However, there are some fine glimpses of the River Severn between the trees to the east and the rolling hillsides to the west, all covered with broad-leaved woodland. Two locks, at Berriew and Brynderwyn, continue the rise towards Newtown, lifting the canal above the level of the Severn, whose waters flow swiftly alongside from Tan-y-fron to Newtown. The two lock keeper's cottages are fine white-washed houses and at Brynderwyn, a former coal wharf, there is a late 19th-C warehouse still standing. Just past bridge 135 there is a llama paddock, at the base of the wooded hills to the east of the canal, looking decidedly out of place in the more traditional farmscape. It is part of Penllwyn Holiday Lodges, where a lake has been created, adjoining the cut. Several of the bridges beyond Tan-y-fron have their dates of construction cast into them: Glanhafren Bridge (143) was built in 1889 and is comparatively ornate with cast iron balustrades, and bridge 147 has elegant white iron railings displaying the date 1853 and Brymbo. Bridge 142 is one of the few remaining swing bridges on the canal.

Berriew
Powys. PO, tel, stores. The village of Berriew lies to the west, climbing the steep slopes of the fast-flowing river which cascades over rocks beneath the houses. In the centre of the village is a handsome 18th-C single-span stone arch across the river; the black and white painted timber-framed and stone houses are ranged on either side. The village is very picturesque, with a unity of style, and has been voted the Best Kept Village in Wales numerous times; but this has not spoilt it, for it is still quiet, pretty and self-contained. The church – a Victorian restoration of a medieval building, dedicated to St Bueno (who miraculously brought St Winifred back to life: *see* St Winifred's Well in the Llanymynech section) – is the centre point of the village, set attractively amongst trees. The vicarage is dated 1616. A two-arched brick aqueduct carries the canal over the beautiful wooded valley of the River Rhiw. Originally built of stone, the aqueduct was reconstructed in 1889 and although it appeared quite sound when the navigation was closed, the canal was piped across it, because of leakage, before the latest renovation work.

Andrew Logan Museum of Sculpture Berriew, Welshpool SY21 8PJ (01686 640689; www.andrewlogan.com). Next to the Talbot Hotel by the river Rhiw. Works of popular poetry and metropolitan glamour by the founder, in 1972, of the Alternative Miss World Contest. Inspired by the excesses of Busby Berkeley, his works are wild, bizarre and exciting, and not at all what you would expect in this village. An enlivening and enriching experience? – George Melly called it 'Fabergé for the Millennium' – you will either love it or hate it. *Open May–Oct, Wed–Sun 12.00–18.00, phone for private visits.* Charge. Café and extraordinary gift shop.

Garthmyl
Powys. Tel. An old village beside the canal. The original wharf buildings can still be identified, looking rather incongruous as the wharf has long vanished. The concentration of remains, such as kiln banks, warehouses and a maltings, is probably due to the fact that the canal terminated here until the extension of the navigation between 1815 and 1821.

THE QUAY TO THE MARCHES
Prior to the building of the Montgomery Canal, the River Severn was a natural artery for trade, navigated above Shrewsbury as far as Pool Quay. Of course such river transport was unreliable, and low water levels would result in long delays. The beams in the Powis Arms (The Quay) were marked for each day the boatmen were stranded for lack of water.
It was from Swan Wharf, opposite the pub, that Montgomeryshire oak was shipped downstream to the naval dockyards at Bristol. In 1712 the *Duchess*, owned by George Bradley, was transporting 40-ton loads to Bristol and back. Until the Montgomery & Ellesmere Canal linked with the main inland waterways network in 1833, Pool Quay remained an important transhipment point.

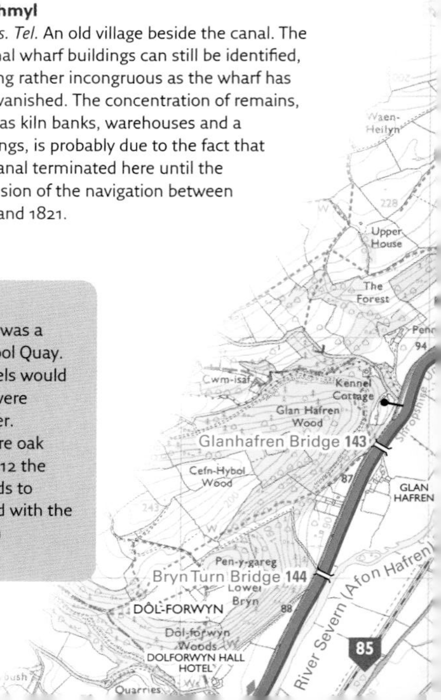

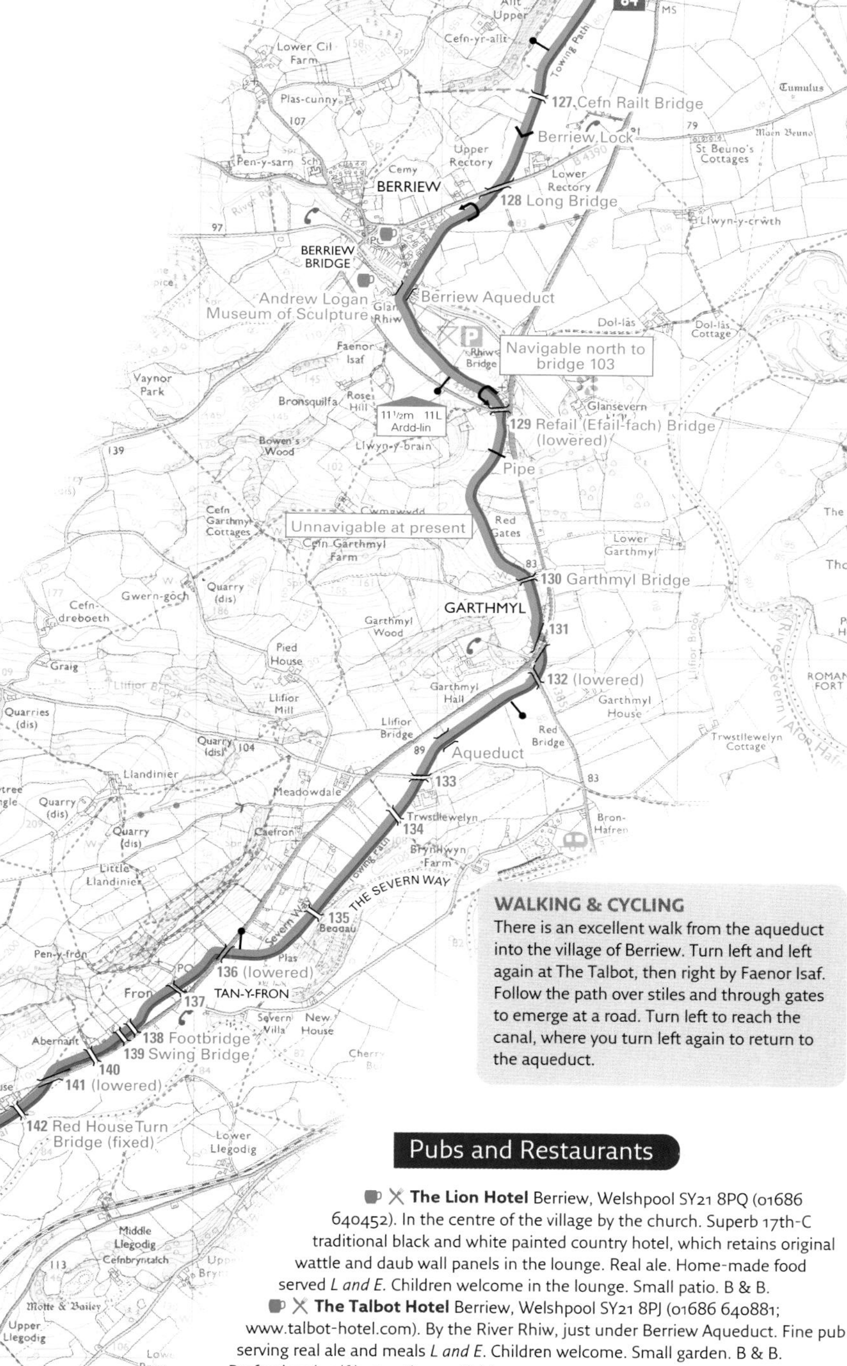

WALKING & CYCLING

There is an excellent walk from the aqueduct into the village of Berriew. Turn left and left again at The Talbot, then right by Faenor Isaf. Follow the path over stiles and through gates to emerge at a road. Turn left to reach the canal, where you turn left again to return to the aqueduct.

Pubs and Restaurants

The Lion Hotel Berriew, Welshpool SY21 8PQ (01686 640452). In the centre of the village by the church. Superb 17th-C traditional black and white painted country hotel, which retains original wattle and daub wall panels in the lounge. Real ale. Home-made food served *L and E*. Children welcome in the lounge. Small patio. B & B.

The Talbot Hotel Berriew, Welshpool SY21 8PJ (01686 640881; www.talbot-hotel.com). By the River Rhiw, just under Berriew Aqueduct. Fine pub serving real ale and meals *L and E*. Children welcome. Small garden. B & B. Professional golf instruction available.

Newtown

The canal continues south west towards Newtown along the wooded west side of the Severn valley. Canal and river flow side by side, the river providing the water for the canal via a feeder at Penarth and at one time by a pumping station at Newtown. Five single locks raise the canal to its summit level at Newtown. Aberbechan aqueduct is triple-arched and spans Bechan Brook, where there are the remains of a corn mill and maltings, hidden between the trees. Bridge 153 south of the aqueduct has the place and date of construction – Brymbo 1862 – cast into it. The canal is dry south of Freestone Lock and the course ends short of its original terminus. The once busy basin and the last half mile or so have vanished under housing, although street names recall what was once there. The entry to Newtown must now be made on foot – it is a pleasant walk.

- **Abermwl**
  Powys. PO, tel, stores. The best feature of the village is the iron bridge carrying the road jointly over the canal and the River Severn. After a plain girder bridge across the canal it develops into a beautiful elegant single-span arch leaping across the river. Into the curve of the arch are cast the words 'This second iron bridge constructed in the county of Montgomeryshire 1852'. By the PO there is a water-pump.
  Pwll Penarth (01938 555654; montwt@cix.co.uk). Once the settling beds for a sewage farm, this is now a Montgomeryshire Wildlife Trust haven for wildlife, where you may see grey wagtails, kingfishers, skylarks and lapwings, along with otters. In the autumn salmon can be seen jumping the fish pass. Access directly from the towpath near Freestone Lock.
- **Newtown**
  Powys. PO, tel, stores, garage, bank, station, cinema, market, leisure centre. Built around the Severn which sweeps through the town in a gentle curve. Prosperous as a woollen manufacturing town from the 18th C; the industry has now ceased. Its growth in the early 19th C prompted the building of the canal as a means of supplying coal and raw materials.

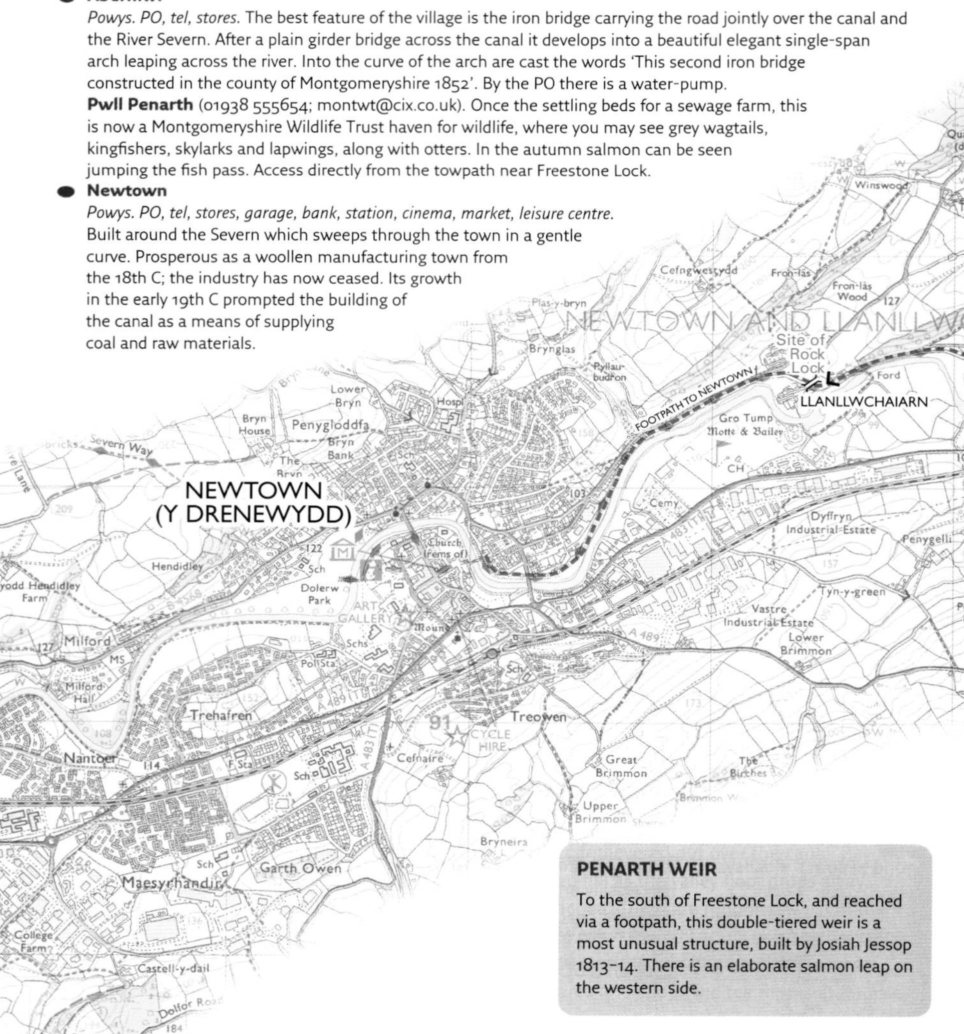

PENARTH WEIR

To the south of Freestone Lock, and reached via a footpath, this double-tiered weir is a most unusual structure, built by Josiah Jessop 1813–14. There is an elaborate salmon leap on the western side.

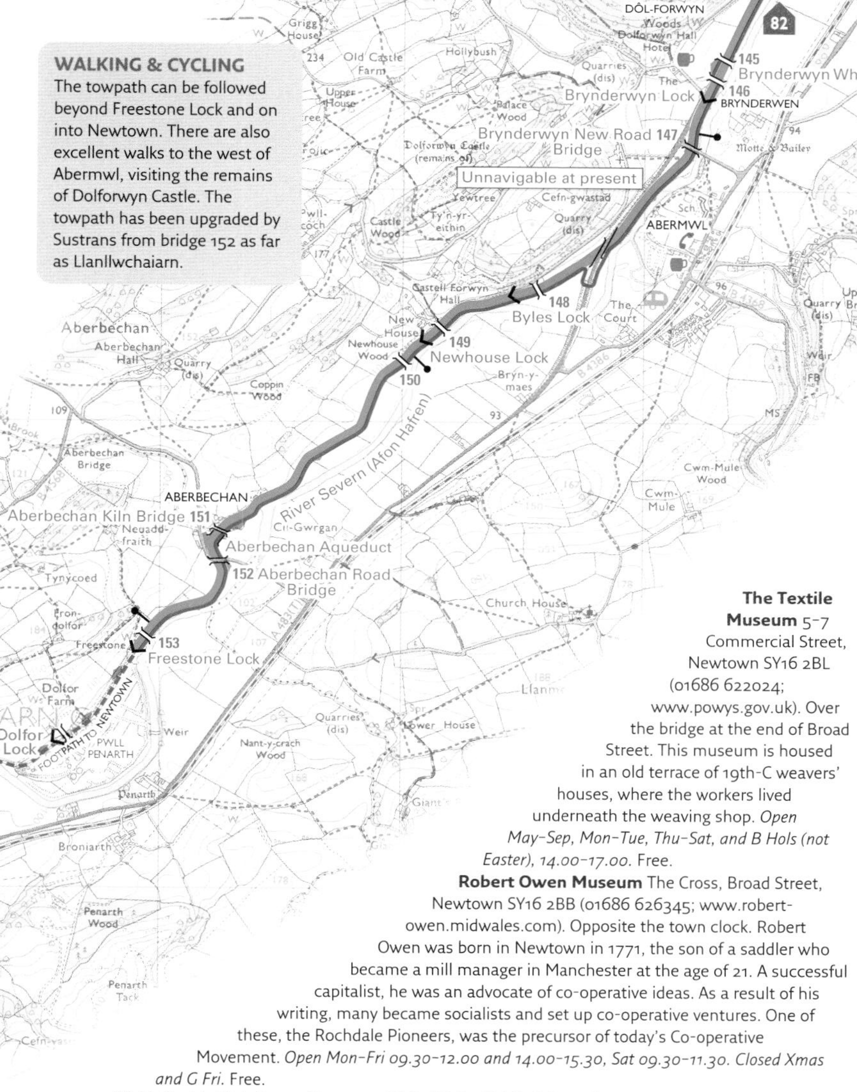

WALKING & CYCLING
The towpath can be followed beyond Freestone Lock and on into Newtown. There are also excellent walks to the west of Abermwl, visiting the remains of Dolforwyn Castle. The towpath has been upgraded by Sustrans from bridge 152 as far as Llanllwchaiarn.

The Textile Museum 5-7 Commercial Street, Newtown SY16 2BL (01686 622024; www.powys.gov.uk). Over the bridge at the end of Broad Street. This museum is housed in an old terrace of 19th-C weavers' houses, where the workers lived underneath the weaving shop. *Open May-Sep, Mon-Tue, Thu-Sat, and B Hols (not Easter), 14.00-17.00.* Free.

Robert Owen Museum The Cross, Broad Street, Newtown SY16 2BB (01686 626345; www.robert-owen.midwales.com). Opposite the town clock. Robert Owen was born in Newtown in 1771, the son of a saddler who became a mill manager in Manchester at the age of 21. A successful capitalist, he was an advocate of co-operative ideas. As a result of his writing, many became socialists and set up co-operative ventures. One of these, the Rochdale Pioneers, was the precursor of today's Co-operative Movement. *Open Mon-Fri 09.30-12.00 and 14.00-15.30, Sat 09.30-11.30. Closed Xmas and G Fri.* Free.

W. H. Smith High Street, Newtown SY16 2NP (01686 626280). All you would expect, housed in a fine recreation of the early shop, with a small museum upstairs.

Tourist Information Centre Central Car Park, Newtown SY16 2PW (01686 625580; www.tourism.powys.gov.uk).

Pubs and Restaurants

Access to Abermwl village is via Brynderwyn Bridge (147) and follow the road, turning right at the roundabout, for about ½ mile.

Abermwl Hotel Abermwl SY15 6ND (01686 630676; www.abermulehotel.co.uk). Friendly and traditional, family-run country pub with an inglenook. Real ale. Food available *L and E (not Tue)*. Children's play area. Patio and garden. B & B, caravan, and camping.

There are plenty of pubs and hotels to be found in Newtown.

SHROPSHIRE UNION CANAL

MAXIMUM DIMENSIONS

Autherley to Nantwich, and Middlewich Branch
Length: 72'
Beam: 7'
Headroom: 8'

Nantwich to Ellesmere Port
Length: 72'
Beam: 9'
Headroom: 8'

MANAGER

enquiries.walesandbordercounties@
britishwaterways.co.uk

MILEAGE

AUTHERLEY JUNCTION (Staffordshire & Worcestershire Canal) *to:*
Norbury: 15½ miles
Market Drayton: 27 miles
HURLESTON JUNCTION (Llangollen Canal): 40¾ miles
Barbridge Junction (Middlewich Branch): 42 miles
Chester Junction with Dee Branch: 58 miles
ELLESMERE PORT JUNCTION with Manchester Ship Canal: 66½ miles
Locks: 47

Middlewich Branch
Middlewich (Trent & Mersey Canal) *to:*
Barbridge Junction: 10 miles
Locks: 4

THE CHESTER CANAL

In 1772 an enabling Act was passed for a canal from the River Dee in Chester to join the Trent & Mersey Canal at Middlewich, with a spur to Nantwich. The building of the Trent & Mersey was the cause of this new venture, for it was seen as a threat to the future of the River Dee Navigation and the port of Chester. The new canal was designed to bolster Chester as an alternative port to Liverpool, and so was planned as a barge canal, with locks 80ft by 14ft 9in. Work started in Chester in the middle of 1772 and progressed slowly. There were engineering and financial problems, and the main line of the new canal was altered to terminate at a basin and warehouses just outside Nantwich: the proposed line to Middlewich was now to be a branch. The Nantwich–Chester link was completed in 1779, but the spur to Middlewich was not built until 54 years later. When the Nantwich–Chester Canal was finished, arguments with the Dee River Company delayed the building of the river lock. By this time competition with the Trent & Mersey was out of the question. Although regular freight and fast passenger services were run, the canal was wholly uneconomic and in 1787 the company collapsed. In 1790 it was revived and the canal repaired, for the directors saw the publication of the plans of the Ellesmere Canal as their last chance to complete the line to Middlewich.

THE BIRMINGHAM & LIVERPOOL JUNCTION CANAL

The future prosperity of the Ellesmere & Chester was limited by the lack of an outlet to the south, without which its trade could never be more than local. So the company was much cheered by the plans for the Birmingham & Liverpool Junction Canal which received its Act in 1825. The line from Nantwich to Autherley, on the Staffordshire & Worcestershire Canal, would give a direct link between Liverpool and the Midlands, and thus with the canal network as a whole. After serious engineering difficulties the canal was opened in 1835, shortly after the opening of the long-planned branch from the Chester Canal to the

Trent & Mersey at Middlewich, providing access to Manchester and the Potteries. Railway competition was close at hand by this date, and so the Birmingham & Liverpool Junction and Ellesmere & Chester companies worked closely together to preserve their profits. Ellesmere Port was greatly enlarged, and by 1840 steam haulage was in use on the Wirral line and on the Mersey itself. In 1845 the two companies merged, and then shortly after were reformed as the Shropshire Union Railways & Canal Company.

THE SHROPSHIRE UNION CANAL

The Shropshire Union Railways & Canal Company was formed under the shadow of railway expansion. Its initial plans were to build railways instead of canals, on the principle that it would halve the construction costs to lay a railway along the bed of an existing canal. By 1849 this plan had been abandoned, for the slow development of railways in Wales had shown the company that canals could still be profitable. Throughout the mid 19th C the Shropshire Union network remained profitable, and did not experience the steady decline of other major canal systems. The London & North Western Railway Company was a major shareholder in the Shropshire Union, and they were happy to let the canals remain as they provided the company with a significant tentacle into Great Western Railway territory. As a result the Shropshire Union was allowed to expand steadily; in 1870 the company owned 213 narrowboats, and in 1889 there were 395. By 1902 this fleet had increased to 450 boats. A few branches were threatened with closure on the grounds of unprofitability, but all remained open. The flourishing trade continued until World War I, which started a pattern of regular heavy losses from which the company was never able to recover. In 1921 the company gave up canal carrying, and sold most of its fleet of boats to private operators. Locks were closed at weekends, and standards of maintenance began to slip. In 1922 the Shropshire Union Company was bought out by the London & North Western Railway, which then was swallowed in turn by the newly-formed London Midland & Scottish Railway. Despite these changes the network remained open, although trade declined rapidly. Many traders were driven away by the lack of maintenance, which meant that most boats could only operate half empty. In 1936 a breach occurred on the Montgomery Canal one mile south of Frankton Junction; the company set out to repair the damage and then changed its mind. (The Weston line had been similarly abandoned after a breach in 1917.) With trade at a standstill there were no complaints, and in 1944 an Act was passed making closure official. This Act also officially abandoned 175 miles of the old Shropshire Union network. Out of this mass closure only the main line and the Middlewich Branch remained, although the Llangollen Branch (*see* page 23) luckily also escaped closure, being originally retained as a water supply channel. The Montgomery Canal also survives and is now the subject of an exciting restoration project (*see* page 71).

MEETING ONESELF COMING BACK

When first constructed the Shroppie relied very heavily on Belvide Reservoir – beside the A5 – for its supplies of water. In its original form the reservoir proved woefully inadequate and its capacity was doubled in 1836 to give a total of 70 million cubic metres of water. Thirty-four years later Barnhurst Sewerage Farm opened at Autherley Junction and, when it later became a treatment works, its entire discharge became available to feed both the Shroppie and the Staffs & Worcs Canal. Today there is rarely a problem of water shortage on the Shroppie, which can largely be attributed to the regular habits of the good people of Wolverhampton.

Autherley Junction

The Shropshire Union Canal leaves the Staffordshire & Worcestershire Canal at Autherley Junction, and runs straight along the side of the former Wolverhampton Aerodrome at Pendeford, now covered with houses. Passing the Wolverhampton Boat Club (visiting boaters welcome), the canal soon enters a short cutting, which is through rock and narrow in places. Emerging briefly into the green and quiet countryside that is found along the whole length of this navigation, the canal (having shrugged off the noisy intrusion of the M54 motorway) again plunges into a deep, long cutting that is typical of this particular stretch. The start of this length is beautifully framed by the arch of bridge 8, beguiling the boater into a tree-lined avenue.

NAVIGATIONAL NOTES

The canal is very narrow south of bridges 5 and 6, and between bridges 8 and 9.

Autherley Junction
An important and busy canal junction, where in 1830 Thomas Telford brought his Birmingham & Liverpool Junction Canal (now part of the Shropshire Union system) to join the much older Staffordshire & Worcestershire Canal (built by James Brindley and opened in 1772). There is a former canal toll office here, also a boatyard and a boatclub. The stop lock has a fall of only about 6in: it was insisted upon by the Staffordshire & Worcestershire Company to prevent the newer canal stealing water from them. Autherley Junction is sometimes confused with Aldersley Junction, 1/2 mile to the south, where the Birmingham Canal Navigations join the Staffordshire & Worcestershire Canal from the east after falling through the Wolverhampton flight of 21 locks.

WALKING & CYCLING

The Shropshire Union Canal offers a delightfully rural cycling and walking corridor from Wolverhampton all the way to the Mersey Estuary. Apart from the historic city of Chester, there is virtually no urban intrusion and little impact from industry or trunk roads and motorways. There is good disabled access to the towpath off Wobaston road, to the north of Bridge 4 and in Wheaton Aston at Bridge 19.

Boatyards

Ⓑ **Oxley Marine** The Wharf, Oxley Moor Road, Wolverhampton WV10 6TZ (01902 789522; www.oxleymarine.co.uk). D Pump out, gas, overnight and long-term mooring, winter storage, slipway, boat and engine sales and repairs, DIY facilities, *emergency call out*. Licensed bar *each evening*, snacks.

Ⓑ **Napton Narrowboats** Autherley Junction, Oxley Moor Road, Wolverhampton WV9 5HW (01926 813644). D E Pump out, gas, narrowboat hire, overnight mooring, long term mooring, winter storage, slipway, chandlery, provisions, books and maps, boat building, DIY facilities, boat repairs, solid fuel, gifts, showers. *Emergency call out.*

Pubs and Restaurants

Pendulum 48 Blaydon Road, Wolverhampton WV9 5NP (01902 623201). North west of Blaydon Road Bridge. Rota of guest ales. Food *L and E (not Sun)*. Children welcome. Outside seating. Pub games. Regular quiz and music nights. Morrisons supermarket next door.

BOAT TRIPS

City of Wolverhampton Passenger Boat Services, Oxley Marine, The Wharf, Oxley Moor Road, Wolverhampton WV10 6TZ (01902 789522; www.oxleymarine.co.uk). ***Nb Stafford*** is a 42-seat boat operating public trips *Apr–Sep on most Sun* and booked charter trips. Also day boat ***Chester*** available throughout the year.

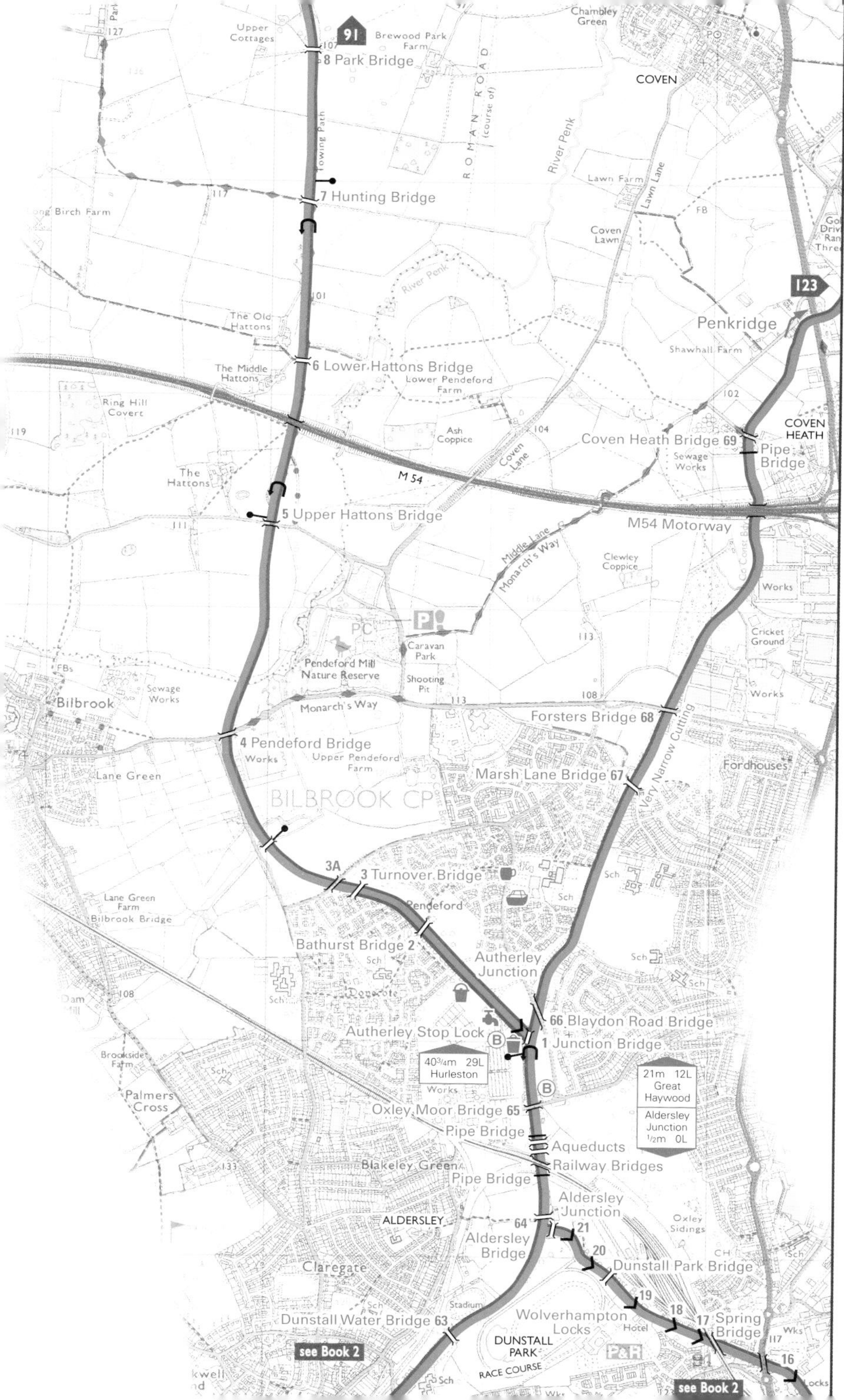

Upper Cottages
91
Brewood Park Farm
8 Park Bridge
Chambley Green
COVEN
Towing Path
ROMAN ROAD (course of)
River Penk
Lawn Farm
Lawn Lane
7 Hunting Bridge
Long Birch Farm
Coven Lawn
FB
River Penk
123
The Old Hattons
Penkridge
Shawhall Farm
6 Lower Hattons Bridge
The Middle Hattons
Lower Pendeford Farm
Ring Hill Covert
102
Ash Coppice
Coven Lane
COVEN HEATH
Coven Heath Bridge 69
Pipe Bridge
Sewage Works
The Hattons
M 54
5 Upper Hattons Bridge
M54 Motorway
Middle Lane
Monarch's Way
Clewley Coppice
Works
PC
P
Caravan Park
Cricket Ground
Pendeford Mill Nature Reserve
Shooting Pit
Works
Sewage Works
Bilbrook
Monarch's Way
Forsters Bridge 68
4 Pendeford Bridge
Works
Upper Pendeford Farm
Lane Green
Marsh Lane Bridge 67
Very Narrow Cutting
Fordhouses
BILBROOK CP
3A
3 Turnover Bridge
Sch
Lane Green Farm
Bilbrook Bridge
Pendeford
Sch
Bathurst Bridge 2
Autherley Junction
Sch
Dovecote
Dam Mill
66 Blaydon Road Bridge
Autherley Stop Lock
1 Junction Bridge
Brookside Farm
40¾m 29L Hurleston
21m 12L Great Haywood
Works
Aldersley Junction ½m 0L
Palmers Cross
Oxley Moor Bridge 65
Pipe Bridge
Aqueducts
Railway Bridges
Blakeley Green
Pipe Bridge
Aldersley Junction
ALDERSLEY
64
21
Oxley Sidings
Aldersley Bridge
20
Claregate
Dunstall Park Bridge
19
Stadium
18
Wolverhampton Locks
17 Spring Bridge
Dunstall Water Bridge 63
Hotel
DUNSTALL PARK
P&R
16
RACE COURSE
see Book 2
see Book 2

Brewood

Leaving the balustraded Avenue Bridge (10), which leads westward to Chillington Hall, the canal curves in a bold cutting past the village of Brewood (moorings by bridge 14) and its attractive wharf - and moves north west along a very straight embankment. The head bank of the big Belvide Reservoir can be seen on the west side; its feeder stream enters the canal just south of Stretton Aqueduct. This solid but elegant cast iron structure carries the canal over the A5. Crossing the aqueduct by boat tends to give the canal traveller an air of great superiority over the teeming motorists below. After another long, wooded cutting the canal reaches Wheaton Aston Lock. This lock marks the end of the long pound from Autherley and the beginning of the 17-mile level that lasts almost to Market Drayton. Reasonably priced diesel can be obtained from Turners Garage by bridge 19, which also holds an amazing stock of boat and bicycle parts and sells a variety of coal.

Brewood
Staffs. PO, tel, stores, bank, chemist, takeaway, garage, butchers, bakers, cashpoint. The name (pronounced Brood) derives from Celtic Bre, meaning hill, thus giving wood on the hill. It originally consisted of a Roman fort on Beacon Hill to defend Watling Street. Dean Street, below the church, is a gem with a great diversity of façades jostling for attention side by side. Most obvious are the tripartite windows of Dean Street House, although lower down the street are Old Smithy Cottages, built c.1350 and once a hall house open to the roof. The village church is a tall, elegant building which has been greatly restored but still contains a 16th-C font and several 16th-C effigies and 17th-C monuments commemorating the Giffard family of Chillington Hall. Speedwell Castle, on the market square, has a most strikingly ornate façade and is a delightful building (some would say folly) erected by an apothecary around 1740. He is reputed to have won handsomely on a horse named Speedwell and used his winnings to build this dwelling. The chemist shop, nearby, has an 18th-C exterior and in 1828 was the birthplace of Thomas Walker, an eminent Victorian engineer, who built the Severn railway tunnel. The entire market square is allegedly riddled with underground vaults and passages interconnecting Speedwell Castle with the pubs and hotels ringing the square.

Chillington Hall Codsall Wood, Wolverhampton WV8 1RE (01902 850236; www.chillingtonhall.co.uk) 1½ miles west of the canal, south west of Brewood, has been the home of the Giffard family since the 12th C. The existing hall was built in the 18th C, and the wooded park in which it stands was designed by Capability Brown. *Open Aug, Wed–Fri and Sun, 14.00–17.00; at other times by appointment.*

Belvide Reservoir A large nature reserve open to naturalists. The Royal Society for the Protection of Birds is developing the reserve to include displays and hides, enabling enthusiasts to have a greater opportunity to observe the many species of birds. There is only private club fishing and no sailing on the reservoir, to preserve the bird sanctuary.

Stretton
Staffs. 1 mile north east of Stretton Aqueduct off the A5. The church was rebuilt in the 19th C but retains its original chancel and fragments of medieval glass in the east window.

Stretton Hall Built in 1620 to designs by Inigo Jones. Most interesting features are the vast fireplace with steps up to it for chimney sweep boys, and the remarkable staircase suspended by chains from the roof. The house is private.

Lapley
Staffs. 3/4 mile north east of bridge 17. The central tower of the church dominates the village. It is an interesting building with fine Norman windows, an old Dutch font and traces of medieval paintings on the nave wall. The church as we see it now was completed in the 15th C.

Wheaton Aston
Staffs. PO, tel, stores, off-licence, cashpoint, garage. Overrun by new housing. The village green around the church (rebuilt in 1857) is a memento of a more pleasant past. The garage beside the canal can repair boat engines and also sells chandlery. There is wheelchair access on both sides of the canal at bridge 19.

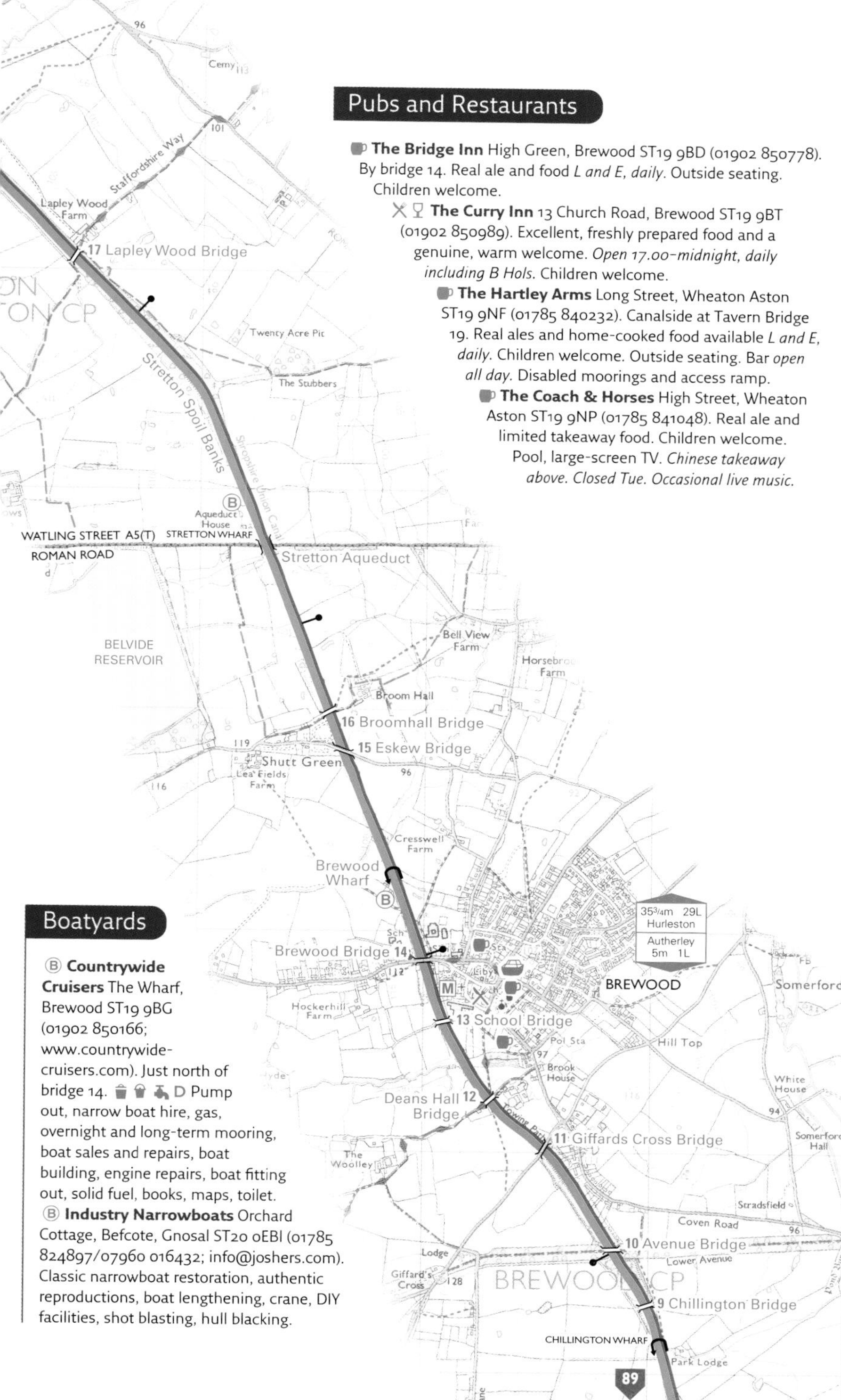

Pubs and Restaurants

The Bridge Inn High Green, Brewood ST19 9BD (01902 850778). By bridge 14. Real ale and food *L and E, daily*. Outside seating. Children welcome.

The Curry Inn 13 Church Road, Brewood ST19 9BT (01902 850989). Excellent, freshly prepared food and a genuine, warm welcome. *Open 17.00–midnight, daily including B Hols.* Children welcome.

The Hartley Arms Long Street, Wheaton Aston ST19 9NF (01785 840232). Canalside at Tavern Bridge 19. Real ales and home-cooked food available *L and E, daily*. Children welcome. Outside seating. Bar *open all day*. Disabled moorings and access ramp.

The Coach & Horses High Street, Wheaton Aston ST19 9NP (01785 841048). Real ale and limited takeaway food. Children welcome. Pool, large-screen TV. *Chinese takeaway above. Closed Tue. Occasional live music.*

Boatyards

Ⓑ **Countrywide Cruisers** The Wharf, Brewood ST19 9BG (01902 850166; www.countrywide-cruisers.com). Just north of bridge 14. D Pump out, narrow boat hire, gas, overnight and long-term mooring, boat sales and repairs, boat building, engine repairs, boat fitting out, solid fuel, books, maps, toilet.

Ⓑ **Industry Narrowboats** Orchard Cottage, Befcote, Gnosal ST20 0EBI (01785 824897/07960 016432; info@joshers.com). Classic narrowboat restoration, authentic reproductions, boat lengthening, crane, DIY facilities, shot blasting, hull blacking.

Church Eaton

The canal now proceeds along the very long pound, alternately in cuttings and on embankments. Both offer interest: the cuttings for their rich vegetation, and the embankments for the excellent views over quiet, unspoilt grazing land.

Pubs and Restaurants

Royal Oak Church Eaton ST20 0AS (01785 823078). Real ale and home-made pies served in a pub that concentrates on live entertainment in the form of *weekend* music, comedy and drama. Outside seating. Food is served *E Thu–Sat and L Sun.*

High Bridge, Grub Street Cutting (see *page 94*)

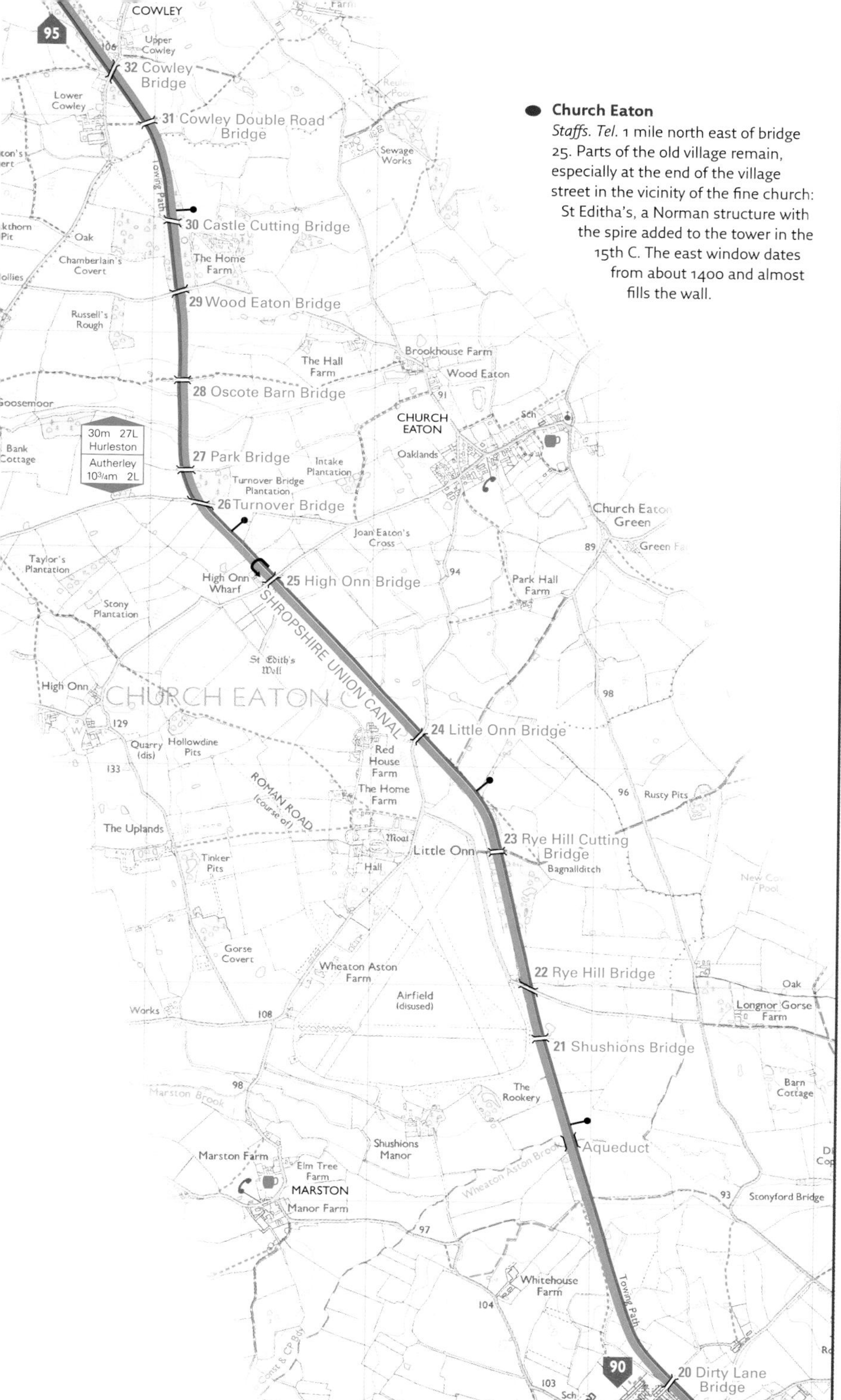

Church Eaton

Staffs. Tel. 1 mile north east of bridge 25. Parts of the old village remain, especially at the end of the village street in the vicinity of the fine church: St Editha's, a Norman structure with the spire added to the tower in the 15th C. The east window dates from about 1400 and almost fills the wall.

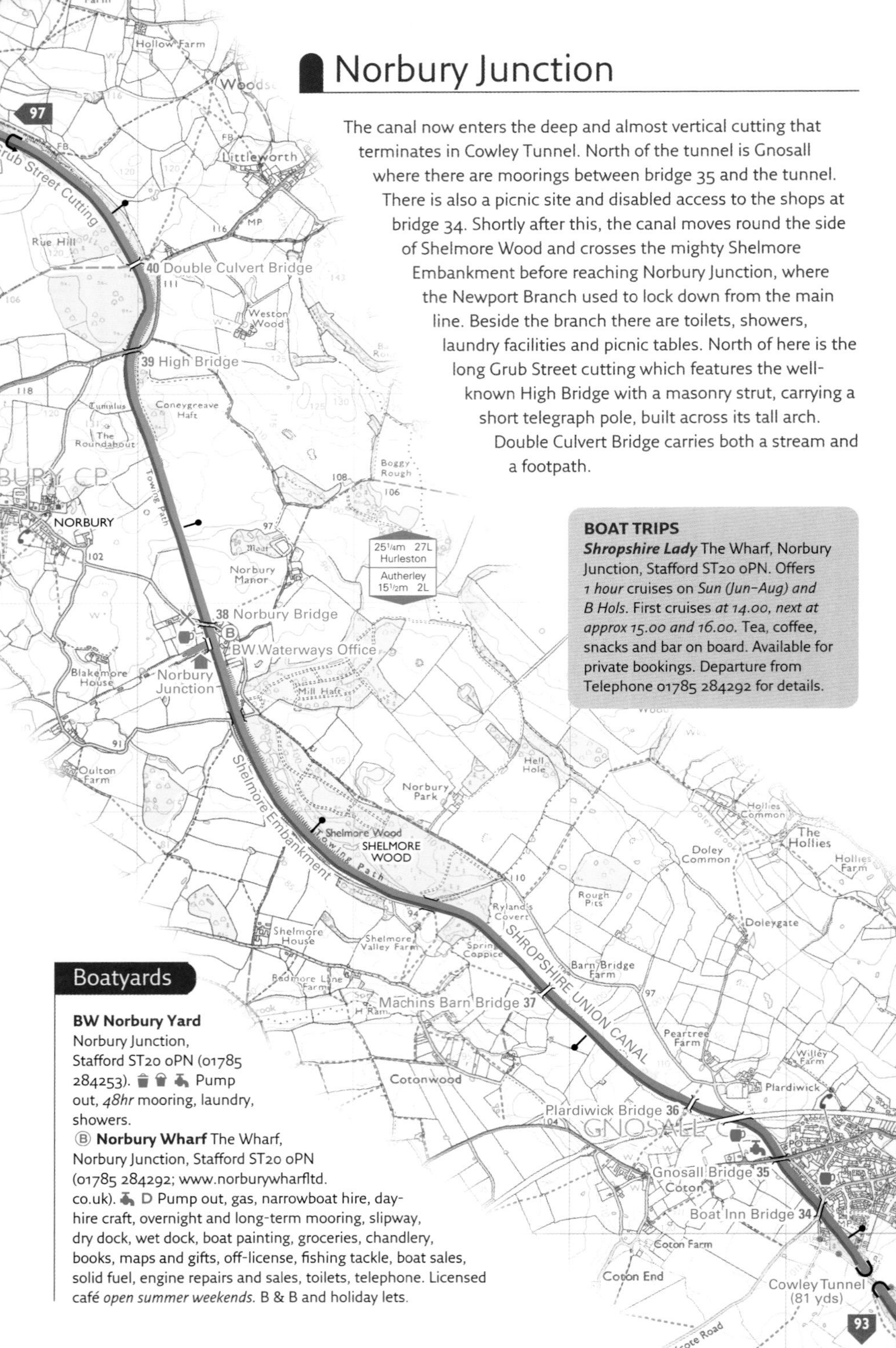

Norbury Junction

The canal now enters the deep and almost vertical cutting that terminates in Cowley Tunnel. North of the tunnel is Gnosall where there are moorings between bridge 35 and the tunnel. There is also a picnic site and disabled access to the shops at bridge 34. Shortly after this, the canal moves round the side of Shelmore Wood and crosses the mighty Shelmore Embankment before reaching Norbury Junction, where the Newport Branch used to lock down from the main line. Beside the branch there are toilets, showers, laundry facilities and picnic tables. North of here is the long Grub Street cutting which features the well-known High Bridge with a masonry strut, carrying a short telegraph pole, built across its tall arch. Double Culvert Bridge carries both a stream and a footpath.

BOAT TRIPS

Shropshire Lady The Wharf, Norbury Junction, Stafford ST20 0PN. Offers *1 hour* cruises on *Sun (Jun–Aug) and B Hols*. First cruises *at 14.00, next at approx 15.00 and 16.00*. Tea, coffee, snacks and bar on board. Available for private bookings. Departure from Telephone 01785 284292 for details.

Boatyards

BW Norbury Yard Norbury Junction, Stafford ST20 0PN (01785 284253). Pump out, *48hr* mooring, laundry, showers.

Ⓑ **Norbury Wharf** The Wharf, Norbury Junction, Stafford ST20 0PN (01785 284292; www.norburywharfltd.co.uk). D Pump out, gas, narrowboat hire, day-hire craft, overnight and long-term mooring, slipway, dry dock, wet dock, boat painting, groceries, chandlery, books, maps and gifts, off-license, fishing tackle, boat sales, solid fuel, engine repairs and sales, toilets, telephone. Licensed café *open summer weekends*. B & B and holiday lets.

- **Cowley Tunnel**
This short tunnel was originally intended to be much longer - 690yds - but most of it was opened out at an early stage during construction (in 1831) because of dangerous faults in the rock, and now only 81yds remain. The tunnel is unlined, and to the south of it a steep narrow cutting through solid rock stretches a considerable distance - an awe-inspiring sight.

- **Gnosall**
Staffs. PO, tel, stores, off-licence, takeaways, garage. East of bridge 35. The main feature of interest in the village is the church of St Laurence, 1 mile east of the canal. It is a 15th-C building with original Norman tower arches. The east window has fine decorated tracery framing modern stained glass.

- **Shelmore Embankment**
The construction of this great embankment, 1 mile long, just south of Norbury Junction, was the source of endless grief and expense to the Birmingham & Liverpool Junction Canal Company in general and to Thomas Telford, the engineer, in particular. It was an enormous task anyway to shift the millions of cubic feet of earth to build the bank; but while the contractors struggled to complete it, the bank slipped and collapsed time and again. By early 1834, Shelmore Embankment was the only unfinished section of the whole canal. It was not until 1835, after 5½ years' solid work on it and well after Telford's death, that the embankment was completed by William Cubitt and the B & LJ Canal was opened as a through route. There are flood gates at each end, to close off the channel in case of a breach. These were closed each night during World War II as a precaution against bombing.

- **Norbury Junction**
This was once the outlet for the Shrewsbury, Newport and Trench branches on to the rest of the Shropshire Union Canal system. There was a long flight of locks from the junction down to Newport, but these are now closed, except for the top lock which is used as a dock.

- **Loynton Moss**
This is a floating bog with an interesting plant community managed by Staffordshire Wildlife Trust (01889 880100). It can be accessed by a footpath immediately north of bridge 39 which links into a circular walk with interpretation boards. **Keep to the footpath** as the moss is potentially dangerous. There are viewpoints around the site.

Pubs and Restaurants

Boat Inn Wharf Road, Gnosall, Stafford ST20 0DA (01785 822208). By bridge 34. Canalside pub serving real ale and a good range of bar meals *L and E, daily.* Children and dogs welcome. Garden, darts, and pool table. Quiz *Sun.* Cash point.

Navigation Newport road, Gnosall, Stafford ST20 0BN (01785 822327). Canalside, at bridge 35. Real ales together with an interesting selection of food served *L and E* in restaurant and bar. Children and dogs welcome. Garden and play area. Darts and pool table. Disabled access and facilities. Moorings.

Royal Oak Newport road, Gnosall, Stafford ST20 0BL (01785 822362). In the village by the railway bridge. Basic bar, and comfortable lounge, where you can enjoy real ale. Home-made food available *L and E, daily.* Children welcome. Garden and play area. Quiz *Sun.*

Junction Inn Norbury Junction, Stafford ST20 0PN (01785 284288; www.norburyjunction.co.uk). Canalside, at Norbury Junction. Superbly situated canal pub serving real ales and food *L and E, daily.* Carvery *Sun L.* Beer garden, patio and children's play area. Pool, darts and juke box.

Old Wharf Tearoom Norbury Junction, Stafford ST20 0PN (01785 284292). Attractive waterside café with an interesting display of Measham teapots. Inexpensive selection of light snacks and refreshments. *Open daily 08.00-18.00.*

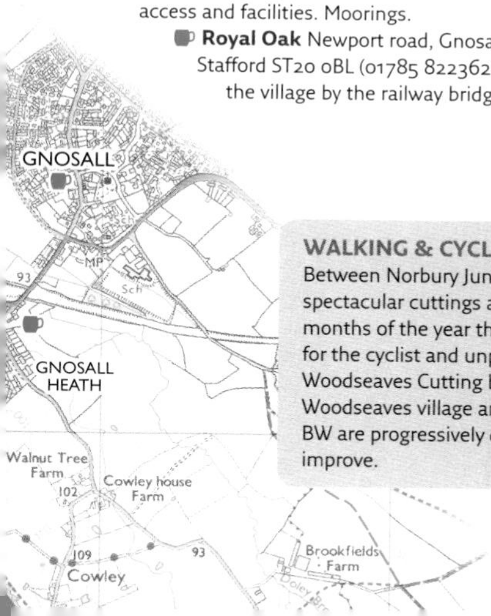

GNOSALL
MP
Sch
93
GNOSALL HEATH
Walnut Tree Farm
102
Cowley house Farm
109
93
Cowley
Brookfields Farm

WALKING & CYCLING

Between Norbury Junction and Nantwich the navigation passes through several spectacular cuttings and many more of lesser magnitude. During the wetter months of the year the towpath can become waterlogged making it impassable for the cyclist and unpleasant for walkers. Probably the worst section is through Woodseaves Cutting between bridges 56 and 59 and a diversion through Woodseaves village and back to the canal at Tyrley Wharf should be considered. BW are progressively draining and upgrading the towpath so the situation will improve.

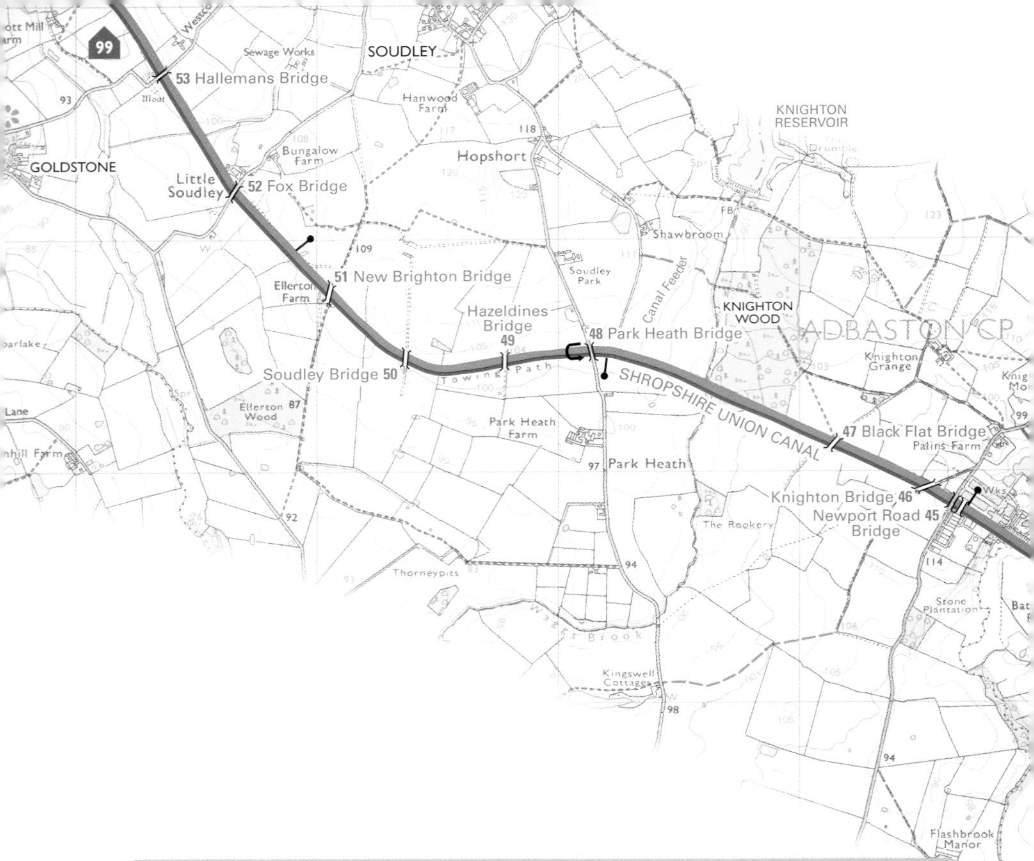

PLANT LIFE

Wood Sorrel is a widespread, charming, creeping perennial. Widespread in moist, shady woods, it is an indicator of ancient woodlands and hedgerows. The trefoil leaves, often purplish beneath and which fold down at night, are borne on long stalks. They have a sharp acid taste and were formerly used as a flavouring, like those of Sorrel. Lilac-veined flowers (April–June) are carried on stalks.

Knapweed is a widespread, hairy perennial of grassy places. The grooved stems branch towards the top. The leaves are narrow and slightly lobed near the base of the plant. The flower heads appear June–September and have brown bracts and purple florets.

Shebdon

The canal moves out of Grub Street cutting, leaving behind the unusual double-arched bridge, containing a small telegraph pole, and, passing the village of High Offley on a hill to the north, continues in a north westerly direction through the quiet open farmland that always accompanies this canal. Along this stretch are two canalside pubs - both amaze the traveller by their very survival, situated as they are on quiet roads and an even quieter canal. The great Shebdon Embankment is heralded by an aqueduct; at the far end is a large ex-chocolate factory (now producing only dried milk), whose goods used to be carried to and from Bournville (on the Worcester & Birmingham Canal) by narrowboat.

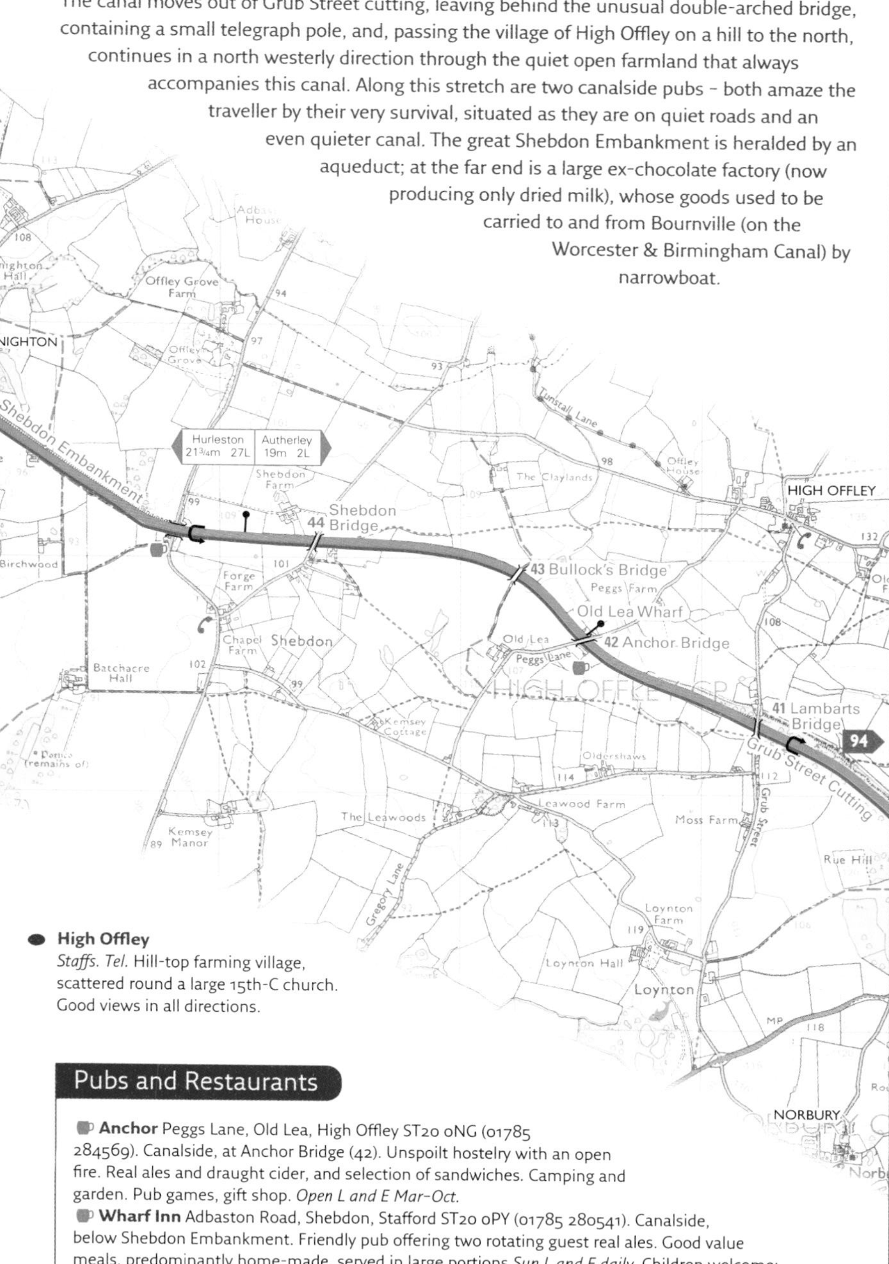

● **High Offley**
Staffs. Tel. Hill-top farming village, scattered round a large 15th-C church. Good views in all directions.

Pubs and Restaurants

Anchor Peggs Lane, Old Lea, High Offley ST20 0NG (01785 284569). Canalside, at Anchor Bridge (42). Unspoilt hostelry with an open fire. Real ales and draught cider, and selection of sandwiches. Camping and garden. Pub games, gift shop. *Open L and E Mar-Oct.*

Wharf Inn Adbaston Road, Shebdon, Stafford ST20 0PY (01785 280541). Canalside, below Shebdon Embankment. Friendly pub offering two rotating guest real ales. Good value meals, predominantly home-made, served in large portions *Sun L and E daily.* Children welcome; dogs in taproom only. Garden.

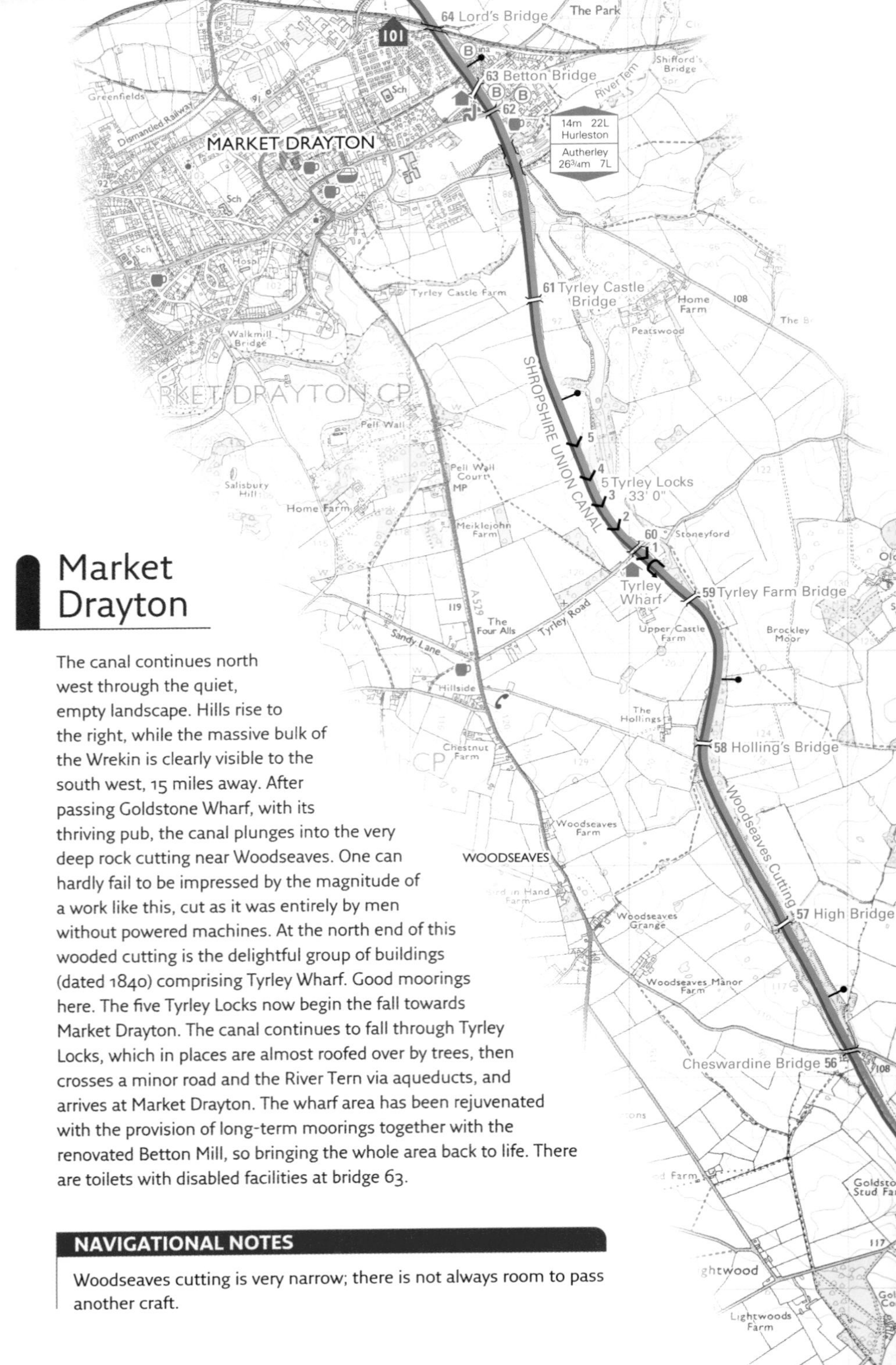

Market Drayton

The canal continues north west through the quiet, empty landscape. Hills rise to the right, while the massive bulk of the Wrekin is clearly visible to the south west, 15 miles away. After passing Goldstone Wharf, with its thriving pub, the canal plunges into the very deep rock cutting near Woodseaves. One can hardly fail to be impressed by the magnitude of a work like this, cut as it was entirely by men without powered machines. At the north end of this wooded cutting is the delightful group of buildings (dated 1840) comprising Tyrley Wharf. Good moorings here. The five Tyrley Locks now begin the fall towards Market Drayton. The canal continues to fall through Tyrley Locks, which in places are almost roofed over by trees, then crosses a minor road and the River Tern via aqueducts, and arrives at Market Drayton. The wharf area has been rejuvenated with the provision of long-term moorings together with the renovated Betton Mill, so bringing the whole area back to life. There are toilets with disabled facilities at bridge 63.

NAVIGATIONAL NOTES

Woodseaves cutting is very narrow; there is not always room to pass another craft.

Market Drayton

Shropshire. PO, tel, stores, garage, banks, laundrette, chemist, garage. On the west bank of the canal, the market centre for the surrounding district, is an attractive town with some splendid old buildings. It received its charter in the 13th C but was destroyed by fire in 1651. However, picturesque black and white timber framing was again used for the rebuilding, the best of which is the Tudor House Hotel in the market square and the adjacent Sandbrook Vaults (1653) in Shropshire Street. The parish church of St Mary is large and well-sited overlooking the Tern valley and dates from the 12th C. The ivy-clad Corbet Arms Hotel is a fine centre-piece to the main square. The town now claims to be the home of gingerbread – there are two bakeries, one producing the original Billingtons recipe which was sold at a weekly market in the Buttercross. The link may be somewhat tenuous, but is based on the town's connection with Clive of India who was known to have returned from the east with a plentiful selection of spices, one of which could well have been ginger!

Swimming Centre Newtown, Market Drayton TF9 1JT (01630 655177). Swimming pool offering a variety of activity programmes: indoor and outdoor pools. *Open daily* – times and activities vary from holiday to term-time so telephone for details.

Tourist Information Centre 49 Cheshire Street, Market Drayton TF9 1PH (01630 652139; www.virtual-shropshire.co.uk). A well-stocked centre *open Apr–Oct, Mon–Fri 10.00–17.00, Sat 10.00–17.30; Nov–Mar, Mon–Fri 10.00–17.00, Sat 10.00–16.00. Closed Sun, B Hol Mon and for two weeks over Xmas.* Interesting range of town trails available including a children's version.

Pubs and Restaurants

The Wharf Tavern Goldstone Wharf, Cheswardine, Market Drayton TF9 2LP (01630 661226). Canalside, at bridge 55. Once a coal wharf and warehouse, now a popular canal venue. Real ale, together with meals *L and E* (book for restaurant meals *at weekends*). Garden with children's play area. Moorings.

The Talbot Newcastle Street, Market Drayton TF9 1HW (01630 654989). Canalside at bridge 62. Warm, friendly, cheerful pub serving real ale and bar food *L and E, daily*. Children's room. Garden. Quiz *Wed*. Moorings.

The Stafford Court Hotel Stafford Street, Market Drayton TF9 1HY (01630 652646). Cosy, comfortable establishment serving real ales and excellent traditional English food *L and E, daily*. Carvery *Wed and Sat*. Children welcome. Outside seating. No electronic machines. Quizzes, discos and bingo, *telephone for details*. B & B.

The Corbet Arms Hotel High Street, Market Drayton TF9 1PY (01630 652037). Georgian coaching inn with a very forward lady ghost in room 7. Real ale. Food available in bar and restaurant *L and E (not Mon, Tue)*. Children welcome if eating. Live music at *weekends*.

The Crown Queen Street, Market Drayton TF9 1PX (01630 655675). This old-fashioned, welcoming single-roomed pub serves real ales and food at *L daily and E Mon–Thu*. They have held the recipe for the famous Clive Pie. Children and dogs welcome. Small garden.

The Salopian Star Stafford Street, Market Drayton TF9 1HX (01630 652530). Real ales from the Salopian Brewery dispensed in an open-plan bar. Children welcome *during the day*. Beer garden and pub games. *Open all day*. There are many other good pubs in Market Drayton.

The Four Alls Newport road, Woodseaves, Market Drayton TF9 2AG (01630 652995; www.thefouralls.com). Large roadside pub with *L and E* food, 10 minutes walk from bridge 60. B & B.

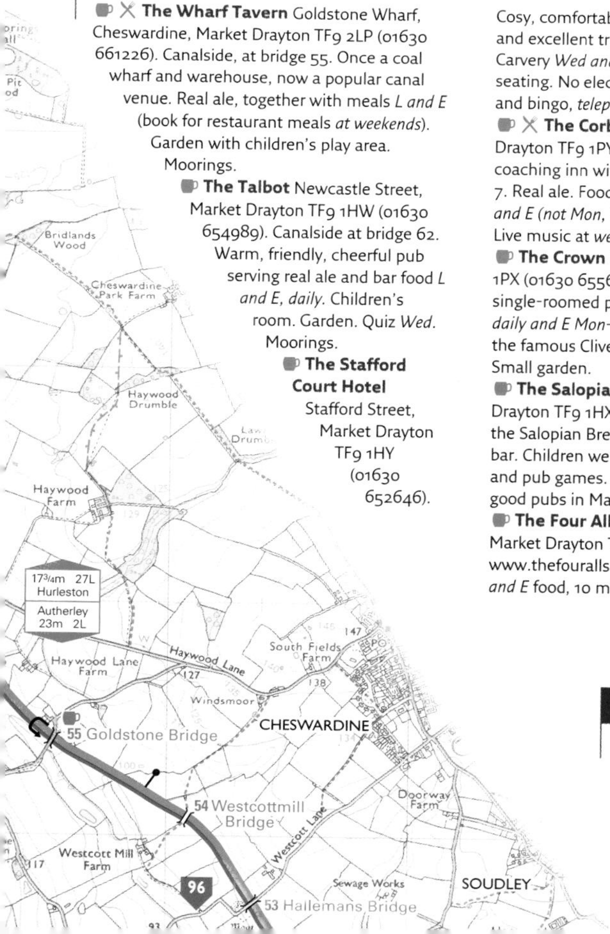

Boatyards

See page 100 for details.

Adderley

The navigation leaves Market Drayton passing new housing development on the offside, somewhat softened by the orderly and colourful line of moored boats. Soon the canal regains its peaceful isolation, passing through a pleasant wooded cutting (which is alleged by the superstitious to shelter a vociferous ghost) before arriving at the five Adderley Locks: the middle of the three main groups of locks between Autherley and Nantwich.

Adderley
Shropshire. PO, tel, stores, garage (no fuel). A rather under-populated village, bisected by the now-closed railway and flanked by the large Shavington and Adderley Parks. The unusual church, set by itself, was rebuilt of red sandstone in 1801 in neo-classical style. In 1958 a large portion of the church was closed to reduce maintenance costs, including the tower dated 1712, the transepts and the chancel. As a result the much smaller interior is better suited to contemporary needs and feels more like a large formal drawing room than a church. The Village Club welcomes visitors and is open Mon-Fri 20.00-23.00.

Boatyards

Ⓑ **Holidays Afloat** Newcastle Road, Market Drayton TF9 1HW (01630 652641). Gas, overnight mooring, long-term mooring, winter storage, slipway, crane, boat and engine sales, chandlery, maps, gifts, solid fuel.

Ⓑ **Betton Mill Wharf** Betton Mill, Betton Road, Market Drayton TF9 1HH (01630 658282). D E Pump out, engine sales and repairs, electric boat recharging, chandlery, boat fitting out, boat painting, wet dock, DIY facilities. For Peter Roden, independent marine engineer, telephone 01270 524383.

Ⓑ **Tom's Moorings** Lord's Bridge, Market Drayton TF9 1HH (01543 414808). Pump out, overnight mooring, long-term mooring, electrical hook up.

Ⓑ **Turley Wharf** at bridge 63. Pump out, toilets and disabled toilet, picnic tables.

Tyrley Top Lock (see *page 98*)

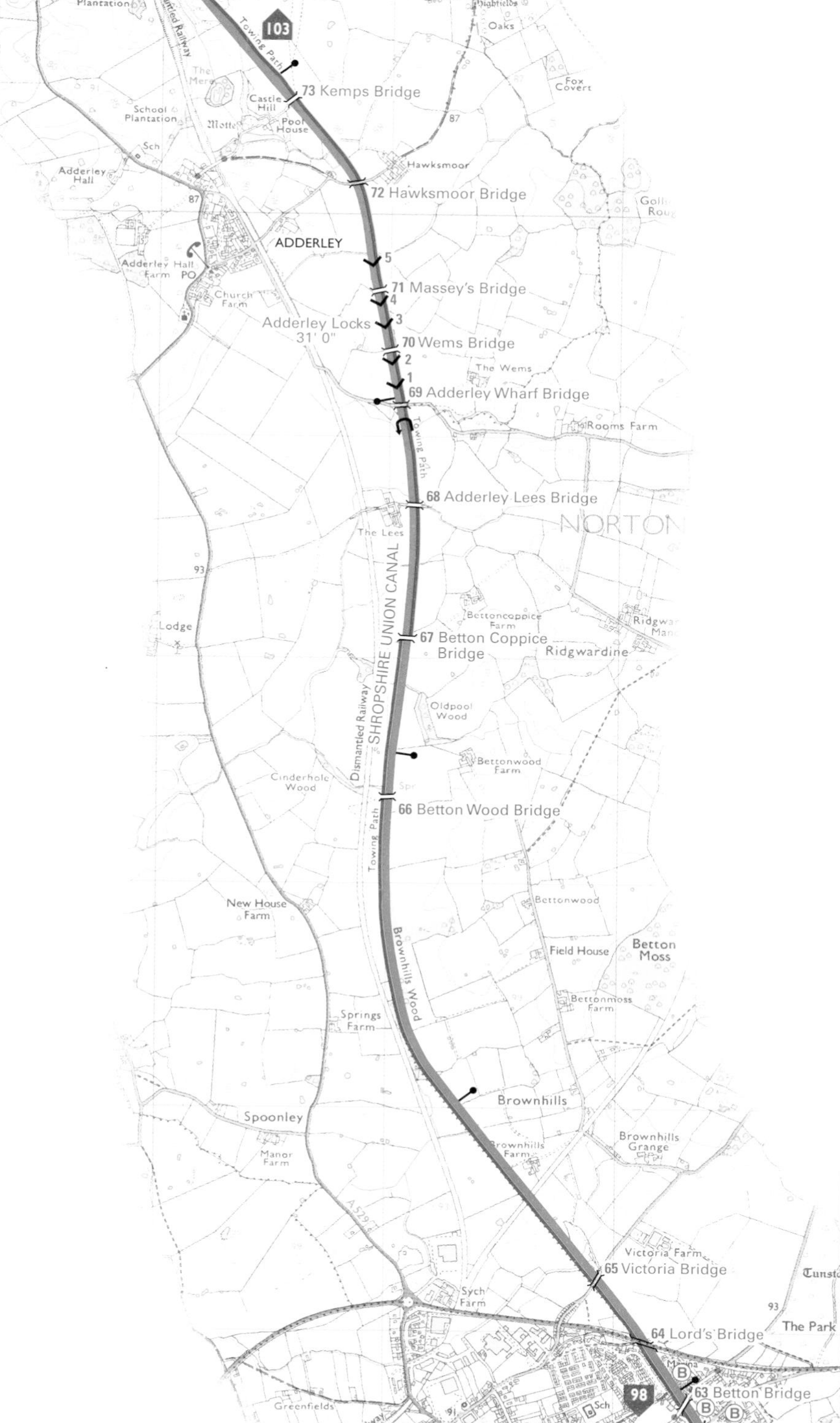
103
Towing Path
73 Kemps Bridge
72 Hawksmoor Bridge
ADDERLEY
Adderley Locks
31' 0"
71 Massey's Bridge
70 Wems Bridge
69 Adderley Wharf Bridge
68 Adderley Lees Bridge
NORTON
SHROPSHIRE UNION CANAL
67 Betton Coppice Bridge
Ridgwardine
66 Betton Wood Bridge
Brownhills Wood
Brownhills
65 Victoria Bridge
64 Lord's Bridge
63 Betton Bridge
62
98
The Mere
Castle Hill
Pool House
Hawksmoor
School Plantation
Adderley Hall
Adderley Hall Farm
Church Farm
The Wems
Rooms Farm
The Lees
Bettoncoppice Farm
Oldpool Wood
Bettonwood Farm
Cinderhole Wood
Dismantled Railway
Lodge
New House Farm
Bettonwood
Field House
Betton Moss
Bettonmoss Farm
Springs Farm
Spoonley
Manor Farm
Brownhills Farm
Brownhills Grange
Victoria Farm
Sych Farm
The Park
Greenfields
Oaks
Fox Covert

Audlem

Adderley Locks are shortly followed by the 15 locks in the Audlem flight, lowering the canal by over 90ft to the dairylands of southern Cheshire. The locks are close together, well maintained, and provide over two hours' energetic navigating. There is an attractive cottage at the top lock, the wharf has a craft shop, and there are two pubs near bridge 78, along with a *general store*. The bottom of the locks is marked by a restored canal stable (base of the Day-Star Theatre Company) and just to the north a minor aqueduct over the infant River Weaver. The canal flows northwards through an undisturbed stretch of pastoral land. Cows graze either side, clearly intent on maintaining Cheshire's reputation as a prime dairy county. It is chilling to reflect that in 1968 hardly a single beast was left alive for miles around here after the ravages of foot and mouth disease. Fortunately this area fared somewhat better in the 2001 outbreak. There is an attractive *picnic area* with *barbecue facilities* at Coole Pilate, just north of bridge 83.

Pubs and Restaurants

Bridge 12 Shropshire Street, Audlem CW3 0DX (01270 811267). Canalside at bridge 78. Friendly pub serving real ale. Food available *all day, every day* in busy restaurant with extensive menu. Conservatory and outside seating. Children welcome.

Shroppie Fly The Wharf, Audlem CW3 0DX (01270 811772). This converted warehouse serves ale from a bar built like a narrowboat, complete with cratch. Real ale and food served *all day*. Children welcome. Canalside seating. Pool and dominoes. Live music *Fri and Sat*.

Lord Combermere The Square, Audlem CW3 0AQ (01270 812277). Pub and restaurant open *L and E*. Garden. Winter fires.

Old Priest House Coffee Shop Stafford Street, Audlem CW3 0AA (01270 811749). Opposite the church. Serves breakfasts, lunches and teas, *09.00–17.00*.

Audlem

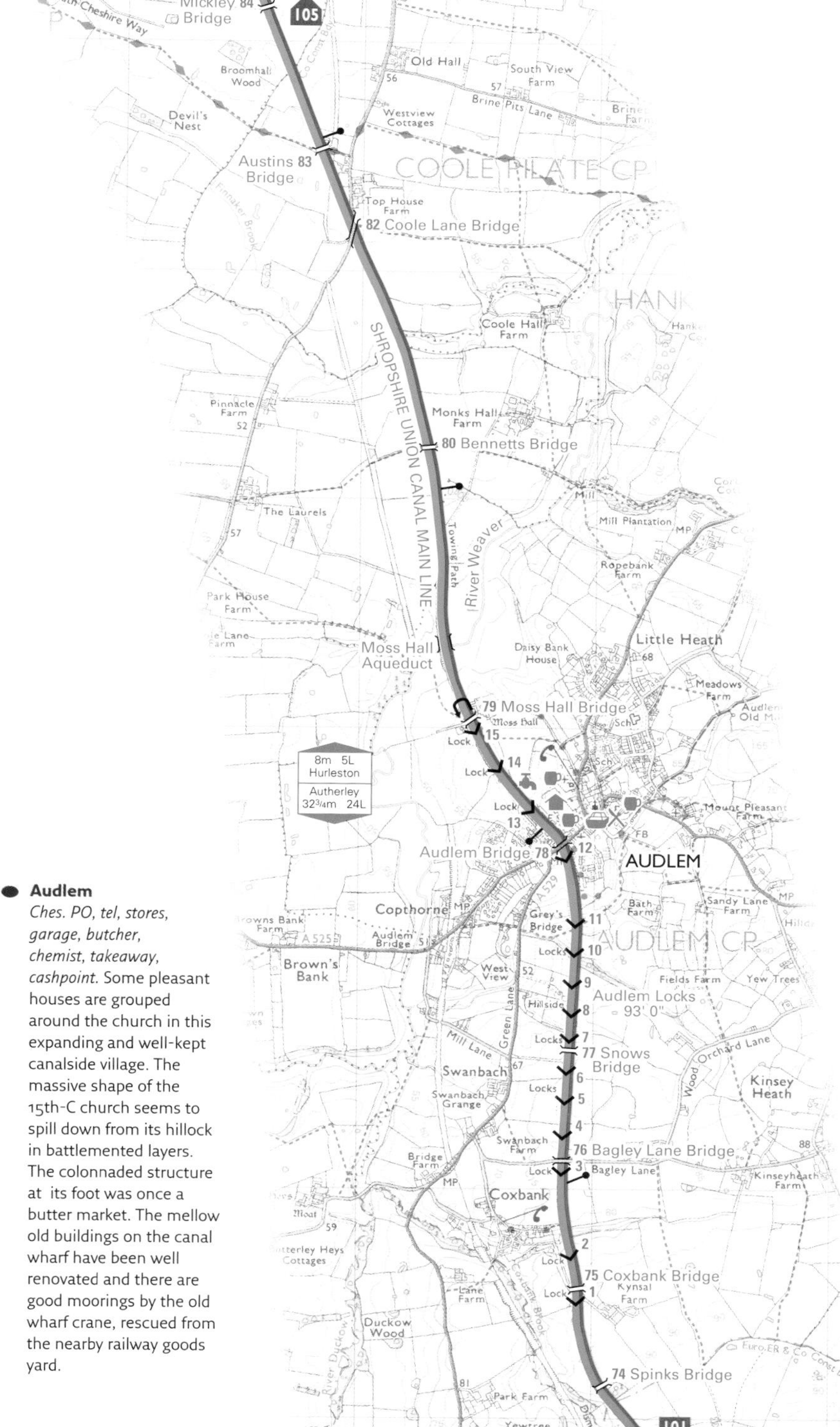

Audlem

Ches. PO, tel, stores, garage, butcher, chemist, takeaway, cashpoint. Some pleasant houses are grouped around the church in this expanding and well-kept canalside village. The massive shape of the 15th-C church seems to spill down from its hillock in battlemented layers. The colonnaded structure at its foot was once a butter market. The mellow old buildings on the canal wharf have been well renovated and there are good moorings by the old wharf crane, rescued from the nearby railway goods yard.

Nantwich

Hack Green Locks briefly interrupt the navigation. The railway which once accompanied the canal has long since closed, although the line crossing from Shrewsbury to Nantwich and Crewe is still open. Swinging round Dorfold Park on a long embankment, the canal crosses the Nantwich–Chester road on a fine cast iron aqueduct and soon reaches an oblique canal junction at Nantwich Basin: this is where Telford's narrow Birmingham & Liverpool Junction Canal joins the older Chester Canal. The wide bridgehole at the next and all subsequent bridges reveals the difference in gauge of the two canals. The Chester Canal's width is complemented by its sweeping course, as it curves gracefully round the hillside towards Hurleston Junction. There is a sculpture trail along the towpath between bridges 91 and 92 to celebrate the restoration of the Nantwich embankment. At bridge 92 a picnic site has been created beside the largest of the sculptures.

NAVIGATIONAL NOTES

If you are heading southwards and wish to take on water at bridge 92, slow down well in advance. The water point is immediately south of the bridge where there are also showers, toilets and rubbish disposal.

Dorfold Hall 1/4 mile south west of Nantwich Basin, CW5 8LD. Built by Ralph Wilbraham in 1616, this beautiful Jacobean house is approached along an avenue of trees. The panelled rooms contain fine furnishings and family portraits. *Open Apr–Oct, Tue and B Hol Mon 14.00–17.00.* Charge.

Nantwich

Ches. All services. Prosperous since Roman times because of its salt springs, Nantwich was the country's main salt-mining centre until the 19th C. The town was devastated by fire in 1583 but rebuilt in fine Tudor style. Two especially interesting buildings on the road into town from the basin are the Cheshire Cat Inn and a tiny cottage built in 1502 and restored in 1971. On Beam Street are the Tollemache Almshouses, built in 1638 by Sir Edmund Wright who became Lord Mayor of London in 1641.

Church of St Mary Church Lane, Nantwich CW5 5RQ (01270 625268; www.stmarysnantwich.org.uk). Focal point of the town centre, it is a large and magnificent red sandstone church which stands behind its former graveyard, now an open green. It dates from the 14th C, though it was greatly restored in 1885. It has an unusual octagonal tower and the vaulted chancel contains 20 ornate 14th-C choir stalls with canopies. Fine collection of kneelers. *Open all year.* Donation. **Visitor Centre** *open Mar–Dec, weekdays 10.00–16.30.* Refreshments.

Hack Green Secret Nuclear Bunker Hack Green, Nantwich CW5 8AQ (01270 629219; www.hackgreen.co.uk). Described as: 'A unique and exciting day out . . . discovering the secret world of Nuclear Government', this highly unusual attraction, beside bridge 85, would have become home to the select few in the event of a nuclear strike. Too sinister for some; for others the chance to see the underground paraphernalia required to support existence in the face of nuclear holocaust. *Open mid March–Oct, daily 10.30–17.30, and Nov–Mar 11.00–16.30, Sat and Sun (closed Dec).* Charge.

Nantwich Museum Pillory Street, Nantwich CW5 5BQ (01270 627104; www.nantwichmuseum.org.uk). An insight into the life and times of an historic market town. Roman and medieval treasures and a cheese-making display. Details on the Civil War Battle of Nantwich. *Open Apr–Sep, Mon–Sat 10.30–16.30 and Oct–Mar as per summer but closed Mon.* Free.

Players Theatre Love Lane, Nantwich CW5 5BG (01270 624556; www.nantwichplayers.com). Regular productions *throughout the year.*

Tourist Information Centre Market Street, Nantwich CW5 5DG (01270 610983; www.crewe-nantwich.gov.uk). *Open weekdays 09.30–17.00; Sat 10.00–16.00 and B Hol Mon 11.00–15.00.*

Acton

Ches. Tel. A small village with a large church of red stone and an old pub with a mounting block outside.

Nantwich Basin

CW5 8LB. A busy canal basin, once the terminus of the isolated Chester Canal from Nantwich to Ellesmere Port. When the B & LJ Canal was first authorised in 1826, Telford intended to bring it from Hack Green across Dorfold Park and straight into Nantwich Basin; but the owner of the park refused to allow it and forced the company to build the long embankment right round the park and the iron aqueduct over the main road. This proved a difficult and costly diversion since, as at Shelmore, the embankment repeatedly collapsed. Today the old canalside cheese warehouses are still in existence and there is a boatyard and a hire base here.

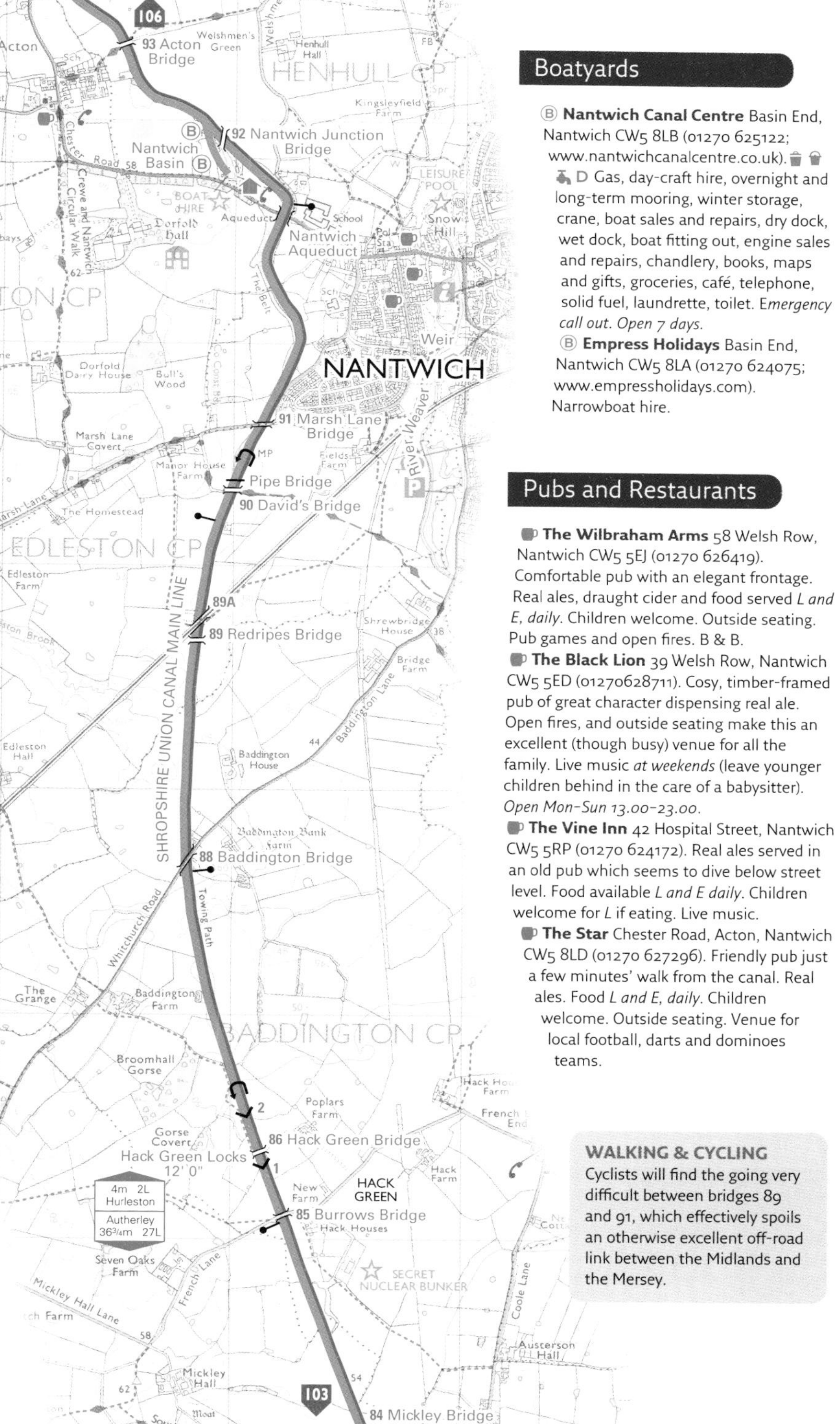

Boatyards

Ⓑ **Nantwich Canal Centre** Basin End, Nantwich CW5 8LB (01270 625122; www.nantwichcanalcentre.co.uk). D Gas, day-craft hire, overnight and long-term mooring, winter storage, crane, boat sales and repairs, dry dock, wet dock, boat fitting out, engine sales and repairs, chandlery, books, maps and gifts, groceries, café, telephone, solid fuel, laundrette, toilet. *Emergency call out. Open 7 days.*

Ⓑ **Empress Holidays** Basin End, Nantwich CW5 8LA (01270 624075; www.empressholidays.com). Narrowboat hire.

Pubs and Restaurants

The Wilbraham Arms 58 Welsh Row, Nantwich CW5 5EJ (01270 626419). Comfortable pub with an elegant frontage. Real ales, draught cider and food served *L and E, daily*. Children welcome. Outside seating. Pub games and open fires. B & B.

The Black Lion 39 Welsh Row, Nantwich CW5 5ED (01270628711). Cosy, timber-framed pub of great character dispensing real ale. Open fires, and outside seating make this an excellent (though busy) venue for all the family. Live music *at weekends* (leave younger children behind in the care of a babysitter). *Open Mon-Sun 13.00-23.00.*

The Vine Inn 42 Hospital Street, Nantwich CW5 5RP (01270 624172). Real ales served in an old pub which seems to dive below street level. Food available *L and E daily*. Children welcome for *L* if eating. Live music.

The Star Chester Road, Acton, Nantwich CW5 8LD (01270 627296). Friendly pub just a few minutes' walk from the canal. Real ales. Food *L and E, daily*. Children welcome. Outside seating. Venue for local football, darts and dominoes teams.

WALKING & CYCLING

Cyclists will find the going very difficult between bridges 89 and 91, which effectively spoils an otherwise excellent off-road link between the Midlands and the Mersey.

Barbridge Junction

At Hurleston Junction the Llangollen Canal branches off up four narrow locks on its way to North Wales (*see* page 24). Meanwhile the main line of the Shropshire Union soon reaches Barbridge where there is a junction with the Middlewich Branch. This branch connects the Shropshire Union system to the Trent & Mersey Canal. The canal moves almost westwards now alongside a busy main road at a level slightly below the wheels of the passing juggernauts. The Middlewich Branch is an attractive and under-rated link canal – with some wonderfully

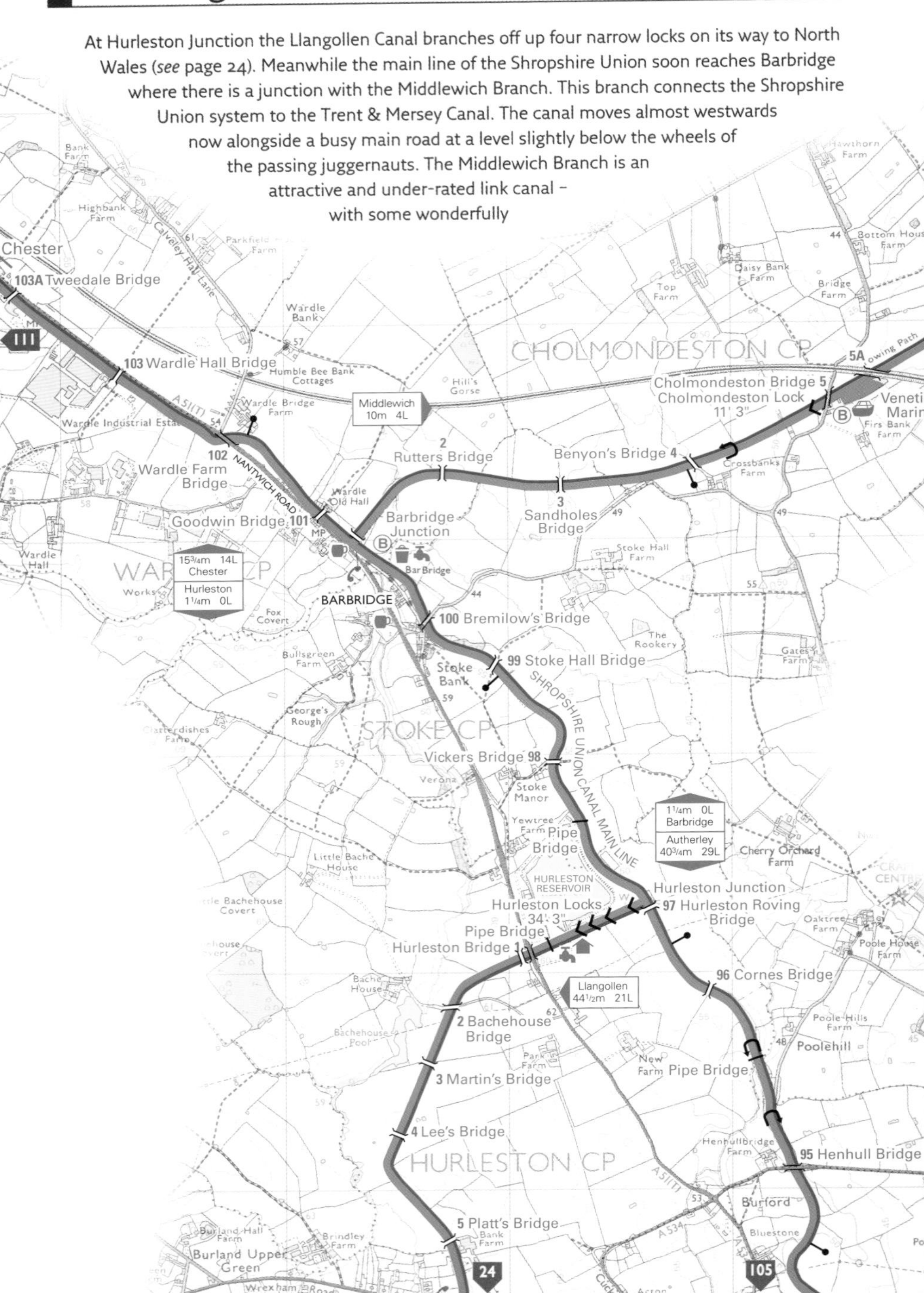

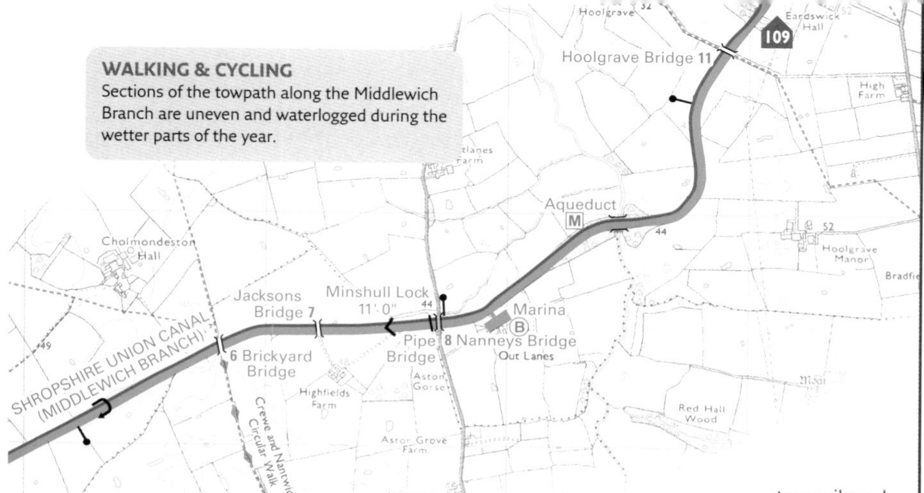

WALKING & CYCLING
Sections of the towpath along the Middlewich Branch are uneven and waterlogged during the wetter parts of the year.

tranquil rural moorings - which leaves the main line at Barbridge Junction, passing a boatyard and heading east through quiet and remote countryside. By Cholmondeston Lock there is a huge marina. After passing another lock, the canal crosses the River Weaver on an aqueduct as it approaches the village of Church Minshull, where L.T.C Rolt and *Cressy* spent an enjoyable sojourn. For those not wishing to navigate as far as Chester there are frequent buses from Barbridge to the centre of the city.

Boatyards

Ⓑ **Midway Boats, Barbridge Marina** Wardle, Nantwich CW5 6BE (01270 528682; www.midwayboats.co.uk). Gas, long-term mooring, slipway, boat sales and repairs, day boat hire, engine sales and repairs, outboard specialist, chandlery, books and maps, boat building, upholstery, toilet.

Ⓑ **Venetian Marina** Cholmondeston Lock, Nantwich CW5 6DA (01270 528251; www.surftech.co.uk/canal/venetian/). D Pump out, gas, long-term mooring, slipway, winter storage, dry dock, wet dock, boat building, boat sales and repairs, engine sales and repairs, groceries, large chandlery, books and maps, gifts, café, telephone, toilets, showers.

Ⓑ **Aqueduct Marina** The Outlanes, Church Minshull, Nantwich CW5 6DX (01270 522284; www.aqueductmarina.co.uk). Large marina due to open 2009. **D** Pump out, long- and short-term moorings, gas, slipway, repairs, brokerage, laundrette, café, shop and chandlery.

Pubs and Restaurants

The Olde Barbridge Inn Old Chester Road, Barbridge CW5 6AY (01270 528443; www.the-olde-barbridge-inn.co.uk). Busy, brewery chain pub. Real ale. Food available *all day, every day*. Children welcome and enclosed play area. Canalside garden. Jazz band *Thu*. Also quiz nights and music at weekends. Moorings.

The Jolly Tar Nantwich Road, Wardle CW5 6BE (01270 528283; www.jollytarpub.co.uk). Real ale together with grills and a range of home-made pub food served *served L and E, daily, all day Sat and Sun*. Children's menu and outside play area including bouncy castle. Regular live music (check website). Pool, darts and dominoes. Dogs welcome.

Middlewich

This is a quiet stretch of canal passing through rich farmland interspersed with woods. There are superb views to the west over the River Weaver and Winsford Top Flash. At bridge 22A the West Coast Main Line makes a noisy crossing. The canal then descends through two locks to Middlewich, where it joins the Trent & Mersey. This last few yards of the Middlewich Branch used to belong to the Trent & Mersey, and the bridge over the entrance to the branch is grandiosely inscribed 'Wardle Canal 1829'. There are good moorings at the boatyard to the left of the junction.

Boatyards

Ⓑ **Kings Lock Boatyard** Booth Lane, Middlewich CW10 OJJ (01606 737564). D Gas, overnight mooring, long-term mooring, winter storage, slipway, engine sales and repairs, boat repairs, chandlery (including mail order), books, maps, gifts, solid fuel. *Emergency call out.*
Ⓑ **Andersen Boats** Wych House, St Anne's Road, Middlewich CW10 9BQ (01606 833668; www.andersenboats.com). Pump out, gas, narrowboat hire, books and maps. Useful DIY shop nearby.
Ⓑ **Middlewich Narrowboats** Canal Terrace, Middlewich CW10 9BD (01606 832460; www.middlewichboats.co.uk). D Pump out, gas, narrowboat hire, overnight mooring (*not Fri*), long-term mooring, dry dock,boat building, groceries, chandlery, books and maps, engine repairs, toilets, laundry service, breakdown service, grit blasting, hull and cabinside painting. *Closed Sun.* Useful tool hire shop next door.

Church Minshull
Ches. Tel. An old and mellow village beside the River Weaver. The notable 18th-C church in the centre of the village is the subject of a preservation order - it is certainly the core of this most attractive place. Midway between bridges 14 and 15 there is a gateway in the hedge providing good access to the village and an opportunity to visit Yankee Candles, Cross Lane CW1 4RG (01270 522252; www.distinctivedesigns-florist.co.uk) who are *open daily* selling gifts, candles, glass and fresh flowers.

Middlewich
Ches. PO, tel, stores, bank, chemist, off-licence, garage. A town that since Roman times has been dedicated to salt extraction. Most of the salt produced here goes to various chemical industries. Subsidence from salt extraction has prevented redevelopment for many years, but a big renewal scheme is now in progress. The canalside area is a haven of peace below the busy streets.
St Michael's Church Queen Street, Middlewich CW10 9AR (01606 833663; www.middlewichparishchurch.org.uk). A handsome medieval church which was a place of refuge for the Royalists during the Civil War. It has a fine interior with richly carved woodwork.

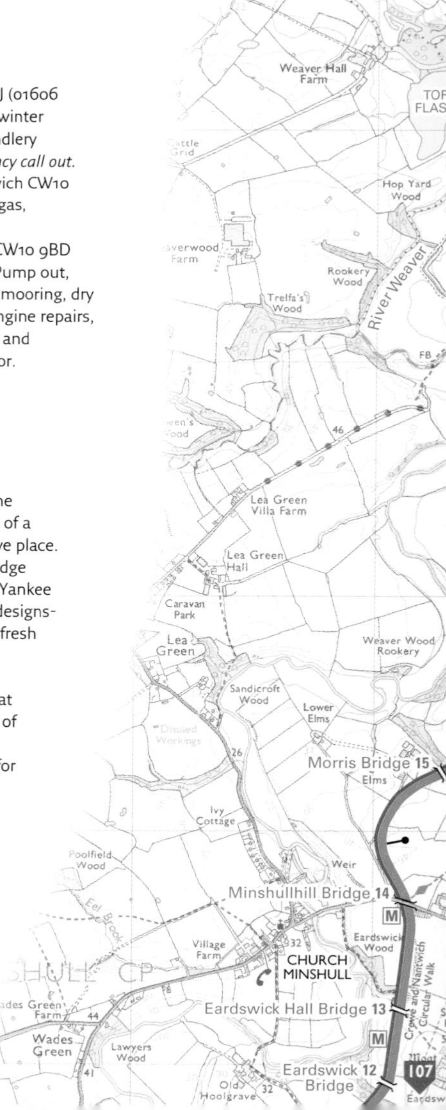

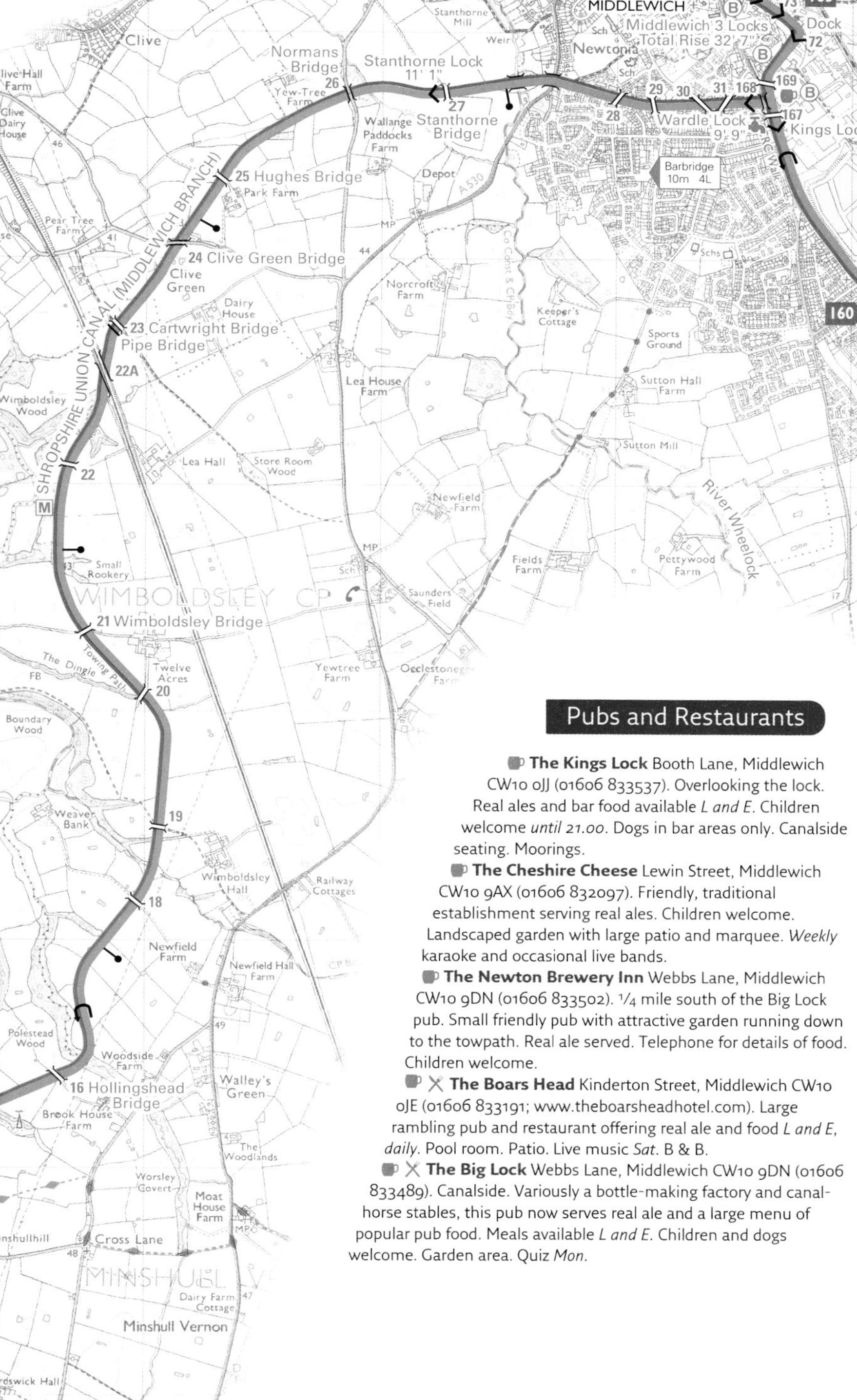

Pubs and Restaurants

The Kings Lock Booth Lane, Middlewich CW10 0JJ (01606 833537). Overlooking the lock. Real ales and bar food available *L and E*. Children welcome *until 21.00*. Dogs in bar areas only. Canalside seating. Moorings.

The Cheshire Cheese Lewin Street, Middlewich CW10 9AX (01606 832097). Friendly, traditional establishment serving real ales. Children welcome. Landscaped garden with large patio and marquee. *Weekly* karaoke and occasional live bands.

The Newton Brewery Inn Webbs Lane, Middlewich CW10 9DN (01606 833502). 1/4 mile south of the Big Lock pub. Small friendly pub with attractive garden running down to the towpath. Real ale served. Telephone for details of food. Children welcome.

The Boars Head Kinderton Street, Middlewich CW10 0JE (01606 833191; www.theboarsheadhotel.com). Large rambling pub and restaurant offering real ale and food *L and E, daily*. Pool room. Patio. Live music *Sat*. B & B.

The Big Lock Webbs Lane, Middlewich CW10 9DN (01606 833489). Canalside. Variously a bottle-making factory and canal-horse stables, this pub now serves real ale and a large menu of popular pub food. Meals available *L and E*. Children and dogs welcome. Garden area. Quiz *Mon*.

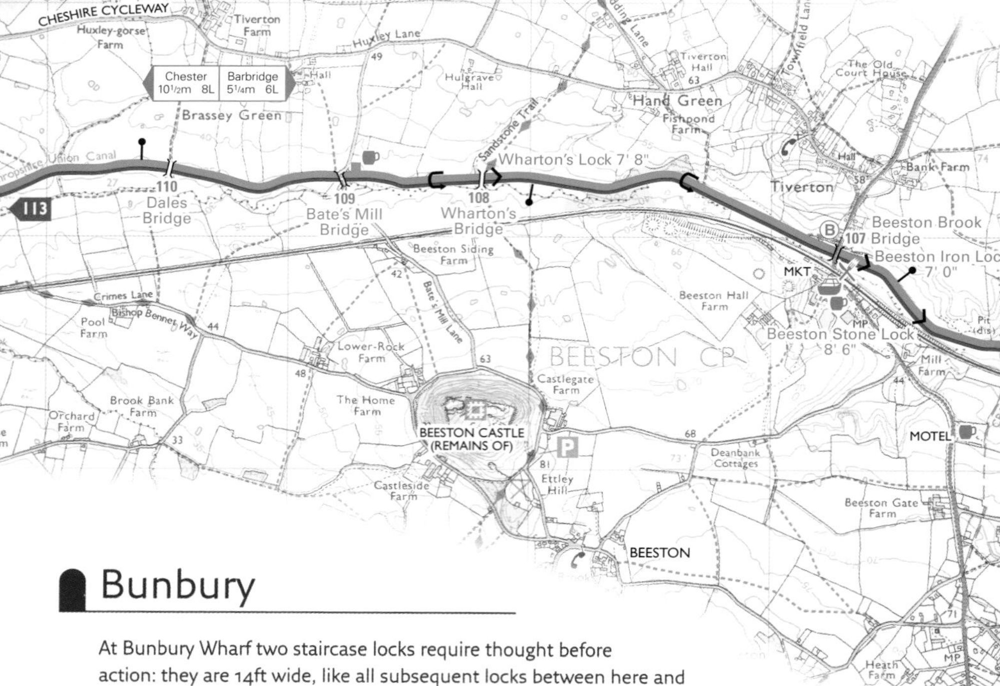

Bunbury

At Bunbury Wharf two staircase locks require thought before action: they are 14ft wide, like all subsequent locks between here and Chester. To the south east of Calveley Bridge 104 there is a full range of facilities including showers and toilets, while close by there is the Calveley Coal Company (01829 261199/260009) selling a range of coal and gas. At Beeston two contrasting lock-chambers are encountered: one is made of stone, the other of cast iron flanged plates to overcome running sand below it. Up the hill to the north of the two locks is Tiverton, now totally devoid of all services. There is a convenient café to the south of bridge 107, *open seven days a week until late* (also groceries available beyond the railway bridge). From Wharton Lock an excellent view is obtained of the massive bulk of Beeston Castle, a landmark which can be seen from places up to 30 miles away. As one moves westward, the romantic-looking turrets of neighbouring Peckforton Castle (of somewhat younger origins) come into view.

Boatyards

Ⓑ **Chas Hardern Beeston** Castle Wharf, Beeston, nr Tarporley CW6 9NH (01829 732595; www.chashardern.co.uk). D Pump out, gas, coal, narrowboat hire, chandlery, books and maps, gifts, boat and engine repairs. *24hr emergency call out.*

Ⓑ **Anglo Welsh** The Canal Wharf, Bunbury, Tarporley CW6 9QB (01829 260957; www.anglowelsh.co.uk). D E Pump out, gas, narrowboat hire, day-hire craft, overnight mooring, long-term mooring, winter storage, slipway, books and maps, DIY facilities, groceries, café, gifts, solid fuel, telephone, toilet. *24hr emergency call out.*

- **Calveley**
  Ches. Tel.
- **Bunbury**
  Ches. PO, tel, stores, garage, butcher, fish & Chips (closed Sun & Mon). 1 mile south west of Bunbury Locks. The church is an outstanding building: supremely light, airy and spacious, it stands as a fine monument to workmanship of the 14th and 15th C.

Bunbury Mill Mill Lane, Bowesgate Road, Bunbury, Tarporely CW6 9PP (01829 261422; www.bunbury-mill.org). Up the hill from Bunbury Wharf, towards the village. Guided tours around a fully restored watermill, working until 1960 when it was destroyed by a massive flood. *Open Easter–Sep, Sun and B Hol Mon's, 13.30–16.30.* Nominal charge. Informal groups and parties catered for. Details may change, so telephone if possible.

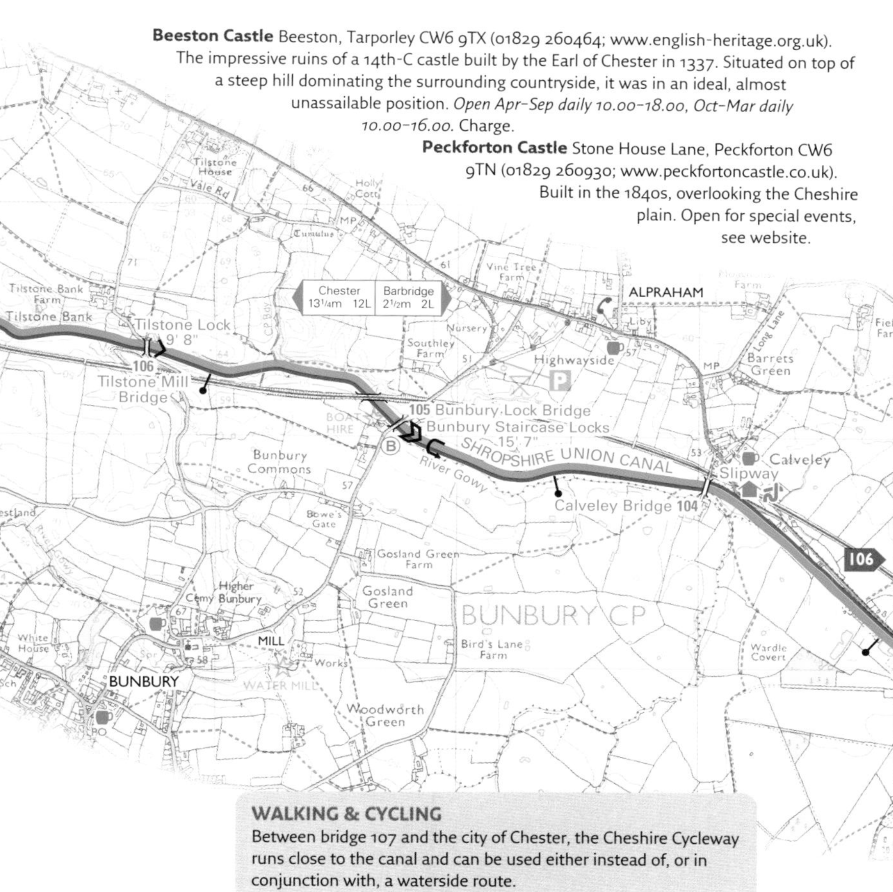

Beeston Castle Beeston, Tarporley CW6 9TX (01829 260464; www.english-heritage.org.uk). The impressive ruins of a 14th-C castle built by the Earl of Chester in 1337. Situated on top of a steep hill dominating the surrounding countryside, it was in an ideal, almost unassailable position. *Open Apr–Sep daily 10.00–18.00, Oct–Mar daily 10.00–16.00.* Charge.

Peckforton Castle Stone House Lane, Peckforton CW6 9TN (01829 260930; www.peckfortoncastle.co.uk). Built in the 1840s, overlooking the Cheshire plain. Open for special events, see website.

WALKING & CYCLING

Between bridge 107 and the city of Chester, the Cheshire Cycleway runs close to the canal and can be used either instead of, or in conjunction with, a waterside route.

Pubs and Restaurants

The Goldmine Bar and Grill Calveley, Tarporley CW6 9JN (01829 262550). Modern pub serving food *all day every day.* Outside seating and childrens play area.

The Dysart Arms Bowes Gate Road, Bunbury CW6 9PH (01829 260183; www.dysartarms-bunbury.co.uk). By the church. Once a farmhouse with stone-flagged floors, it now serves real ale. Large range of food available *L and E, daily.* Children welcome when eating or in the attractive gardens. Pub games. Dogs welcome away from dining areas.

The Nags Head Long Lane, Bunbury CW6 9RN (01829 260027). In centre of the village, a 300-year-old building featuring attractively decorated façade with a horse's head picked out in a central plaster frieze, and an inglenook fireplace. Real ale and food available *L and E (not L midweek).* Children welcome *until 21.00 (22.00 in summer),* dogs at all times. Relaxing garden with children's play area.

The Wild Boar Hotel Whitchurch Road, Beeston CW6 9NW (01829 260309; www.wildboarhotel.co.uk). ½ mile past Beeston Castle Hotel, on A49. Restaurant in a large Tudor building serving food *L and E, daily.* Garden. Children welcome. B & B.

Beeston Castle Hotel Whitchurch Road, Beeston CW6 9NJ (01829 260234). Below bridge 107. Real ale and an attractive restaurant serving meals *L and E, daily,* in this market-side hotel. À la carte menu (booking *at weekends*) and snacks in the bar. Children welcome. Garden. B & B.

The Shady Oak Bates Mill Lane, nr Beeston CW6 9UE (01829 730717). Canalside, at Bate's Mill Bridge. Friendly, canalside pub serving real ale and home-cooked food *L and E, daily.* Children's menu. Groups and parties catered for.

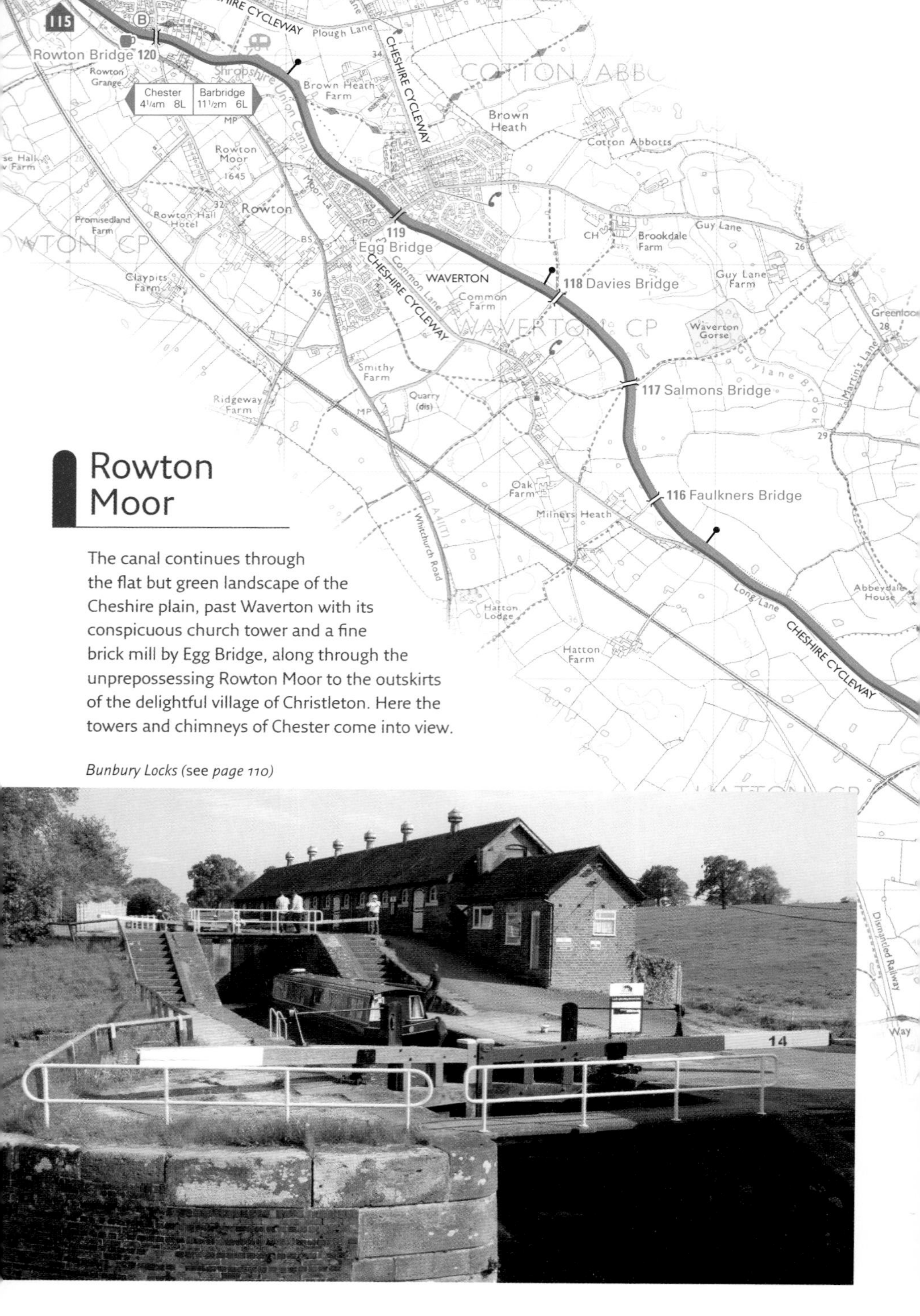

Rowton Moor

The canal continues through the flat but green landscape of the Cheshire plain, past Waverton with its conspicuous church tower and a fine brick mill by Egg Bridge, along through the unprepossessing Rowton Moor to the outskirts of the delightful village of Christleton. Here the towers and chimneys of Chester come into view.

Bunbury Locks (see *page 110*)

Pubs and Restaurants

The Poacher's Pocket Tattenhall Road, Tattenhall CH3 9BD (01829 771010). South of Crow's Nest Bridge 113. Inexpensive home-cooked food available *all day, every day*, together with takeaways and real ales. Children's outdoor play area. Garden.

The Cheshire Cat Whitchurch Road, Christleton, Chester CH3 6AE (01244 332200). Large and imposing canalside hostelry, *open all day*, serving real ales and food *all day, every day*. Children welcome. Moorings. B & B.

Battle of Rowton Moor It was here, 3 miles from Chester, that one of the last major battles of the Civil War took place in 1645. The Parliamentarians completely routed the Royalists who, still under fierce attack, retreated to Chester. It is said that King Charles I watched the defeat from the walls of Chester, but it is more probable that he saw only the final stages under the walls of the city. Charles fled, leaving 800 prisoners and 600 dead and wounded.

Waverton
Ches. PO, tel, stores, takeaway (east of bridge 119). *Store open 6.00–22.00 daily*. The church is pleasing and well worth visiting.

Boatyards

Ⓑ **The Workshop** The Moorings, Rowton Bridge, Christleton, Chester CH3 7BD (01244 332633). Overnight mooring, long-term mooring, winter storage, slipway, engine sales and repairs (including outboards). *Emergency call out*.

Ⓑ **Crow's Nest Boat Services** CW11 3PT Beside Crow's Nest bridge 113. (01829 772592). D Pump out, gas, mooring, winter storage, alterations, engine repairs. Emergency call-out.

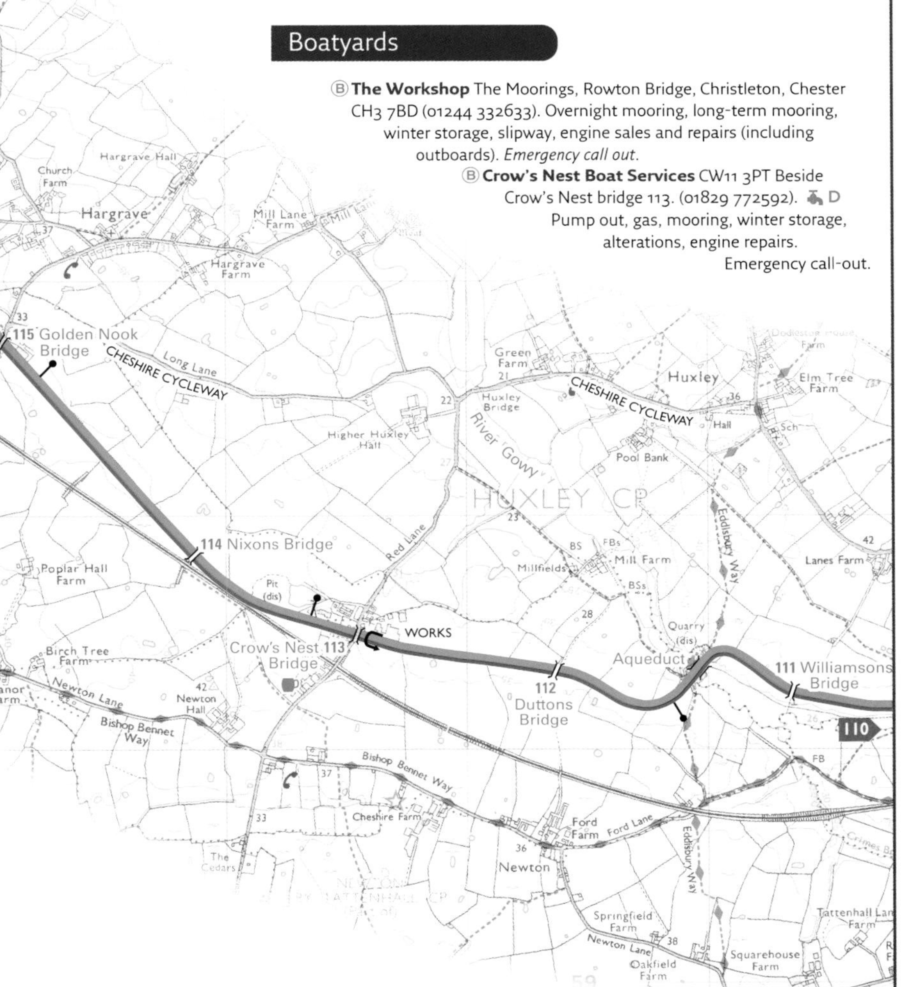

Chester

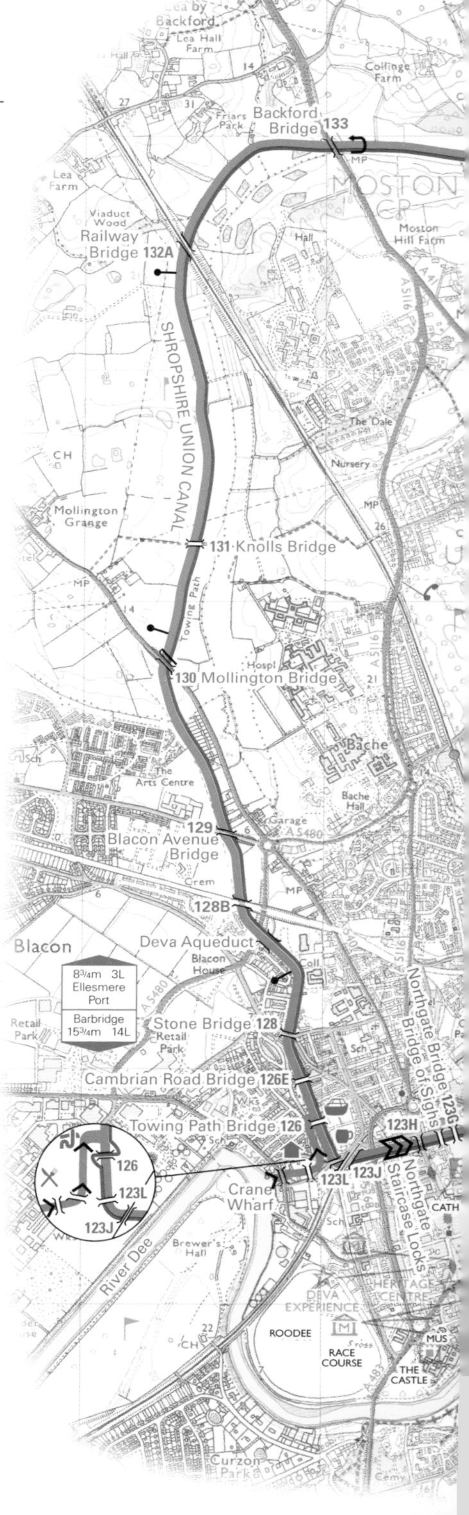

Leaving Christleton, the waterway soon begins the descent into the ancient city of Chester through five locks; none of these have top gate paddles, and they all take rather long to fill. The canal goes straight through the middle of the town. Passing the site of an old lead works, and a great variety of bridges, the navigation approaches the old city and suddenly curves round into a very steep rock cutting. Soon the Northgate Locks (a staircase) are reached: at the bottom is a sharp right turn to Tower Wharf. The area is a little run down but some parts are being re-developed. Here the line of the original Chester Canal once led straight down, via a further two locks (long since abandoned), into the River Dee. At the head of the arm leading down into the Dee there is the site of an historic boatyard and a handy store on the off-side next to bridge 128. Chester city centre is easily accessed from the canal at bridge 123E and there is a useful selection of shops, including a laundrette, to the north east of bridge 126.

Boatyards

Ⓑ **David Jones Boatbuilders** Taylor's Boatyard, Upper Cambrian View, Chester CH1 4DE (01244 390363). At junction with Dee Branch. Winter storage, slipway. Shipwrights, wood and steel boats built, all repairs and specialize in classic craft. *Emergency call out. Open Mon–Fri, weekends by appointment.*

Ⓑ **BW Chester Yard** Tower Wharf, Chester (01244 390372). (charge) Pump out, slipway, dry dock (bookings and charge).

- **Christleton**
  Ches. PO, tel, stores. A very pleasant village near the canal, well worth visiting.
- **Chester**
  Ches. All services. There is a wealth of things to see in this Roman city. It is in fact an excellent town to see on foot, because of the amazing survival of almost all the old city wall. This provides Chester with its best and rarest feature – one can walk right round the city on this superb footpath, over the old city gates and past the defensive turrets, including King Charles' Tower above the canal. Other splendid features are the race course – the Roodee – (just outside the city wall and therefore well inside the modern town) where Chester Races are held each year in *May and Jul–Sep* (it can easily be overlooked for free from the road that runs above and beside it), the superb old

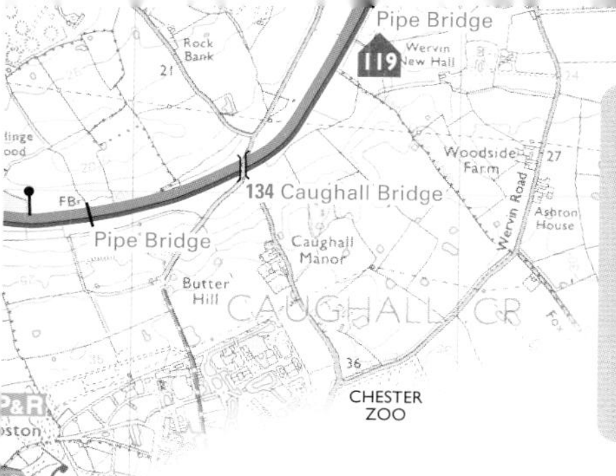

BOAT TRIPS

A range of luncheon and dinner cruises from the **Mill Hotel** Milton Street, Chester CH1 3NF (01244 350035; www.millhotel.com). *Two-hour cruises for up to 45 people, most days,* in both directions along the canal. Also bicycle hire.

Chester Boat Souters Lane, Chester CH1 1SD (01244 325394; www.chesterboat.co.uk). On the River Dee, just off City Walls. A range of river trips introducing the canal boater to Chester's historic river. *Open throughout the year.* Telephone or visit website for further details.

cathedral, the bold new theatre, the Rows (unique double-tier medieval shopping streets), and the immense number of old and fascinating buildings throughout the town.

Abbey Square Outside the cathedral, opposite the Victorian town hall, the square is entered through a massive gateway built in 1377.

Chester Cathedral Northgate Street, Chester CH1 2HU (01244 324756; www.chestercathedral.com). A magnificent building of dark-red stone on the site of a 10th-C minster. In 1092 the Earl of Chester and St Anselm founded a Benedictine abbey which was dissolved in 1540, but in the following year it was made a cathedral and the seat of a bishop. In 1742 Handel gave his first public performance of the *Messiah* in the cathedral and a copy of his marked score is on display. *Open daily 09.00–17.00.*

Church of St John the Baptist St John's Street, Chester. Impressive 12th-C church that was built on the site of an earlier Saxon church. Licensed restaurant and shop. Charge.

Chester Castle Grosvenor Road, Chester (01244 327617). The original timber structure, c.1069, was replaced by stone walls and towers by Henry III. Unfortunately, in 1789 the defensive walls were removed to make way for the incongruous Thomas Harrison group of buildings, which include the Grand Entrance and Assize Courts. The main part of the castle is occupied by troops of the Cheshire Regiment, but the 13th-C Agricola Tower is open to the public.

Chester Heritage Tours Chester Visitor Centre, Chester CH1 1QX (0870 7656850; www.chesterheritagetours.co.uk). See highlights of Historic Chester from an open-top 1930s-vintage omnibus. More details from the Visitor Centre or TIC. Charge.

Chester Market Princess Street, Chester (01244 402340). There has been a traditional market in the city since the 14thC and today's undercover shopping experience features up to 100 stalls selling fresh produce. *Open Mon-Sat 08.00-17.30.*

Cheshire Military Museum The Castle, Chester CH1 2DN (01244 327617; www.chester.ac.uk/militarymuseum). Situated inside the tower of the castle. Experience 300 years of history amidst this inter-active display. *Open daily 09.00–17.00. Closed Xmas to New Year. Last entry 16.30.* Charge.

Chester Visitor & Craft Centre Vicar's Lane, Chester CH1 1QX (01244 351609; www.chestertourism.com). Working craft shops and café. Brass rubbing, video theatre, Hall of Names and much more. *Open Apr-Sep Mon-Sat 09.00–17.30 & Oct-Mar 09.30–17.00; Sun 10.00–16.00 all year.* Free.

City Sightseeing Chester Visitor Centre, Chester CH1 1QX (01244 347352; www.city-sightseeing.com). *55-minute* tours in an open-top bus. Your ticket lasts all day so get on and off as you please.

Dewa Roman Experience Pierpoint Lane, off Bridge Street, Chester CH1 1NL (01244 343407; www.dewaromanexperience.co.uk). Reconstruction of Roman Chester together with its sights, sounds and smells. Shop. *Open daily 09.00-17.00 (Dec & Jan 10.00-16.00).* Charge.

Grosvenor Museum 27 Grosvenor Street, Chester CH1 2DD (01244 402008; www.chester.gov.uk). Award-winning museum that introduces Chester's past, in particular the Roman fortress of Deva and its inhabitants. *Open Mon-Sat 10.30-17.00 and Sun 13.00-16.00.* Free.

Grosvenor Park Miniature Railway Grosvenor Park, Chester CH1 1QQ (07967 533324; www.gpmr.co.uk). One of Chester's premier children's (9-90 years old) attractions laid out in Grosvenor Park amidst ducks, moorhens and geese. Steam *most summer Sun. Open Apr-Oct Sat, Sun & school hols 10.30-17.00 & Nov-Mar Sun 11.00-16.00 (winter weather permitting).* Charge.

Guided Walks (01244 405626; www.chester.gov.uk). Several themed walks examining Chester's past. Telephone or visit website for further details. Charge.

Tourist Information Centre Town Hall, Northgate Street, Chester CH1 2HJ (01244 402111; www.chestertourism.com). *Open Mon-Fri 09.00-17.00, Sat & Sun 10.00-16.00.*

Travel Contact Traveline on 0870 608 2 608 or visit

NAVIGATIONAL NOTES

Ellesmere Port Bottom Lock Entry into the Manchester Ship Canal from the Shropshire Union is restricted by a swing bridge over the first lock (adjacent to the Holiday Inn) which is not under the control of BW. Boaters wishing to enter the canal must first contact Ellesmere Port & Neston Borough Council (0151 356 6543) to make arrangements for the bridge to be swung. Any difficulties in obtaining assistance should be referred to BW (01606 723800).

Manchester Ship Canal Harbour Master, Queen Elizabeth II Dock, Eastham, Wirral (0151 327 1461; www.shipcanal.co.uk). The ship canal currently carries 2,500 vessel movements each year, and this number is increasing. A great deal of it is hazardous, petro-chemical traffic and therefore a no smoking regime is enforced. The canal company is happy to allow pleasure boat use on the understanding that certain conditions are adhered to. It is not a navigation for the novice boater and should be viewed as a transit corridor for the experienced boat owner (not hire boater) to access the River Weaver, the River Mersey, the Shropshire Union Canal or the cruising waterways above Pomona Lock.

1 The boat must carry £1 million third party insurance cover.
2 The boat is subject to an annual Certificate of Seaworthiness.
3 The appropriate fee is paid, currently set at £18.00 plus £18.00 for each lock used.
4 The boater must contact the harbourmaster at least 48 hours in advance of passage to obtain copies of:
   a) Pleasure Craft Transit Notes
   b) Port of Manchester Navigation Bylaws
   At this juncture one can discuss appropriate times of arrival and departure to coincide with scheduled shipping movements.
5 At all times the boater is required to act in a responsible manner and be aware that this is a daytime transit route only, with no lay-by facilities. One should familiarise oneself with the geography of the canal before setting out.
6 VHF radio equipment is desirable (the Manchester Ship Canal Company call and operate on channel 14 in the canal and channel 7 on the River Mersey) and if not available a mobile phone should be considered essential.

Weston Marsh Lock Access to the River Weaver via Weston Marsh Lock is available by giving prior notice to BW at Northwich (01606 723800; enquiries.walesandbordercounties@britishwaterways.co.uk).

www.merseytravel.gov.uk. for regular departures to Liverpool and The Wirral.

- **Northgate Locks**
Hewn out of solid rock, these three staircase locks lower the canal by 33ft, an impressive feat of engineering and a suitable complement to the deep rock cutting nearby.
- **The Dee Branch**
This branch into the tidal River Dee runs through three wide locks from the boatyard near Tower Wharf. There used to be a large basin below the second lock, but this has now been filled in. The bottom lock and bridge are new, having been built to replace an old single-tracked swing bridge on a main road. There is a very sharp bend into the branch from Tower Wharf. Anyone wishing to take a boat into the River Dee *must* give *7 days* notice to BW on 01244 390372 during office hours. Charge. (The bottom lock has to be kept padlocked to prevent silting up at high water.) It is practicable to enter or leave the River Dee at this point for *only four hours either side of high water*, since there is insufficient water at the entrance for the rest of the time. *Boaters should check with their insurance company that their cover extends to navigation of the River Dee.*

WALKING & CYCLING
Between Chester and Ellesmere Port the towpath is in excellent condition with a hard surface throughout and for the most part is used by National Cycle Route 56.

Pubs and Restaurants

The Old Trooper Whitchurch Road, Christleton, near Chester CH3 6AE (01244 335784). By Christleton Bridge. Harvester pub/restaurant serving real ale and food *L and E all day, every day*. Children welcome. Outside seating.

There are many pubs in Chester including:

The Frog and Nightingale Cow Lane, Chester CH1 3LH (01244 347278). Canalside next to bridge 123E. Real ales and bar meals and snacks *all day Mon-Sun*. Regular live music during *week*. Outside seating.

The Albion Park Street, Chester CH1 1RN (01244 340345; www.albioninnchester.co.uk). City centre pub of great character – a genuine living memorial to the memory of World War I and the last Victorian corner pub in Chester. Real ales. Food *L and E, daily*. No children. Dogs welcome.

The Olde Custom House Watergate Street, Chester CH1 2LB (01244 324435). Comfortable city pub, not far from the racecourse, serving real ale along with food. Outside seating. *Open all day*.

Alexander's Rufus Court, Chester CH1 2JW (01244340005; www.alexandersjazz.com). Situated in a picturesque courtyard, this establishment is a continental-style café by day and a jazz, blues and comedy venue by night. Real ales, fine wines, snacks and meals are available and children are welcome *during the day. In the evening* you can reserve a table with a meal or just turn up at the door. Outside seating. *Open Mon-Sat 11.00-02.00 & Sun 12.00-00.30*.

The Old Harkers Arms 1 Russell Street, Chester CH3 5AL (01244 344525; www.harkersarms-chester.co.uk). Atmospheric converted canalside warehouse serving real ales and food *L and E Mon-Fri & all day Sat & Sun*. Children welcome *until 19.00. Open all day.*

The Mill Hotel Milton Street, Chester CH1 3NF (01244 350035; www.millhotel.com). Interesting and ever-changing range of guest real ales. Bar and restaurant food *L and E, daily*. Children welcome. B & B. *L and E* canal cruises. Moorings.

Telford's Warehouse Canal Basin, Tower Wharf, Chester CH1 4EZ (01244 390090; www.telfordswarehouse.com). Canalside on the wharf beside the BW office. Regular music venue, host to a varied range of bands, catering for most tastes and serving a selection of home-made bar meals and snacks, together with real ale. The Gallery Restaurant – home to regular art exhibitions – offers a similar well-priced and interesting menu as the pub downstairs.

The Galley 1/2 Old Port Street, Earls Port, Chester CH1 4JP (01244 378614). On the Dee Arm, just before it meets the river. Licensed coffee shop serving freshly prepared meals and snacks *for breakfast, lunch and tea*. Children welcome. *Open weekdays 09.00-15.00; Sat & Sun 11.00-16.00*.

Wirral

Sweeping northwards along the lock-free pound from Chester to the Mersey, the canal enters open country for the last time as it crosses Wirral. The handsome stone railway viaduct over the navigation carries the Chester-Birkenhead line. The docks and basins of Ellesmere Port itself, where the Shropshire Union Canal meets the Manchester Ship Canal, are – or were – very extensive. Telford's famous warehouses in which the narrowboats and barges were loaded and discharged under cover were regrettably set alight by local hooligans and had to be demolished in the interests of safety. But now part of the old dock complex is the home of the Boat Museum, a large sub-aqua centre and the headquarters of the British Sub-Aqua Club. The sprawling museum site, making excellent use of the multitude of different buildings once part of the docks complex, plays host to a wide range of festive activity from boating jamborees to a variety of musical events. It has more than once been the venue for an excellent weekend of Cajun music and dance, the boats forming a strikingly colourful backdrop to non-stop revelling. Whatever one's interests, making the journey beyond Chester is always well worthwhile. There is still access for boats from the Shropshire Union through several wide locks down into the Manchester Ship Canal. But no pleasure boat may enter the ship canal without giving notice to the Ship Canal Company (*see* details on page 116). Those wishing to use it as a transit corridor to the River Weaver should also contact BW on 01606 723800; enquiries.walesandbordercounties@britishwaterways.co.uk to arrange for the operation of Weston Marsh Lock *during duty hours only*. The North West Region of the Inland Waterways Association publishes an excellent guide to navigating the Ship Canal: visit www.waterways.org.uk and search for 'Manchester Ship Canal'.

● **Stoak**

Ches. Tel. Also spelt Stoke, there is little of interest in this scattered village, except a pleasant country pub and a small, pretty church.

Chester Zoo Caughall Street, Upton, Chester CH2 1LH (01244 380280; www.chesterzoo.org.uk). 1/2 mile south of Caughall Bridge (134). Wide variety of animals, shown as much as possible without bars and fences, enhanced by attractive flower gardens and its own miniature canal. Largest elephant house in the world. *Open daily 10.00–dusk. Closed Xmas.* Charge.

● **Ellesmere Port**

Ches. All services. An industrial town of little interest apart from its once fine Victorian railway station.

The Boat Museum South Pier Road, Ellesmere Port CH65 4FW (0151 355 5017; www.nwm.org.uk/ellesmere). Established in the old Ellesmere Port basins. Exhibits, models and photos trace the development of the canal system from early times to its heyday in the 19th C. Vessels on display in the basin include a diverse and widely representative array of narrowboats, a tunnel tug, a weedcutter plus some larger vessels. Restored period cottages. An exciting and expanding venture in a splendid setting beside the ship canal, and not to be missed. Our canal heritage is still alive. *Open Apr–Oct, daily 10.00–17.00; Nov–Mar, Sat & Sun 11.00–16.00. Closed Xmas Day and Boxing Day.* Charge.

Tourist Information Centre Unit 22b, McArthurGlen Designer Outlet, Ellesmere Port CH65 9JJ (0151 356 7879; www.welcometoellesmereneston.com). *Open Mon-Fri 10.00-20.00; Sat 10.00-19.00 & Sun 10.00-17.00.*

● **Wirrall**

*Ches. All services.*A peninsula defined by the River Mersey on its east side and the River Dee along its west shore. Birkenhead is the focal town but it is the whole area that is now promoted rather than just a single habitation.The area's history dates back to the foundation of a Benedictine Priory created in 1150 and it was the monks who first established the ferry route across the Mersey. More recently shipbuilding became the dominant industry with the arrival of William Laird who, in 1825 set up his first shipyard here.

Birkenhead Market Birkenhead CH41 2YH (0151 666 3194/5; www.birkenheadmarket.co.uk). Over 300 indoor and outdoor stalls to choose from. *Open Mon-Sat. 09.00-17.00.*

Birkenhead Park Park Office, Grand Entrance (North Lodge), Conway Street, Birkenhead (0151 652 5197; www.wirral.gov.uk). This elaborate park, designed by Joseph Paxton (of Crystal Palace fame) in 1847, was the first publicly funded park in Europe and it went on to inspire the designs for Central Park in New York.

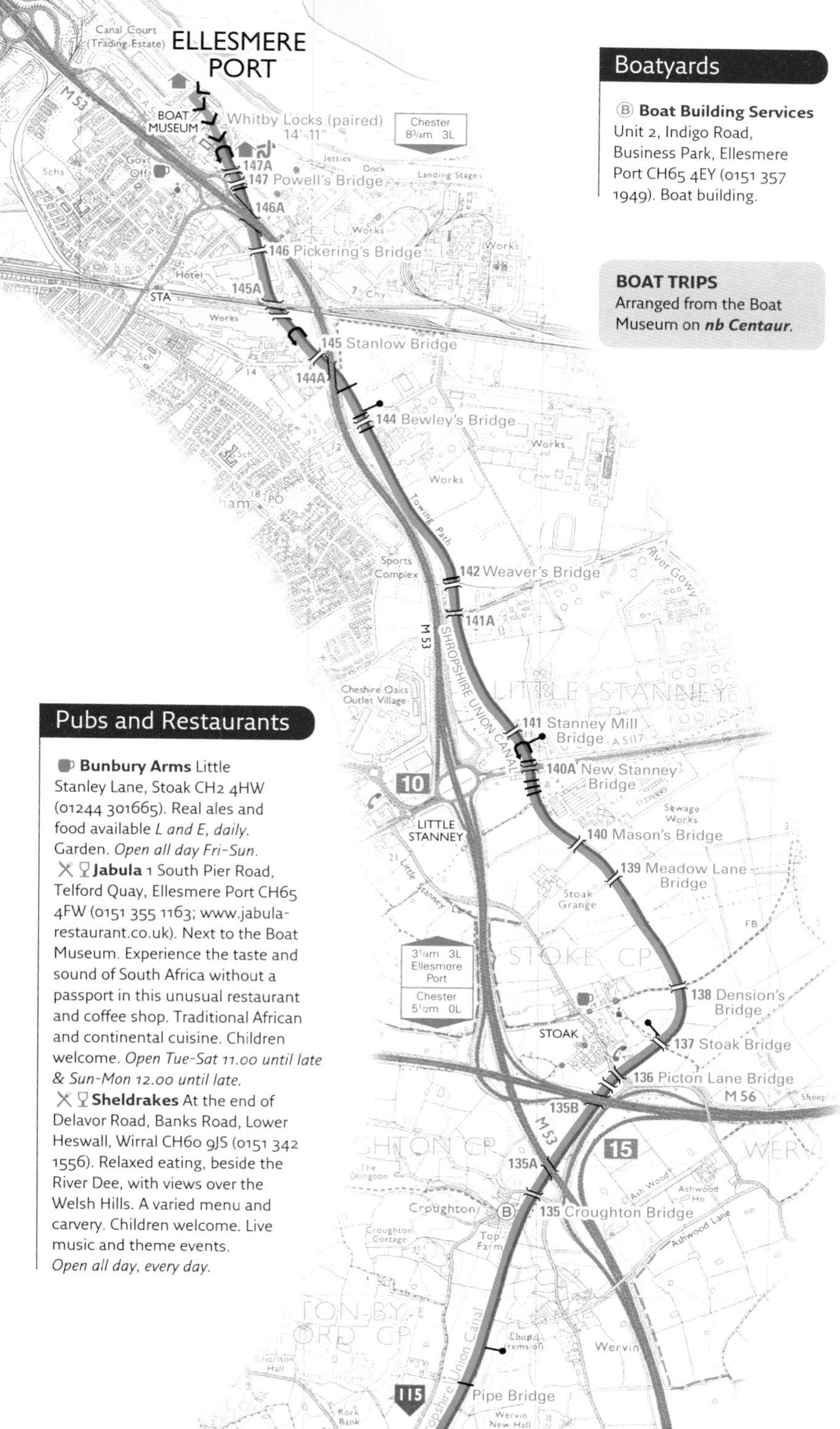

Boatyards

Ⓑ **Boat Building Services** Unit 2, Indigo Road, Business Park, Ellesmere Port CH65 4EY (0151 357 1949). Boat building.

BOAT TRIPS
Arranged from the Boat Museum on ***nb Centaur***.

Pubs and Restaurants

Bunbury Arms Little Stanley Lane, Stoak CH2 4HW (01244 301665). Real ales and food available *L and E, daily*. Garden. *Open all day Fri-Sun*.

Jabula 1 South Pier Road, Telford Quay, Ellesmere Port CH65 4FW (0151 355 1163; www.jabula-restaurant.co.uk). Next to the Boat Museum. Experience the taste and sound of South Africa without a passport in this unusual restaurant and coffee shop. Traditional African and continental cuisine. Children welcome. *Open Tue-Sat 11.00 until late & Sun-Mon 12.00 until late.*

Sheldrakes At the end of Delavor Road, Banks Road, Lower Heswall, Wirral CH60 9JS (0151 342 1556). Relaxed eating, beside the River Dee, with views over the Welsh Hills. A varied menu and carvery. Children welcome. Live music and theme events. *Open all day, every day.*

Birkenhead Tramway and Transport Museum 1 Taylor Street, Birkenhead CH41 1BG (0151 647 2128; www.wirral.gov.uk). Travel back in time on either a genuine Hong Kong Tram or the 1901 beautifully restored Birkenhead tram. Also trams and buses in various stages of restoration and the Baxter Collection of cars and motorcycles. *Open Apr-Oct Sat-Sun 13.00-17.00 & Nov-Mar Sat-Sun 12.00-16.00; also Wed-Fri during Easter & summer Hols.* Free. Other examples of the area's industrial heritage are the **Shore Road Pumping Station** (0151 650 1182) *– open as per Tramway and Transport Museum* - and the **Egerton Bridge.** These are all visited as part of the Birkenhead Heritage Trail. Free.

Blue Planet Aquarium Longlooms Road, Little Stanney, Ellesmere Port CH65 9LF (0151 357 8804; www.blueplanetaquarium.com). West of bridge 140A and M53 junction 10. New aquarium with two floors of interactive exhibits, themed restaurant, Caribbean reef, Amazon Jungle and Oil-Rig shop. An excellent all-weather attraction, but entry will cost a family of four more than £40. *Open daily 10.00–18.00 (closes at 17.00 Mon–Fri during term time).*

Bromborough Pool Village Wirral (0151 649 6481; www.riverside.org.uk). Constructed in the shadow of its more famous neighbour – Port Sunlight – and today surrounded by modern factory complexes, this delightful village was the brainchild of the Prices family and was built to house their candle factory workers. It still retains its charm and tranquility and remains an historical example of Victorian philanthropy. Follow the Heritage Trail, visit the parish church or delve into the past via the Heritage Centre in the village hall. *There are no opening time restrictions on the village.* Trains from Ellesmere Port or Chester to Port Sunlight.

Cajobah Hamilton Square, Birkenhead CH415AR (0151 647 9577). An intriguing little gallery and tearooms. set in a Grade I listed building, which also stocks a wide range of textiles, jewellery and pottery as well as offering short craft courses.

Floral Pavilion Theatre New Brighton CH45 2LH (0151 666 0007; www.floralpavilion.co.uk). A traditional-style theatre with a full and varied programme of entertainment throughout the summer months.

Mersey Ferries Pier Head, Liverpool L3 1DP (0151 330 1444; www.merseyferries.co.uk). *50-min cruises daily* together with *regular cross-river ferry services.* Also cruises further afield including the Manchester Ship Canal. *Cruises Mon-Fri 10.00-15.00 & Sat-Sun 10.00-18.00.* Café and shop. Charge. Free activity pack with every child's return ticket. Operates from ferry terminals at Woodside and Seacombe on Wirral and Pier Head, Liverpool.

Ness Botanic Gardens Ness, Neston, South Wirral CH64 4AY (0151 353 0123; www.nessgardens.org.uk). Originating from the first seeds planted by Arthur Kilpin Bulley in 1898, a Liverpool cotton broker and founder of Bees Seeds Ltd. His insatiable appetite for rare and unusual species led him to sponsor early pioneer plant hunters on expeditions to the temperate regions of the Far East, in search of exotic species that could be cultivated in our climate. A striking location, set on the banks of the Dee, with views out over North Wales; in all 64 acres. Shop, tea room and plant sales. *Open daily, Mar-Oct 09.30-17.00 & Nov-Feb 09.30-16.00.* Charge.

Pacific Road Arts Centre Pacific Road, Birkenhead CH41 1LJ (0151 647 0752; www.pacificroad.co.uk). Wirral's premier arts centre.

Port Sunlight Village, the Heritage Centre and the Lady Lever Art Gallery Port Sunlight, Wirral CH62 5DX (0151 644 6466; www.portsunlightvillage.com). Picturesque style 19th-C model village built by the soap baron William Hesketh Lever for his workers, together with a collection of art treasures in a sumptuous gallery, dedicated to his wife. Village *always open*; Heritage Centre *open daily 10.00–16.00 & Nov–Mar, Sat and Sun 11.00–16.00*; gallery *open daily 10.00–17.00*. Also **Gladstone Theatre** (0151 643 8757; www.gladstone.uk.com). Originally the men's dining hall, opened in 1891, today it is a venue for a variety of entertainment. Telephone for programme. Trains from Ellesmere Port or Chester to Port Sunlight for village and theatre and to Bebington for gallery.

Tam O'Shanter Urban Farm Boundary Road, Bidston CH43 7PD (0151 653 9332; www.visitliverpool.com). Small city farm on the edge of Bidston Hill. A safe place for children to visit, with a small but varied collection of farm animals. Café, picnic area, play area and nature trail. *Open daily 09.30–16.30.* Free but donations welcome.

Space Port Victoria Place, Seacombe, Wallasey, Wirral CH44 6QY (0151 330 1444; www.spaceport.org.uk). Based in the Grade II listed Seacombe Ferry Terminal Annexe, this attraction offers visitors the chance to partake in a fun and informative virtual journey through space. Interactive exhibits, real life stories, trips into the past and into the future all contrive to make us consider the weird and wonderful cosmos of which we are all a part. Café and shop. *Open Tue–Sun 10.30–18.00 (also open Mon during school holidays).* Charge. Bus or ferry from Hamilton Square, Birkenhead.

Tourist Information Centre Woodside Ferry Booking Hall, Birkenhead CH41 6DU (0151 647 6780; www.visitwirral.com). *Open daily 10.00-17.00.* Starting point for the Birkenhead Heritage Trail.

Williamson Art Gallery and Museum Slatey Road, Birkenhead L43 4UE (0151 652 4177; www.wirral.gov.uk). A permanent collection together with a wide range of changing exhibitions with particular relevance to the area. *Open Tue-Sun 10.00-17.00 & B Hol Mon.* Free.

Wirral Museum Hamilton Square, Birkenhead CH41 5BR (0151 666 4010; www.wirral.gov.uk/). A wide range of exhibits housed in the Grade II listed Town Hall.*Open as per Williamson Art Gallery.* Free.

STAFFORDSHIRE & WORCESTERSHIRE CANAL: NORTH

MAXIMUM DIMENSIONS

Length: 70'
Beam: 7'
Headroom: 6' 6"

MANAGER

0121 200 7400
enquiries.westmidlands@britishwaterways.co.uk

MILEAGE

AUTHERLEY JUNCTION to:
GREAT HAYWOOD JUNCTION: 20½ miles

Locks: 12

Construction of this navigation was begun immediately after that of the Trent & Mersey, to effect the joining of the rivers Trent, Mersey and Severn. Engineered by James Brindley, the Staffordshire & Worcestershire was opened throughout in 1772, at a cost of rather over £100,000. It stretched 46 miles from Great Haywood on the Trent & Mersey to the River Severn, which it joined at Stourport. The canal was an immediate success. It was well placed to bring goods from the Potteries down to Gloucester, Bristol and the West Country; while the Birmingham Canal, which joined it half-way along at Aldersley Junction, fed manufactured goods northwards from the Black Country to the Potteries via Great Haywood. In 1815 the Worcester & Birmingham Canal opened, offering a more direct but heavily locked canal link between Birmingham and the Severn. The Staffordshire & Worcestershire answered this threat by gradually extending the opening times of the locks until, by 1830, they were open 24 hours a day. When the Birmingham & Liverpool Junction Canal was opened from Autherley to Nantwich in 1835, traffic bound for Merseyside from Birmingham naturally began to use this more direct, modern canal. The Staffordshire & Worcestershire lost a great deal of traffic over its length as most of the boats now passed along only the ½-mile stretch of the Staffordshire & Worcestershire Canal between Autherley and Aldersley Junctions. The company levied absurdly high tolls for this tiny length. The B & LJ Company therefore co-operated with the Birmingham Canal Company in 1836 to promote in Parliament a Bill for the Tettenhall & Autherley Canal and Aqueduct. This project was to be a canal flyover, going from the Birmingham Canal right over the profiteering Staffordshire & Worcestershire and locking down into the Birmingham & Liverpool Junction Canal. The Staffordshire & Worcestershire company had to give way, and reduced its tolls to an acceptable level. In spite of this set back, the Staffordshire & Worcestershire maintained a good profit, and high dividends were paid throughout the rest of the 19th C. From the 1860s onwards, railway competition began to bite, and the company's profits began to slip. Several modernisation schemes came to nothing, and the canal's trade declined. Now the canal is used almost exclusively by pleasure craft. It is covered in full in *Guide 2* of this series.

Autherley Junction

Autherley Junction is marked by a big white bridge on the towpath side. The stop lock just beyond marks the entrance to the Shropshire Union: there is a useful boatyard just to the north of it. Leaving Autherley, the Staffordshire & Worcestershire passes new housing before running through a very narrow cutting in rock, once known as 'Pendeford Rockin', after a local farm: there is only room for boats to pass in the designated places, so a good look out should be kept for oncoming craft. After passing the motorway the navigation leaves behind the suburbs of Wolverhampton and enters pleasant farmland. The bridges need care: although the bridgeholes are reasonably wide, the actual arches are rather low.

- **Autherley Junction**
  A busy canal junction with a full range of boating facilities close by.
- **Coven**
  Staffs. PO, tel, stores, garage, fish & chips. The only true village on this section, Coven lies beyond a dual carriageway north west of Cross Green Bridge. There is a large number of shops, including a laundrette.

Pubs and Restaurants

Fox & Anchor Inn Brewood Road, Cross Green, Wolverhampton WV10 7PW (01902 790786). Canalside by Cross Green Bridge. Large and friendly pub with roof-top terrace. Real ale, and meals available *all day*. Menu is traditional English, along with steaks and *Sun* roast. Children's menu, garden and good moorings.

WALKING & CYCLING
The towpath is generally in good condition for both walkers and cyclists.

Boatyards

Ⓑ **Napton Narrowboats** Autherley Junction, Oxley Moor Road, Wolverhampton WV9 5HW (01926 813644). D E Pump out, gas, narrowboat hire, overnight mooring, long term mooring, winter storage, slipway, chandlery, provisions, books and maps, boat building, DIY facilities, boat repairs, solid fuel, gifts, showers. *Emergency call out.*

Ⓑ **Oxley Marine** The Wharf, Oxley Moor Road, Wolverhampton WV10 6TZ (01902 789522; www.oxleymarine.co.uk). D Pump out, gas, overnight and long-term mooring, winter storage, slipway, boat and engine sales and repairs, DIY facilities, *emergency call out.* Licensed bar *each evening*, snacks.

BOAT TRIPS
City of Wolverhampton Passenger Boat Services, The Wharf, Oxley Moor Road, Wolverhampton WV10 6TZ. ***Nb Stafford*** Carrying up to 42 passengers, with a bar and food. Public trips on *most Sun Apr–Sep*, plus private charter. For details telephone 01902 789522.

BIRD LIFE
The *Long-Tailed Tit* is a charming resident of woods, heaths and hedgerows. Feeding flocks of these birds resemble animated feather dusters. Their plumage can look black and white, but at close range there is a pinkish wash to the underparts and pinkish buff on the backs. The long-tailed tit has a tiny, stubby bill, a long tail, and an almost spherical body.

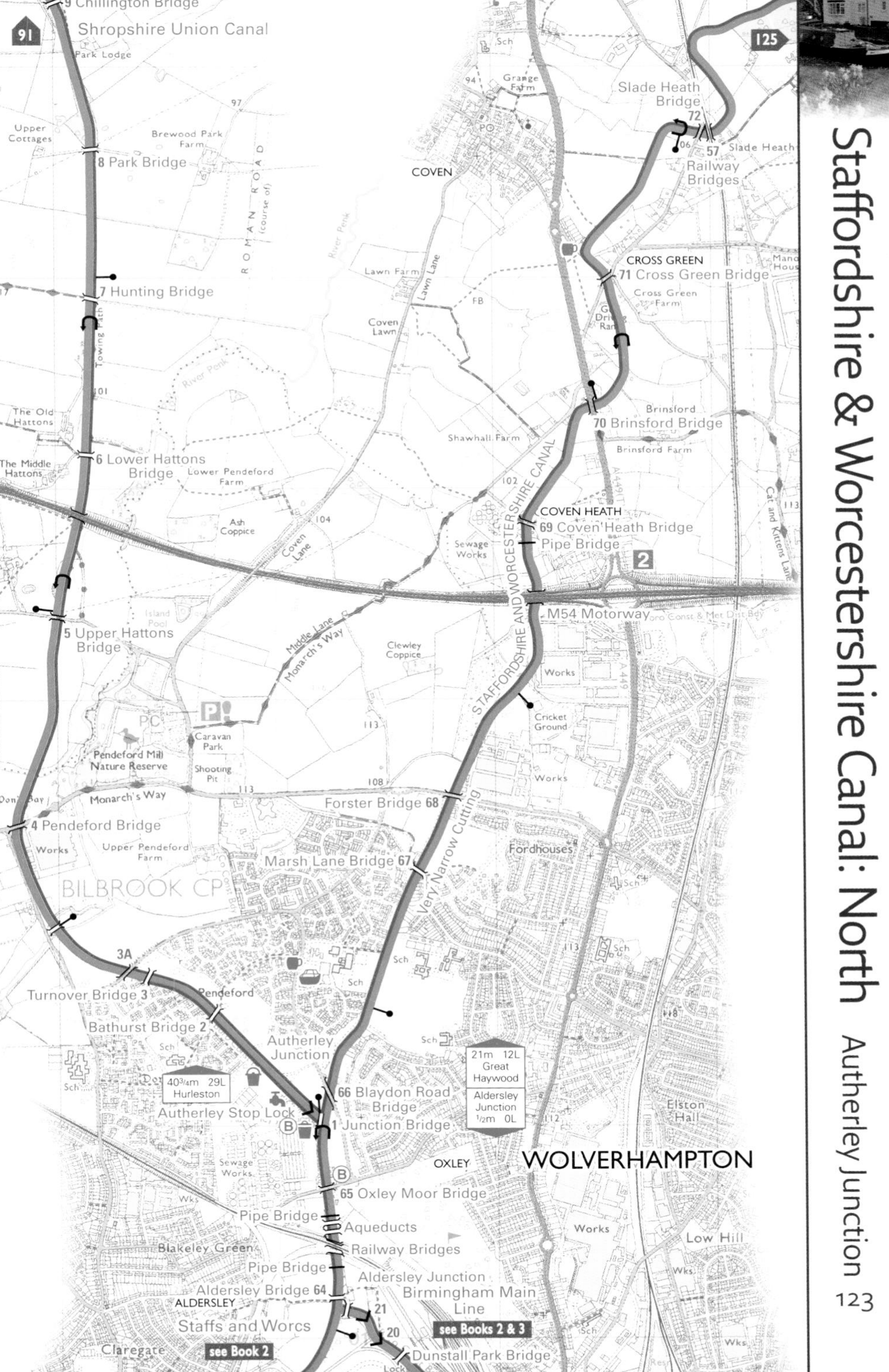

Staffordshire & Worcestershire Canal: North

Autherley Junction

Gailey Wharf

The considerable age of this canal is shown by its extremely twisting course, revealed after passing the railway bridge. There are few real centres of population along this stretch, which comprises largely former heathland. The canal widens just before bridge 74, where Brindley incorporated part of a medieval moat into the canal. Hatherton Junction marks the entrance of the former Hatherton Branch of the Staffordshire & Worcestershire Canal into the main line. This branch used to connect with the Birmingham Canal Navigations. It is closed above the derelict second lock, although the channel remains as a feeder for the Staffordshire & Worcestershire Canal. There is a campaign for its restoration. There is a marina at the junction. A little further along, a chemical works is encountered, astride the canal in what used to be woodlands. This was once called the 'Black Works', as lamp black was produced here. Gailey Wharf is about a mile further north: it is a small canal settlement that includes a boatyard and a large, round, toll keeper's watch-tower, containing a useful canal shop. The picturesque Wharf Cottage opposite has been restored as a bijou residence. The canal itself disappears under Watling Street and then rapidly through five locks towards Penkridge. These locks are very attractive, and some are accompanied by little brick bridges. The M6 motorway, and the traffic noise, comes alongside for 1/2 mile, screening the reservoirs which feed the canal.

Pillaton Old Hall Penkridge, ST19 5RZ (01785 712200). South east of bridge 85. Only the gate house and stone-built chapel remain of this late 15th-C brick mansion built by the Littleton family, although there are still traces of the hall and courtyard. The chapel contains a 13th-C wooden carving of a saint. Visiting is by appointment only: telephone 01785 712200. The modest charge is donated to charity.

Gailey and Calf Heath reservoirs 1/2 mile east of Gailey Wharf, either side of the M6. These are feeder reservoirs for the canal, though rarely drawn on. The public has access to them as nature reserves to study the wide variety of natural life, especially the long-established heronry which is thriving on an island in Gailey Lower Reservoir. In Gailey Upper, fishing is available to the public from the riparian owner. In Gailey Lower a limited number of angling tickets are available on a season ticket basis each year from BW. There is club sailing on two of the reservoirs.

Boatyards

Ⓑ **Otherton Boat Haven** Otherton, Otherton, Penkridge ST19 5NX (01785 712515; mobile 07966 184182; www.othertonboathaven.co.uk). D Pump out, gas, overnight and long-term mooring, boat and engine sales and repairs, toilets, coal, laundry facilities.

Ⓑ **J D Boat Services** The Wharf, Gailey, Stafford ST19 5PR (01902 791811; www.jdboats.co.uk). D Pump out, gas, boat and engine repairs, engine sales, boat building, breakdown service. Gifts and provisions, chandlery and maps opposite in the Roundhouse.

Ⓑ **Viking Afloat** At J D Boat Services (01905 610660; www.viking-afloat.com). Narrowboat hire.

Pubs and Restaurants

Misty's Bar & Restaurant King's Road, Calf Heath, near Wolverhampton WV10 7DU (01902 790570). Restaurant serving excellent and reasonably priced home-cooked food *L and E*. Children welcome. Garden.

Cross Keys Filance Lane, Penkridge ST19 5HJ (01785 712826). Canalside, at Filance Bridge (84). Once a lonely canal pub, now it is modernised and surrounded by housing estates. Family orientated, it serves real ale and food *L and E*. Garden, with *summer* barbecues. There is a useful Spar shop 100yds north, on the estate.

BOAT TRIPS

Hatherton Belle 45-seater trip boat with a bar. Details from Misty's Bar and Restaurant.

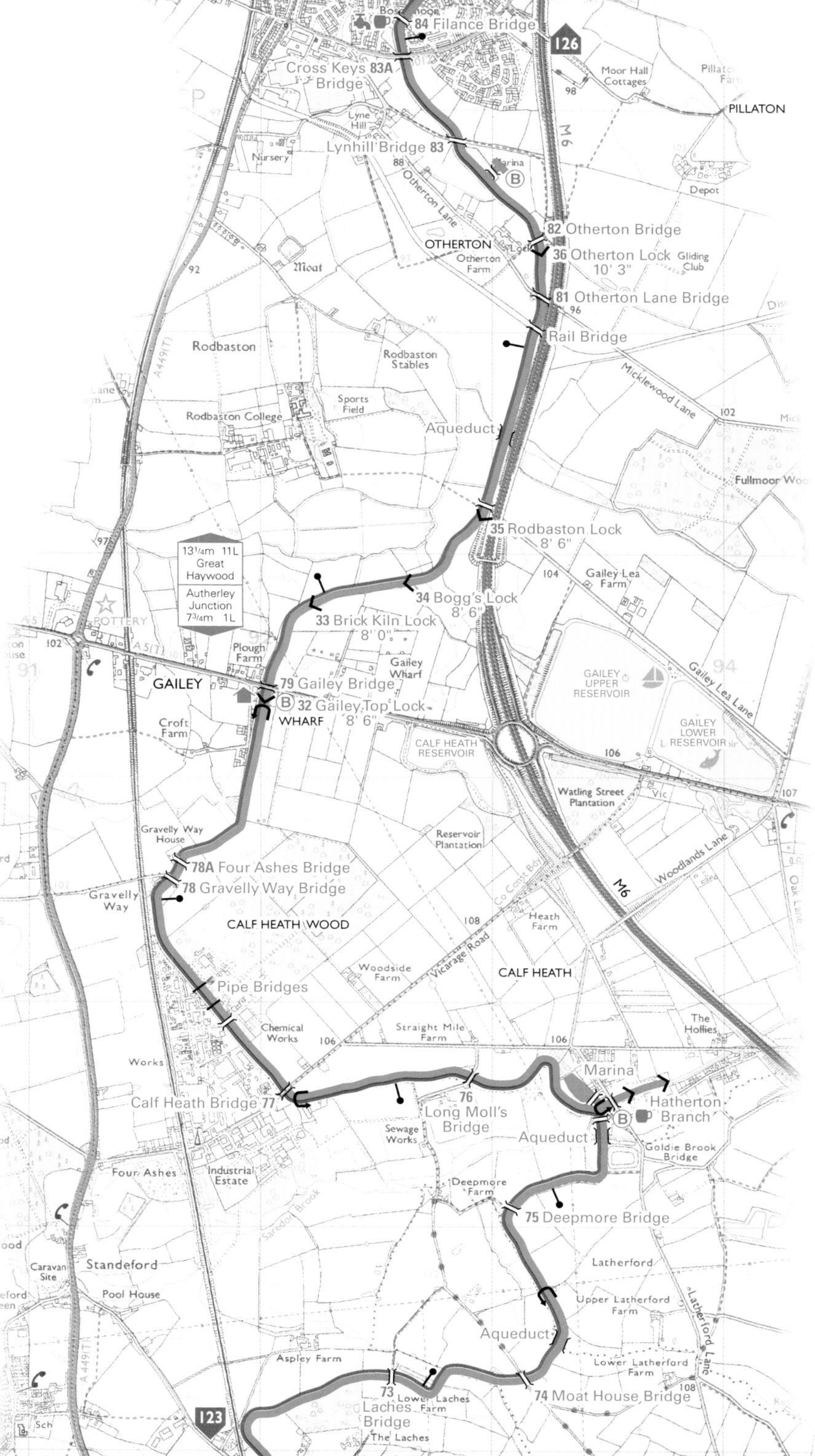
84 Filance Bridge
126
Cross Keys 83A Bridge
Moor Hall Cottages
PILLATON
Lyne Hill
Lynhill Bridge 83
Nursery
Otherton Lane
Marina
M6
Depot
82 Otherton Bridge
OTHERTON
Otherton Farm
Moat
36 Otherton Lock 10' 3"
Gliding Club
81 Otherton Lane Bridge
Rail Bridge
Rodbaston
Rodbaston Stables
Micklewood Lane
Sports Field
Rodbaston College
Aqueduct
Fullmoor Wood
35 Rodbaston Lock 8' 6"
13¼m 11L Great Haywood
Autherley Junction 7¾m 1L
Gailey Lea Farm
34 Bogg's Lock 8' 6"
33 Brick Kiln Lock 8' 0"
POTTERY
A5(T)
Plough Farm
Gailey Wharf
GAILEY
79 Gailey Bridge
32 Gailey Top Lock 8' 6"
WHARF
GAILEY UPPER RESERVOIR
Gailey Lea Lane
Croft Farm
CALF HEATH RESERVOIR
GAILEY LOWER RESERVOIR
Watling Street Plantation
Gravelly Way House
Reservoir Plantation
Woodlands Lane
78A Four Ashes Bridge
78 Gravelly Way Bridge
Gravelly Way
CALF HEATH WOOD
Vicarage Road
Heath Farm
Woodside Farm
CALF HEATH
Pipe Bridges
Chemical Works
Straight Mile Farm
The Hollies
Works
Marina
Calf Heath Bridge 77
76 Long Moll's Bridge
Hatherton Branch
Sewage Works
Aqueduct
Goldie Brook Bridge
Four Ashes
Industrial Estate
Deepmore Farm
75 Deepmore Bridge
Standeford
Caravan Site
Latherford
Pool House
Upper Latherford Farm
Latherford Lane
Aqueduct
Aspley Farm
Lower Latherford Farm
73 Laches Bridge
Lower Laches Farm
74 Moat House Bridge
123
The Laches
A449(T)

Penkridge

The navigation now passes through Penkridge and is soon approached by the little River Penk: the two water courses share the valley for the next few miles. The Cross Keys at Filance Bridge (*see* page 124) was once an isolated canal pub – now it is surrounded by housing, which spreads along the canal in each direction. Apart from the noise of the motorway this is a pleasant valley: there are plenty of trees, a handful of locks and the large Teddesley Park alongside the canal. At Acton Trussell the M6 roars off to the north west and once again peace returns to the waterway. Teddesley Park Bridge was at one time quite ornamental, and became known as 'Fancy Bridge'. It is less so now. At Shutt Hill an iron post at the bottom of the lock is the only reminder of a small wharf which once existed here. The post was used to turn the boats into the dock.

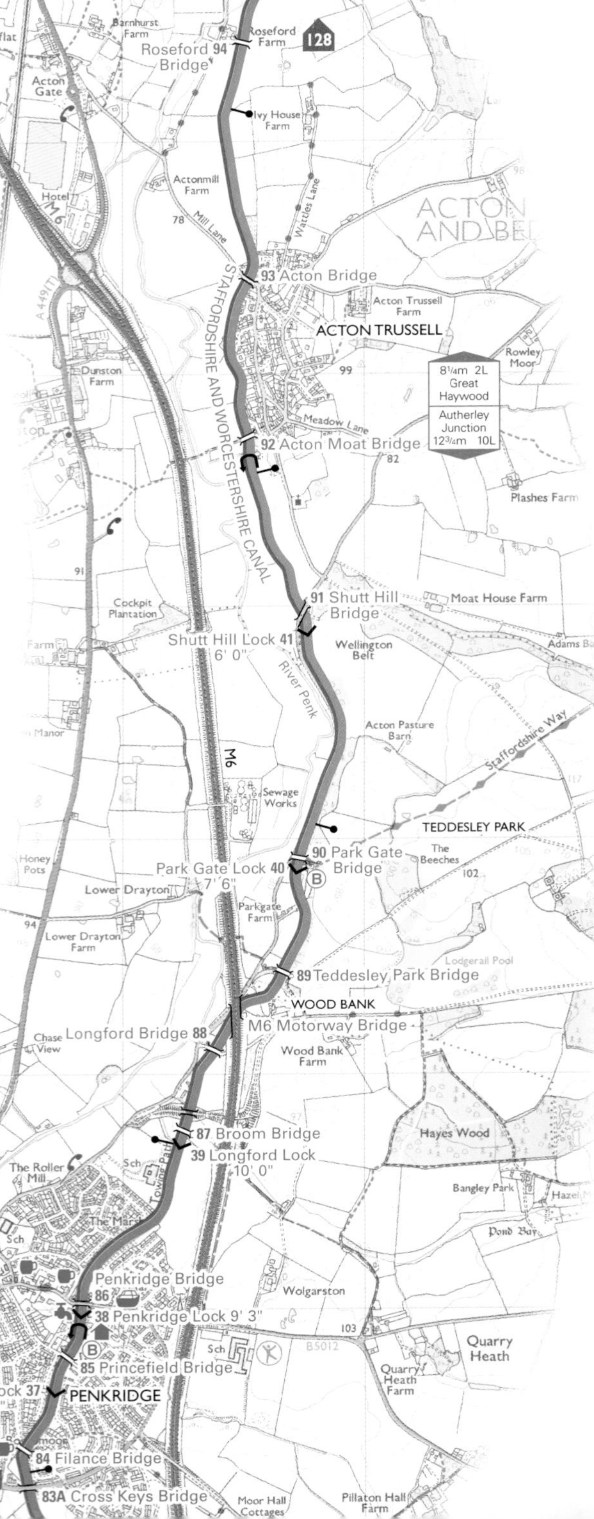

Penkridge

Staffs. PO, tel, stores, garage, bank, station, butchers, takeaway and chemist. Above Penkridge Lock is a good place to tie up in this relatively old village. It is bisected by a trunk road, but luckily most of the village lies to the east of it. The church of St Michael is tall and sombre, and is well-kept. A harmonious mixture of styles, the earliest part dates from the 11th C, but the whole was restored in 1881. There is a fine Dutch 18th-C wrought iron screen brought from Cape Town, and the tower is believed to date from c.1500. There are fine monuments of the Littletons of Pillaton Hall (*see* page 120), dating from 1558 and later.

Teddesley Park On the east bank of the canal. The Hall, once the family seat of the Littletons, was used during World War II as a prisoner-of-war camp, but has since been demolished. Its extensive wooded estate still remains.

Acton Trussell

Staffs. Tel, stores. A village overwhelmed by modern housing: much the best way to see it is from the canal. The church stands to the south, overlooking the navigation. The west tower dates from the 13th C, topped by a spire built in 1562.

Boatyards

Ⓑ **Teddesley Boat Company** Park Gate Lock, Teddesley Road, Penkridge ST19 5RH (01785 714692; www.narrowboats.co.uk). D Pump out, gas, narrowboat hire, overnight and long-term mooring, winter storage, crane, boat and engine sales and repairs, boat building, telephone, books and maps. For chandlery telephone 01785 712437.

Ⓑ **Tom's Moorings** Cannock Road, Penkridge ST19 5DT (01543 414808). Above Penkridge Lock. Pump out, gas, overnight and long-term mooring.

PLANT LIFE

The *Bluebell* is a familiar bulbous perennial, often carpeting whole woodland floors if the situation suits its requirements. The leaves are narrow and all basal. Bell-shaped flowers in one-sided spikes appear April–June.

Pubs and Restaurants

The Boat Cannock Road, Penkridge ST19 5DT (01785 714178). Canalside, by Penkridge Lock. Mellow and friendly red-brick pub dating from 1779, with plenty of brass and other bits and pieces in the homely bars. Real ale. Food is available *L and E, all day.* Children welcome, garden.

Star Market Place, Penkridge ST19 5DJ (01785 712513). Fine old pub serving real ale and bar meals *12.00–17.00 in summer, reduced hours in winter.* Children welcome. Outside seating.

White Hart Stone Cross, Penkridge ST19 5AS (01785 712242). This historic former coaching inn, visited by Mary, Queen of Scots, and Elizabeth I, has an impressive frontage, timber framed with three gables. It serves real ale, and meals *L and E.* Outside seating.

Railway Clay Street, Penkridge ST19 5AF (01785 712685). Real ale is available in this listed and historic main road pub, along with meals *L and E.* Children welcome and there is a wonderful garden.

Littleton Arms St Michael's Square, Penkridge ST19 5AL (01785 716300; www.thelittletonarms.com). Hotel, bar and restaurant. Real ale and excellent food L and E. Outside seating. Children welcome. B & B.

Flames Mill Street, Penkridge ST19 5AY (01785 712955). Contemporary eastern cuisine.

WALKING & CYCLING

The Staffordshire Way crosses the canal between bridges 89 and 90. This 90-mile path stretches from Mow Cop in the north (near the Macclesfield Canal) to Kinver Edge in the south, using the Caldon Canal towpath on the way. It connects with the Gritstone Trail, the Hereford & Worcester Way and the Heart of England Way. A guide book is available from local Tourist Information Centres.

Tixall

Continuing north along the shallow Penk valley, the canal soon reaches Radford Bridge, the nearest point to Stafford. It is about 1½ miles to the centre of town: there is a frequent bus service. A canal branch used to connect with the town via Baswich Lock and the River Sow. If you look carefully west of bridge 101 you can just about deduce where the connection was made - some remains of brickwork are the clue. A mile further north the canal bends around to the south east and follows the pretty valley of the River Sow, and at Milford crosses the river via an aqueduct - an early structure by James Brindley, carried heavily on low brick arches. Tixall Lock offers some interesting views in all directions: the castellated entrance to Shugborough Railway Tunnel at the foot of the thick woods of Cannock Chase and the distant outline of the remarkable Tixall Gatehouse. The canal now completes its journey to the Trent & Mersey Canal at Great Haywood. It is a length of waterway quite unlike any other. Proceeding along this very charming valley, the navigation enters Tixall Wide - an amazing and delightful stretch of water more resembling a lake than a canal, said to have been built in order not to compromise the view from Tixall House (alas, no more), and navigable to the edges. The Wide is noted for its kingfisher population. Woods across the valley conceal Shugborough Hall. The River Trent is met, on its way south from Stoke-on-Trent, and is crossed on an aqueduct. There is a wharf, and fresh produce can be purchased at the farm north of bridge 74 on the Trent & Mersey, which is entered through an elegantly arched bridge. The bridge is the subject of a very famous photograph taken by the canal historian Eric de Maré.

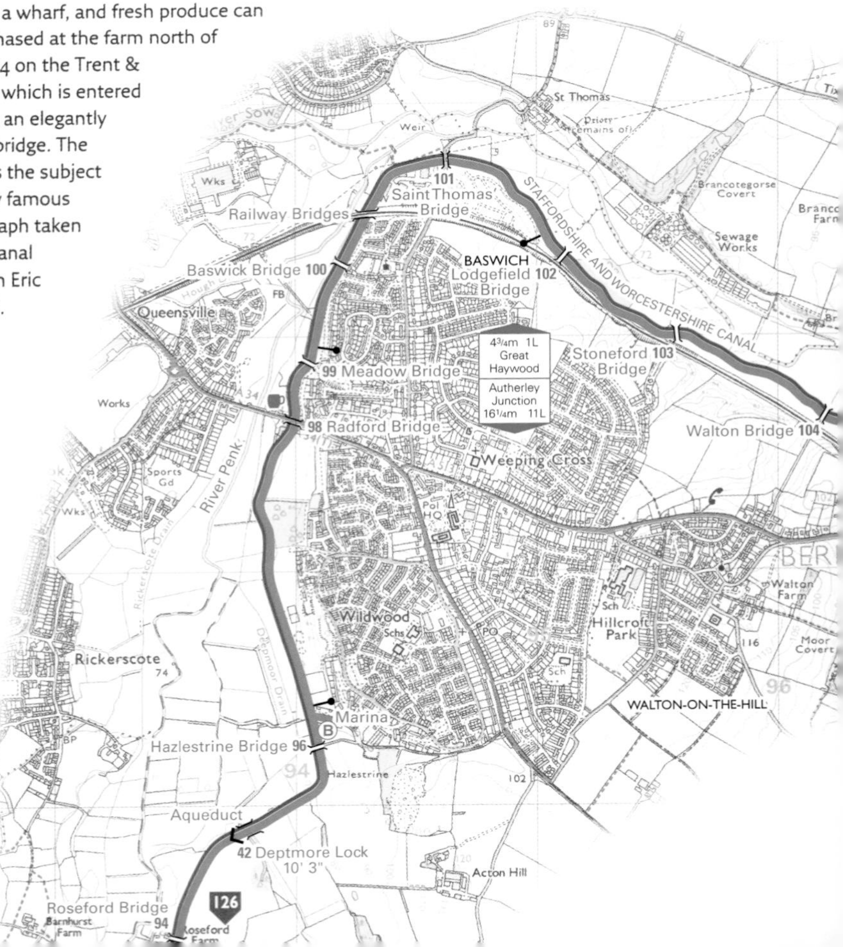

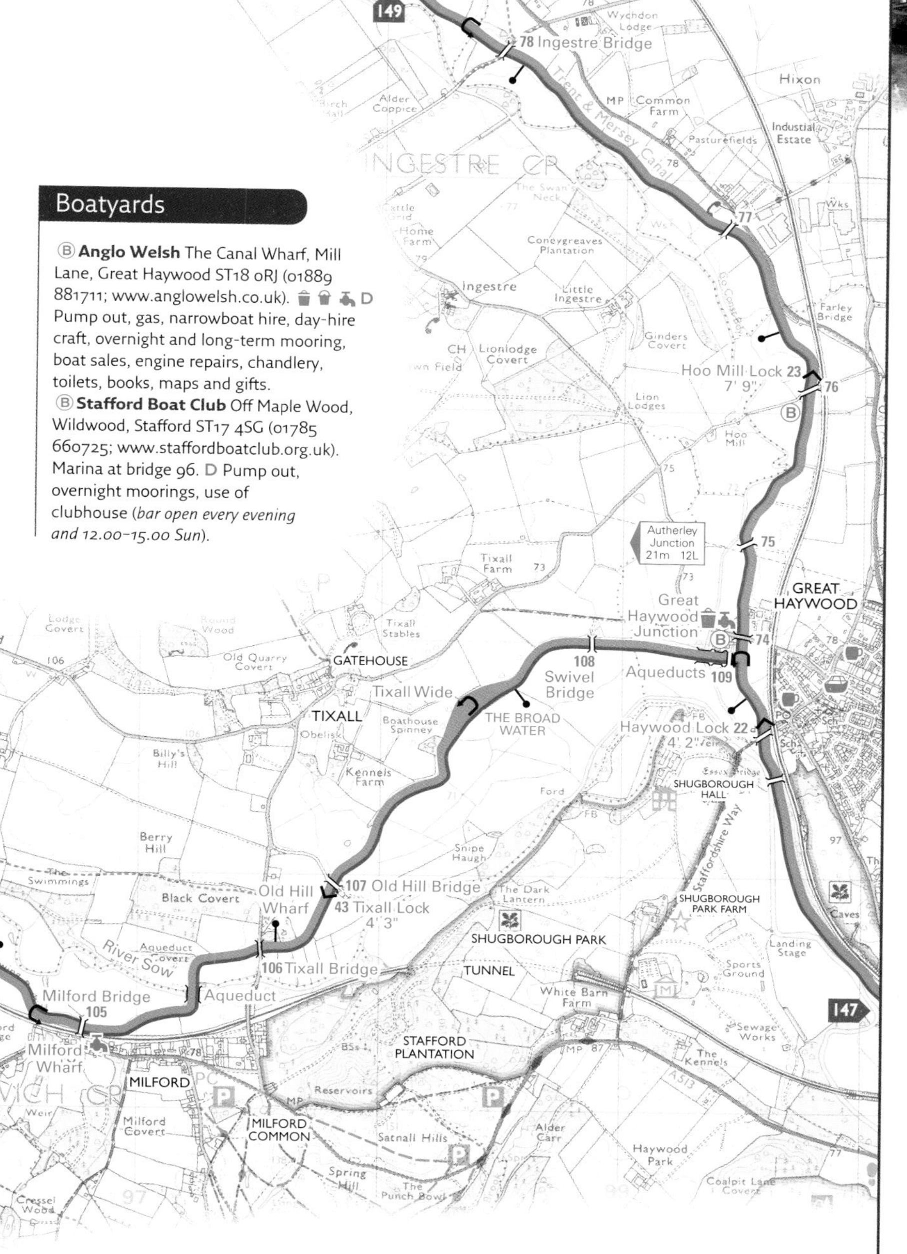

Boatyards

Ⓑ **Anglo Welsh** The Canal Wharf, Mill Lane, Great Haywood ST18 0RJ (01889 881711; www.anglowelsh.co.uk). D Pump out, gas, narrowboat hire, day-hire craft, overnight and long-term mooring, boat sales, engine repairs, chandlery, toilets, books, maps and gifts.

Ⓑ **Stafford Boat Club** Off Maple Wood, Wildwood, Stafford ST17 4SG (01785 660725; www.staffordboatclub.org.uk). Marina at bridge 96. D Pump out, overnight moorings, use of clubhouse (*bar open every evening and 12.00–15.00 Sun*).

WALKING & CYCLING

There is a Nature Trail at Milford Common, and visitors to Shugborough Hall can enjoy excellent walks in the park.

Stafford

Staffs. All services. This town is well worth visiting, since there is a remarkable wealth of fine old buildings. These include a handsome City Hall complex of ornamental Italianate buildings, c.1880. The robust-looking gaol is nearby; and the church of St Mary stands in very pleasing and spacious grounds. There are some pretty back alleys: Church Lane contains a splendid-looking eating house, and at the bottom of the lane a fruiterer's shop is in a thatched cottage built in 1610.

The Shire Hall Gallery Market Square, Stafford ST16 2LD (01785 278345; www.staffordshire.gov.uk). A stimulating variety of work by local artists, craftsmen, printmakers, jewellers, photographers and others. *Open Mon–Sat 09.30–17.00, Sun 13.00–16.00.* Free.

Tourist Information Centre Market Street, Stafford ST16 2LD (01785 619619; www.visitstafford.org).

The Stafford Branch

Just west of bridge 101 there was once a lock taking a branch off the Staffordshire & Worcestershire to Stafford. One mile long, it was unusual in that it was not a canal but the canalised course of the River Sow.

Milford

Staffs. PO, tel, stores, garage. Best reached from Tixall Bridge (106). Milford Hall is hidden by trees.

Tixall

Staffs. Tel, stores. Just to the east are the stables and the gatehouse of the long-vanished Tixall Hall. This massive square Elizabethan building dates from 1598 and is fully four storeys high. It stands alone in a field and is considered to be one of the most ambitious gatehouses in the country. The gatehouse is now available for holiday lets: telephone the Landmark Trust (01628 825925) for details.

Great Haywood

Staffs. PO, tel, stores. Centre of the Great Haywood and Shugborough Conservation Area, the village is attractive in parts, but it is closely connected in many ways to Shugborough Park, to which it is physically linked by the very old Essex Bridge, where the crystal clear waters of the River Sow join the Trent on its way down from Stoke.

Shugborough Hall *NT.* Milford, near Stafford ST17 0XB (01889 881388; www.shugborough.org.uk). Walk south along the road from bridge 106 to the A513 at Milford Common. The main entrance is on your left. The present house dates from 1693, but was substantially altered by James Stuart around 1760 and by Samuel Wyatt around the turn of the 18th C. The Trust has leased the whole to Staffordshire County Council who now manage it. The house has been restored at great expense. There are some magnificent rooms and treasures inside.

Museum of Staffordshire Life This excellent establishment, Staffordshire's County Museum, is housed in the old stables adjacent to Shugborough Hall (*see* above). Open since 1966, it is superbly laid out and contains all sorts of exhibits concerned with old country life in Staffordshire.

Shugborough Park There are some remarkable sights in the large park that encircles the Hall. Thomas Anson, who inherited the estate in 1720, enlisted in 1744 the help of his famous brother, Admiral George Anson, to beautify and improve the house and the park. In 1762 he commissioned James Stuart, a neo-Grecian architect, to embellish the grounds. 'Athenian' Stuart set to with a will, and the spectacular results of his work can be seen scattered round the park.

The Park Farm Within Shugborough Park. Designed by Samuel Wyatt, it contains an agricultural museum, a working mill and a rare breeds centre. Traditional country skills such as bread-making, butter-churning and cheese-making are demonstrated.
Open Apr–Oct daily 11.00–17.00. Charge. Parties must book. Tea rooms, shop.

Pubs and Restaurants

Radford Bank Inn Radford Bank, Stafford ST17 4PG (01785 2428250). Canalside at bridge 98. Food is served *all day, every day until 21.00*, along with real ale. Children are welcome, *until 21.00 and in the restaurant*, and there is a garden.

The Clifford Arms Main Road, Great Haywood ST18 0SR (01889 881321). There has apparently been a pub on this site for hundreds of years. At one time it was a coaching inn. Now it is a friendly village local with an open fire, serving real ale and bar and restaurant meals *L and E*. Small garden with yews. Moorings.

Lockhouse Restaurant Trent Lane, Great Haywood ST18 0ST (01889 881294). Friendly and handy for Anglo-Welsh visitors. Morning and afternoon tea, coffee and cakes, hot and cold carvery *L daily* and home-cooked English food . Real ale is available for the thirsty. Canalside garden, and just a couple of minutes' walk from the village.

TRENT & MERSEY CANAL

MAXIMUM DIMENSIONS

Derwent Mouth to Horninglow Basin, Burton upon Trent
Length: 72'
Beam: 14'
Headroom: 7'
Stenson lock is very tight for 14ft beam craft and Weston Lock is tight for boats of 72ft length.

Burton upon Trent to south end of Harecastle Tunnel
Length: 72'
Beam: 7'
Headroom: 6' 3"

Harecastle Tunnel
Length: 72'
Beam: 7'
Headroom: 5' 9"

North end of Harecastle Tunnel to Croxton Aqueduct
Length: 72'
Beam: 7'
Headroom: 7'

Croxton Aqueduct to Preston Brook Tunnel
Length: 72'
Beam: 8' 2"
Headroom: 6' 3"

MANAGER:

Derwent Mouth to bridge 27a Willington:
01636 704481
enquiries.emidlands@britishwaterways.co.uk
Willington bridge 27a to Great Haywood bridge 75:
01827 252000
enquiries.westmidlands@britishwaterways.co.uk
Great Haywood bridge 75 to Preston Brook:
01606 723800
enquiries.walesandbordercounties@britishwaterways.co.uk

MILEAGE

DERWENT MOUTH to:
Swarkestone Lock: 7 miles
Willington: 12¼ miles
Horninglow Wharf: 16½ miles
Barton Turn: 21¼ miles
Fradley, junction with Coventry Canal: 26¼ miles
Great Haywood, junction with Staffordshire & Worcestershire Canal: 39 miles
Stone: 48½ miles
Stoke Top Lock, junction with Caldon Canal: 58 miles
Harding's Wood, junction with Macclesfield Canal: 63¾ miles
King's Lock, Middlewich, junction with Middlewich Branch: 76¼ miles
Anderton Lift, for River Weaver: 86½ miles
PRESTON BROOK north end of tunnel and Bridgewater Canal: 93½ miles

Locks: 76

This early canal was originally conceived partly as a roundabout link between the ports of Liverpool and Hull, while passing through the busy area of the Potteries and mid-Cheshire, and terminating either in the River Weaver or in the Mersey. Its construction was promoted by Josiah Wedgwood (1730–95), the famous potter, aided by his friends Thomas Bentley and Erasmus Darwin. In 1766 the Trent & Mersey Canal Act was passed by Parliament, authorising the building of a navigation from the River Trent at Shardlow to Runcorn Gap, where it would join the proposed extension of the Bridgewater Canal from Manchester.
The ageing James Brindley was appointed engineer for the canal. Construction began at once and in 1777 the Trent & Mersey Canal was opened. In the total 93 miles between Derwent Mouth and Preston Brook, the Trent & Mersey gained connection with no fewer than nine other canals or significant branches.
By the 1820s the slowly-sinking tunnel at Harecastle had become a serious bottle-neck, so Thomas Telford recommended building a second tunnel beside the old one. His recommendation was eventually accepted by the company and the new tunnel was completed in under three years, in 1827. Although the Trent & Mersey was taken over in 1845 by the new North Staffordshire Railway Company, the canal flourished until World War I.
Look out for the handsome cast iron mileposts, which actually measure the mileage from Shardlow, not Derwent Mouth. There are 59 originals, from the Rougeley and Dixon foundry in Stone, and 34 replacements, bearing the mark of the Trent & Mersey Canal Society – T & MCS 1977.

Shardlow

The Trent & Mersey Canal begins at Derwent Mouth, some 2½ miles upstream of the point where the Soar Navigation enters the River Trent at a complicated waterways junction. Navigators leaving the Soar and heading towards the Trent & Mersey should turn LEFT (west), thus avoiding Thrumpton Weir, which lies beyond the large railway bridge. The entrances to the Cranfleet Cut and Erewash Canal (Trent Lock) are passed, both lying to the north, while continuing upstream to the railway bridge the paired Sawley Locks (power-operated, by the keeper) will be seen at the entrance to the Sawley Cut. The flood lock is usually open, but should it need operating, be sure to leave a paddle open at each end after you have passed through. Keep to the LEFT when travelling upstream, or to the RIGHT when travelling downstream, to avoid another large weir by the M1 motorway bridge. The Trent is navigable virtually to Shardlow (turn left under the concrete footbridge if you wish to explore as far as Cavendish Bridge). The 1758 tolls are engraved on a plaque on the bridge – it was washed away in the floods in 1947, and was re-erected in 1960. The first lock on the Trent & Mersey is Derwent Mouth Lock, beyond which is Shardlow, one of the most interesting inland canal ports on the whole inland waterway network. Note, for example, the old salt warehouse by Shardlow Lock.

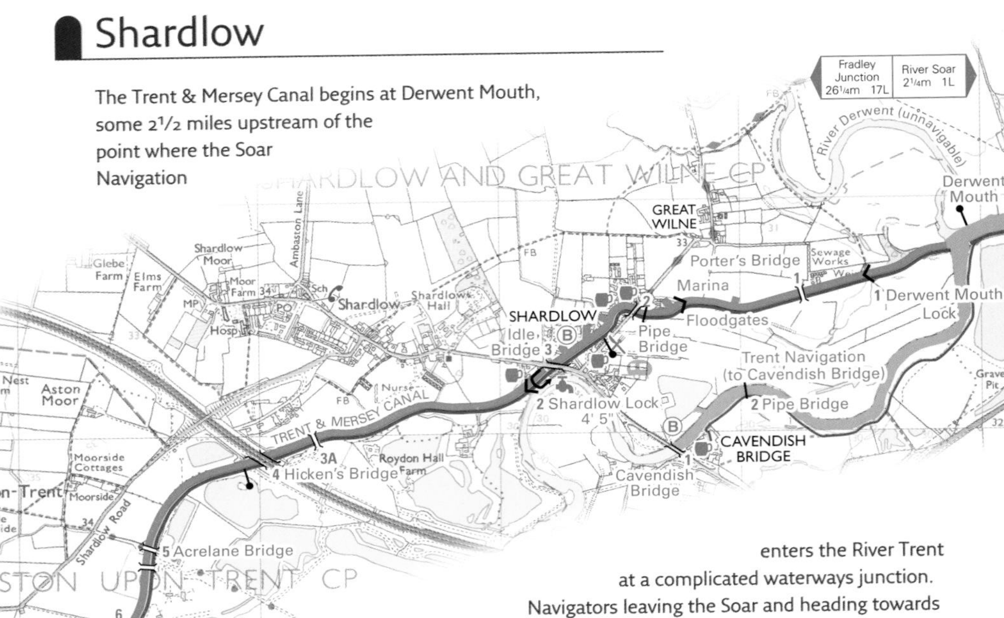

Boatyards

Ⓑ ✕ **Sawley Marina** Long Eaton, Nottingham NG10 3AE (01159 734278; www.bwml.co.uk). P D Pump out, gas, overnight and long-term mooring, winter storage, slipway, crane, boat and engine sales, engine repairs, telephone, chandlery, solid fuel, toilets, showers, restaurant, laundrette, groceries.

Ⓑ **Dobsons Boatyard** The Wharf, Shardlow DE72 2GH (01332 792271; sales@millermarine.com). D Pump out, gas, overnight and long-term mooring, slipway, chandlery, boat building, boat and engine sales, engine repairs, wet dock, books and maps.

Ⓑ ✕ **Shardlow Marina** London Road, Shardlow DE72 2GL (01332 792832). On the River Trent. D Pump out, gas, overnight and long-term mooring, winter storage, slipway, boat sales, chandlery, laundrette, toilets and showers. Caravan and camping site. Bar and restaurant on site.

BOAT TRIPS

Nb Pochard carries up to 70 people, with a bar and buffet. Based at Sawley Marina, NG10 3AE (01509 813311).

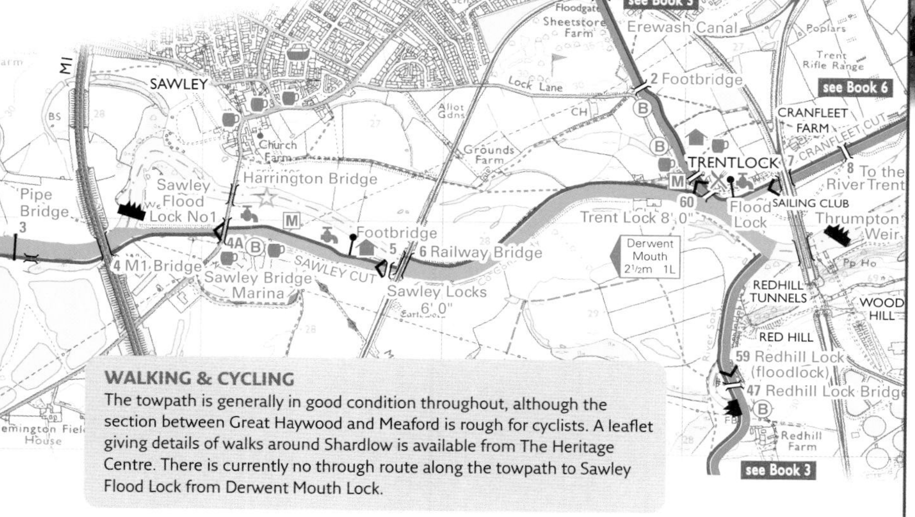

WALKING & CYCLING

The towpath is generally in good condition throughout, although the section between Great Haywood and Meaford is rough for cyclists. A leaflet giving details of walks around Shardlow is available from The Heritage Centre. There is currently no through route along the towpath to Sawley Flood Lock from Derwent Mouth Lock.

NAVIGATIONAL NOTES

1 Those leaving the canal and heading towards the River Trent should not pass Shardlow floodgates if the warning light shows red.
2 The Derwent is not navigable north of Derwent Mouth.

● **Sawley Cut**
In addition to a large marina and a well-patronised BW mooring site, the Derby Motor Boat Club has a base on the Sawley Cut. There are windlasses for sale at Sawley Lock, as well as the more conventional facilities, and BW showers. It is beautifully tended, with lots of flowers and some jokey sculptures. Have a look at the flood level markers – they are astonishing!

● **Shardlow**
Derbs. PO, tel, stores, garage. Few canal travellers will want to pass through Shardlow without stopping. Everywhere there are living examples of large-scale canal architecture, as well as long-established necessities such as canal pubs. By the lock is the biggest and best of these buildings – the 18th-C Trent Mill, now the Clock Warehouse. Restored in 1979, it has a large central arch where boats once entered to unload.

Shardlow Heritage Centre London Road, Shardlow DE72 2GA (adjacent to the Clock Warehouse (www.homepages.which.net/~shardlow.heritage/). Exhibitions of local canal history and replica of a narrowboat back cabin. Plus a calendar of canal-centred events. *Open Easter–Oct, Sat, Sun and B Hols 12.00–17.00.* Modest entry charge.

Pubs and Restaurants

The Clock Warehouse London Road, Shardlow DE72 2GA (01332 792844). Real ale, and food *L and E, all day.* Children welcome, and there is a garden. Moorings.

The Old Marina Bar & Restaurant Shardlow Marina, London Road, Shardlow DE72 2GA (01332 799797; www.theoldmarinabar.co.uk). Meals *L and E;* carvery *Sun 12.00–16.00;* specials during *week*. Outside seating. Children welcome. Live music *Fri and Sat.*

The Navigation Inn 143 London Road, Shardlow DE722HJ (01332 792918). By bridge 3. Haunted pub, serving real ale, and home-made food *L and E,* including *Sun* carvery. Garden with children's play area. Moorings. Live music *Fri.*

The Malt Shovel 49 The Wharf, Shardlow DE72 2GH (01332 799763). By bridge 2. Friendly canalside pub, built in 1779 and serving real ale. Excellent food with home-made specials *L only (not Sun).* Children welcome. Outside seating.

The New Inn The Wharf, Shardlow DE72 2HG (01332 793330). Next to the Malt Shovel. Real ale, and bar meals *L and E.* Children welcome. Garden and outside seating.

The Thai Kitchen 3 Wilne Lane, Shardlow DE72 2HA (01332 792331). Authentic Thai food *L and E* in a restaurant haunted by the 'lady in grey'. Children welcome.

The Old Crown Cavendish Bridge, Shardlow DE72 2HL (01332 792392). Friendly riverside pub. Real ale. Bar meals *L* , and *E Mon–Thu.* Children welcome. Garden with play area. B & B.

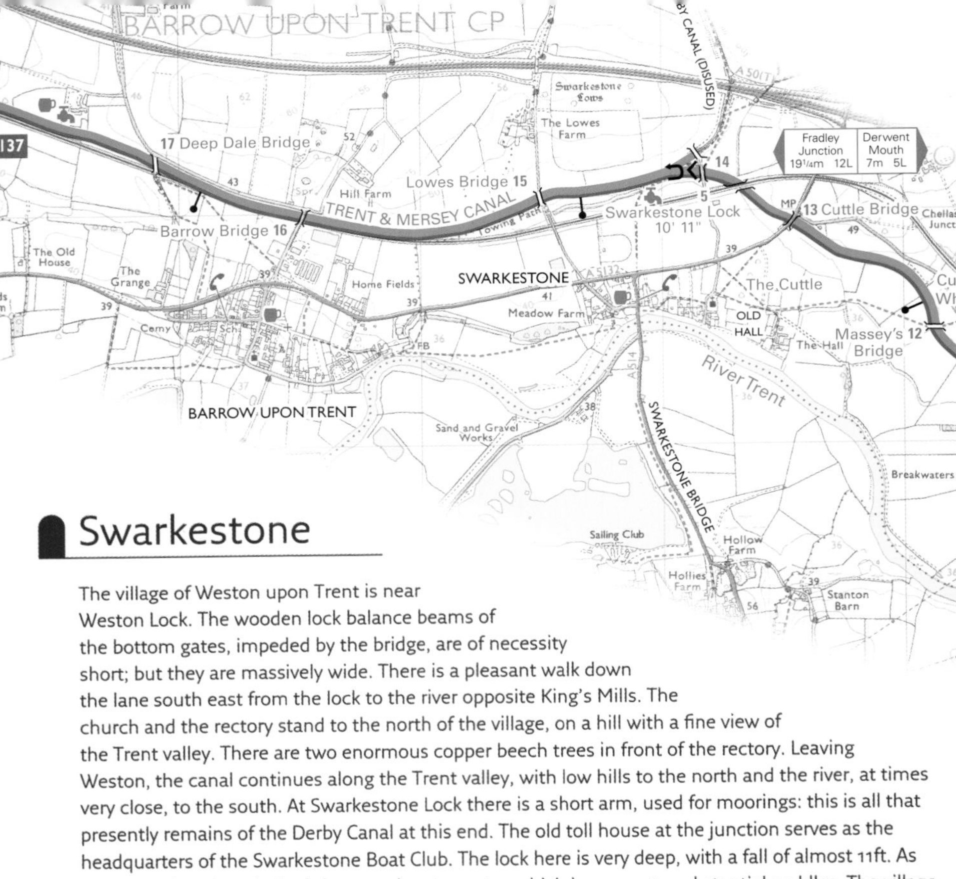

Swarkestone

The village of Weston upon Trent is near Weston Lock. The wooden lock balance beams of the bottom gates, impeded by the bridge, are of necessity short; but they are massively wide. There is a pleasant walk down the lane south east from the lock to the river opposite King's Mills. The church and the rectory stand to the north of the village, on a hill with a fine view of the Trent valley. There are two enormous copper beech trees in front of the rectory. Leaving Weston, the canal continues along the Trent valley, with low hills to the north and the river, at times very close, to the south. At Swarkestone Lock there is a short arm, used for moorings: this is all that presently remains of the Derby Canal at this end. The old toll house at the junction serves as the headquarters of the Swarkestone Boat Club. The lock here is very deep, with a fall of almost 11ft. As with the other deep locks, it has very low top gates which incorporate substantial paddles. The village of Barrow upon Trent lies between the canal and the river – the countryside is green and pleasant, with only the occasional train rumbling by to disturb the peace.

Weston upon Trent

Derbs. Tel, stores. A scattered village that is in fact not very close to the Trent. The isolated church is splendidly situated beside woods on top of a hill, its sturdy tower crowned by a short 14th-C spire. Inside are fine aisle windows of the same period. The lock gardens make the approach from the canal particularly attractive.

Swarkestone

Derbs. Tel, stores. The main feature of Swarkestone is the 18th-C five-arch stone bridge over the main channel of the River Trent. An elevated causeway then carries the road on stone arches all the way across the Trent's flood plain to the village of Stanton by Bridge. It was at Swarkestone that Bonnie Prince Charlie, in the rising of 1745, gave up his attempt for the throne of England and returned to his defeat at Culloden. In a field nearby are the few remains of Sir Richard Harpur's Tudor mansion, which was demolished before 1750. The Summer House, a handsome, lonely building, overlooks a square enclosure called the Cuttle. Jacobean in origin, it is thought that it may have been the scene of bull-baiting, although it seems more likely it was just a 'bowle alley'. Restored by the Landmark Trust, it is available for holiday lets – telephone (01628) 825925 for details. The Harpurs moved to Calke following the demolition of their mansion after the Civil War. The pub in the village, and monuments in the church, which is tucked away in the back lanes, are a reminder of the family.

Barrow upon Trent

Derbs. Tel, stores. A small, quiet village set back from the canal. A lane from the church leads down to the River Trent. Opposite there is a 'pinfold', once an enclosure for stray animals. The surviving lodge house stands opposite a mellow terrace of old workmen's cottages.

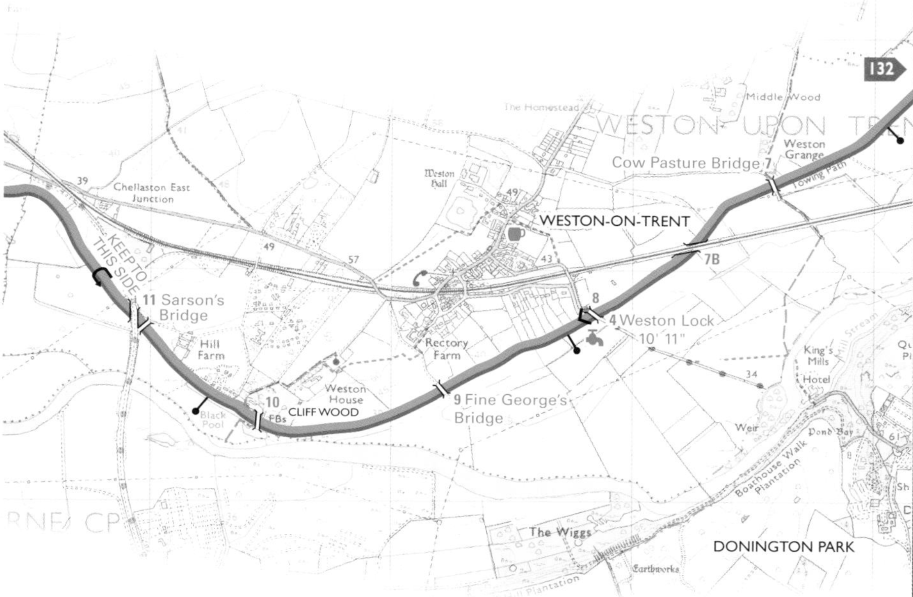

Pubs and Restaurants

The Old Plough Inn 1 Main Street, Weston-upon-Trent DE72 2BL (01332 700331). Attractive pub serving real ale. Food, with good choice for children, available *L and E*. Outside seating.

The Crew & Harpur Arms Woodshop Lane, Swarkestone DE73 1JA (01332 700641). By the river bridge. Real ale, and bar meals served *all day* in this handsome pub. Riverside seating and garden. Moorings.

The Ragley Boat Stop Deepdale Lane, off Sinfin Lane, Barrow-on-Trent DE73 1HH (01332 703919; www.king-henrys-taverns.co.uk). Large pub 300yds west of bridge 17, serving real ale. Food is available *L and E, and all day Sun*. Extensive vegetarian and children's menus. Children welcome. Outside seating in a 3-acre garden. Good moorings.

A HOP, A SKIP, AND A JUMP TO DERBY

The Derby Canal, which left the Trent & Mersey at Swarkestone and joined the Erewash at Sandiacre, has long been disused. One condition of its building, and a constant drain on its profits, was the free carriage of 5000 tons of coal to Derby each year, for the use of the poor.

But one of the most unusual loads was transported on 19 April 1826, when 'a fine lama, a kangaroo, a ram with four horns, and a female goat with two young kids, remarkably handsome animals' arrived in Derby by canal 'as a present from Lord Byron to a Gentleman whose residence is in the neighbourhood, all of which had been picked up in the course of the voyage of the *Blonde* to the Sandwich Islands in the autumn of 1824'.

Willington

Just by bridge 18 is Arleston House, an attractive old building with ground-floor walls of stone and the upper tiers of brick. This is followed by Stenson Lock, the last of the wide locks until Middlewich – it has a massive fall of 12ft 4in, and is overlooked by a useful coffee shop. Stenson is a small farming centre and a popular mooring spot with a large marina. After passing through a railway bridge, the canal changes course and heads off in a south easterly direction towards Burton upon Trent.

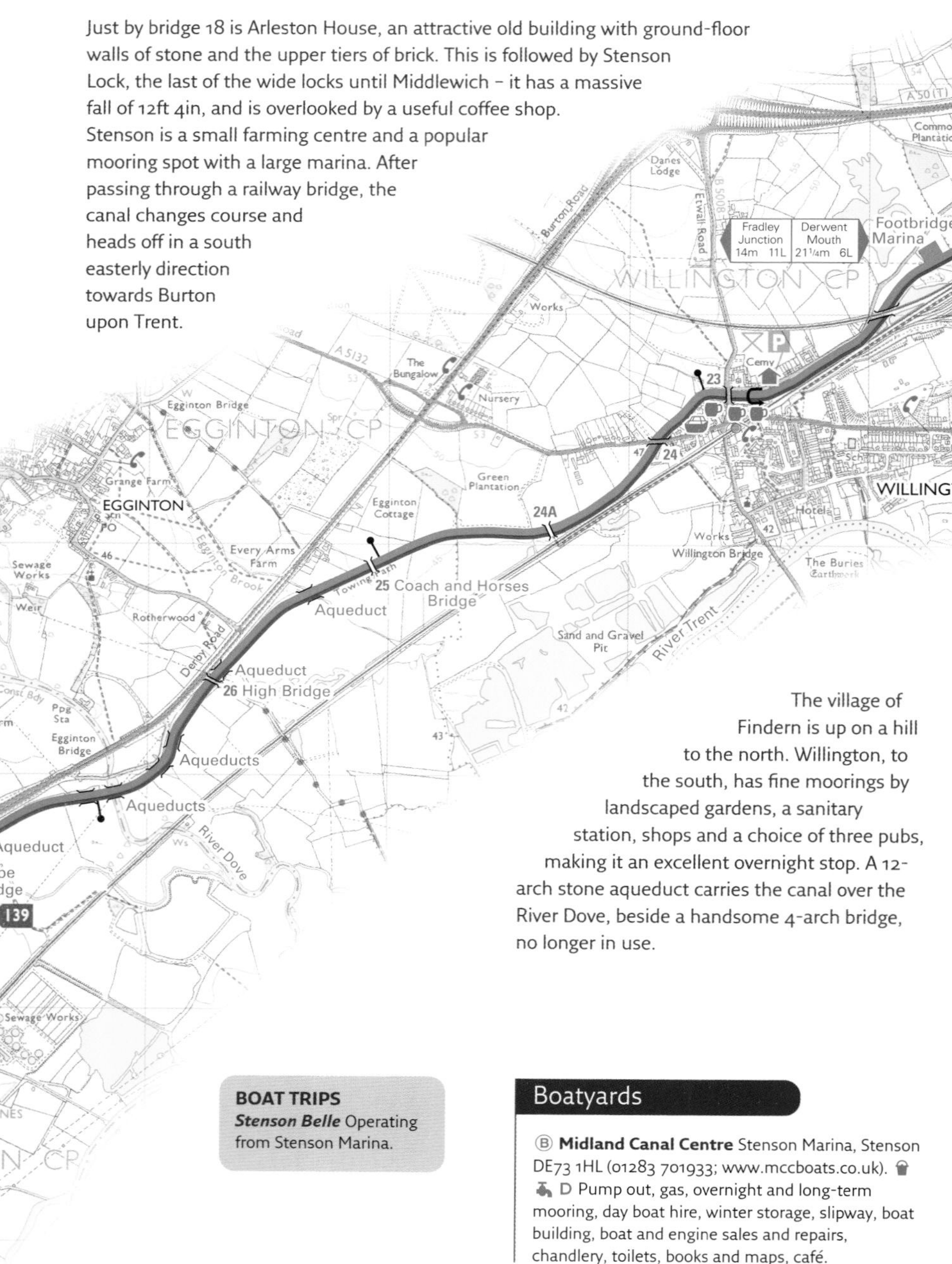

The village of Findern is up on a hill to the north. Willington, to the south, has fine moorings by landscaped gardens, a sanitary station, shops and a choice of three pubs, making it an excellent overnight stop. A 12-arch stone aqueduct carries the canal over the River Dove, beside a handsome 4-arch bridge, no longer in use.

BOAT TRIPS
Stenson Belle Operating from Stenson Marina.

Boatyards

Ⓑ **Midland Canal Centre** Stenson Marina, Stenson DE73 1HL (01283 701933; www.mccboats.co.uk). D Pump out, gas, overnight and long-term mooring, day boat hire, winter storage, slipway, boat building, boat and engine sales and repairs, chandlery, toilets, books and maps, café.

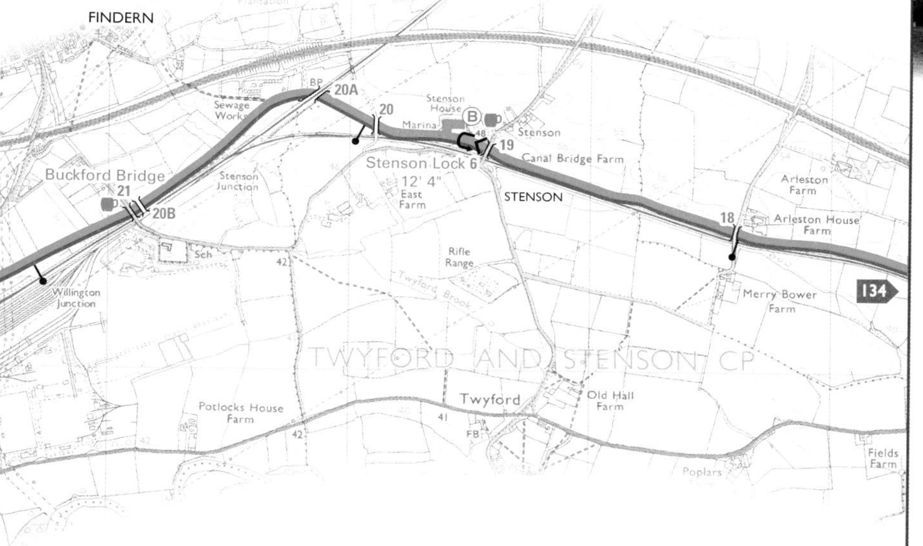

Repton
Derbs. PO. 1½ miles south east of Willington (over the River Trent) is Repton, one of the oldest towns in England, which was once the capital of Mercia. The crypt below St Wystan's Church was built in the 10th C. One of the finest examples of Saxon architecture in the country, this crypt was completely forgotten until the end of the 18th C when a man fell into it while digging a grave. Repton public school dates from 1557, and there is much of historical interest in the school and the town.

Willington
Derbs. PO, tel, stores, delicatessen. The railway bisects this busy little village on an embankment. There are three pubs, all close together.

Findern
Derbs. PO, tel, stores. A small, quiet village where Jedekiah Strutt, the inventor of the ribbed stocking frame, served a 7-year apprenticeship with the local wheelwright. At one time the village green was no more than a waste patch used by cars as a short cut, and a parking place. When suggestions were made to turn it into a formal cross roads, the indignant Women's Institute galvanised the villagers into actually uprooting all traces of tarmac from the green and turfing the whole area properly.

Egginton
Derbs. A quiet village lying off the A38. The church, set apart from the village, is pleasingly irregular from the outside, with a large chancel and a squat tower.

Pubs and Restaurants

The Bubble Inn Stenson DE73 1HL (01283 703113; www.thebubbleinn.com). Alongside Stenson Lock and Marina, this modern pub in a converted barn serves real ale and bar meals *L and E (not L & E Sun).* Children welcome. Garden.

The Wheel Inn Main Street, Findern DE65 6AG (01283 703365; www.thefindernwheel.co.uk). Meals available *L and E, daily.* Garden, barbecue and children's play area. Quiz *Wed and Sun.*

The Rising Sun The Green, Willington DE65 6BP (01283 702116). Friendly village pub serving real ale. Reasonably priced bar food,including home-made pies, available *L and E.* Children welcome. Outside seating. Occasional live music.

The Green Dragon 11 The Green, Willington DE65 6BP (01283 702327). Popular and welcoming pub, with plenty of low beams. Real ale. Wide range of food available *L and E.* Garden. Children welcome away from the bar. Moorings.

Nadee Heath Lane, Findern DE65 6AR (01283 701333; www.nadeerestaurant.co.uk). Adjacent to canal at bridge 21. Bar and Indian restaurant. Landscaped garden, including a 5-a-side football pitch. Children welcome. *Open all day during season, E only during winter.*

Burton upon Trent

Logs, coal and *diesel* are available between bridges 28 and 29. *Fish & chips* can be obtained 100yds north of Horninglow Basin, which has some services and a butterfly garden. The canal then passes along one side of Burton upon Trent, without entering the town. Many of the old canalside buildings have been demolished, but the waterside has been nicely tidied up, making the passage very pleasant. The lovely aroma of brewing - malt and hops - often pervades the town, usually strongest to the west. Dallow Lock is the first of the narrow locks, an altogether easier job of work than the wider ones to the east. Shobnall Basin is now used by a boatyard, and visitor moorings nearby are available from which to explore the town. The A38 then joins the canal, depriving the navigator of any peace. On the hills to the north west is the well-wooded Sinai Park - the moated 15th-C house here, now a farm, used to be the summer home of the monks from Burton Abbey. There is a fine canalside pub at bridge 34, and a *shop* selling provisions, home-made cakes and crafts. It is *open Easter-Oct, daily 09.00-18.00*. The canal enters the National Forest at bridge 30 - indeed an intricately carved seat reminds us of this - and will leave it just beyond Alrewas. The Bass Millennium Woodland, to the west of Branston Lock, is part of this major project.

Burton upon Trent
Staffs. All services. Known widely for its brewing industry, which originated here in the 13th C, when the monks at Burton Abbey discovered that an excellent beer could be brewed from the town's waters, because of their high gypsum content. At one time there were 31 breweries producing 3 million barrels of ale annually: alas, now only a few remain. The advent of the railways had an enormous effect on the street geography of Burton, for gradually a great network of railways took shape, connecting with each other and with the main line. These branches were mostly constructed at street level, and until recent years it was common for road traffic to be held up by endless goods trains chugging all over the town. Only the last vestiges of this system now remain. The east side of the town is bounded by the River Trent, on the other side of which are pleasant hills. The main shopping centre lies to the east of the railway station.
Marston's Brewery Visitor Centre Shobnall Road, Burton upon Trent DE14 2BW (01283 507391; www.marstonsbeercompany.co.uk). Tours of the brewery, including the unique and world-famous Burton Union system are available *Mon-Fri*. At the end of the tour you can enjoy a drink of real ale in the Visitor Centre. *Please telephone or visit website to check availability and to book.*
Brewhouse Arts Centre Union Street, Burton upon Trent DE14 1EB (01283 508100; www.little-theatre.co.uk). Live entertainment in a 230-seat theatre, plus a gallery and bistro bar.
Tourist Information Centre 183 High Street, Burton upon Trent DE14 1NG (01283 508111).

Shobnall Basin
This is all that remains of the Bond End Canal, which gave the breweries the benefit of what was modern transport, before the coming of the railways.

Branston
Staffs. PO, tel, stores, garage, butcher, Chinese takeaway, fish & chips. This is apparently the place where the famous pickle originated.

Boatyards

Ⓑ **Jannel Cruisers** Shobnall Marina, Shobnall Road, Burton upon Trent DE14 2AU (01283 540006; www.jannel.co.uk). In Shobnall Basin. D Pump out, gas, narrowboat hire, overnight mooring, long-term mooring, winter storage, slipway, dry dock, chandlery, books and maps, boat-fitting, boat sales, engine sales and repairs, toilets.

WALKING & CYCLING

Cycle Route 54 uses the towpath north of Burton upon Trent. It links Lichfield with Derby. Three walking trails around Burton upon Trent are available from the TIC. There are pleasant walks through Branston Water Park - telephone 01283 508573 for more information.

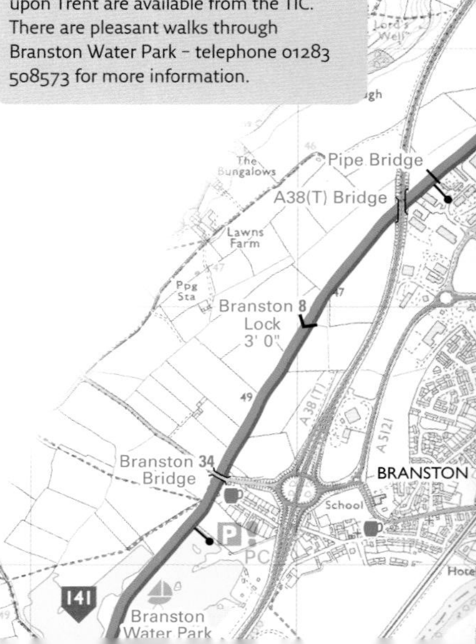

NAVIGATIONAL NOTES

A BW key is needed for Dallow Lock.

Pubs and Restaurants

The Mill House Milford Drive, Stretton Park DE13 0LA (01283 535133). Family friendly pub nicely situated by the canal. Real ale. Food available *all day*, with a children's menu. *24hr* mooring. Children's soft play area.

The Brewhouse Union Street, Burton upon Trent DE14 1EB (01283 508100; www.little-theatre.co.uk). At the Arts Centre. Coffee and meals, *L and E (up to 1 hour before a performance).*

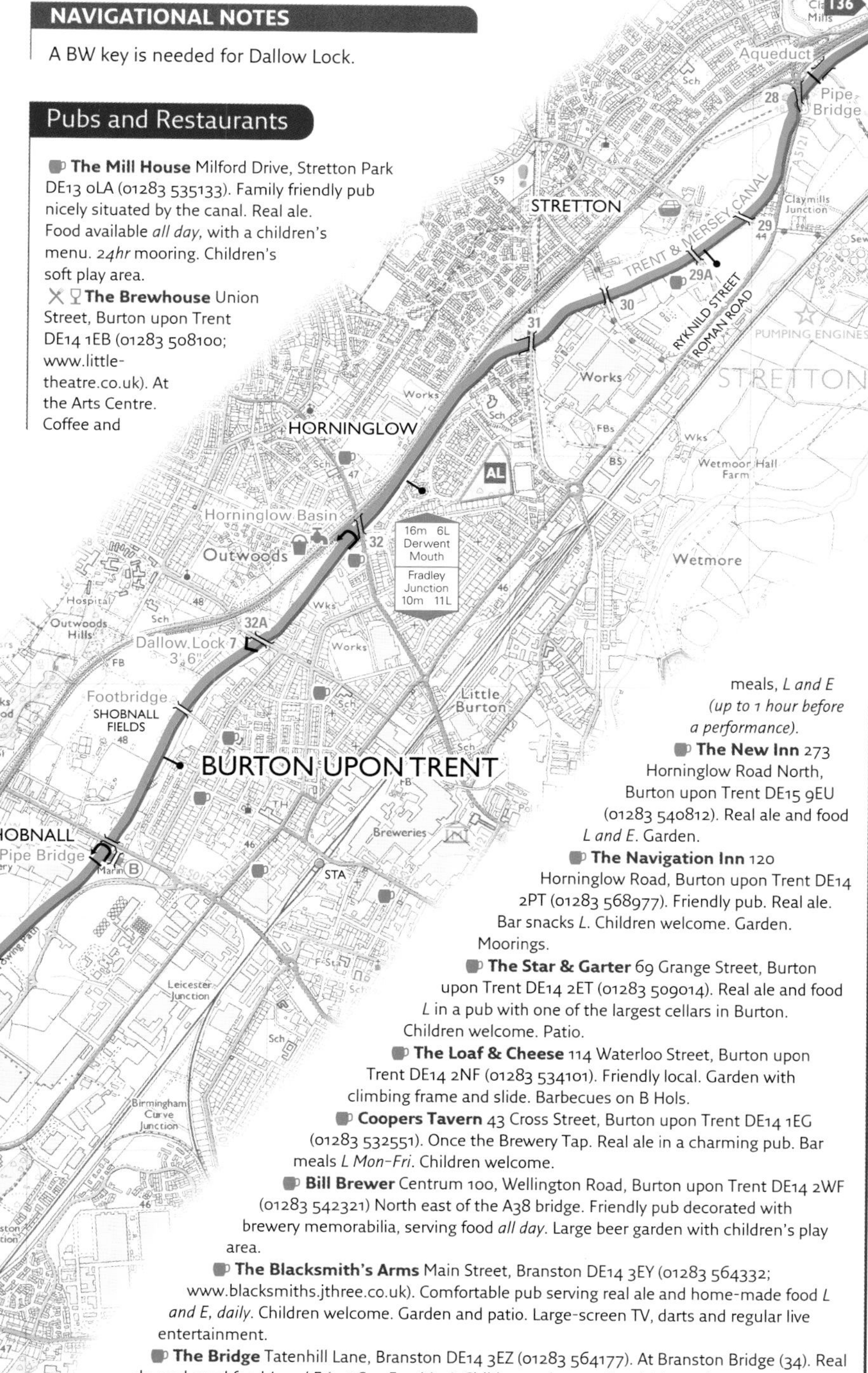

The New Inn 273 Horninglow Road North, Burton upon Trent DE15 9EU (01283 540812). Real ale and food *L and E*. Garden.

The Navigation Inn 120 Horninglow Road, Burton upon Trent DE14 2PT (01283 568977). Friendly pub. Real ale. Bar snacks *L*. Children welcome. Garden. Moorings.

The Star & Garter 69 Grange Street, Burton upon Trent DE14 2ET (01283 509014). Real ale and food *L* in a pub with one of the largest cellars in Burton. Children welcome. Patio.

The Loaf & Cheese 114 Waterloo Street, Burton upon Trent DE14 2NF (01283 534101). Friendly local. Garden with climbing frame and slide. Barbecues on B Hols.

Coopers Tavern 43 Cross Street, Burton upon Trent DE14 1EG (01283 532551). Once the Brewery Tap. Real ale in a charming pub. Bar meals *L Mon–Fri*. Children welcome.

Bill Brewer Centrum 100, Wellington Road, Burton upon Trent DE14 2WF (01283 542321) North east of the A38 bridge. Friendly pub decorated with brewery memorabilia, serving food *all day*. Large beer garden with children's play area.

The Blacksmith's Arms Main Street, Branston DE14 3EY (01283 564332; www.blacksmiths.jthree.co.uk). Comfortable pub serving real ale and home-made food *L and E, daily*. Children welcome. Garden and patio. Large-screen TV, darts and regular live entertainment.

The Bridge Tatenhill Lane, Branston DE14 3EZ (01283 564177). At Branston Bridge (34). Real ale, and good food *L and E (not Sun E or Mon)*. Children welcome. Canalside garden.

Barton Turn

Beside Tatenhill Lock there is an attractive cottage; at the tail of the lock is yet another of the tiny narrow brick bridges that are such an engaging feature of this navigation. Note the very fine National Forest seat just north of the lock – there is another at Bagnall Lock, along with a 'living willow' sculpture. After passing flooded gravel pits and negotiating another tiny brick arch at bridge 36, the canal and the A38, the old Roman road, come very close together – thankfully the settlement of Barton Turn has been bypassed, leaving the main street (the old Roman road of Ryknild Street) wide and empty. It is with great relief that Wychnor Lock, with its diminutive crane and warehouse, is reached – here the A38 finally parts company with the canal, and some peace returns. To the west is the little 14th-C Wychnor church. Before Alrewas Lock the canal actually joins the River Trent – there is a large well-marked weir which should be given a wide berth. The canal then winds through the pretty village of Alrewas, passing the old church, several thatched cottages and a charming brick bridge.

- **Barton-under-Needwood**
  Staffs. PO, tel, stores, bank, garage. Many years ago, when there were few roads and no canals in the Midlands, the only reasonable access to this village was by turning off the old Roman road, Ryknild Street: hence, probably, the name Barton Turn. The village is indeed worth turning off for, although unfortunately it is nearly a mile from the canal. A pleasant footpath from Barton Turn Lock leads quietly to the village, which is set on a slight hill. Its long main street has many attractive pubs. The church is battlemented and surrounded by a very tidy churchyard. Pleasantly uniform in style, it was built in the 16th C by John Taylor, Henry VIII's private secretary, on the site of his cottage birthplace. The former Royal Forest of Needwood is to the north of the village.
- **Wychnor**
  Staffs. A tiny farming settlement around the church of St Leonards.
- **Alrewas**
  Staffs. PO, tel, stores, garage, butcher, chemist, tearoom, fish & chips. Just far enough away from the A513, this is an attractive village whose rambling back lanes harbour some excellent timbered cottages. The canal's meandering passage through the village, passing well tended gardens and a bowling green, and the presence of the church and its pleasant churchyard creates a friendly and unruffled atmosphere. The River Trent touches the village, and once fed the old Cotton Mill (now converted into dwellings), and provides it with a fine background which is much appreciated by fishermen. The somewhat unusual name Alrewas, pronounced 'olrewus', is a corruption of the words Alder Wash – a reference to the many alder trees which once grew in the often-flooded Trent valley and gave rise to the basket weaving for which the village was once famous.

Alrewas Church Mill End Lane, Alrewas DE13 7BT. A spacious building of mainly 13th-C and 14th-C construction, notable for the old leper window, which is now filled by modern stained glass.

Boatyards

Ⓑ **Barton Turns Marina** Barton Turn, Barton-under-Needwood DE13 8DZ (01283 711666; www.bartonmarina.co.uk). D Pump out, gas, overnight and long-term mooring, winter storage, slipway, boat sales and repairs, engine repairs, chandlery, toilets, showers, books, maps and gifts, laundrette. Also pub, restaurant and shops, including a deli and bakery/butcher.

Boat Doctor (01332 771622). Marine engineer with *24hr emergency breakdown call out.*

Ⓑ **Wychnor Moorings** Wychnor, Burton upon Trent DE13 8BY (07778 668388). Pump out, gas, long-term mooring, coal.

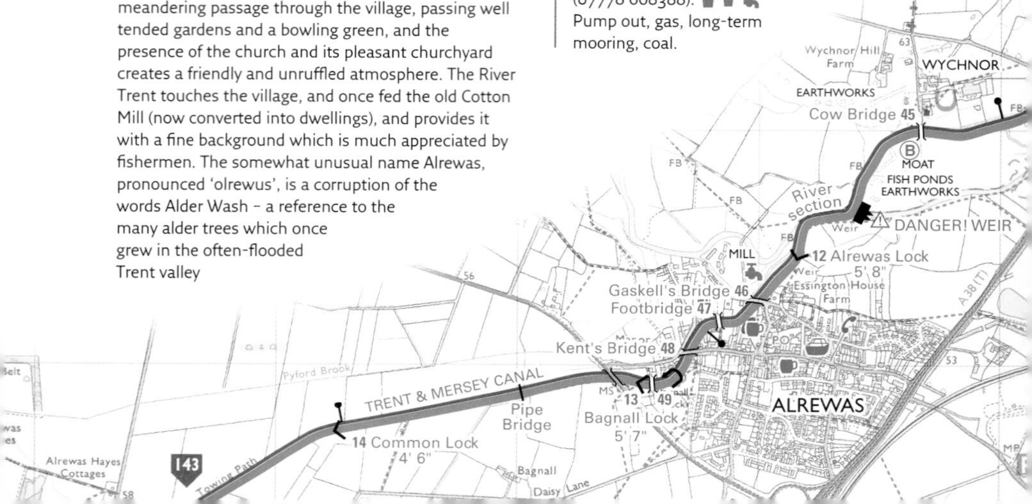

NAVIGATIONAL NOTES

In times of flood great caution should be exercised along the stretch immediately north of Alrewas Lock – keep well over to the towpath side at all times.

Pubs and Restaurants

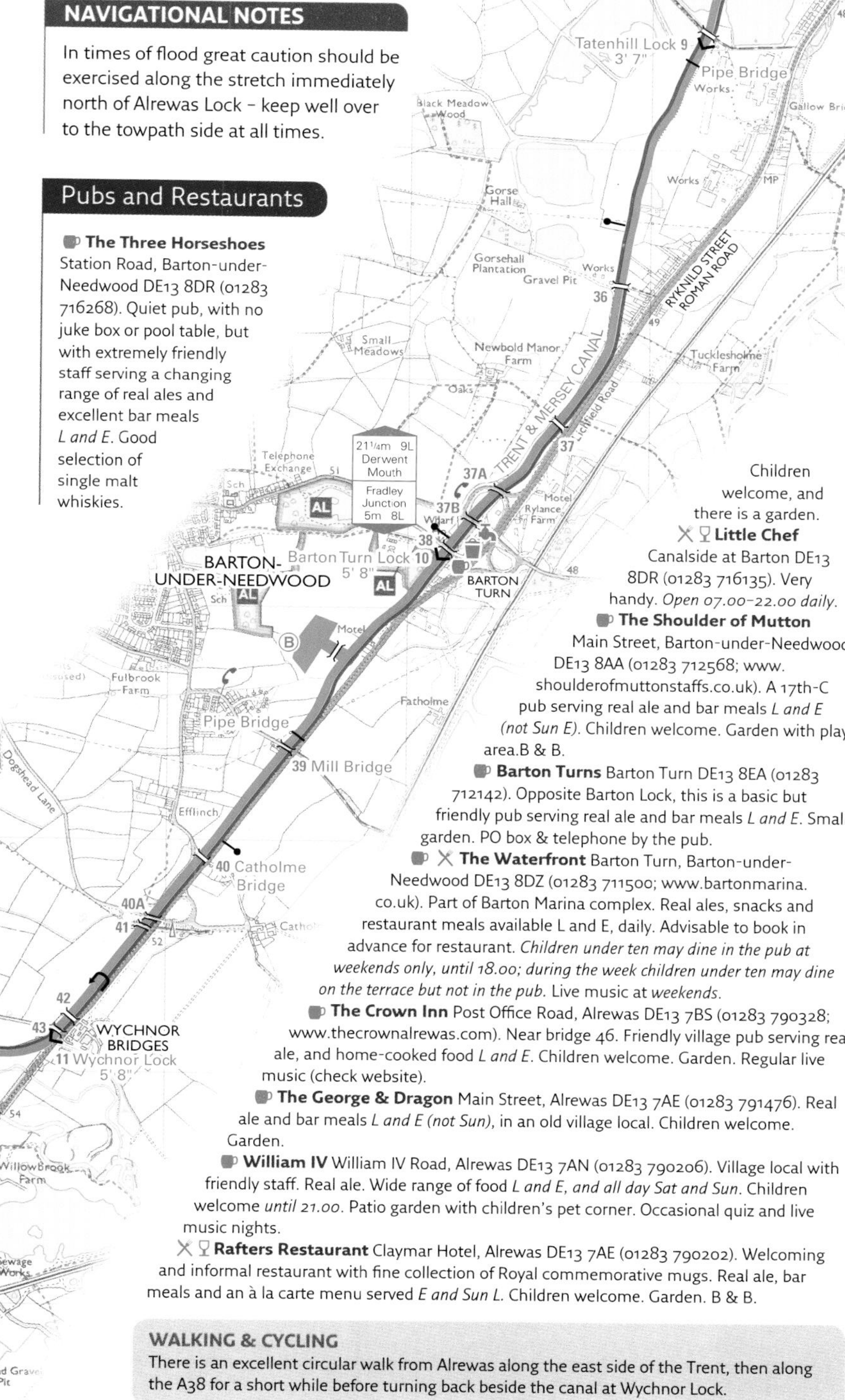

The Three Horseshoes Station Road, Barton-under-Needwood DE13 8DR (01283 716268). Quiet pub, with no juke box or pool table, but with extremely friendly staff serving a changing range of real ales and excellent bar meals *L and E*. Good selection of single malt whiskies. Children welcome, and there is a garden.

Little Chef Canalside at Barton DE13 8DR (01283 716135). Very handy. *Open 07.00–22.00 daily.*

The Shoulder of Mutton Main Street, Barton-under-Needwood DE13 8AA (01283 712568; www.shoulderofmuttonstaffs.co.uk). A 17th-C pub serving real ale and bar meals *L and E (not Sun E)*. Children welcome. Garden with play area.B & B.

Barton Turns Barton Turn DE13 8EA (01283 712142). Opposite Barton Lock, this is a basic but friendly pub serving real ale and bar meals *L and E*. Small garden. PO box & telephone by the pub.

The Waterfront Barton Turn, Barton-under-Needwood DE13 8DZ (01283 711500; www.bartonmarina.co.uk). Part of Barton Marina complex. Real ales, snacks and restaurant meals available L and E, daily. Advisable to book in advance for restaurant. *Children under ten may dine in the pub at weekends only, until 18.00; during the week children under ten may dine on the terrace but not in the pub.* Live music at *weekends*.

The Crown Inn Post Office Road, Alrewas DE13 7BS (01283 790328; www.thecrownalrewas.com). Near bridge 46. Friendly village pub serving real ale, and home-cooked food *L and E*. Children welcome. Garden. Regular live music (check website).

The George & Dragon Main Street, Alrewas DE13 7AE (01283 791476). Real ale and bar meals *L and E (not Sun)*, in an old village local. Children welcome. Garden.

William IV William IV Road, Alrewas DE13 7AN (01283 790206). Village local with friendly staff. Real ale. Wide range of food *L and E, and all day Sat and Sun*. Children welcome *until 21.00*. Patio garden with children's pet corner. Occasional quiz and live music nights.

Rafters Restaurant Claymar Hotel, Alrewas DE13 7AE (01283 790202). Welcoming and informal restaurant with fine collection of Royal commemorative mugs. Real ale, bar meals and an à la carte menu served *E and Sun L*. Children welcome. Garden. B & B.

WALKING & CYCLING

There is an excellent circular walk from Alrewas along the east side of the Trent, then along the A38 for a short while before turning back beside the canal at Wychnor Lock.

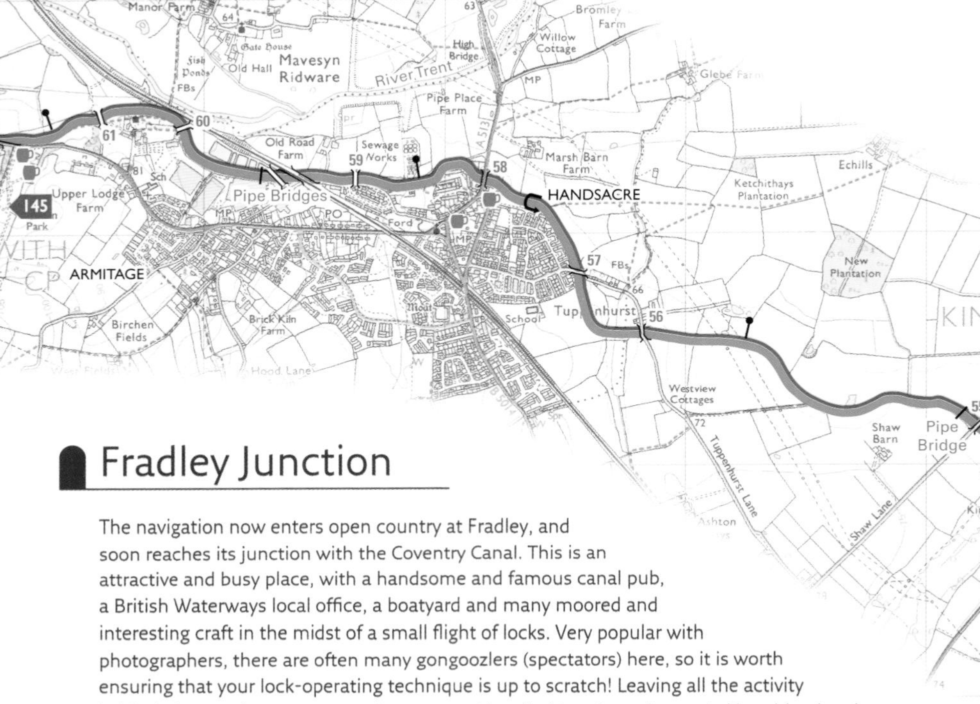

Fradley Junction

The navigation now enters open country at Fradley, and soon reaches its junction with the Coventry Canal. This is an attractive and busy place, with a handsome and famous canal pub, a British Waterways local office, a boatyard and many moored and interesting craft in the midst of a small flight of locks. Very popular with photographers, there are often many gongoozlers (spectators) here, so it is worth ensuring that your lock-operating technique is up to scratch! Leaving all the activity behind, the canal soon enters quiet countryside, climbing through wooded heathland and abruptly changing its course from south west to north west, a direction it generally maintains right through to its terminus at Preston Brook, over 67 miles away. The isolated Woodend Lock introduces a further stretch of woodland; beyond this the canal winds towards Handsacre. Armitage soon follows as the railway crosses and the Trent comes very close. There is a useful *general store* 500yds south of bridge 59, and *fish & chips* and a *café* near bridge 58.

NAVIGATIONAL NOTES

West of bridge 61 the canal is very narrow, due to the removal of Armitage Tunnel, and wide enough for one boat only. Check that the canal is clear before proceeding.

Boatyards

Ⓑ **Swan Line Cruisers** Fradley Junction, Alrewras DE13 7DN (01283 790332). D Pump out, gas, narrowboat hire, overnight mooring, long term mooring, boat building, boat sales and engine repairs, chandlery, books and maps, gifts, groceries.

Ⓑ **King's Bromley Wharf Marina** Lichfield Road, Bromley Hayes WS13 8HT (01543 417209; www.kingsbromleymarina.co.uk). D Pump out, gas, overnight and long-term mooring, slipway, boat sales, chandlery, coal, toilets, showers, laundrette.

Fradley Junction
Alrewas DE13 7DN. A long-established canal centre where the Coventry Canal joins the Trent & Mersey. Like all the best focal points on the waterways, it is concerned solely with the life of the canals, and has no relationship with local roads or even with the village of Fradley. The junction bristles with boats for, apart from it being an inevitable meeting place for canal craft, there is a boatyard, a British Waterways information centre and café (01283 790236, guided tours), BW moorings, a boat club, a popular pub and another café at the holiday park – all in the middle of a 5-lock flight.

- **Kings Bromley**

  Staffs. PO, tel, stores. A village 1½ miles north of bridge 54, along the A515. There are some pleasant houses and an old mill to be seen here, as well as what is reputed to have been Lady Godiva's early home. The Trent flows just beyond the church, which contains some old glass. A large cross in the southern part of the churchyard is known locally as Godiva's cross.

- **Armitage**

  Staffs. PO, tel, stores, garage. A main road village, whose church is interesting: it was rebuilt in the 19th C in a Saxon/Norman style, which makes it rather dark. The organ is 200 years old and it is enormous: it came from Lichfield Cathedral and practically deafens the organist at Armitage.

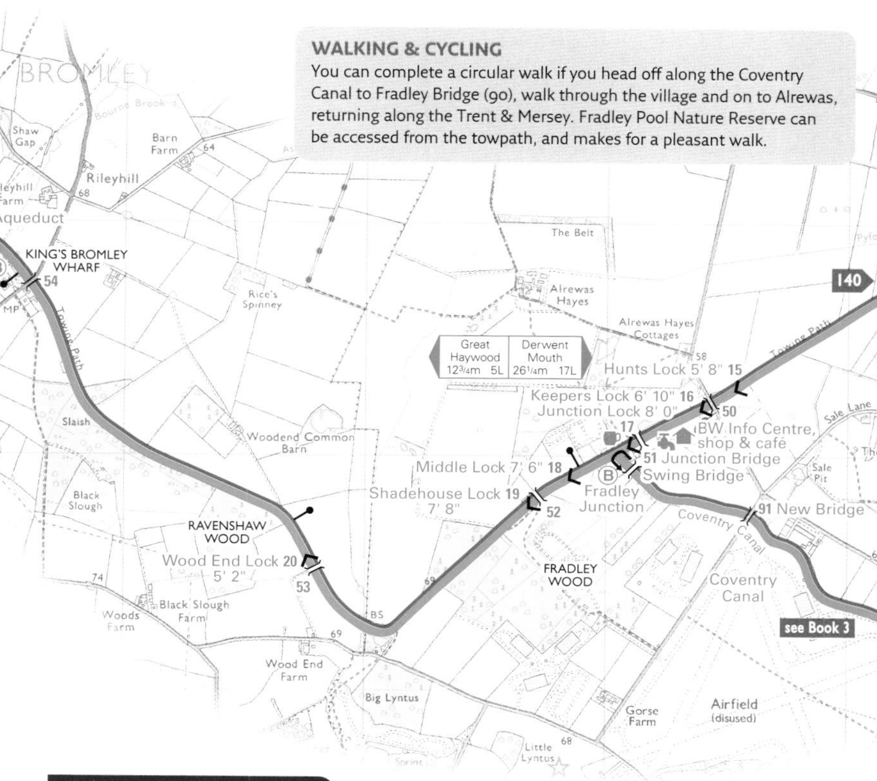

WALKING & CYCLING

You can complete a circular walk if you head off along the Coventry Canal to Fradley Bridge (90), walk through the village and on to Alrewas, returning along the Trent & Mersey. Fradley Pool Nature Reserve can be accessed from the towpath, and makes for a pleasant walk.

Pubs and Restaurants

The Swan Fradley Junction, Alewras DE13 7DN (01283 790330; www.theswanatfradley.co.uk). Known as 'The Mucky Duck'. Canalside, it is the focus of the junction and justly famous, this is reputedly one of the most photographed pubs in the country! It is in a 200-year-old listed building, with a fine public bar warmed by a coal fire, a comfortable lounge, and a vaulted cellar room. Real ale, and bar meals are served *L and E*, with a carvery *Sun L*. There is a flowered patio at the rear.

The Crown The Green, Handsacre WS15 4DT (01543 490239). At bridge 58. Welcoming 300-year-old pub serving real ale. Family room, and a garden. Good moorings. Occasional entertainment.

Old Peculiar The Green, Handsacre WS15 4DP (01543 491891). Traditional English pub. Real ale, and food available *L and E (not Mon or Tue L)*. Pretty garden. Children welcome.

The Spode Cottage Lower Lodge, Armitage WS15 4AT (01543 490353). Attractive pub serving real ale and meals *all day*. Children welcome. Outside seating, garden and children's play area. Live entertainment *first Sat of month*.

The Plum Pudding Brasserie Rugeley Road, Armitage WS15 4AZ (01543 490330; www.plumpudding.co.uk). Modern, award-winning restaurant serving real ale and meals *L and E*. Children welcome for meals only. Outside seating, including large, covered, canalside area used for eating and drinking. B & B.

Rugeley

The A513 crosses the canal on a new bridge where the short, 130yds long, Armitage Tunnel used to run before its roof was removed in 1971 to combat the subsidence effects of coal being mined nearby. To the west stands Spode House, a former home of the pottery family. The huge power station at Rugeley, tidied up now, comes into view – and takes a long time to recede. There are pleasant moorings at Rugeley, by bridge 66, with the town centre and shops only a short walk away. North of the town, the canal crosses the River Trent via a substantial aqueduct. It then enters an immensely attractive area full of interest. Accompanied by the River Trent, the canal moves up a narrowing valley bordered by green slopes on either side, Cannock Chase being clearly visible to the south. Wolseley Hall has gone, but Bishton Hall (now a school) still stands: its very elegant front faces the canal near Wolseley Bridge. There is a pub, an Indian restaurant and an antique, craft and garden centre just a short way to the south.

- **Spode House** WS15 1PU Spode House and Hawkesyard Priory stand side by side. The priory was founded in 1897 by Josiah Spode's grandson and his niece Helen Gulson when they lived at Spode House. The Priory is now known as Hawkesyard Hall, and is a restaurant and spa.
- **Rugeley**
  Staffs. PO, tel, stores, garage, banks, station, cinema. A bustling and much re-developed town, with many shops at the centre. There are two churches by bridge 67; one is a 14th-C ruin, the other is the parish church built in 1822 as a replacement.
- **Cannock Chase**
  Covering an area of 26 square miles, and designated as an Area of Outstanding Natural Beauty in 1949, the Chase is all that remains of what was once a Norman hunting ground known as the King's Forest of Cannock. Large parts are recognised as Sites of Special Scientific Interest, and exceptional flora and fauna are abundant. This includes a herd of fallow deer whose ancestors have grazed in this region for centuries. An area of 4½ square miles forms a Country Park, one of the largest in Britain. Near the Sherlock Valley an area was chosen in 1964 as the site of the Deutscher Soldatenfriedhof, and was built by the German War Graves Commission. It contains the graves of 2143 German servicemen from World War I, and 2786 from World War II. It is an intentionally sombre place. A small area is devoted to the crews of German airships, shot down over the UK in 1916 and 1917. There were two huge army camps on the Chase during World War I, but today little remains, apart from some anonymous and overgrown concrete foundations.
  Museum of Cannock Chase Valley Road, Hednesford WS12 1TD (01543 877666; www.cannockchasedc.gov.uk). This site was at one time the Valley Colliery. Local history and interactive galleries. *Open Jan-Mar, Mon-Fri 11.00-16.00; Apr-Oct, daily 11.00-17.00.* Free. Coffee shop, gift shop, visitor information and walks.

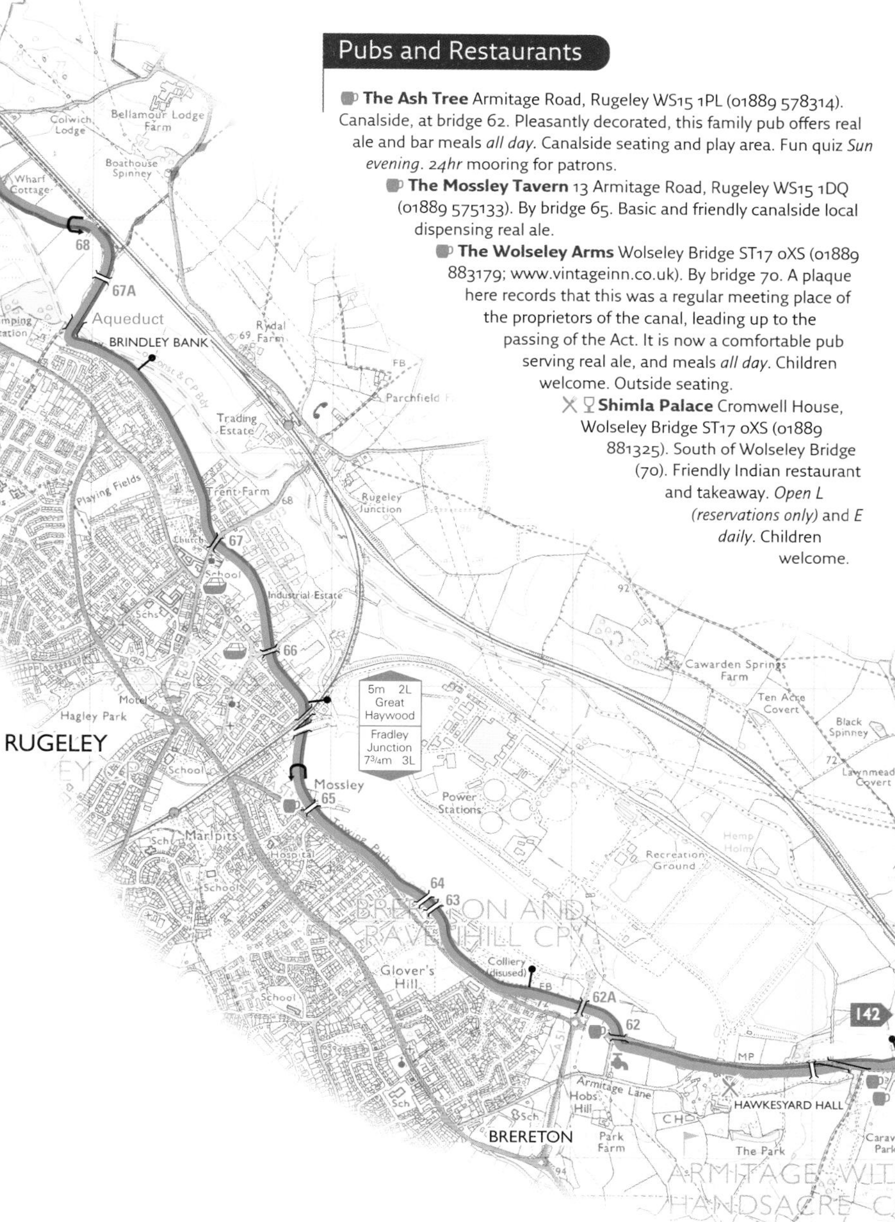

Pubs and Restaurants

The Ash Tree Armitage Road, Rugeley WS15 1PL (01889 578314). Canalside, at bridge 62. Pleasantly decorated, this family pub offers real ale and bar meals *all day*. Canalside seating and play area. Fun quiz *Sun evening*. *24hr* mooring for patrons.

The Mossley Tavern 13 Armitage Road, Rugeley WS15 1DQ (01889 575133). By bridge 65. Basic and friendly canalside local dispensing real ale.

The Wolseley Arms Wolseley Bridge ST17 0XS (01889 883179; www.vintageinn.co.uk). By bridge 70. A plaque here records that this was a regular meeting place of the proprietors of the canal, leading up to the passing of the Act. It is now a comfortable pub serving real ale, and meals *all day*. Children welcome. Outside seating.

Shimla Palace Cromwell House, Wolseley Bridge ST17 0XS (01889 881325). South of Wolseley Bridge (70). Friendly Indian restaurant and takeaway. *Open L (reservations only)* and *E daily*. Children welcome.

Great Haywood

The pleasant surroundings continue as the canal passes Colwich. As the perimeter of Shugborough Park is reached the impressive façade of the Hall can be seen across the parkland. Haywood Lock and a line of moored craft announce the presence of Great Haywood and the junction with the Staffordshire & Worcestershire Canal (*see* page 129), which joins the Trent & Mersey under a graceful and much photographed towpath bridge: just the other side there is a useful boatyard. Beyond the junction the Trent valley becomes much broader and more open. There is another boatyard by Hoo Mill Lock.

- **Little Haywood**
Staffs. PO box, stores. An elegant residential village, with a shop and two pubs.
- **Great Haywood**
Staffs. PO, tel, stores. Centre of the Great Haywood and Shugborough Conservation Area, the village is not particularly beautiful, but it is closely connected in many ways to Shugborough Park, to which it is physically linked by the very old Essex Bridge, where the crystal clear waters of the River Sow join the Trent on its way down from Stoke. Haywood Lock is beautifully situated between this packhorse bridge (which is an ancient monument) and the unusually decorative railway bridge that leads into Trent Lane. The lane consists of completely symmetrical and very handsome terraced cottages: they were built by the Ansons to house the people evicted from the former Shugborough village, the site of which is now occupied by the Arch of Hadrian within the park, built to celebrate Anson's circumnavigation of the globe in 1740-44. About 100yds south of Haywood Lock is an iron bridge over the canal. This bridge, which now leads nowhere, used to carry a private road from Shugborough Hall which crossed both the river and the canal on its way to the church just east of the railway. This was important to the Ansons, since the packhorse bridge just upstream is not wide enough for a horse and carriage, and so until the iron bridge was built the family had to *walk* the 300yds to church on Sunday mornings!

Shugborough Hall *NT.* Milford, near Stafford ST17 0XB (01889 881388; www.shugborough.org.uk). Walk west from Haywood Lock and through the park. The present house dates from 1693, but was substantially altered by James Stuart around 1760 and by Samuel Wyatt around the turn of the 18th C. It was at this time that the old village of Shugborough was bought up and demolished by the Anson family so that they should enjoy more privacy and space in their park. Family fortunes fluctuated greatly for the Ansons, the Earl of Lichfield's family; and crippling death duties in the 1960s brought about the transfer of the estate to the National Trust. The Trust has leased the property to Staffordshire County Council who now manage the whole estate. The house has been restored at great expense, and there are some magnificent rooms and many treasures inside.

Museum of Staffordshire Life This excellent establishment, Staffordshire's County Museum, is housed in the old stables adjacent to Shugborough Hall. Open since 1966, it is superbly laid out and contains all sorts of exhibits concerned with old country life in Staffordshire. Amongst many things it contains an old-fashioned laundry, the old gun-room and the old estate brew-house, all completely equipped. Part of the stables contains harness, carts, coaches and motor cars. There is an industrial annexe up the road, containing a collection of preserved steam locomotives and some industrial machinery.

Shugborough Park There are some remarkable sights in the large park which encircles the Hall. Thomas Anson, who inherited the estate in 1720, enlisted in 1744 the help of his famous brother, Admiral George Anson, to beautify and improve the house and the park. In 1762 he commissioned James Stuart, a neo-Grecian architect, to embellish the park. 'Athenian' Stuart set to with a will, and the spectacular results of his work can be seen scattered round the grounds. The stone monuments that he built have deservedly extravagant names such as the Tower of the Winds, the Lanthorn of Demosthenes and so on.

The Park Farm Designed by Samuel Wyatt, it contains an agricultural museum, a working mill and a rare breeds centre. Traditional country skills such as bread-making, butter-churning and cheese-making are demonstrated.
Open Apr-Oct daily 11.00-17.00. Charge. Parties must book. Tea rooms, shop.

Boatyards

Ⓑ **Anglo Welsh** The Canal Wharf, Mill Lane, Great Haywood ST18 0RJ (01889 881711; www.anglowelsh.co.uk). D Pump out, gas, narrowboat hire, day-hire craft, overnight and long-term mooring, boat sales, engine repairs, chandlery, toilets, books, maps and gifts.

Ⓑ **Engineering & Canal Services** Hoo Mill Boatyard, Hoo Mill Lane, Great Haywood ST18 0RG (01889 882611; mobile 07721 487561; engcanal@globalnet.co.uk) (modest charge) D Pump out, gas, overnight and long-term mooring, winter storage, boat and engine sales and repairs, toilets, showers, laundrette.

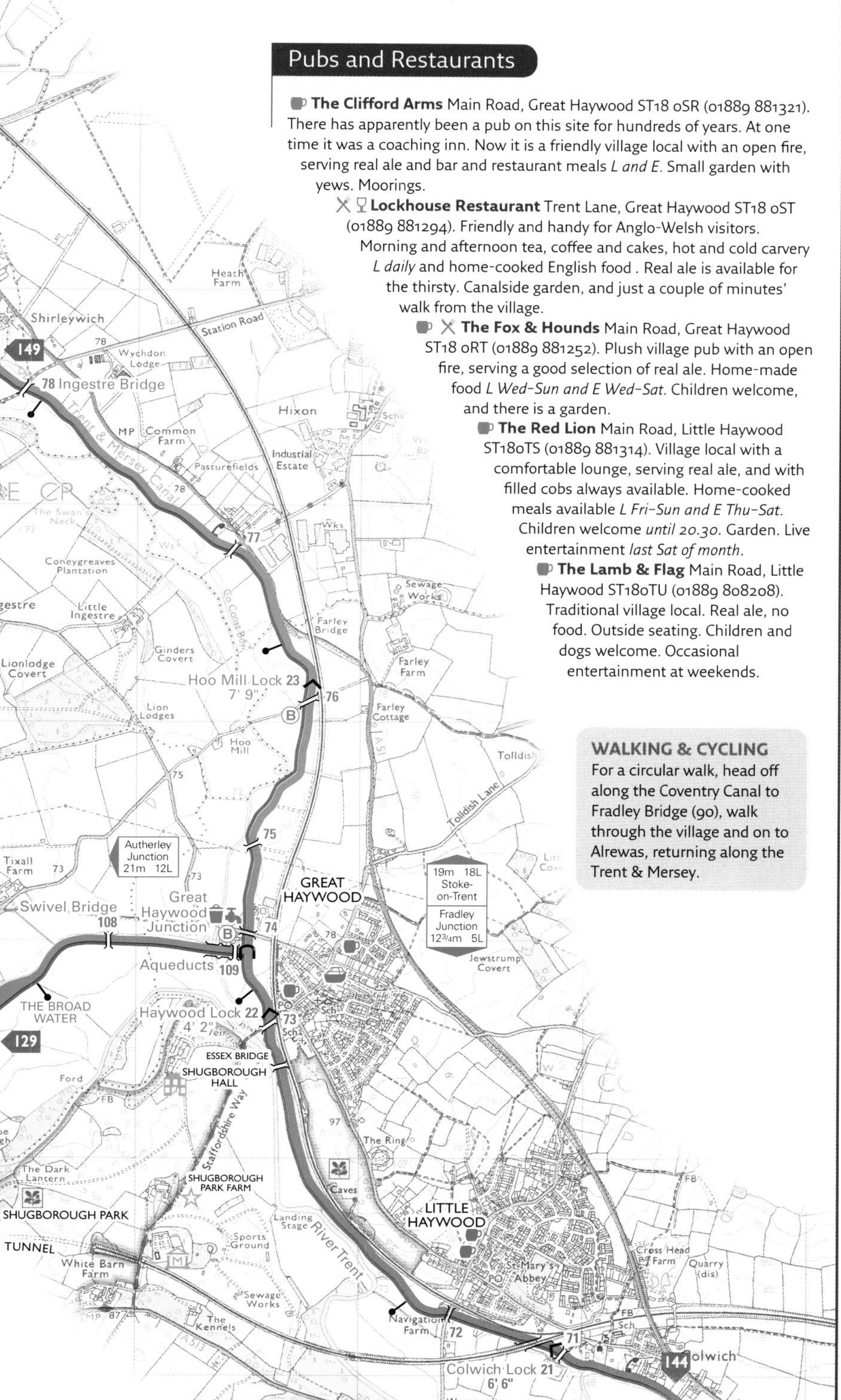

Pubs and Restaurants

The Clifford Arms Main Road, Great Haywood ST18 0SR (01889 881321). There has apparently been a pub on this site for hundreds of years. At one time it was a coaching inn. Now it is a friendly village local with an open fire, serving real ale and bar and restaurant meals *L and E.* Small garden with yews. Moorings.

Lockhouse Restaurant Trent Lane, Great Haywood ST18 0ST (01889 881294). Friendly and handy for Anglo-Welsh visitors. Morning and afternoon tea, coffee and cakes, hot and cold carvery *L daily* and home-cooked English food . Real ale is available for the thirsty. Canalside garden, and just a couple of minutes' walk from the village.

The Fox & Hounds Main Road, Great Haywood ST18 0RT (01889 881252). Plush village pub with an open fire, serving a good selection of real ale. Home-made food *L Wed-Sun and E Wed-Sat.* Children welcome, and there is a garden.

The Red Lion Main Road, Little Haywood ST18 0TS (01889 881314). Village local with a comfortable lounge, serving real ale, and with filled cobs always available. Home-cooked meals available *L Fri-Sun and E Thu-Sat.* Children welcome *until 20.30.* Garden. Live entertainment *last Sat of month.*

The Lamb & Flag Main Road, Little Haywood ST18 0TU (01889 808208). Traditional village local. Real ale, no food. Outside seating. Children and dogs welcome. Occasional entertainment at weekends.

WALKING & CYCLING

For a circular walk, head off along the Coventry Canal to Fradley Bridge (90), walk through the village and on to Alrewas, returning along the Trent & Mersey.

Weston upon Trent

The canal now leaves behind the excitement and interest of Great Haywood to continue its quiet north westerly passage through a broad valley towards Stone and Stoke-on-Trent. Hoo Mill Lock is a busy spot with many moored boats, and a useful boatyard. North of the lock a main road joins the hitherto quiet canal for a while. To the west is Ingestre Hall: beyond here the locks are broadly spaced and, although roads are never far away, the atmosphere is one of remoteness and peace. The village of Weston upon Trent is pretty, and there are pleasant pubs to visit.

● **Great Haywood**
See previous section.
Ingestre Hall Ingestre ST18 0RF (01889 270225). 1/2 mile south west of bridge 78. Originally a Tudor building and a former home of the Earls of Shrewsbury, the Hall was rebuilt in neo-Gothic style following a fire in 1820. It is surrounded by large attractive gardens, and is now a residential arts centre *not open to the public.*
Battle of Hopton Heath An inconclusive Civil War battle fought on 19 March 1643 1 1/2 miles west of Weston. Supported by Roaring Meg – a 29-pound cannon – the Royalists took the initiative, making several bold and effective cavalry charges against the Roundheads. However, the Roundheads' musketry fought back strongly, and after the Royalist leader (the Earl of Northampton) was killed, the Cavaliers weakened and fell back. Eventually both sides were exhausted and nightfall brought an end to the battle. Casualties – at under 200 – were surprisingly light, and neither side could claim victory.

● **Weston upon Trent**
Staffs. PO, tel, stores (by A51 junction). A pretty village of cottages and new houses, stretching away from St Andrew's church.

Boatyards

Ⓑ **Great Haywood Marina** Canalside Farm, Mill Lane, Great Haywood ST18 0RQ (01889 883713/07771 685 731; www.gjp-marinas.co.uk). D Pump out, gas, slipway, workshop, laundrette, toilets, showers, members' lounge, adjacent farm shop.

The Trent Aqueduct at Great Haywood (see page 146)

Pubs and Restaurants

The Saracen's Head Stafford Road, Weston ST18 0HT (01889 270286). About 20yds from the canal at bridge 80, this is a traditional country pub with open fires and a conservatory, serving a wide range of freshly cooked food *L and E*, including speciality dishes. Choice of real ales. Children are welcome *until 21.00*, and there is a large garden with a play area and panoramic views.

The Woolpack The Village Green, Weston ST18 0JH (01889 270238). Attractive 17th-C pub with a real fire serving home-cooked food *L and E (Sun until 18.00)*, along with real ale. Children welcome. Garden.

The Holly Bush Inn Salt, near Stafford ST18 0BX (01889 508234; www.hollybushinn.co.uk). Access from a stile near bridge 82; then walk up the lane. A 16th-C thatched country inn, reputedly the oldest in Staffordshire, serving real ale and meals *all day every day*. Children welcome. Large award-winning garden with outdoor pizza oven.

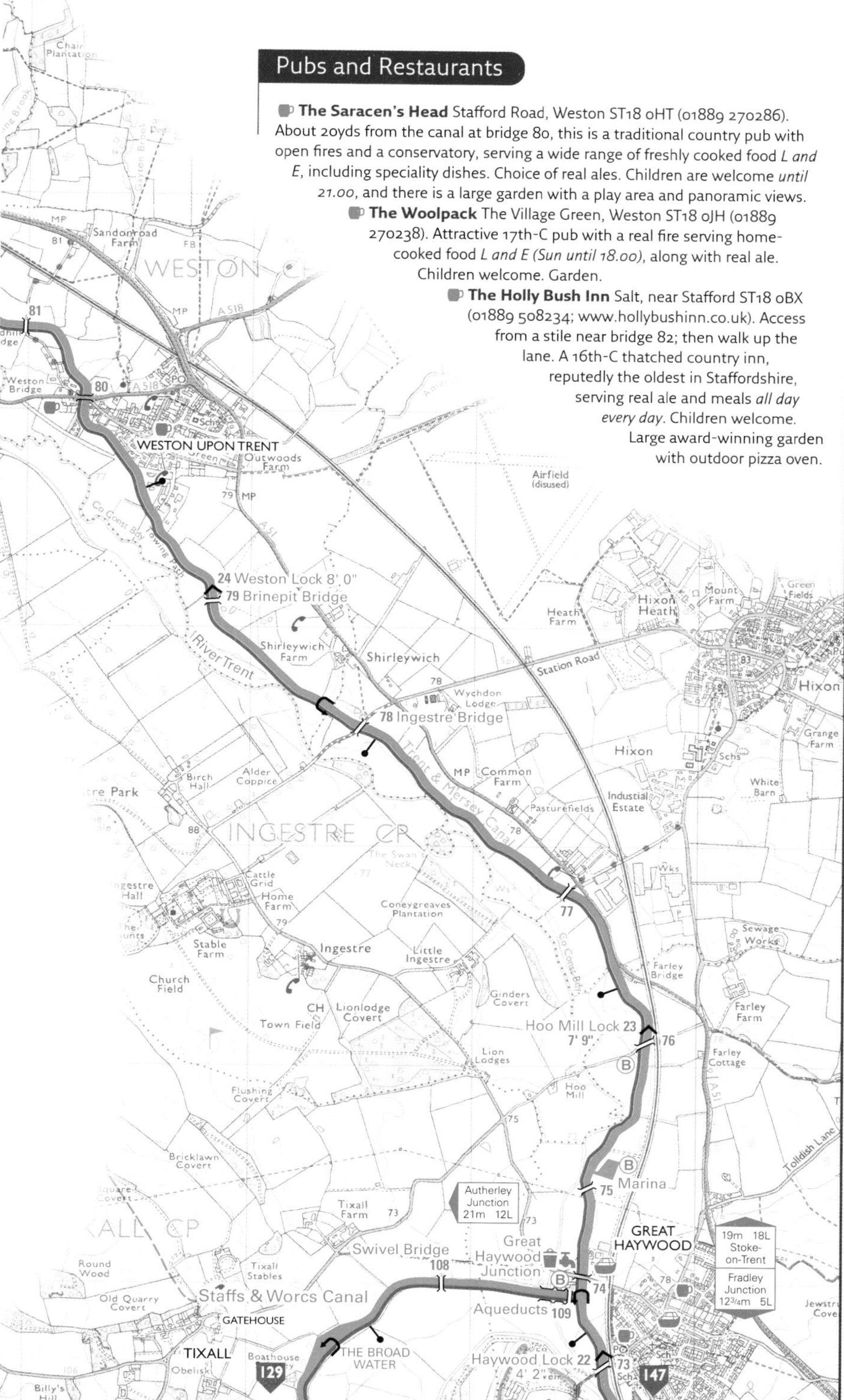

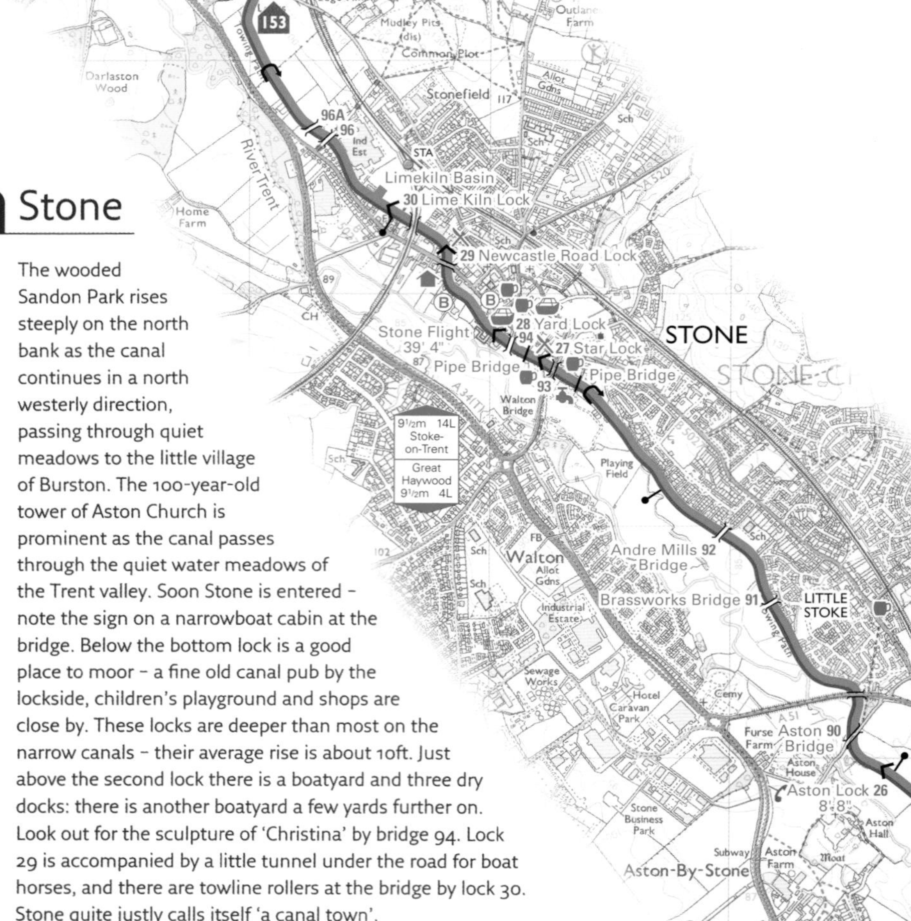

Stone

The wooded Sandon Park rises steeply on the north bank as the canal continues in a north westerly direction, passing through quiet meadows to the little village of Burston. The 100-year-old tower of Aston Church is prominent as the canal passes through the quiet water meadows of the Trent valley. Soon Stone is entered - note the sign on a narrowboat cabin at the bridge. Below the bottom lock is a good place to moor - a fine old canal pub by the lockside, children's playground and shops are close by. These locks are deeper than most on the narrow canals - their average rise is about 10ft. Just above the second lock there is a boatyard and three dry docks: there is another boatyard a few yards further on. Look out for the sculpture of 'Christina' by bridge 94. Lock 29 is accompanied by a little tunnel under the road for boat horses, and there are towline rollers at the bridge by lock 30. Stone quite justly calls itself 'a canal town'.

Sandon
Staffs. PO, tel, stores. A small estate village clustered near the main gates to Sandon Park. The main road bisecting the place is enough to send any canal boatman scurrying back to the safety of the relative peace and quiet of Sandon Lock. There is a pub, however, opposite the park gates.

Burston
Staffs. Tel. A hamlet apparently untouched by modern times, in spite of the proximity of three transport routes. Most of the village is set around the village pond. A surprisingly quiet place.

Stone
Staffs. PO, tel, stores, garage, bank, station, laundrette. A very busy and pleasant town with strong canal associations, and excellent boating and shopping facilities. The old priory church began to fall down in 1749, so in 1753 an Act of Parliament was obtained to enable the parishioners to rebuild it. The canalside is splendid, with dry docks, wharves and the impressive old Joules brewery buildings having a timeless air. There are always interesting craft to admire.

BOAT TRIPS

Brindleys Narrowboat Restaurant Stone ST15 8ZR (01785 812210; www.brindleysofstone.co.uk). Onboard ***Aquarius***, a restaurant with fully licensed bar, with a capacity of 32 persons seated at tables for two and four persons. *Fri and Sat E, and Sun L throughout the year.* Available for charter.

Roman Trips *daily 10.00-16.00 in summer* on this pretty little boat moored by Newcastle Road Bridge.

Pubs and Restaurants

The Dog & Doublet Inn Sandon ST18 0DJ (01889 508331). Friendly pub, serving real ale and bar food *L and E*. Children welcome. Garden with children's playthings. B & B.

The Greyhound Inn Burston ST18 0DR (01889 508263). A 10-minute walk up the lane east of bridge 86. Real ale. Good traditional bar and restaurant food *L and E*. Children welcome. Small garden.

The Three Crowns Little Stoke, Stone ST15 8QU (01785 819516). Welcoming stone and thatch pub dating from the 1700s, with open fires. Food available *L and E*, and real ale is served. Children welcome. Garden.

The Star Inn Stafford Street, Stone ST15 8UW (01785 813096). By Stone bottom lock. Traditional lockside pub, which apparently dates from the 14th C and is one of the oldest on the waterways, where none of the rooms are on the same level (it is noted in the *Guinness Book of Records* for this fact). Real ale. Good food served *L and E (all day at weekends)*. Children's room. Outside seating.

La Dolce Vita Stafford Street, Stone ST15 8QW (01785 817985). English and Italian food in a restaurant with gardens beside Star Lock. *Open L and E (all day Sun)*. Children welcome

The Crown Hotel 38 High Street, Stone ST15 8AS (01785 813535) Real ale. Food served *L and E*. Outside seating. Children welcome.

The Red Lion 25 High Street, Stone ST15 8AJ (01785 814500). Traditional town pub. Real ale. Food not served but you are welcome to bring your own sandwiches, etc.

The Swan 18 Stafford Street, Stone ST15 8QW (01785 815570). Traditional English pub serving real ale. Food served *L, daily*. Children not welcome. Live music every *week*.

Hatters Restaurant Newcastle Road, Stone ST15 8LB (01785 819292; www.hattersrestaurant.co.uk) adjacent to canal atl ock 29. Choices from a set price menu in comfortable, relaxed atmosphere. *Open E Tue–Sat*.

Boatyards

Ⓑ **Canal Cruising Co** Crown Street, Stone ST15 8QN (01785 813982; www.canalcruising.co.uk). D Pump out, gas, narrowboat hire, boat and engine repairs, dry dock. Supermarket adjacent, telephone nearby. 100yds along from boatyard.

Ⓑ **Stone Boatbuilding** Newcastle Road, Stone ST15 8JZ (01785 812688; www.stoneboatbuilding.co.uk). D Pump out, gas, overnight and long-term mooring, winter storage, slipway, boat building, boat repairs, engine sales and repairs, solid fuels, chandlery, toilets, books, maps, and gifts.

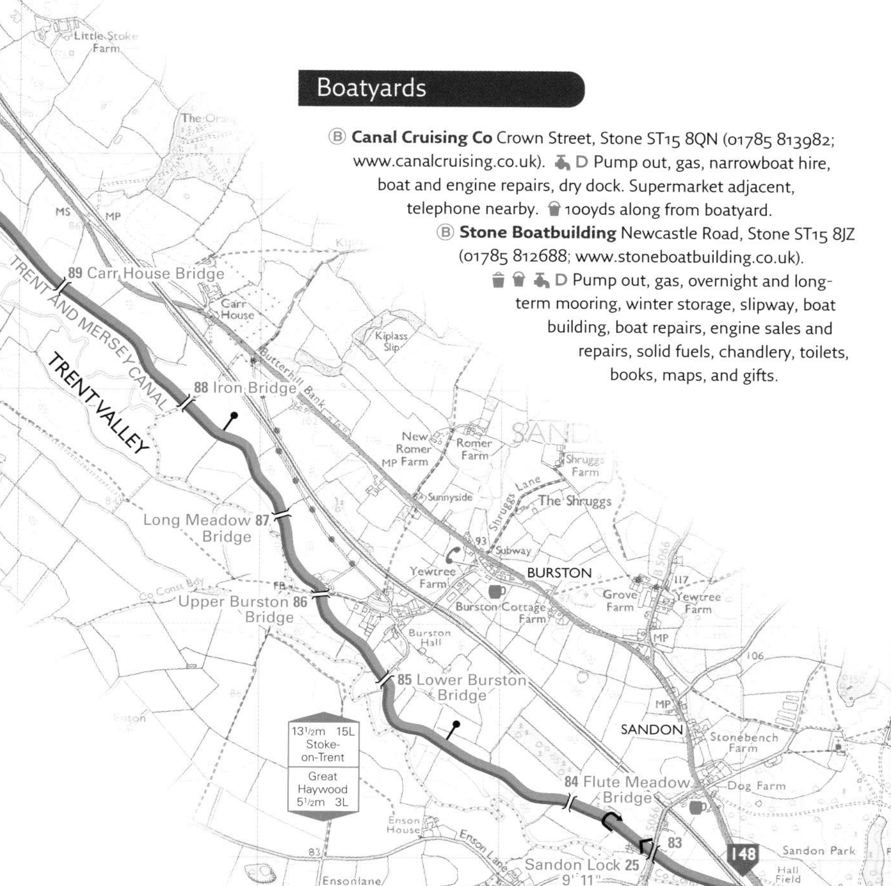

Barlaston

Stone Locks are soon followed by another flight of four, climbing up the valley to Meaford. The present Meaford Locks replaced an earlier staircase of three, the remains of which can be seen by lock 33. Here the railway line draws alongside, while the valley widens out and becomes flatter and less rural. The railway continues to flank the canal as it approaches the straggling village of Barlaston (*PO*). Just before Trentham Lock, where there are good moorings, is the Wedgwood Pottery, set back from the canal. The factory is conveniently served by Wedgwood Halt. North of Hemheath Bridge, where there is also a *PO*, *delicatessen* and useful *shop* in the *petrol station*, looms Stoke-on-Trent. A sign gives details of the nearby Newstead Wood and Hem Heath Nature Reserves, both refreshing open spaces before you tackle Stoke.

Wedgwood Factory King Street, Fenton, Near Longton, Stoke-on-Trent ST4 3FB (01782 204141; www.thewedgwoodvisitorcentre.com). The Wedgwood Group is the largest china and earthenware manufacturer in the world. It was started in 1759 in Burslem by the famous Josiah Wedgwood, the Father of English Potters, who came from a small pottery family. By 1766 he was sufficiently prosperous to build a large new house and factory which he called Etruria – a name suggested by his close friend Dr Erasmus Darwin – and to use the canal, of which he was a promoter, for transport. It was here that he produced his famous Jasper unglazed stoneware with white classical portraits on the surface. He revolutionised pottery-making with his many innovations and after his death in 1795 the company continued to expand. In the 1930s the Wedgwoods decided to build a new factory because mining subsidence had made Etruria unsuitable. The Etruria factory has unfortunately since been demolished but the large new factory began production in 1940 in Barlaston and is still the centre of the industry, with six electric tunnel ovens which produce none of the industrial smoke that is commonly associated with the Potteries. The Wedgwood Museum at Barlaston has a vast range of exhibits of Wedgwood pottery. The works is only a few yards from the canal, accessible from bridge 104. The visitor centre is *open Mon–Fri 09.00–17.00, Sat and Sun 10.00–17.00*. Charge. Self-guided tours. There are demonstrations, a shop, a museum, bistro and a restaurant. Parties of 12 people and over must book. A stop here should be on every canal traveller's itinerary.

WILDLIFE

Northwich Woodlands (www.northwichwoodlands.org.uk) are a network of country parks, woodlands, meadows, waterways and open water lying just to the north east of Northwich, through which both the Trent & Mersey Canal and the River Weaver flow. Many different species of butterfly have been seen in the woodlands including the *Speckled Wood*. This is a double-brooded butterfly, flying April–June and July–September. It favours clearings and is fond of sunbathing. The upperwings are dark brown with pale markings; the underwings are rufous brown. The caterpillars feed on grasses.

The *Large Skipper* favours grassy places of all kinds and flies during June and July. The upperwings are dark brown and orange-brown with pale markings. The underwings are buffish orange with paler spots. In common with most other skipper butterflies, at rest the Large Skipper often holds its wings at an angle and can look rather moth-like. The caterpillars feed on grasses.

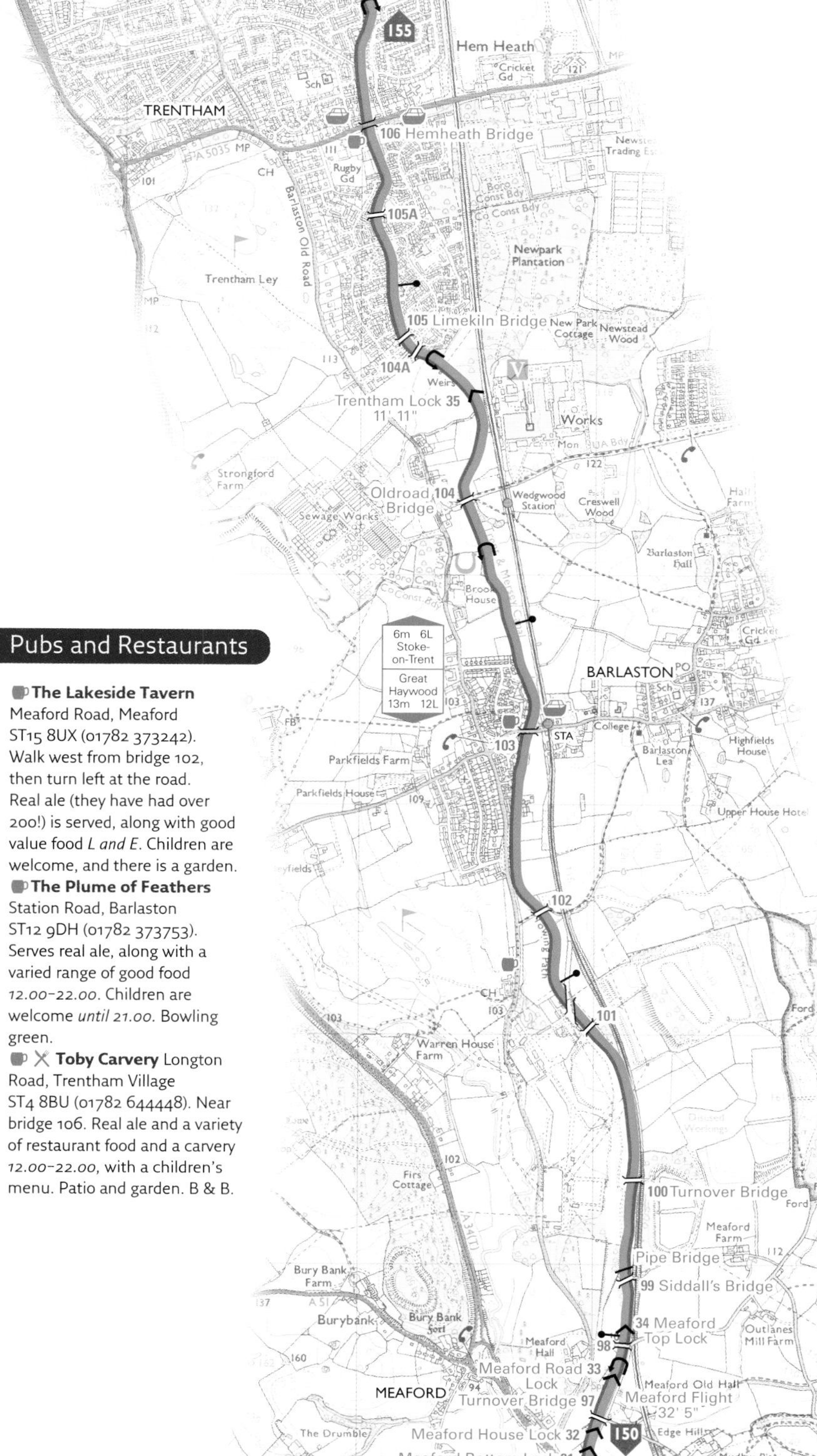

Pubs and Restaurants

The Lakeside Tavern Meaford Road, Meaford ST15 8UX (01782 373242). Walk west from bridge 102, then turn left at the road. Real ale (they have had over 200!) is served, along with good value food *L and E*. Children are welcome, and there is a garden.

The Plume of Feathers Station Road, Barlaston ST12 9DH (01782 373753). Serves real ale, along with a varied range of good food *12.00–22.00*. Children are welcome *until 21.00*. Bowling green.

Toby Carvery Longton Road, Trentham Village ST4 8BU (01782 644448). Near bridge 106. Real ale and a variety of restaurant food and a carvery *12.00–22.00*, with a children's menu. Patio and garden. B & B.

Stoke-on-Trent

This is a fascinating length of canal, not always (if ever) beautiful but all extremely interesting, passing right through the centre of Stoke-on-Trent, where all was once factories and warehouses – but which are now being rebuilt. Signs of the pottery industry still survive, its most remarkable manifestation being the bottle kilns – the brick furnaces shaped like gigantic bottles about 30ft high that still stand, cold and disused (but, happily, to be preserved), at the side of the canal. The Caldon Canal (*see* page 16) leaves the main line just above Stoke Top Lock. A statue of James Brindley, who built the Trent & Mersey Canal, stands near the junction. The Trent & Mersey then passes a marina and a pub, built for the National Garden Festival, before heading towards the south portal of the great Harecastle Tunnel. The Roundhouse, the very last remains of the original Wedgwood factory built in 1769, is easily missed – it stands beside bridge 117. Further along, by bridge 119, moor to visit the Royal Doulton shop.

Stoke-on-Trent
Staffs. All services. The city was formed in 1910 from a federation of six towns (Burslem, Fenton, Hanley, Longton, Stoke and Tunstall) but became known as the Five Towns in the novels of Arnold Bennett. The thriving pottery industries are the source of the city's great prosperity. The town hall, in Glebe Street, is an imposing and formal 19th-C building. Opposite the town hall is the parish church of St Peter, which contains a commemorative plaque to Josiah Wedgwood. Festival Park has been built on the site of the old Shelton Steelworks, with a dry ski slope, Waterworld and a multi-screen cinema amongst other attractions.

The Potteries Museum & Art Gallery Bethesda Street, Hanley, Stoke-on-Trent ST1 3D (01782 232323; www.stoke.gov.uk). The home of the world's finest collection of Staffordshire ceramics. Also a Mark XVI Spitfire. *Open Mar–Oct, Mon–Sat 10.00–17.00, Sun 14.00–17.00; Nov–Feb, Mon–Sat 10.00–16.00, Sun 13.00–16.00.* Free.

Churchill China Marlborough Pottery, High Street, Sandyford, Tunstall ST6 5NZ (01782 745899; www.churchill-direct.com). Close to bridge 112, this factory shop sells fine bone china and giftware. *Open Mon–Sat 09.00–17.00, Sun 10.00–16.00.*

Etruria Industrial Museum Lower Bedford Street, Etruria, Hanley ST4 7AF (01782 233144; www.stoke.gov.uk). Beside the canal, at the junction with the Caldon. This is a Victorian steam-powered potter's miller's works, built in 1857, which ground bone, flint and stone for the pottery industry, until closure in 1972. It has now been restored as part of an industrial complex incorporating a blacksmith's shop with working steam-powered machinery. Originally the raw materials and ground products were transported by canal, and present-day canal travellers will find plenty of moorings available. *Open Wed–Sun 12.00–16.30, but telephone to check.* Guided tours. Charge. Tearoom and shop.

Gladstone Pottery Museum Uttoxeter Road, Longton, Stoke-on-Trent ST3 1PQ (01782 237777; www.stoke.gov.uk). The last remaining Victorian pottery factory. *Open 10.00–17.00.* Charge.

Ceramica The Old Town Hall, Market Place, Burslem, Stoke-on-Trent ST1 3DW (10782 832001; www.ceramicauk.com). Follow the path of ceramics from clay right through to a finished product. *Open Tue–Sat 10.30–16.30.* Charge.

The Dudson Centre Hope Street, Hanley, Stoke-on-Trent ST1 5DD (01782 285286; www.dudson.co.uk). The 200-year history of the oldest surviving business in the ceramic table ware industry. Café & shop.

Waterworld Festival Park, Etruria, Stoke-on-Trent ST1 5PU (01782 205747; www.waterworld.co.uk). Indoor tropical aqua park, outdoor pool, lots of different water rides, aqua disco. *Open daily (telephone to confirm times).* Charge.

Pubs and Restaurants

Toby Carvery Marina Way, Festival Park, Etruria ST1 5PA (01782 260199). Canalside at Stoke Marina. Large lounge, a carvery restaurant. Real ale, and meals *all day*. Garden and moorings.

The New Rendezvous 67 Etruria Old Road, Etruria ST1 5PE (01782 279330). West of bridge 117A. Quaint pub in a listed building, serving real ale and food *L and E*. Children welcome, garden.

The Bird in Hand 79 Etruria Vale Road, Etruria ST4 5NX (01782 205048). Real ale. Bar meals and snacks are served *L and E*. Children welcome, and there is a garden.

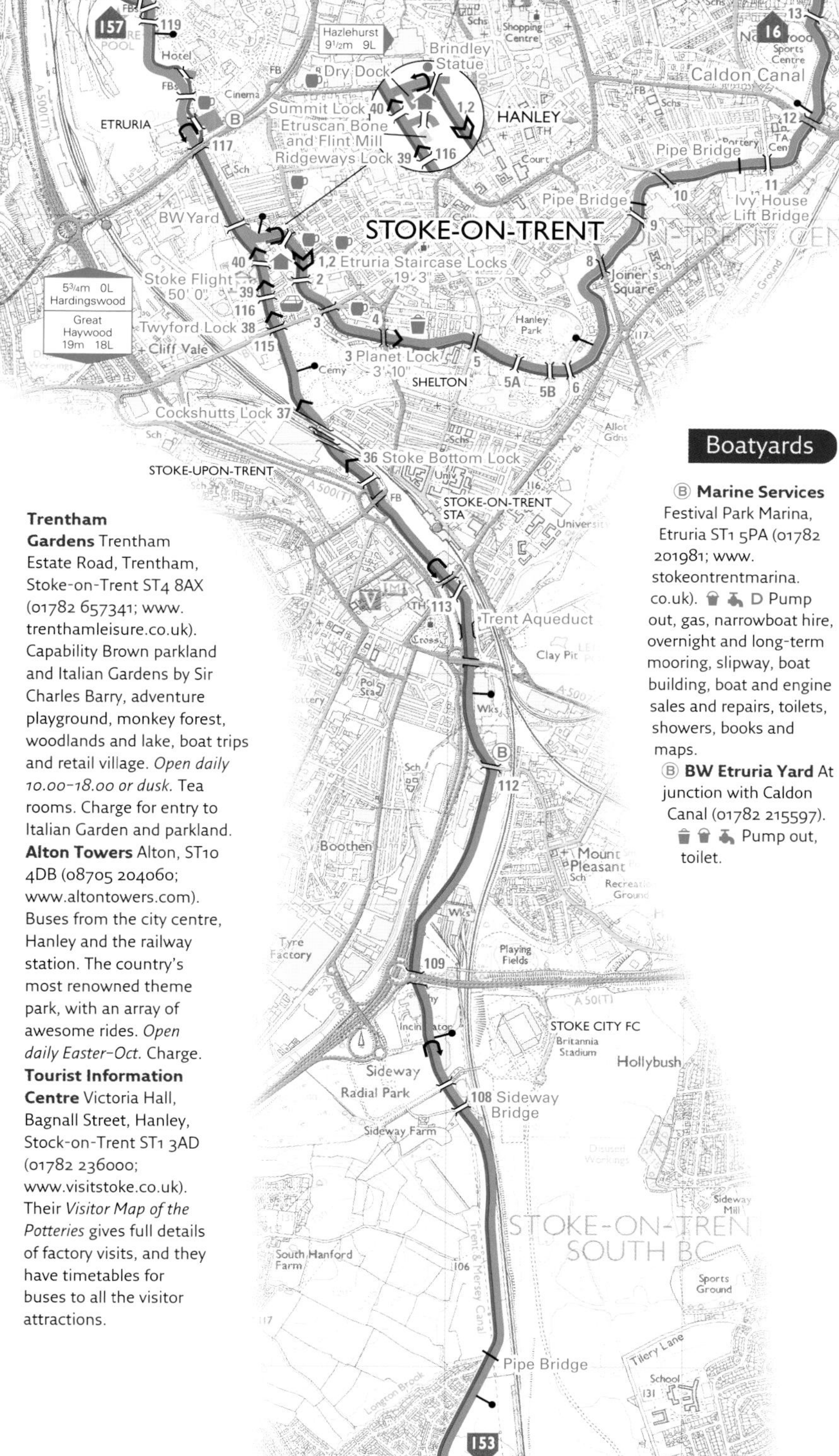

Trentham Gardens Trentham Estate Road, Trentham, Stoke-on-Trent ST4 8AX (01782 657341; www.trenthamleisure.co.uk). Capability Brown parkland and Italian Gardens by Sir Charles Barry, adventure playground, monkey forest, woodlands and lake, boat trips and retail village. *Open daily 10.00–18.00 or dusk.* Tea rooms. Charge for entry to Italian Garden and parkland.

Alton Towers Alton, ST10 4DB (08705 204060; www.altontowers.com). Buses from the city centre, Hanley and the railway station. The country's most renowned theme park, with an array of awesome rides. *Open daily Easter–Oct.* Charge.

Tourist Information Centre Victoria Hall, Bagnall Street, Hanley, Stock-on-Trent ST1 3AD (01782 236000; www.visitstoke.co.uk). Their *Visitor Map of the Potteries* gives full details of factory visits, and they have timetables for buses to all the visitor attractions.

Boatyards

Ⓑ **Marine Services** Festival Park Marina, Etruria ST1 5PA (01782 201981; www.stokeontrentmarina.co.uk). D Pump out, gas, narrowboat hire, overnight and long-term mooring, slipway, boat building, boat and engine sales and repairs, toilets, showers, books and maps.

Ⓑ **BW Etruria Yard** At junction with Caldon Canal (01782 215597). Pump out, toilet.

Harecastle Tunnel

The canal swings past what was the junction with the old Burslem Arm (hopefully to be restored) which headed north for about a ¼ of a mile just before bridge 123, and continues through the flattened remains of an industrial area, before reaching the weathered and evocative red-brick and slate buildings of the Middleport Pottery, with kilns, cranes and cobbles right beside the canal. A large boatyard, with boats moored almost across the width of the canal then follows, with a couple of pubs and an excellent fish & chip shop close-by. Before long the navigation passes the open expanse of Westport Park Lake, popular with fishermen, and finally abandons its very twisting course to make a beeline for Harecastle Hill and the famous 2926yd tunnel. There were once two tunnels here: only one is now navigable. Beyond lies Kidsgrove and Hardings Wood Junction.

The Three Harecastle Tunnels

There are altogether three parallel tunnels through Harecastle Hill. The first, built by James Brindley, was completed in 1777, after 11 years' work. To build a 9ft-wide tunnel 13/4 miles long represented engineering on a scale quite unknown to the world at that time, and the world was duly impressed. Since there was no towpath in the tunnel the boats – which were of course all towed from the bank by horses at that time – had to be legged through by men lying on the boat's cabin roof and propelling the boat by walking along the tunnel roof. The towing horse would, in the meantime, have to be walked over the top of the hill. This very slow means of propulsion, combined with the great length of the narrow tunnel and the large amount of traffic on the navigation, made Harecastle a major bottle-neck for canal boats. So in 1822 the Trent & Mersey Canal Company called in Thomas Telford, who recommended that a second tunnel be constructed alongside the first one. This was done: the new tunnel was completed in 1827, with a towpath (now removed), after only three years' work. Each tunnel then became one-way until in the 20th C Brindley's bore had sunk so much from mining subsidence that it had to be abandoned. Its entrance can still be seen to the west of the newer tunnel mouth. An electric tug was introduced in 1914 to speed up traffic through Telford's tunnel; this service was continued until 1954. The third tunnel through Harecastle Hill was built years after the other two, and carried the Stoke-Kidsgrove railway line. It runs 40ft above the canal tunnels and is slightly shorter. This tunnel was closed in the 1960s: the railway line now goes round the hill and through a much shorter tunnel. Thus two out of the three Harecastle tunnels are disused.

WILDLIFE

Another butterfly seen in Northwich Woodlands (*see* page 146) is the Holly Blue, which appears silvery in flight. The violet-blue upperwings are seldom seen well as it rests showing white, black-dotted underwings. There are two broods, flying April–May, laying eggs on holly; flying August–September and laying eggs on ivy.

The *Orange-Tip* is an attractive spring butterfly, seen flying between April and June. The male has an orange patch on the dark-tipped forewing, which is absent in the female. The hind underwing of both sexes is marbled green and white. The larvae feed mainly on the cuckoo flower.

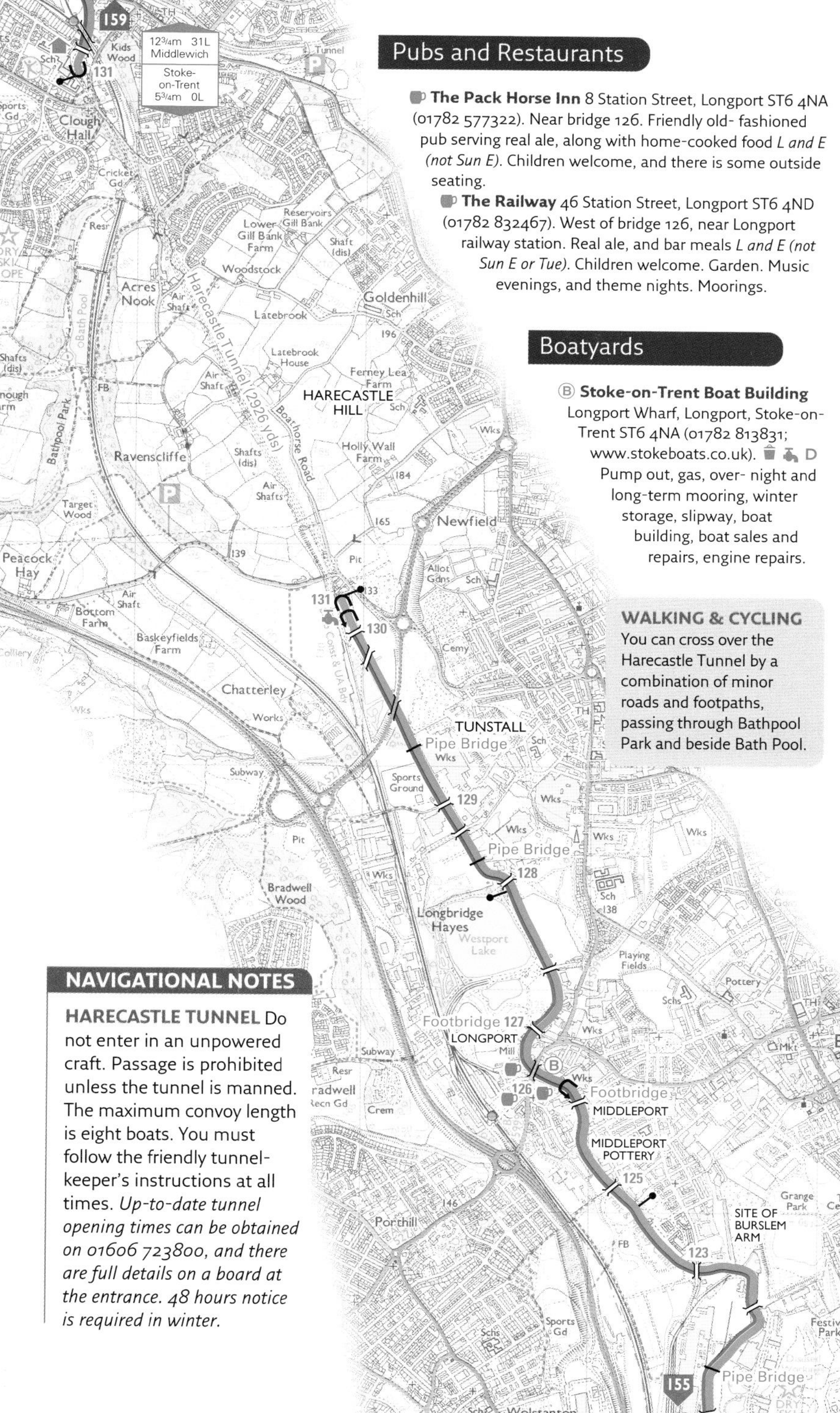

Pubs and Restaurants

The Pack Horse Inn 8 Station Street, Longport ST6 4NA (01782 577322). Near bridge 126. Friendly old- fashioned pub serving real ale, along with home-cooked food *L and E (not Sun E)*. Children welcome, and there is some outside seating.

The Railway 46 Station Street, Longport ST6 4ND (01782 832467). West of bridge 126, near Longport railway station. Real ale, and bar meals *L and E (not Sun E or Tue)*. Children welcome. Garden. Music evenings, and theme nights. Moorings.

Boatyards

Ⓑ **Stoke-on-Trent Boat Building** Longport Wharf, Longport, Stoke-on-Trent ST6 4NA (01782 813831; www.stokeboats.co.uk). D Pump out, gas, over- night and long-term mooring, winter storage, slipway, boat building, boat sales and repairs, engine repairs.

WALKING & CYCLING

You can cross over the Harecastle Tunnel by a combination of minor roads and footpaths, passing through Bathpool Park and beside Bath Pool.

NAVIGATIONAL NOTES

HARECASTLE TUNNEL Do not enter in an unpowered craft. Passage is prohibited unless the tunnel is manned. The maximum convoy length is eight boats. You must follow the friendly tunnel-keeper's instructions at all times. *Up-to-date tunnel opening times can be obtained on 01606 723800, and there are full details on a board at the entrance. 48 hours notice is required in winter.*

Harding's Wood Junction

At the north end of Harecastle Tunnel (2926yds long) the navigation passes Kidsgrove station and a coal yard; there is also a *shower* in the facilities block beside the north tunnel portal. Beyond is Harding's Wood and the junction with the Macclesfield Canal, which crosses the T & M on Poole Aqueduct. There are *showers, laundry facilities and toilets* at the BW yard at Red Bull. The canal continues to fall through a heavily locked stretch sometimes called 'heartbreak hill' but known to the old boatmen as the 'Cheshire Locks'.

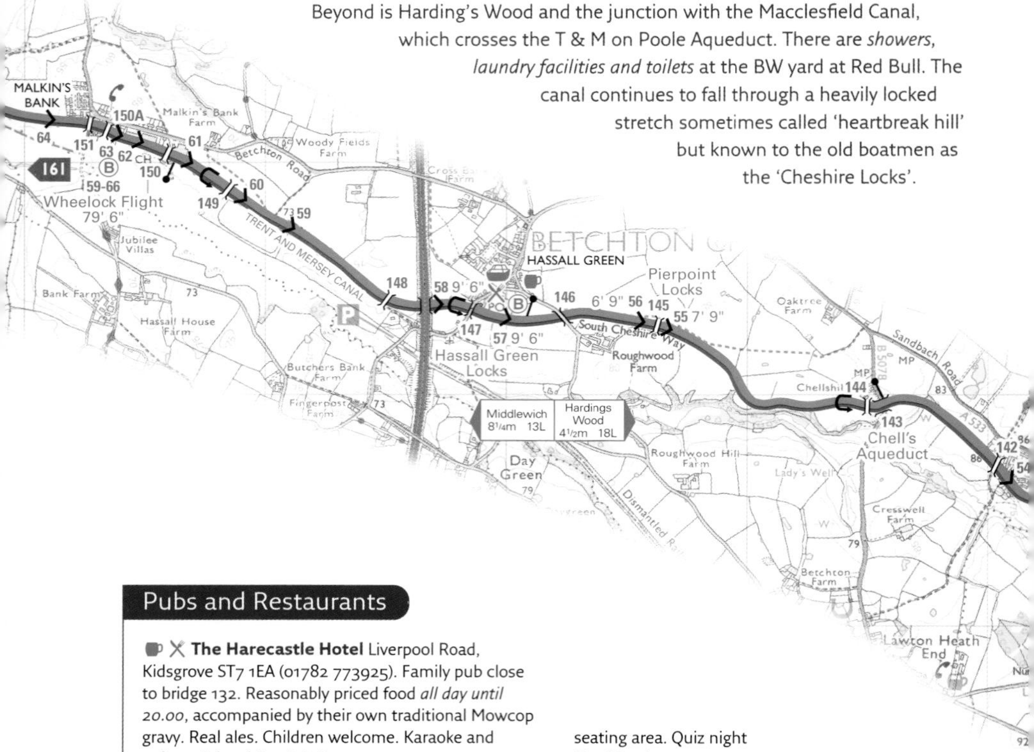

Pubs and Restaurants

The Harecastle Hotel Liverpool Road, Kidsgrove ST7 1EA (01782 773925). Family pub close to bridge 132. Reasonably priced food *all day until 20.00*, accompanied by their own traditional Mowcop gravy. Real ales. Children welcome. Karaoke and quizzes *Fri and Sat*. B & B.

The Blue Bell 25 Hardingswood, Kidsgrove ST7 1EG (01782 774052; www.bluebellkidsgrove.co.uk). Canalside, at Hardings Wood Junction. Friendly, quiet, one-bar local, winnner of many CAMRA awards. Real ale, plus a range of specialist bottled beers, including many from Belgium, plus real cider and perry. No juke box, pool table or gaming machines. Note the trapdoor in the lounge ceiling. Well-behaved children welcome *until 21.00*. Snacks are available *at weekends. Open Tue-Fri 19.30-23.00; Sat 13.00-16.30, 19.00-23.00; Sun 12.00-16.30, 19.00-22.30 (all day during summer). Closed Mon.*

The Canal Tavern Hardingswood Road, Kidsgrove ST7 1EF (01782 775382). Canalside by bridge 133. Food served *L and E*. Children welcome *until 19.30*. Large garden. Karaoke at *weekends*.

The Red Bull Hotel Congleton Road South, Church Lawton ST7 3AJ (01782 782600). By lock 43. Popular pub close to Hardings Wood Junction, serving real ale and bar meals, including fish dishes *L and E*, along with good wine. Children welcome. Canalside seating area. Quiz night *Tue*. Moorings.

The Broughton Arms Mill Mead, Rode Heath ST7 3RX 01270 878661). Canalside at Rode Heath. Friendly family pub, with comfortable bars and canalside seating. Range of real ale. Food available in bar and dining area *L and E*. Children welcome away from the bar. Waterside garden with patio heaters. Quiz *Tue.*

Lockside 57 The Canal Centre, Hassall Green CW11 4YB (01270 762266; www.lock57.co.uk). A well-restored 18th-C building beside the canal. Appetising range of reasonably priced dishes (vegan by arrangement) served *breakfast, L and E (seasonal). Sun* roast. Children's menu. Lockside seating. Cyclists and walkers warmly welcomed. *See* also under Boatyards.

The Romping Donkey Hassall Green CW11 4YA (01270 765202). Haunted 17th-C pub serving real ale, and home-made bar meals and snacks *L and E.* Children welcome, and there is a garden.

Two minor aqueducts are encountered, and most of the locks are narrow pairs – the chambers side by side. At Hassall Green there is a *PO, tel and stores* incorporating a canal shop, restaurant and limited boatyard services.

- **Kidsgrove**
  Staffs. All services. Originally an iron and coal producing town, Kidsgrove was much helped by the completion of the Trent & Mersey Canal. James Brindley is buried here.
- **Rode Heath**
  Cheshire. PO, tel, stores. A useful shopping area right by bridge 140. A butcher's shop at bridge 139.
  Rode Heath Rise ST7 3QX Once the site of a salt works, it has now been landscaped and restored as a wildflower meadow. Telephone 01477 534115 for further information.

NAVIGATIONAL NOTES

HARECASTLE TUNNEL Do not enter in an unpowered craft. With the complete removal of the towpath, headroom is no longer the problem it once was. A one-way system operates, so follow the instructions of the tunnel keepers. *For updated tunnel opening times, telephone 01782 785703.*

Boatyards

Ⓑ **Smithsons Solid Fuel and Caravan Centre** Liverpool Road, Kidsgrove ST7 1EA (01782 787887). Near bridge 132. D Calor gas, solid fuel, lubricants and caravan fittings which can be used as chandlery. Also bicycles and bicycle spares for sale.

Ⓑ **Canal Centre** Hassall Green, Sandbach CW11 4YB (01270 762266). D Gas, groceries, books and maps, coal, short-term mooring, chandlery, toilets. Also PO general store, off-licence, gifts, licensed restaurant and tearoom, coal.

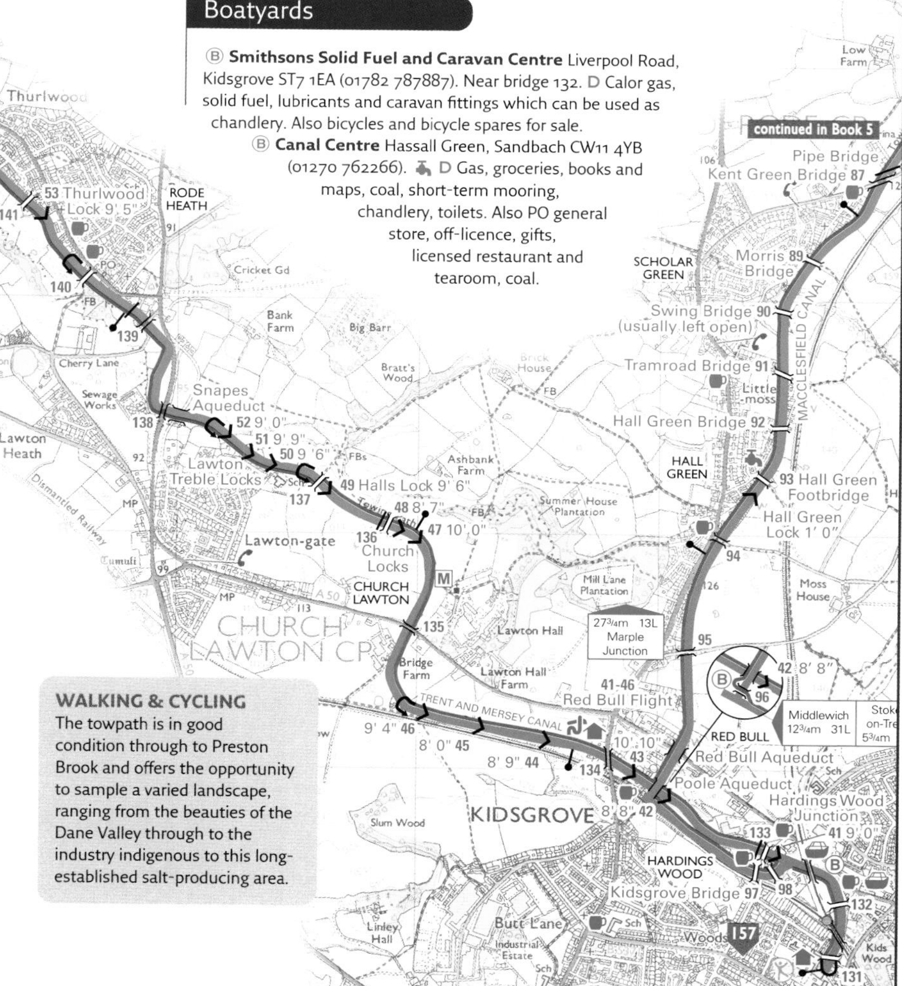

continued in Book 5

WALKING & CYCLING

The towpath is in good condition through to Preston Brook and offers the opportunity to sample a varied landscape, ranging from the beauties of the Dane Valley through to the industry indigenous to this long-established salt-producing area.

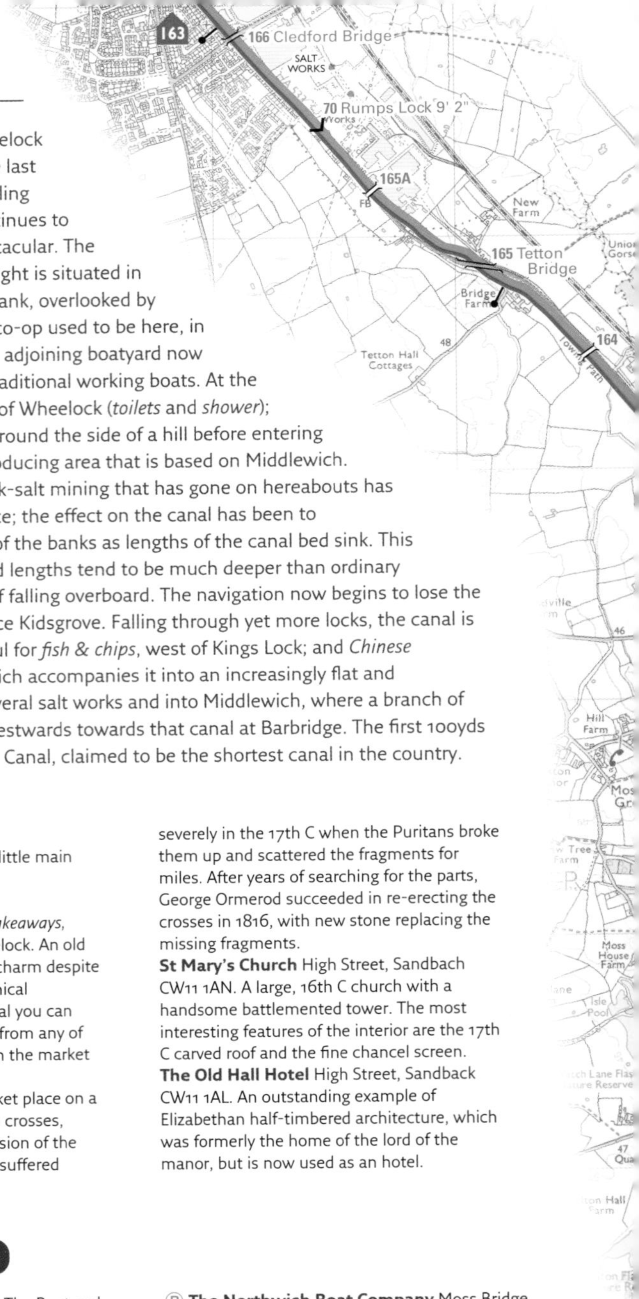

Wheelock

The canal now descends the Wheelock flight of eight locks, which are the last paired locks one sees when travelling northwards. The countryside continues to be quiet and unspoilt but unspectacular. The pair of locks half-way down the flight is situated in the little settlement of Malkin's Bank, overlooked by terraced houses. The boatman's co-op used to be here, in the small terrace of cottages. The adjoining boatyard now specialises in the restoration of traditional working boats. At the bottom of the flight is the village of Wheelock (*toilets* and *shower*); west of here the navigation curls round the side of a hill before entering the very long-established salt-producing area that is based on Middlewich. The 'wild' brine pumping and rock-salt mining that has gone on hereabouts has resulted in severe local subsidence; the effect on the canal has been to necessitate the constant raising of the banks as lengths of the canal bed sink. This of course means that the affected lengths tend to be much deeper than ordinary canals. Non-swimmers beware of falling overboard. The navigation now begins to lose the rural character it has enjoyed since Kidsgrove. Falling through yet more locks, the canal is joined by a busy main road (useful for *fish & chips*, west of Kings Lock; and *Chinese takeaway*, west of bridge 166) which accompanies it into an increasingly flat and industrialised landscape, past several salt works and into Middlewich, where a branch of the Shropshire Union leads off westwards towards that canal at Barbridge. The first 100yds or so of this branch is the Wardle Canal, claimed to be the shortest canal in the country.

- **Wheelock**
  Ches. PO, tel, stores, fish & chips. Busy little main road village on the canal.
- **Sandbach**
  Ches. PO, tel, stores, garage, chemist, takeaways, bank, station. 1½ miles north of Wheelock. An old market town that has maintained its charm despite the steady growth of its salt and chemical industries. After walking from the canal you can refresh yourself with a pint of real ale from any of the seven pubs visible from the seat in the market place.

  Ancient Crosses In the cobbled market place on a massive base stand two superb Saxon crosses, believed to commemorate the conversion of the area to Christianity in the 7th C. They suffered severely in the 17th C when the Puritans broke them up and scattered the fragments for miles. After years of searching for the parts, George Ormerod succeeded in re-erecting the crosses in 1816, with new stone replacing the missing fragments.

  St Mary's Church High Street, Sandbach CW11 1AN. A large, 16th C church with a handsome battlemented tower. The most interesting features of the interior are the 17th C carved roof and the fine chancel screen.

  The Old Hall Hotel High Street, Sandback CW11 1AL. An outstanding example of Elizabethan half-timbered architecture, which was formerly the home of the lord of the manor, but is now used as an hotel.

Boatyards

Ⓑ **Malkins Bank Canal Services** The Boatyard, Betchton Road, Malkins Bank, Sandbach CW11 4XN (01270 764595). Long-term mooring, slipway, boat building and historic boat restoration, boat repairs. *Breakdown service.*

Ⓑ **The Northwich Boat Company** Moss Bridge Cottage, Moss Lane, Sandbach CW11 3PW (01270 760160; www.thenorthwichboat.com). Also (01270 760770; www.carefreecruising.com) on same site. Boat building and fitting out.

Pubs and Restaurants

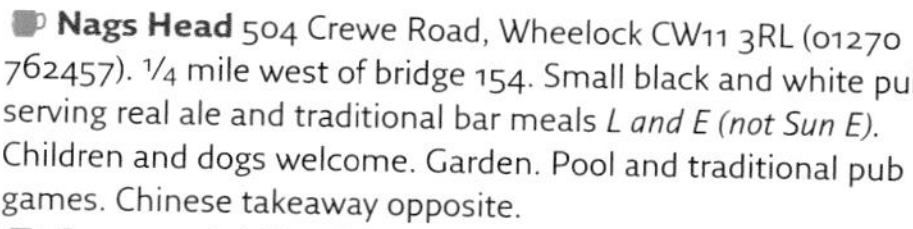

Nags Head 504 Crewe Road, Wheelock CW11 3RL (01270 762457). 1/4 mile west of bridge 154. Small black and white pub serving real ale and traditional bar meals *L and E (not Sun E)*. Children and dogs welcome. Garden. Pool and traditional pub games. Chinese takeaway opposite.

Commercial Hotel Game Street, Wheelock CW113RR (01270 760122). Near bridge 154. Set in a Georgian house with an old-fashioned and spacious feel this pub serves real ale, real cider and bar meals. *Open all day*. Children and dogs welcome. Beer garden, snooker room, darts and dominoes.

Cheshire Cheese 466 Crewe Road, Wheelock CW11 3RL (01270 760319). Heavily beamed, canalside pub serving real ale and a range of meals and snacks *L and E, daily*. Children and dogs welcome (dogs in the garden). Large beer garden. Moorings.

Market Tavern Market Square, Sandbach CW11 1AT (01270 762099). Opposite the crosses. Lively, old, traditional town pub serving real ale and home-cooked bar food *L Mon-Sat*. Children's menu and beer garden. One of the many real ale pubs in, or close to, the square. Regular live music.

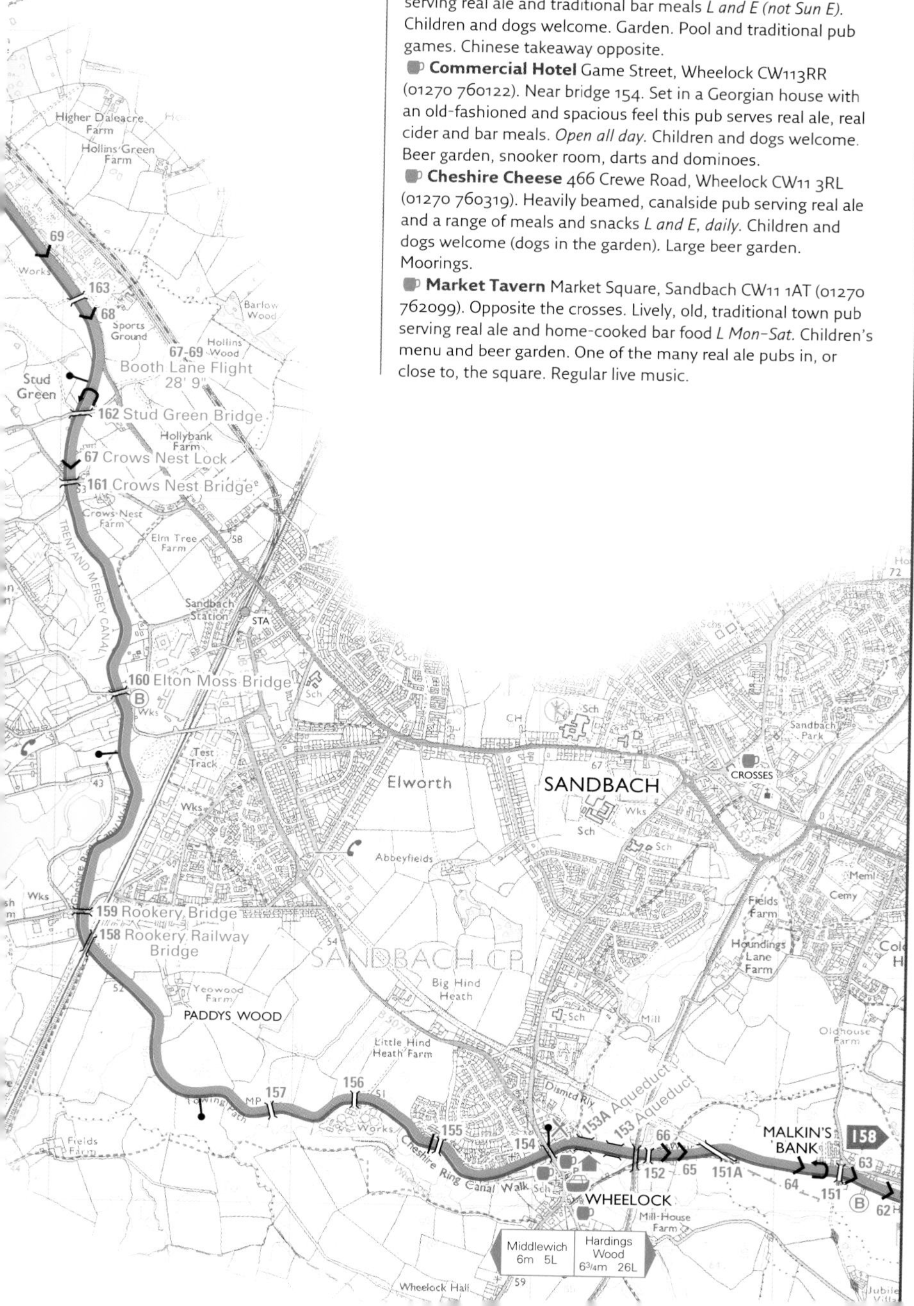

Middlewich 6m 5L | Hardings Wood 6¾m 26L

Middlewich

The Trent & Mersey skirts the centre of the town, passing lots of moored narrowboats and through three consecutive narrow locks, arriving at a wide (14ft) lock (which has suffered from subsidence) with a pub beside it. This used to represent the beginning of a wide, almost lock-free navigation right through to Preston Brook, Manchester and Wigan (very convenient for the salt industry when it shipped most of its goods by boat), but Croxton Aqueduct had to be replaced many years ago, and is now a steel structure only 8ft 2in wide. The aqueduct crosses the River Dane, which flows alongside the navigation as both water courses leave industrial Middlewich and move out into fine open country. Initially, this is a stretch of canal as beautiful as any in the country. Often overhung by trees, the navigation winds along the side of a hill as it follows the delightful valley of the River Dane. There are pleasant moorings with picnic tables and barbecue facilities, created by the Broken Cross Boating Club in old clay pits, just north of bridge 176, on the off-side. The parkland on the other side of the valley encompasses Bostock Hall, a school for children with learning difficulties. At Whatcroft Hall (privately owned), the canal circles around to the east, passing under a railway bridge before heading for the industrial outskirts of Northwich and shedding its beauty and solitude once again.

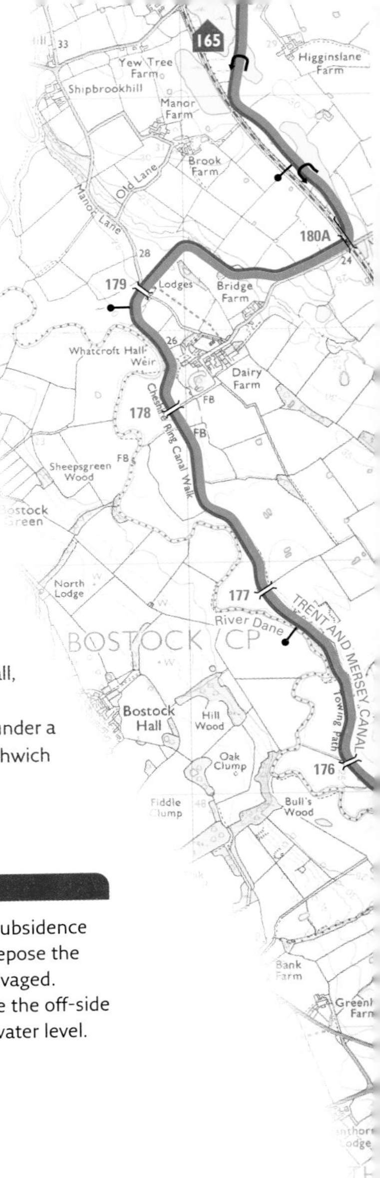

NAVIGATIONAL NOTES

There are several privately owned wide 'lagoons' caused by subsidence along this section of the Trent & Mersey, in some of which repose the hulks of abandoned barges and narrowboats, lately being salvaged. Navigators should be wary of straying off the main line, since the off-side canal bank is often submerged and invisible just below the water level.

Boatyards

Ⓑ **Kings Lock Boatyard** Booth Lane, Middlewich CW10 0JJ (01606 737564). D Gas, overnight mooring, long-term mooring, winter storage, slipway, engine sales and repairs, boat repairs, chandlery (including mail order), books, maps, gifts, solid fuel. *Emergency call out.*

Ⓑ **Andersen Boats** Wych House, St Anne's Road, Middlewich CW10 9BQ (01606 833668; www.andersenboats.com). Pump out, gas, narrowboat hire, books and maps. Useful DIY shop nearby.

Ⓑ **Middlewich Narrowboats** Canal Terrace, Middlewich CW10 9BD (01606 832460; www.middlewichboats.co.uk). D Pump out, gas, narrowboat hire, overnight mooring (*not Fri*), long-term mooring, dry dock, boatbuilding, groceries, chandlery, books and maps, engine repairs, toilets, laundry service, breakdown service, grit blasting, hull and cabinside painting. *Closed Sun.* Useful tool hire shop next door.

Pubs and Restaurants

The Kings Lock 1 Booth Lane, Middlewich CW10 0JJ (01606 833537). Overlooking the lock. Real ales and bar food available *L and E*. Children welcome *until 21.00*. Dogs in bar areas only. Canalside seating. Moorings.

The Cheshire Cheese Lewin Street, Middlewich CW10 9AX (01606 832097). Friendly, traditional establishment serving real ales. Children welcome. Landscaped garden with large patio and marquee. *Weekly* karaoke and occasional live bands. Wide-screen TV.

The Newton Brewery Inn Webbs Lane, Middlewich CW10 9DN (01606 833502). 1/4 mile south of Big Lock. Small friendly pub with an attractive garden running down to the towpath. Real ale. Telephone for details of food. Children welcome.

The Boars Head Kinderton Street, Middlewich CW10 0JE (01606 833191; www.theboarsheadhotel.com). Large rambling pub offering real ale and food *L and E, daily*. Pool room. Patio. Live music *Sat*. B & B.

The Big Lock Webbs Lane, Middlewich CW10 9DN (01606 833489). Canalside. Variously a bottle-making factory and canal-horse stables, this pub now serves real ale. Bar snacks and an à la carte menu available *L and E*. Children and dogs welcome. Garden area. Quiz *Mon*.

Middlewich

Ches. PO, tel, stores, chemist, takeaways, bank, garage. A town that since Roman times has been dedicated to salt extraction. Most of the salt produced here goes to various chemical industries. Subsidence from salt extraction has prevented redevelopment for many years, but a big renewal scheme is now in progress. The canalside area is a haven of peace below the busy streets. There is an interesting town trail depicting Roman Middlewich as a Romano-British saltworks settlement in the period 150-250 AD. Interpretation boards can be found on the towpath north of Bridge 172 and beside the Newton Brewery Inn.

St Michael's Church Queen Street, Middlewich CW10 9AR. A handsome medieval church which was a place of refuge for the Royalists during the Civil War. It has a fine interior with richly carved woodwork.

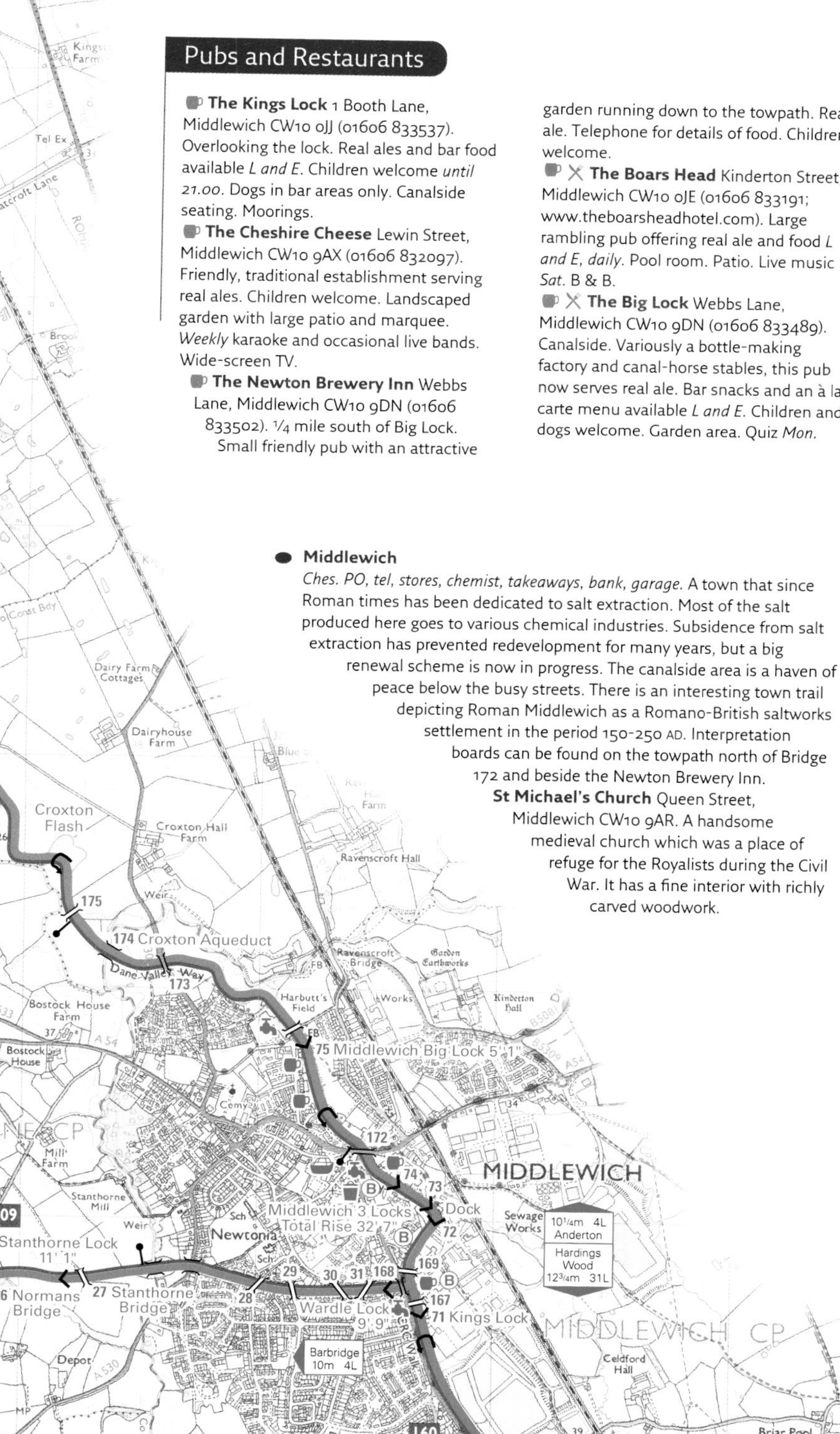

Anderton Lift

The outlying canal settlement of Broken Cross acts as a buffer between the beauty and solitude of the Dane Valley and the industrial ravages around Northwich. Beyond is another length in which salt mining has determined the nature of the scenery.

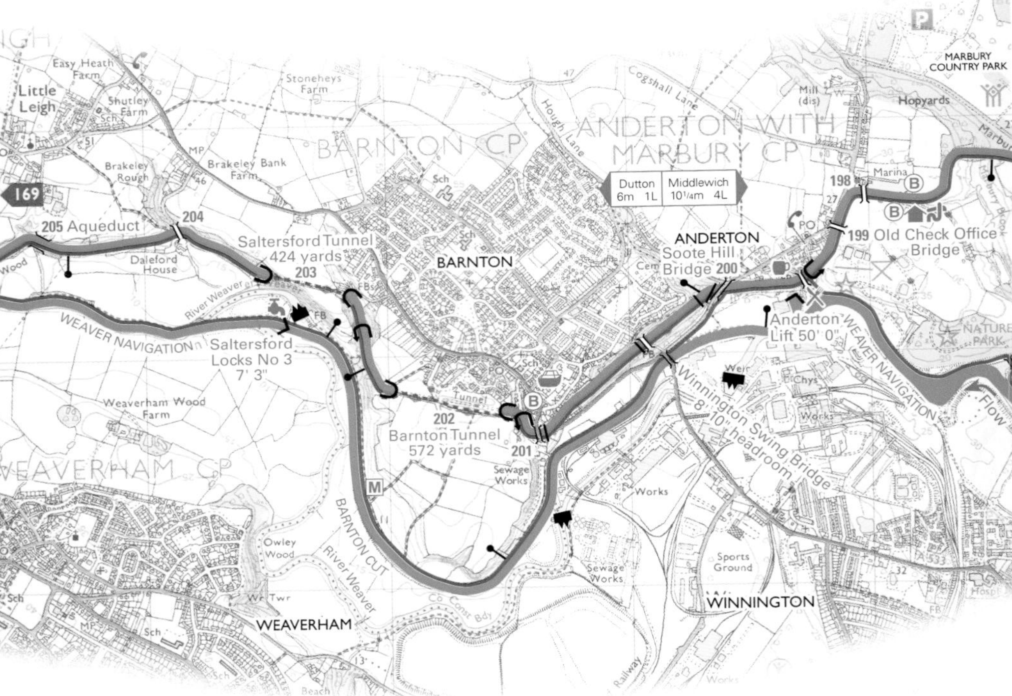

Part of it is heavily industrial, with enormous ICI works dominating the scene; much of it is devastated but rural (just), some of it is nondescript, and some of it is superb countryside. Donkey engines can still be seen in surrounding fields pumping brine. Leaving the vicinity of Lostock Gralam (licensed grocer 100yds east of bridge 189 open daily until 22.00) and the outskirts of Northwich, one passes Marston (late opening stores and tel) and Wincham (PO, tel, stores). Just west of the village, one travels along a ½-mile stretch of canal that was only cut in 1958, as the old route was about to collapse into – needless to say – underground salt workings. Beyond the woods of Marbury Country Park (attractive short-stay moorings) and before Bridge 198, there are a full range of facilities including toilets, showers and washing machines, followed by Anderton (PO, tel, stores) – the short entrance canal to the famous boat lift down into the Weaver Navigation is on the left. The main line continues westwards, winding along what is now a steep hill and into Barnton Tunnel. There is a useful range of shops, up the hill from the east end of the tunnel, including a laundrette, chemist and butcher. You then emerge onto a hillside overlooking the River Weaver, with a marvellous view straight down the huge Saltersford Locks. Now Saltersford Tunnel is entered: beyond it you are in completely open country again. There are good moorings in the basins to the east of both tunnels.

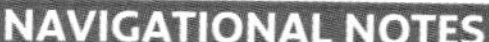

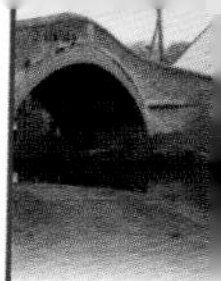

NAVIGATIONAL NOTES

1 Saltersford Tunnel is crooked, affording only a brief glimpse of the other end. Two boats cannot pass in this or Barnton Tunnel, so make sure they are clear before proceeding.

2 *See* notes on page 177 covering use of the Anderton Boat Lift.

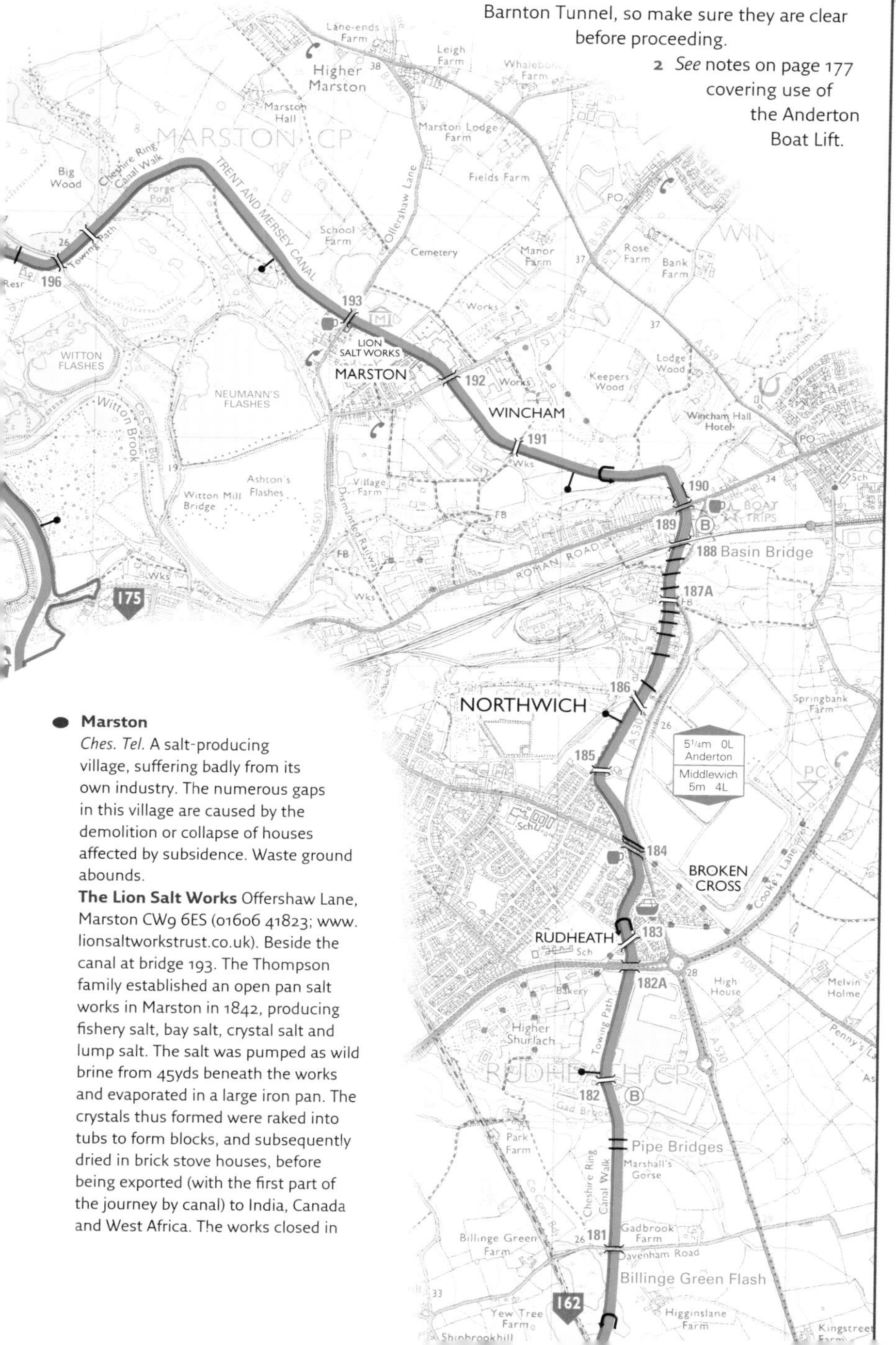

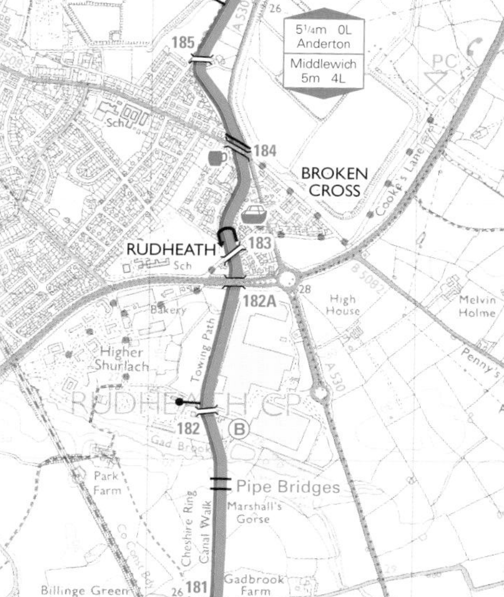

Lane-ends Farm
Higher Marston
Leigh Farm
Whalebone Farm
Marston Hall
MARSTON CP
Marston Lodge Farm
Big Wood
Cheshire Ring Canal Walk
Forge Brook
Forge Pool
TRENT AND MERSEY CANAL
Fields Farm
Ollershaw Lane
School Farm
Cemetery
Manor Farm
PO
Rose Farm
Bank Farm
Towing Path
196
Resr
193
LION SALT WORKS
MARSTON
WITTON FLASHES
NEUMANN'S FLASHES
Works
192
WINCHAM
Keepers Wood
Lodge Wood
A559
Wincham Hall Hotel
191
Witton Brook
Ashton's Flashes
Witton Mill Bridge
Village Farm
Dismantled Railway
190
189
BOAT TRIPS
188 Basin Bridge
ROMAN ROAD
187A
175
NORTHWICH
186
185
A530
5¼m 0L Anderton
Middlewich 5m 4L
Springbank Farm
184
BROKEN CROSS
Cooke's Lane
RUDHEATH
183
182A
High House
Melvin Holme
Higher Shurlach
Bakery
RUDHEATH CP
182
Gad Brook
Park Farm
Pipe Bridges
Marshall's Gorse
Cheshire Ring Canal Walk
Billinge Green Farm
181
Gadbrook Farm
Davenham Road
Billinge Green Flash
162
Yew Tree Farm
Higginslane Farm
Kingstreet Farm
Shipbrookhill

● **Marston**

Ches. Tel. A salt-producing village, suffering badly from its own industry. The numerous gaps in this village are caused by the demolition or collapse of houses affected by subsidence. Waste ground abounds.

The Lion Salt Works Offershaw Lane, Marston CW9 6ES (01606 41823; www.lionsaltworkstrust.co.uk). Beside the canal at bridge 193. The Thompson family established an open pan salt works in Marston in 1842, producing fishery salt, bay salt, crystal salt and lump salt. The salt was pumped as wild brine from 45yds beneath the works and evaporated in a large iron pan. The crystals thus formed were raked into tubs to form blocks, and subsequently dried in brick stove houses, before being exported (with the first part of the journey by canal) to India, Canada and West Africa. The works closed in

1986 but is currently being restored and is well worth visiting. Audio-visual display and many exhibits. *Open Sun–Thu 13.30–16.30, groups by appointment.* Charge. Also information on the attractive countryside of Vale Royal and its rich industrial heritage.

Marbury Country Park Comberbach CW9 6AT (01606 77741; www.cheshire.gov.uk). Two-hundred-acre park occupying the landscaped gardens of the former Marbury Hall and estate, once the home of the Barry and Smith-Barry families. Overlooking Budworth Mere, the house was demolished in 1968 and the much-neglected gardens restored to their former glory by Cheshire County Heritage and Recreation service. The Information Centre (½ mile north of bridge 196) houses a display of Marbury's wildlife and history, including its use as a POW camp during World War II. Visitor's moorings and picnic area.

Anderton Lift

Lift Lane, Anderton CW9 6FW (01606 786777; www.andertonboatlift.co.uk). An amazing and enormous piece of machinery built in 1875 by Leader Williams (later engineer of the Manchester Ship Canal) to connect the Trent & Mersey to the flourishing Weaver Navigation, 50ft below. As built, the lift consisted of two water-filled tanks counterbalancing each other in a vertical slide, resting on massive hydraulic rams. It worked on the very straightforward principle that making the ascending tank slightly lighter – by pumping a little water out – would assist the hydraulic rams (which were operated by a steam engine and pump) in moving both tanks, with boats in them, up or down their respective slide. In 1908 the lift had to have major repairs, so it was modernised at the same time. The troublesome hydraulic rams were done away with; from then on each tank – which contained 250 tons of water – had its own counterweights and was independent of the other tank. Electricity replaced steam as the motive power. One of the most fascinating individual features of the canal system, it draws thousands of sightseers every year. Restoration to full working order is now complete, following the original 1875 hydraulic design, using oil as the motive force rather than the chemically contaminated water that was the cause of the 1908 failure. The more recent counter balance weights, together with their ungainly supporting structure, have been retained to demonstrate the engineering development of the lift.

Northwich

Ches. All services. Regular buses from Barnton. A rather attractive town at the junction of the Rivers Weaver and Dane. (The latter brings large quantities of sand down into the Weaver Navigation, necessitating a heavy expenditure on dredging.) As in every other town in this area, salt has for centuries been responsible for the continued prosperity of Northwich. The Weaver Navigation has of course been another very prominent factor in the town's history, and the building and repairing of barges, narrowboats, and small seagoing ships has been carried on here for over 200 years. Nowadays this industry has been almost forced out of business by foreign competition, and the last private shipyard on the river closed down in 1971. (This yard – Isaac Pimblott's – used to be between Hunt's Locks and Hartford Bridge. Their last contract was a tug for Aden.) However, the big BW yard in the town continues to thrive; some very large maintenance craft are built and repaired here. The wharves by Town Bridge are empty, and are an excellent temporary mooring site for anyone wishing to visit the place. The town centre is very close; much of it has been completely rebuilt very recently. There is now an extensive shopping precinct. Although the large number of pubs has been whittled down in the rebuilding process, there are still some pleasant old streets. The Weaver and the big swing bridges across it remain a dominant part of the background.

Tourist Information Centre 1 The Arcade, Northwich CW9 5AS (01606 353534; www2.valeroyal.gov.uk). *Open Mon–Fri 09.00–17.00; Sat Apr–Oct 10.00–14.00 and Nov–Mar 09.30–12.30.*

Dock Road Edwardian Pumping Station Weir Street, Northwich CW9 8AB (01257 260157). Intriguing listed building housing unique pumps and gas-powered engines fully restored to working order. Building open and engines working *Easter–Sep Sun and B Hols 14.00–17.00, groups by arrangement.* Charge.

Salt Museum Weaver Hall, London Road, Northwich CW9 8AB (01606 41331; www.saltmuseum.org.uk). The history of the salt industry from Roman times to the present day, housed in the town's former workhouse. Look out for the remarkable model ship, made from salt of course. *Open all year Tue–Fri 10.00–17.00; Sat and Sun 14.00–17.00 (12.00–17.00 during Aug); B Hol Mon 10.00–17.00.* Audio visual introduction. Charge

NAVIGATIONAL NOTES

1. The Anderton Boat Lift is available for use 7 days a week and pre-booked passage is essential by telephoning 01606 786777. *Open Apr–Sep 09.00–18.00 with reduced operating hours Oct–Mar.*
2. Boaters should differentiate between the holding moorings at the top and bottom of the lift, which are solely for lift use, and the visitor moorings.

Boatyards

Ⓑ **Orchard Marina** School Road, Gadbrook Park, Rudheath, Northwich CW9 7RG (01606 42082; www.orchardmarina.com). Beside bridge 182. D Pump out, gas, overnight/long-term mooring, dry dock, boat and engine repairs, boat fitting out, boat and engine sales, DIY facilities, books, maps, solid fuel, toilets, showers, laundrette. *Emergency call out.*

Ⓑ **Colliery Narrowboat Co** Wincham Wharf, Lostock Gralam, Northwich CW9 7NT (01606 44672). Beside bridge 189. D Pump out, gas, overnight/long-term mooring, slipway, crane, storage, dry dock, boat building, boat sales, boat and engine repairs, wet dock, DIY facilities, toilets.

Ⓑ **Alvechurch Boat Centres** Anderton Marina, Uplands Road, Anderton CW9 6AQ (01606 79642; www.alvechurch.com). Services are on the canal. D E Pump out, gas, narrowboat hire, overnight mooring, long-term mooring, slipway, sales, engine sales and repairs, boat painting, covered wet docks for hire, chandlery, gifts, restaurant, telephone, toilets.

Ⓑ **Barnton Wharf** Barnton Road, Northwich CW8 4EP (01606 783320). D Pump out, gas, day craft hire, long-term mooring, boat and engine sales, boat and engine repairs, boat fitting out, solid fuel. *24hr emergency call out.*

Ⓑ **Travelreign** Uplands Road, Anderton CW9 6AQ (07931 323747). Overnight and long-term mooring, winter storage, slipway, wet dock.

BIRD LIFE

The *Kingfisher* is a dazzlingly attractive bird, but its colours often appear muted when the bird is seen sitting in shade or vegetation. It has orange-red underparts and mainly blue upperparts; the electric blue back is seen to the best effect when the bird is observed in low-level flight speeding along a river. It is invariably seen near water and uses overhanging branches to watch for fish. When a feeding opportunity arises, the Kingfisher plunges headlong into the water, catching its prey in its bill: the fish is swallowed whole. Kingfishers nest in holes excavated in the river bank.

Pubs and Restaurants

Old Broken Cross Broken Cross Place, Rudheath, Northwich CW9 7EB (01606 40431). Canalside, at bridge 184. Real ale and food *L and E, all day.* Children and dogs welcome. Monthly entertainment. Small canalside garden. Moorings. *Chemist, grocer, laundrette and other shops are ½ mile past pub, towards Northwich.*

Wharf Wincham Wharf, Manchester Road, Lostock Gralam, Northwich CW9 7NT (01606 46099). Canalside by bridge 189. Converted warehouse, reputed to be the oldest on the Trent & Mersey. Real ale is served, together with inexpensive bar meals *L and E (until 19.00 unless by prior arrangement).* Children welcome. Music, karaoke and quiz nights. Large-screen TV upstairs.

Salt Barge Ollershaw Lane, Marston CW9 6ES (01606 43064). Opposite the Lion Salt Works, beside bridge 193. Deceptively large pub with a friendly atmosphere, neatly divided into cosy areas, and with an inviting family room. Real ales and good food available *L and E, daily.* Children's menu and *Sunday* lunch. Garden. Quiz *Thu* and live music at *weekends.*

The Moorings Anderton Marina, Uplands Road, Anderton CW9 6AJ (01606 79789; www.mooringsrestaurant.co.uk). Canalside seating. Boaters please moor outside the basin. Small, independent restaurant and bar overlooking Anderton Marina and the Trent & Mersey Canal. *Open all day.* Wide variety of food with emphasis on fresh fish and fresh produce, served *L and E (not Mon E or Tue all day).* Children and dogs welcome. Patio and terrace.

Anderton Boat Lift Café Lift Lane, Anderton, Northwich CW9 6FW (01606 786777; www.andertonboatlift.co.uk). Café inside the Lift Operations Centre serving tea, coffee, hot and cold snacks, ice creams, etc. Children welcome. *Open as per the Lift Centre.*

Stanley Arms Old Road, Anderton CW9 6AG (01606 75059; www.stanleyarmsnorthwich.co.uk). Canalside, right opposite the Anderton Lift *(also PO, stores).* Friendly real ale pub where children are welcome. Bar food served *all day, every day.* Outside seating and children's play area. The landlord keeps a collection of local tourist information leaflets. Excellent 'bottom of garden' moorings.

Dutton

This, the northernmost stretch of the Trent & Mersey, is a very pleasant one and delightfully rural. Most of the way the navigation follows the south side of the hills that overlook the River Weaver. From about 60ft up, one is often rewarded with excellent views of this splendid valley and the very occasional large vessels that ply up and down it. At one point one can see the elegant Dutton railway viaduct in the distance; then the two waterways diverge as the Trent & Mersey enters the woods preceding Preston Brook Tunnel. There is a stop lock south of the tunnel just beyond a pretty covered dry dock; there are often fine examples of restored working boats moored here. At the north end of the tunnel a notice announces that from here onwards one is on the Bridgewater Canal (*see Guide 5*). There are good moorings north of bridge 213, and to the south of Dutton stop lock.

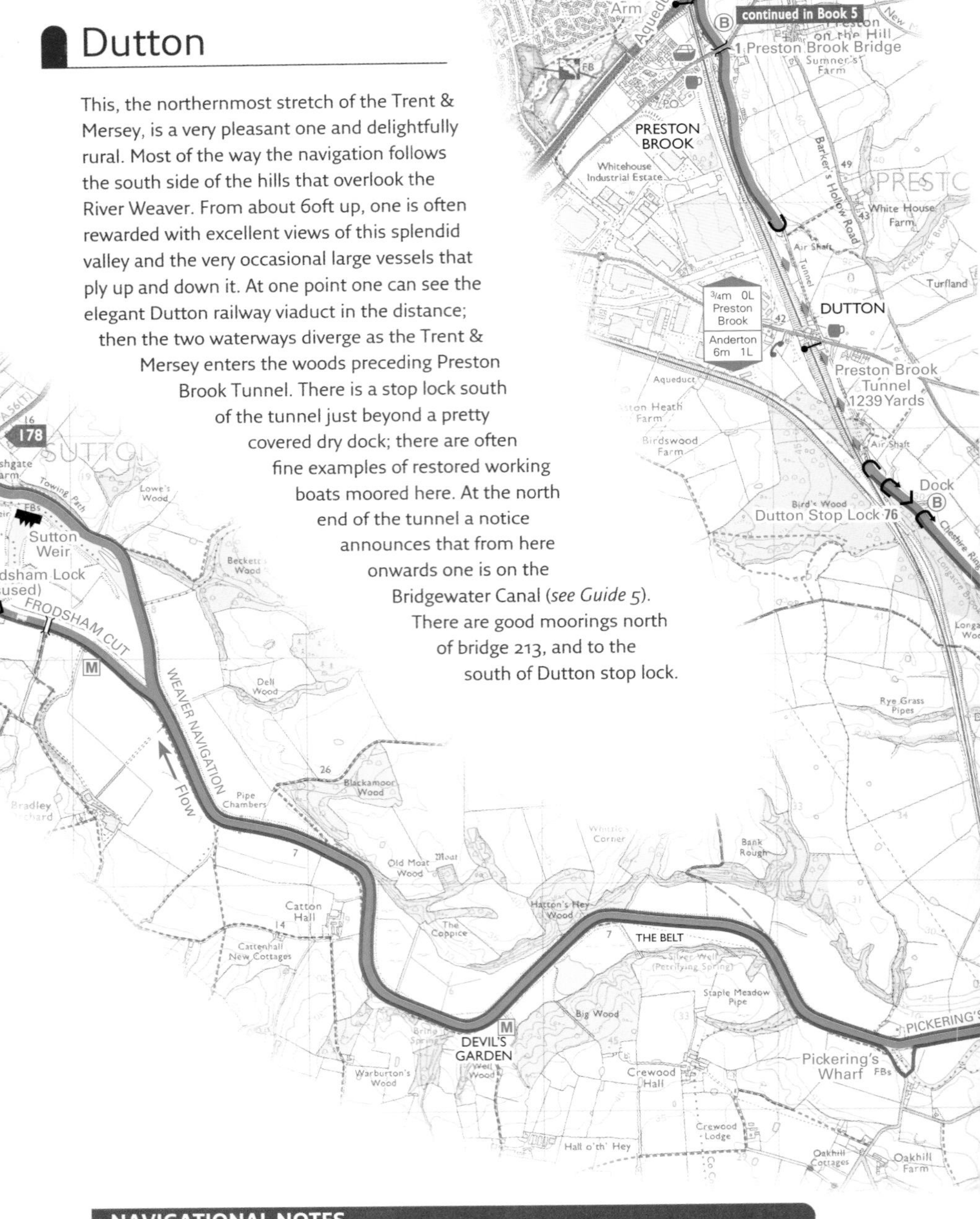

NAVIGATIONAL NOTES

1 Access to Preston Brook Tunnel is restricted to *northbound on the hour to 10 minutes past the hour; southbound on the ½ hour to 20 mins to the hour.*

2 North of Preston Brook Tunnel you are on the Bridgewater Canal, which is owned by the Manchester Ship Canal Company, and is described in detail in *Guide 5*.

3 A British Waterways licence is valid for seven consecutive days on this canal.

Pubs and Restaurants

Leigh Arms Warrington Road, Little Leigh, Northwich CW8 4QT (01606 853327; www.leigharms.co.uk). 1/4 mile south of bridge 209, overlooking the Weaver and Acton Swing Bridge. Attractive old coaching inn with large restaurant area serving real ales and an extensive menu of home-made food *all day, every day*. Children and dogs welcome. Patio and garden seating, children's play area. Live music *Thu/Fri*. Moorings.

Horns Inn Warrington Road, Little Leigh, Northwich CW8 4QT (01606 852192). 200yds south of bridge 209 on the A49, by Acton Swing Bridge. Friendly, roadside pub serving meals *L and E, daily*. Cosy bars, large garden and children's play area.

Hollybush Warrington Road, Little Leigh, Northwich CW8 4QY (01606 853196). 1/4 mile north of bridge 209. Listed, timber-framed building, one of the oldest farmhouse pubs in the country, with unique charm and character. Wide range of interesting, home-cooked food served in bar and restaurant *L and E, daily*. Children welcome. Garden with children's play area, including bouncy castle. Traditional pub games. Curry night *Fri*; quiz night *Sun*. B & B.

Tunnel Top Northwich Road, Dutton, Warrington WA4 4JY (01928 718181). Family pub serving real ale and excellent food *L and E; carvery Fri–Sun*. Children and dogs welcome. Large garden.

Boatyards

Ⓑ **Black Prince Holidays** Bartington Wharf, Acton Bridge, Northwich CW8 4QU (01606 852945; www.black-prince.com). D E Pump out, gas, electric boat recharging, narrowboat hire, day-hire craft, long-term mooring, engine repairs, groceries, books and maps, toilets, gifts, coal.

Ⓑ **Dutton Dry Dock** Tunnel End, Dutton, Warrington WA4 4LA (01928 716701; duttondock@onetel.co.uk). Dry dock, historic boat repairs, boat blacking, boat repairs, engineering and machine shop, vintage engine repairs.

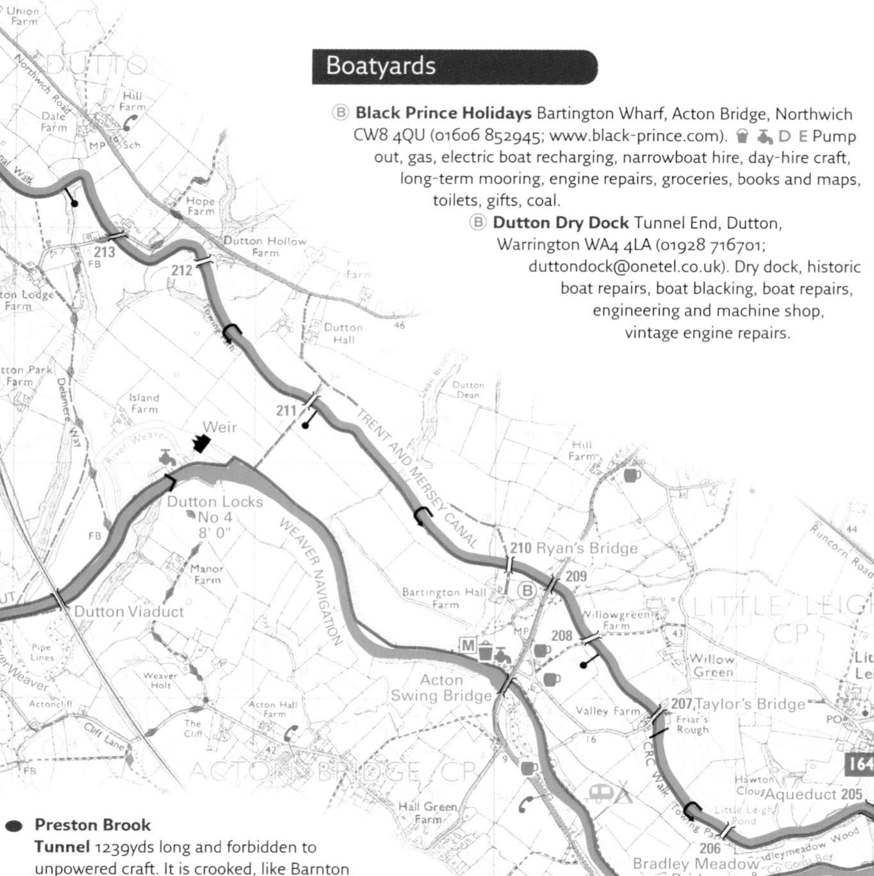

● **Preston Brook Tunnel** 1239yds long and forbidden to unpowered craft. It is crooked, like Barnton and Saltersford tunnels, and there is no towpath.

● **Dutton** *Ches. Tel, garage.* Small settlement on top of Preston Brook Tunnel, at the end of the lane uphill from the south end of the tunnel.

WILDLIFE

The *Reed Warbler*, as the name suggests is almost always associated with reed beds. It is a summer visitor from May to August. These singing birds clamber up reeds, or occasionally use bushes, to deliver a grating, chattering song that includes some mimetic elements. The Reed Warbler has rather nondescript sandy-brown upperparts, paler underparts and dark legs. It constructs a woven, cup-shaped nest attached to upright reed stems, and feeds on insects.

Tree Sparrows, although distributed widely throughout the country, are decidedly scarce. They are occasionally found on the outskirts of villages but are more usually associated with untidy arable farms, taking advantage of frequent grain spills along with buntings and finches. The sexes are similar and easily distinguished from house sparrows by the chestnut cap and nape, and the black patch on an otherwise white cheek. The plumage is otherwise streaked brown on the backs, with pale underparts. The juveniles lack the black cheek patches. Tree sparrows utter house sparrow-like chirps but also a sharp 'tik tik' in flight. They form flocks in winter, sometimes feeding in stubble fields.

The *Southern Hawker* is a large, active species of dragonfly, associated with ponds, lakes, rivers and canals. It patrols a regular patch of water when hunting but can also be seen hawking along woodland rides well away from water. The southern hawker shows broad green stripes on the thorax and abdomen, with markings of a similar colouration on the abdomen except for the last three segments of the male, where the markings are blue. It flies from June to October.

The *Banded Demoiselle* is an attractive damselfly, often found resting among waterside vegetation. The males can be seen in small, fluttering groups hovering over water; the flight of the females is rather feeble. They favour clean steams where the nymphs live partly buried in muddy sediment. The male has a blue body with a metallic sheen; smoky wings show a conspicuous blue 'thumbprint' mark. The female has a green body with a metallic sheen and greenish brown wings. Banded demoiselles fly May to August.

The *Teasel* is a biennial of damp grassland on heavy, often disturbed soils. It produces a rosette of spine-coated leaves in the first year. In the second year, conical heads of purple flowers are borne on tall, angled and spined stems July–August. The dead heads persist. In flower, teasels are popular with bees; the seedheads are particularly favoured by goldfinches.

The *Buddleia*, beloved by butterflies and bees, is a common garden shrub, also widely naturalised on wasteground and around coasts. It has long, narrow leaves which are darker above than below. The showy, often drooping spikes of purple flowers appear June–September.

RIVER WEAVER

MAXIMUM DIMENSIONS

Anderton to Winsford
Length: 196' 6"
Beam: 35' 0"
Draught: 9' 6"
Headroom: 29' 6"

Western Marsh Lock to Anderton
Length: 213' 0"
Beam: 3' 6"
Draught: 10' 6"
Headroom: 59' 0"

Anderton Lift Branch
Length: 72' 0"
Beam: 14' 4"
Draught: 4' 7"
Headroom: 8' 2"

MANAGER

01606 723800
enquiries.wbc@britishwaterways.co.uk

MILEAGE

WINSFORD BRIDGE to:
Northwich: 5½ miles
Anderton Lift (Trent & Mersey Canal): 7 miles
Acton Bridge: 11 miles
Sutton Bridge: 17 miles

WESTON POINT DOCKS (Manchester Ship Canal): 20 miles
Weston Marsh Lock: 19 miles

Locks: 5

The river itself, which rises in the Peckforton Hills and proceeds via Wrenbury, Audlem, Nantwich, Church Minshull and Winsford to Northwich and Frodsham, is just over 50 miles long. Originally a shallow and tidal stream, it was long used for carrying salt away from the Cheshire salt area. The mineral was carried down by men and horses to meet the incoming tide. The sailing barges would load at high water, then depart with the ebbing tide.

In the 17th C the expansion of the salt industry around Northwich, Middlewich and Winsford gave rise to an increasing demand for a navigation right up to Winsford. In 1721, three gentlemen of Cheshire obtained an Act of Parliament to make and maintain the river as a navigation from Frodsham to Winsford, 20 miles upstream. By 1732 the Weaver was fully navigable for 40-ton barges up to Winsford.

When in 1765 the Trent & Mersey was planned to pass along the River Weaver the trustees of the Weaver were understandably alarmed; but in the event the new canal provided much traffic for the river, for although the two waterways did not join, they were so close at Anderton that in 1793 chutes were constructed on the Trent & Mersey directly above a specially built dock on the River Weaver, 50ft below. Thereafter salt was transhipped in ever-increasing quantities by dropping it down the chutes from canal boats into Weaver flats (barges) on the river. This system continued until 1871, when it was decided to construct the great iron boat lift beside the chutes at Anderton. This remarkable structure, now completely restored and in full operation, thus effected a proper junction between the two waterways.

The Weaver Navigation did well throughout the 19th C, mainly because continual and vigorous programmes of modernisation kept it thoroughly attractive to carriers, especially when compared to the rapidly dating narrow canals. Eventually coasters were able to navigate the river right up to Winsford.

In spite of this constant improvement of the navigation, the Weaver's traditional salt trade was affected by 19th-C competition from railways and the new pipelines. However, the chemical industry began to sprout around the Northwich area at the same time and, until recently, Brunner Mond's works at Winnington supplied virtually all the remaining traffic on the river.

Winsford

Although Winsford Bridge (fixed at 10ft 8in) is the upper limit of navigation for shipping and the limit of British Waterways jurisdiction, canal boats can easily slip under the bridge and round the bend into the vast, wonderful and deceptively shallow Winsford Bottom Flash. Navigation upstream of the Bottom Flash is unreliable, for the channel is shallow and winding, but can apparently be done by adventurous persons with small craft. The Top Flash is situated just beside and below the Middlewich Branch of the Shropshire Union Canal, but there is no junction between them here. Downstream of Winsford Bridge is a winding stretch that runs past the oldest and deepest rock salt mine in the country: each bank is piled high with the industrial leftovers of chemical industries and rock salt. But soon the horizon clears as one arrives at Newbridge, beyond which is the superb stretch known as Vale Royal Cut. The Vale Royal Cut typifies the Weaver at its most attractive. The river flows along a closely defined flat green valley floor, flanked by mature woods climbing the steep hillsides that enclose the valley. No buildings or roads intrude upon this very pleasant scene. Vale Royal Locks are at the far end of the cut; the remains of the old Vale Royal Abbey (believed to have been founded by Edward I and dissolved by Henry VIII) are just up the hill nearby. Beyond is a tall stone railway viaduct.

NAVIGATIONAL NOTES

1. The operating times for locks and bridges are *Mon–Thu 08.00–16.15, Fri 08.00–15.45*. Lunch break *12.00–12.45 approx*. Weekend operation of **locks only**: *Apr–Sep 10.00–18.00 & Oct 10.00–16.00. This includes B Hols*. All craft to arrive *30 mins before closing time* to be guaranteed passage. Weston Marsh Lock will be *open at weekends Apr–Oct* for vessels with the necessary paperwork and clearance for the Manchester Ship Canal **but** notice must be given to the Weaver Office *by 16.30 on the previous Thu*. Contact 01606 723800; enquiries.wbc@britishwaterways.co.uk for further details. All locks and bridges are manned.
2. The Weaver is a river navigation that occasionally carries commercial traffic – transported not in canal boats or barges, but in small seagoing ships displacing up to 1000 tonnes, which can use the navigation at all times of day or night. The locks are correspondingly large and often paired. The bridges are either very high or are big swing bridges operated by BW staff. With the exception of Town Bridge in Northwich and Newbridge below Winsford (6ft 4in) none of these bridges need to be swung for any boat with a height above water of less than 8ft. Those craft which do require the bridges to be opened should give prior notice to British Waterways by telephoning 01606 723900. Unless there has been heavy rain, the current is quite gentle – however, as on any river navigation, an anchor and rope should be carried, and the rules should be adhered to. There are few facilities for pleasure craft.

Winsford

Ches. All services (station 1 mile east). A busy salt-mining town astride the Weaver. The centre of town used to be very close to the river, but now a huge new shopping precinct has shifted the heart of the town well away from it. Up the hill, east of the river, there is a pub, takeaway and stores (straight on at the roundabout). Turn left at the roundabout for a large supermarket and garage. To the south west of Winsford Bridge there is a cycle shop and another garage. Up the High street, west of the bridge, there are shops and the Golden Lion Pub.

Winsford Bottom Flash

This very large expanse of water, in an attractive setting among wooded slopes, was created by subsidence following salt extraction in the vicinity. Three caravan sites and a sailing club are based along its banks and anglers crouch in the waterside bushes. It is, however, quite shallow in places – those in canal craft *beware!*

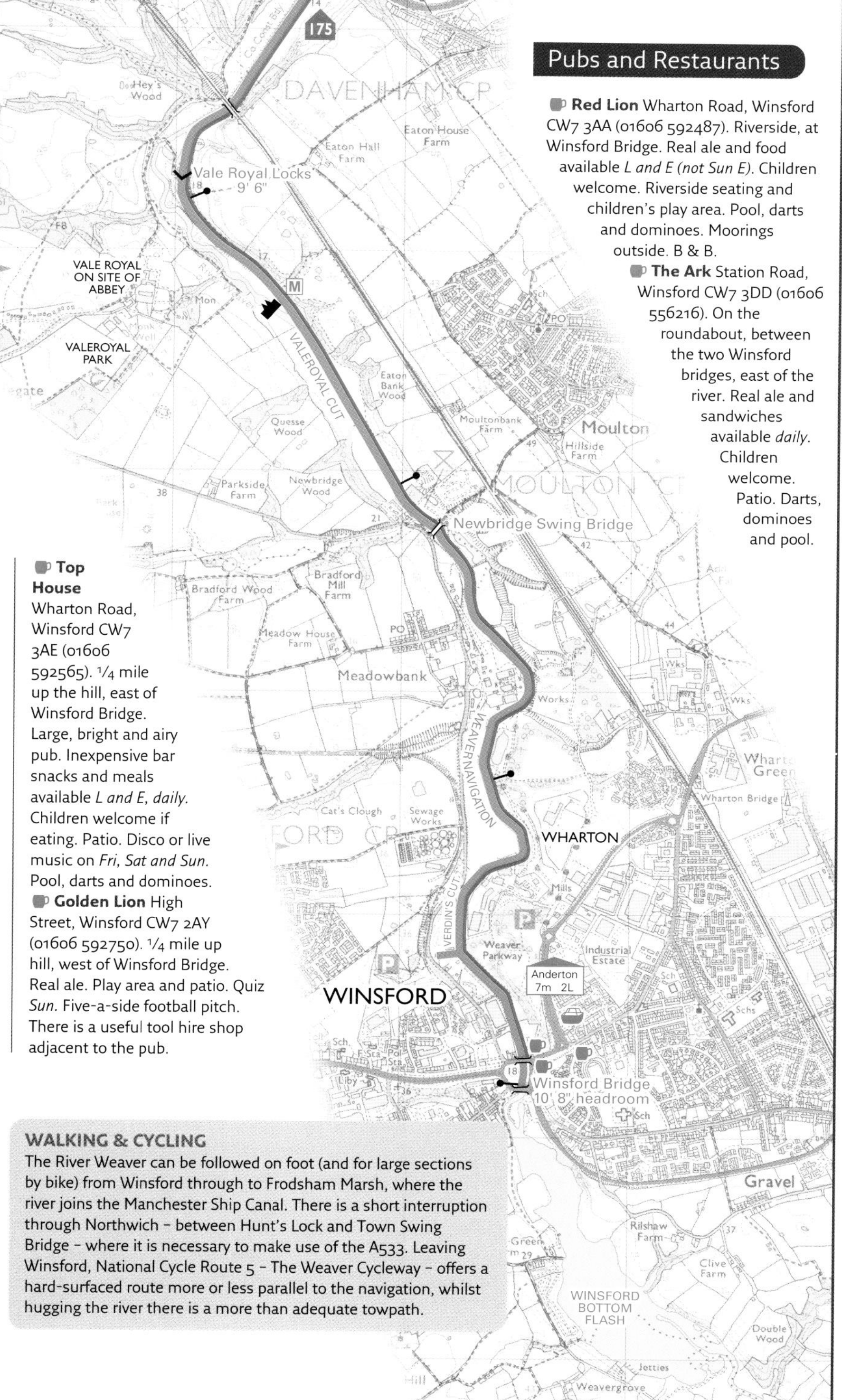

Pubs and Restaurants

Red Lion Wharton Road, Winsford CW7 3AA (01606 592487). Riverside, at Winsford Bridge. Real ale and food available *L and E (not Sun E)*. Children welcome. Riverside seating and children's play area. Pool, darts and dominoes. Moorings outside. B & B.

The Ark Station Road, Winsford CW7 3DD (01606 556216). On the roundabout, between the two Winsford bridges, east of the river. Real ale and sandwiches available *daily*. Children welcome. Patio. Darts, dominoes and pool.

Top House Wharton Road, Winsford CW7 3AE (01606 592565). 1/4 mile up the hill, east of Winsford Bridge. Large, bright and airy pub. Inexpensive bar snacks and meals available *L and E, daily*. Children welcome if eating. Patio. Disco or live music on *Fri, Sat and Sun*. Pool, darts and dominoes.

Golden Lion High Street, Winsford CW7 2AY (01606 592750). 1/4 mile up hill, west of Winsford Bridge. Real ale. Play area and patio. Quiz *Sun*. Five-a-side football pitch. There is a useful tool hire shop adjacent to the pub.

WALKING & CYCLING

The River Weaver can be followed on foot (and for large sections by bike) from Winsford through to Frodsham Marsh, where the river joins the Manchester Ship Canal. There is a short interruption through Northwich – between Hunt's Lock and Town Swing Bridge – where it is necessary to make use of the A533. Leaving Winsford, National Cycle Route 5 – The Weaver Cycleway – offers a hard-surfaced route more or less parallel to the navigation, whilst hugging the river there is a more than adequate towpath.

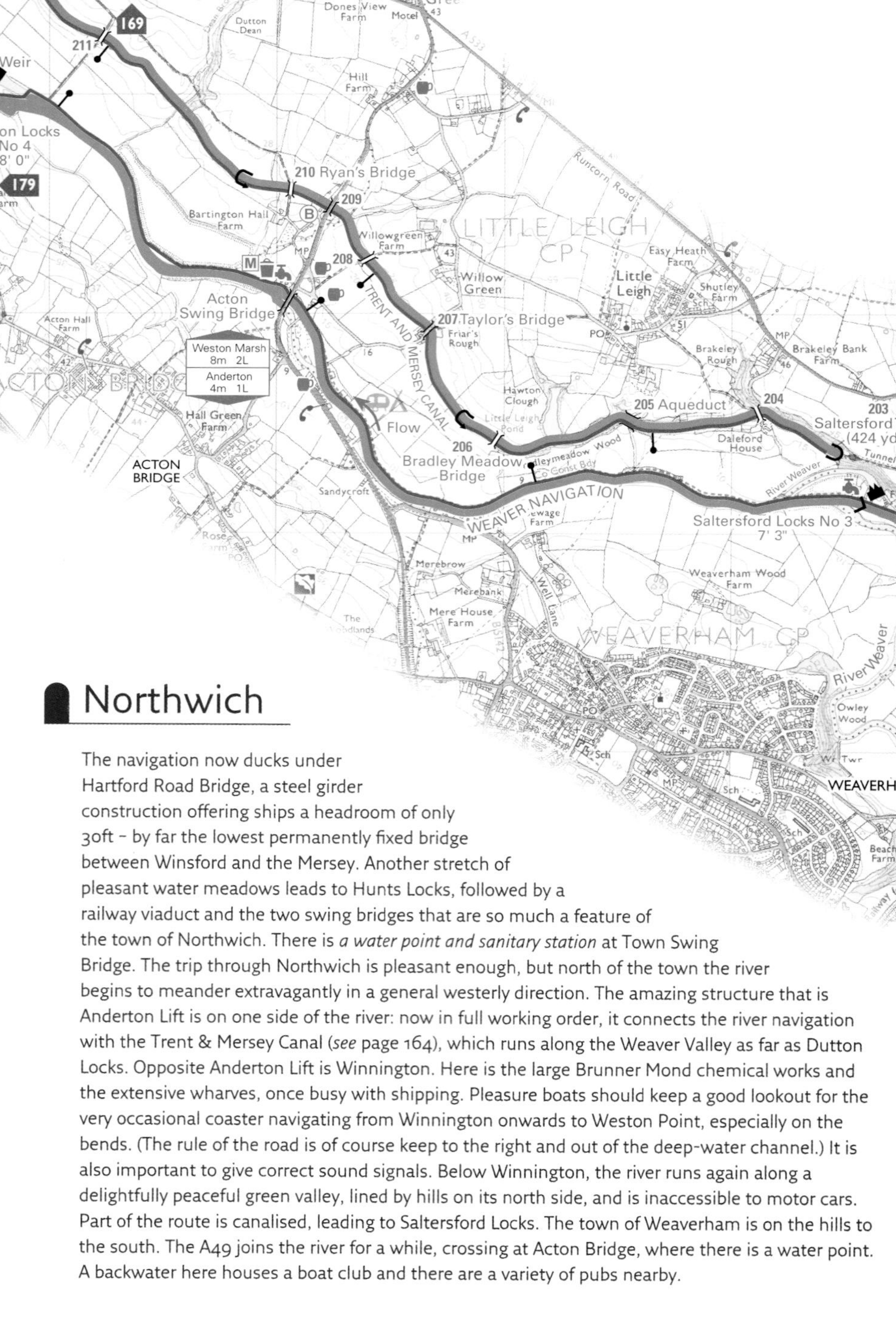

Northwich

The navigation now ducks under Hartford Road Bridge, a steel girder construction offering ships a headroom of only 30ft – by far the lowest permanently fixed bridge between Winsford and the Mersey. Another stretch of pleasant water meadows leads to Hunts Locks, followed by a railway viaduct and the two swing bridges that are so much a feature of the town of Northwich. There is *a water point and sanitary station* at Town Swing Bridge. The trip through Northwich is pleasant enough, but north of the town the river begins to meander extravagantly in a general westerly direction. The amazing structure that is Anderton Lift is on one side of the river: now in full working order, it connects the river navigation with the Trent & Mersey Canal (*see* page 164), which runs along the Weaver Valley as far as Dutton Locks. Opposite Anderton Lift is Winnington. Here is the large Brunner Mond chemical works and the extensive wharves, once busy with shipping. Pleasure boats should keep a good lookout for the very occasional coaster navigating from Winnington onwards to Weston Point, especially on the bends. (The rule of the road is of course keep to the right and out of the deep-water channel.) It is also important to give correct sound signals. Below Winnington, the river runs again along a delightfully peaceful green valley, lined by hills on its north side, and is inaccessible to motor cars. Part of the route is canalised, leading to Saltersford Locks. The town of Weaverham is on the hills to the south. The A49 joins the river for a while, crossing at Acton Bridge, where there is a water point. A backwater here houses a boat club and there are a variety of pubs nearby.

BOAT TRIPS

Sovereign Cruises trips from Northwich Marina (Chester Way, Northwich CW9 5JJ) and the top of the Anderton Boat Lift (Anderton CW9 6FW) by the main car park. Telephone 01606 76204

Edwin Clark (01606 786777; www.andertonboatlift.co.uk). British Waterways' glass-topped trip boat offering trips up and down the lift and along the connecting waterways. Telephone or visit website for further details.

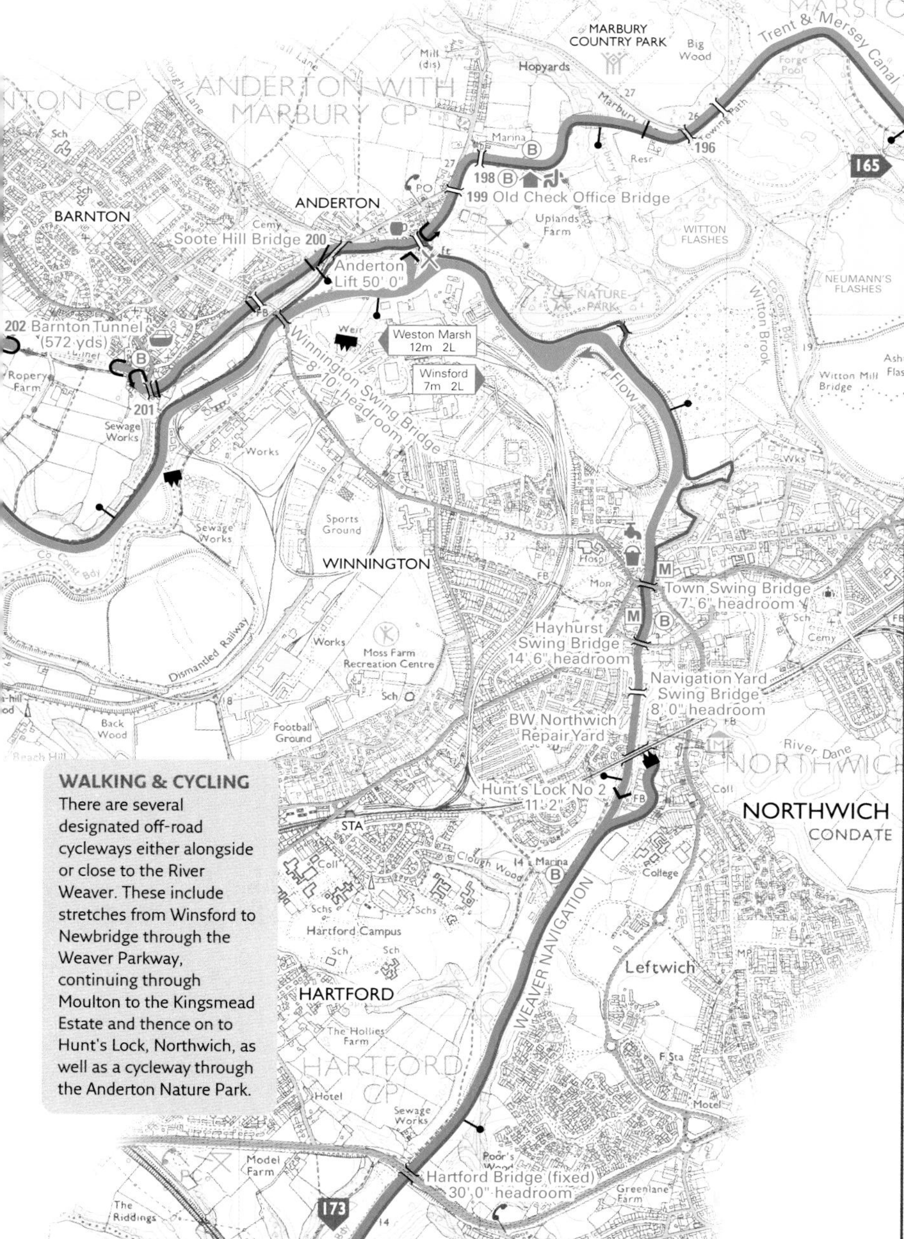

WALKING & CYCLING

There are several designated off-road cycleways either alongside or close to the River Weaver. These include stretches from Winsford to Newbridge through the Weaver Parkway, continuing through Moulton to the Kingsmead Estate and thence on to Hunt's Lock, Northwich, as well as a cycleway through the Anderton Nature Park.

Boatyards

British Waterways North West Region Offices and Repair Yard Navigation Road, Northwich CW8 1BH (01606 74321). Alongside the extensive workshops is the NW Region office – formerly the Weaver Navigation Trustee's offices. As usual, this yard contains many mellow 18th-C buildings. There is also an elegant clock tower on the office block that has been completely refurbished.

Ⓑ **Jalsea Marine** Weaver Shipyard, off Darwin Street, Northwich CW8 1LB (01606 77870; www.jalsea.co.uk). D Overnight and long-term mooring, winter storage, undercover storage and workshops, slipway, crane (30 tons), boat sales, engine sales and repairs, specialist refits and repairs on older wooden boats, boat building, painting, sandblasting, fabrication and repairs, welding, DIY facilities, chandlery, books, maps, gifts, telephone, toilets, showers. Will make arrangements for transit passage to the sea via the Manchester Ship Canal including mandatory certificate of seaworthiness. Special package available for Anderton Lift users.

Ⓑ **Northwich Marina** Hayhurst Boatyard, Chester Way, Northwich CW9 5JJ (01606 44475; www.northwichmarina.co.uk). D Gas, overnight and long-term mooring, winter storage, covered slipway, side slip, crane (6 tons), boat sales and repairs, engine sales and repairs including outboards, chandlery, boat fitting out, DIY facilities, toilets.

The following are on the Trent & Mersey Canal.

Ⓑ **Alvechurch Boat Centres** Anderton Marina, Uplands Road, Anderton CW9 6AQ (01606 79642; www. alvechurch.com). Services are on the canal. D E Pump out, gas, narrowboat hire, overnight mooring, long-term mooring, slipway, sales, engine repairs, boat painting, covered wetdocks for hire, chandlery, gifts, restaurant, telephone, toilets.

Ⓑ **Barnton Wharf** Tunnel Road, Northwich CW8 4EP (01606 783320; barntonwharf@ talk21.com). D Pump out, gas, day-craft hire, long-term mooring, boat and engine sales, boat and engine repairs, boat fitting out, solid fuel. *24hr emergency call out.*

Ⓑ **Black Prince Holidays** Bartington Wharf, Acton Bridge, Northwich CW8 4QU (01606 852945; www. black-prince.com). D E Pump out, gas. *See* page 169 for further details – note that pump out machine is mobile and will attend boats at Acton Bridge.

Northwich

Ches. All services. A rather attractive town at the junction of the Rivers Weaver and Dane. (The latter brings large quantities of sand down into the Weaver Navigation, necessitating a heavy expenditure on dredging.) As in every town in this area, salt has for centuries been responsible for the continued prosperity of Northwich. The town's motto is *Sal est Vita*, Salt is Life, and there is a salt museum in London Road. The Brine Baths at Moss Farm Sports Complex are still *open throughout the year* for the benefit of salt-water enthusiasts. The Weaver Navigation has of course been another very prominent factor in the town's history, and the building and repairing of barges, narrowboats, and small seagoing ships has been carried on here for over 200 years. Nowadays this industry has been almost forced out of business by foreign competition, and the last private shipyard on the river closed down in 1971. The wharves by Town Bridge are empty, and are an excellent temporary mooring site for anyone wishing to visit the place. The town centre is very close; much of it has been completely rebuilt, with an extensive shopping precinct. Although the large number of pubs has been whittled down in the rebuilding process, there are still some pleasant old streets. The Weaver and the big swing bridges across it remain a dominant part of the background.

Anderton Lift

An amazing and enormous piece of machinery built in 1875 by Leader Williams (later engineer of the Manchester Ship Canal) to connect the Trent & Mersey to the flourishing Weaver Navigation, 50ft below. As built, the lift consisted of two water-filled tanks counterbalancing each other in a vertical slide, resting on massive hydraulic rams. It worked on the very straightforward principle that making the ascending tank slightly lighter – by pumping a little water out – would assist the hydraulic rams (which were operated by a steam engine and pump) in moving both tanks, with boats in them, up or down their respective slide. In 1908 the lift had to have major repairs, so it was modernised at the same time. The troublesome hydraulic rams were done away with; from then on each tank – which contained 250 tons of water – had its own counterweights and was independent of the other tank. Electricity replaced steam as the motive power. One of the most fascinating individual features of the canal system, it draws thousands of sightseers every year. Restoration to full working order is now complete, following the original 1875 hydraulic design, using oil as the motive force rather than the chemically contaminated water that was the cause of the 1908 failure. The more recent counterbalance weights, together with their ungainly supporting structure, have been retained on site to demonstrate the engineering development of the lift.

Anderton Boat Lift Centre Lift Lane, Anderton, Northwich CW9 6FW (0161 786777; www.andertonboatlift.co.uk). In 1983 the Anderton Boat Lift structure was declared unsafe and in a dangerous condition and was closed pending sufficient funds becoming available for restoration. This took nearly two decades and the lift was finally reopened as a visitor attraction in March 2002 after a £7m renovation. Today there is a large Operations Centre building housing an extensive interactive exhibition with comprehensive interpretation of the whole site. Also a shop and café with a seating area offering good views out over the River Weaver. Outside there is a children's play area, a maze constructed from the old counterbalance weights that used to hang on the structure and a picnic area. *Open daily Easter-Sep 10.00-17.00; Oct Wed-Sun 11.00-16.00 & Nov Thu-Sun 11.00-16.00 (no boat trips). Closed Dec-Feb.* Entrance to the site and exhibition is free.

Dock Road Edwardian Pumping Station Weir Street, Northwich (07970 207 941; www.pauline-roscoe.co.uk). Intriguing listed building housing unique pumps and gas-powered engines fully restored to working order. Building open and engines working *Easter-Sep Sun and B Hols 14.00-17.00, groups by arrangement.* Charge.

Salt Museum Weaver Hall, London Road, Northwich CW9 8AB (01606 271640; www.saltmuseum.org.uk). The history of the salt industry from Roman times to the present day, housed in the town's former workhouse. Look out for the remarkable model ship, made from salt of course. *Open all year Tue-Fri 10.00-17.00; Sat and Sun 14.00-17.00 (12.00-17.00 during Aug); B Hol Mon 10.00-17.00.* Audio visual introduction. Charge.

Tourist Information Centre 1 The Arcade, Northwich CW9 5AS (01606 353534; www.valeroyal.gov.uk). *Open Mon-Fri 09.00-17.00; Sat Apr-Oct 10.00-14.00 and Nov-Mar 09.30-12.30.*

● **Weaverham**

Ches. PO, tel, stores, chemist, takeaways, garage. The heart of this town contains many old timbered houses and thatched cottages - but these are now heavily outnumbered by council housing estates. The church of St Mary is an imposing Norman building containing several items of interest.

● **Acton Swing Bridge**

An impressive structure weighing 650 tonnes, which uses a very small amount of electricity to open it; 560 tonnes of its weight is borne by a floating pontoon. It was built in 1933, and extensively refurbished in 1999.

NAVIGATIONAL NOTES

1 The Anderton Boat Lift is available for use *7 days a week* and passage can be pre-booked by contacting (01606) 786777; www.andertonboatlift.co.uk. Charge. However, long-term BW licence holders can turn up on the day and take the first available slot without charge. *Open Apr-Sep 11.00-18.00 with reduced operating hours Oct-Mar.*

2 Boaters should differentiate between the holding moorings at the top and bottom of the lift, which are solely for lift use, and the visitor moorings beside Anderton Nature Park on the Weaver. Similar short-stay visitor moorings are available on the Trent & Mersey.

Pubs and Restaurants

There are plenty of pubs in Northwich.

The Floatel London Road, Northwich CW9 5HD (01606 44443). Close to Northwich Marine at the junction of the Rivers Dane and Weaver. This low budget floating hotel complex was launched some 18 years ago and was built locally. It's a family run establishment serving bar snacks, à la carte and carvery menus, *L and E (not Sat and Sun L).* Children welcome. Riverside veranda and own moorings. Cabin B & B.

Hollybush Warrington Road, Little Leigh, Acton Bridge CW8 4QY (01606 853196; www.thehollybush.net). 1/4 mile north of bridge 209. Listed, timber-framed building, one of the oldest farmhouse pubs in the country, with unique charm and character. Real ale and wide range of interesting, home-cooked food served in bar and restaurant *L and E, daily.* Curry night *Fri.* Children welcome. Garden with children's play area. Traditional pub games. Quiz night *Sat.* B & B.

Stanley Arms Old Road, Anderton, Northwich CW9 6AG (01606 75059; www.stanleyarmsnorthwich.co.uk). Canalside, right opposite the Anderton Lift *(also PO, stores).* Friendly real ale pub where children are welcome. Bar food and restaurant meals served *all day, every day.* Garden. The landlord keeps a collection of local tourist information leaflets. Excellent 'bottom of garden' moorings. Quiz night *Wed,* live music *Thu.*

Anderton Boat Lift Café Lift Lane, Anderton, Northwich CW9 6FW (01606 786777; www.andertonboatlift.co.uk). Café inside the Lift Operations Centre serving tea, coffee, hot and cold snacks, ice creams, etc. Children welcome. *Open as per the Lift Centre.*

Riverside Inn Warrington Road, Acton Bridge CW8 3QD (01606 852310; www.marstonsinnsandtaverns.co.uk). Traditional pub offering real ale and serving meals *all day.* Conservatory, patio and garden. Children welcome. Moorings.

Leigh Arms Warrington Road, Acton Bridge CW8 4QT (01606 853327; www.leigharms.co.uk). 1/4 mile south of bridge 209, overlooking the Weaver and Acton Swing Bridge. Footpath between river and garden. Attractive old coaching inn with large restaurant area serving real ales and an extensive menu of home-made food *all day, every day.* Children and dogs welcome. Patio and garden seating. Large children's play area. Curry night *Mon;* live music *Thu.*

Horns Inn Warrington Road, Acton Bridge CW8 4QT (01606 852192). 200yds south of bridge 209 on the A49, by Acton Swing Bridge. Friendly, roadside pub serving home-made meals *L and E, daily.* Cosy bars, garden and children's play area.

Frodsham

A mile further on, Dutton Locks lead to the Dutton railway viaduct, whose elegant stone arches carry the main electrified West Coast Main Line. Beyond the viaduct one comes to Pickering's Wharf, the site of a swing bridge long gone. From here down to Frodsham, the Weaver Valley is a beautiful green, narrow cutting reminiscent of Vale Royal. Woods are ranged along the hills on either side. There are no roads, and no houses except for one farm. It is a delightfully secluded rural setting.

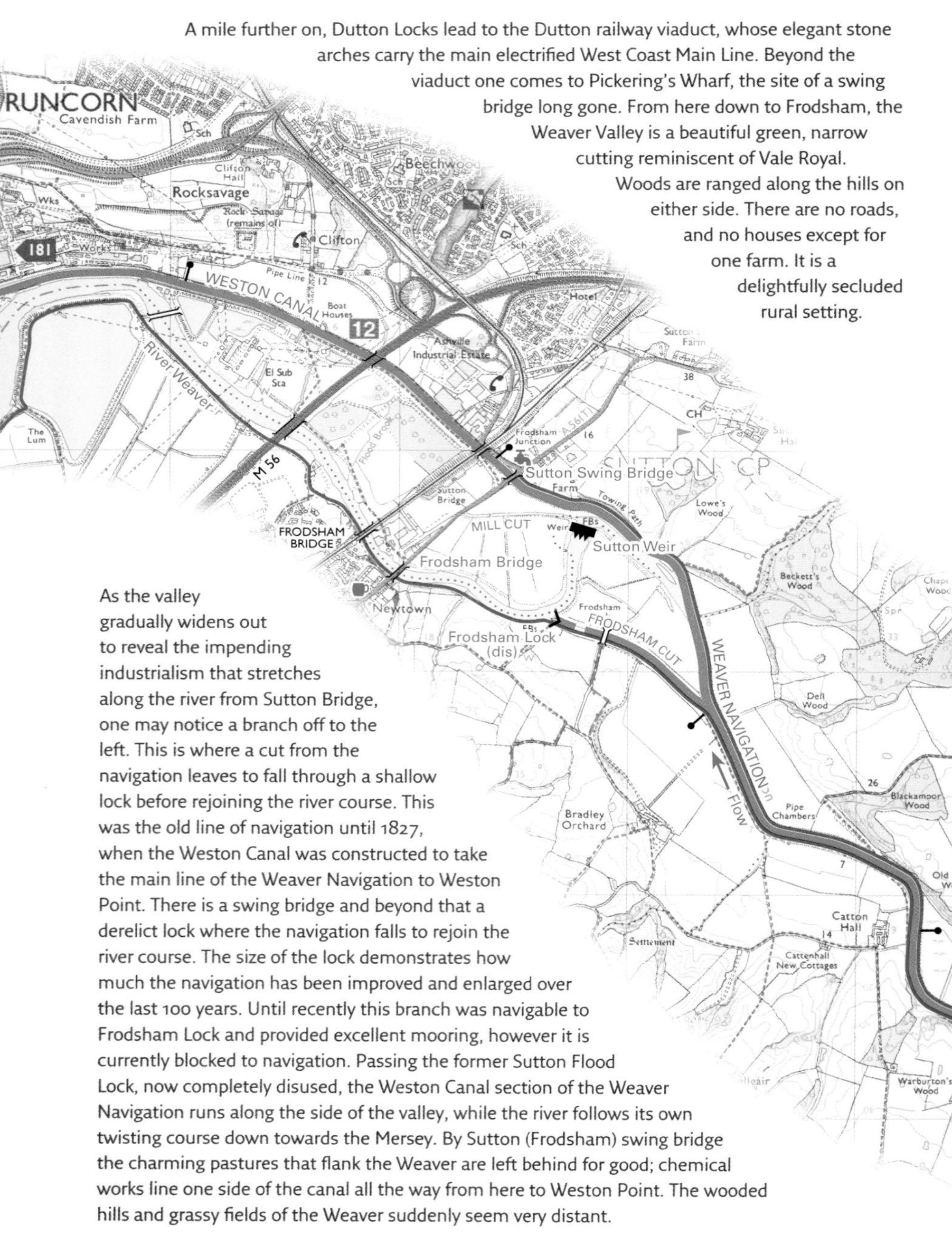

As the valley gradually widens out to reveal the impending industrialism that stretches along the river from Sutton Bridge, one may notice a branch off to the left. This is where a cut from the navigation leaves to fall through a shallow lock before rejoining the river course. This was the old line of navigation until 1827, when the Weston Canal was constructed to take the main line of the Weaver Navigation to Weston Point. There is a swing bridge and beyond that a derelict lock where the navigation falls to rejoin the river course. The size of the lock demonstrates how much the navigation has been improved and enlarged over the last 100 years. Until recently this branch was navigable to Frodsham Lock and provided excellent mooring, however it is currently blocked to navigation. Passing the former Sutton Flood Lock, now completely disused, the Weston Canal section of the Weaver Navigation runs along the side of the valley, while the river follows its own twisting course down towards the Mersey. By Sutton (Frodsham) swing bridge the charming pastures that flank the Weaver are left behind for good; chemical works line one side of the canal all the way from here to Weston Point. The wooded hills and grassy fields of the Weaver suddenly seem very distant.

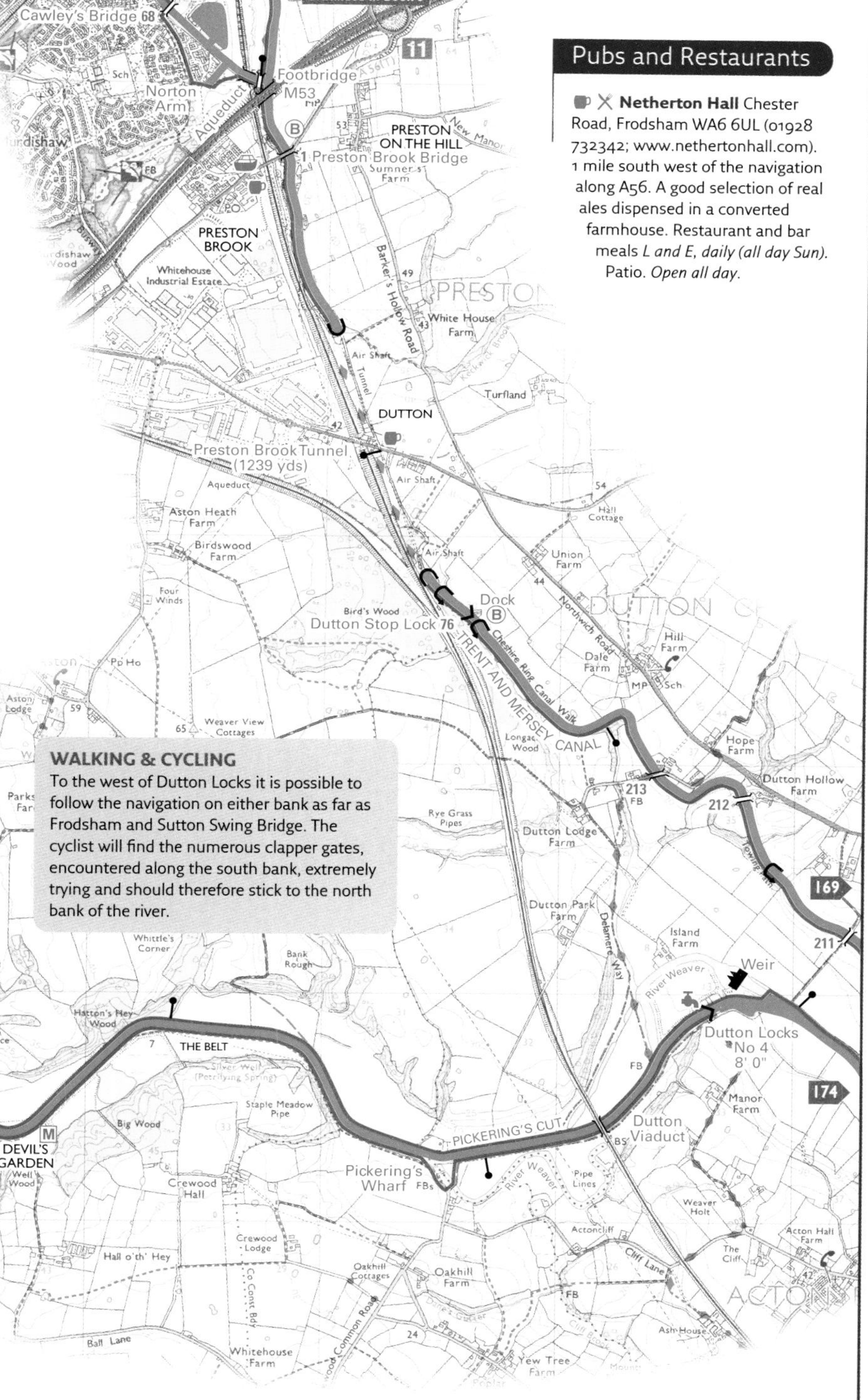

Pubs and Restaurants

Netherton Hall Chester Road, Frodsham WA6 6UL (01928 732342; www.nethertonhall.com). 1 mile south west of the navigation along A56. A good selection of real ales dispensed in a converted farmhouse. Restaurant and bar meals *L and E, daily (all day Sun)*. Patio. *Open all day*.

WALKING & CYCLING

To the west of Dutton Locks it is possible to follow the navigation on either bank as far as Frodsham and Sutton Swing Bridge. The cyclist will find the numerous clapper gates, encountered along the south bank, extremely trying and should therefore stick to the north bank of the river.

Weston Point

At Weston Marsh there is a lock down into the Manchester Ship Canal (*see* Navigational Note below). Beyond here the navigation goes right alongside the Ship Canal from which it is separated by a tall bank. Eventually, after passing the entrance lock up into the abandoned Runcorn & Weston Canal, one arrives at a low (about 5ft) swing bridge. Beyond it are the Weston Point Docks and another lock into the Ship Canal. There are *shops, fish & chips* and *pubs* at Weston Point, through the dock gates.

NAVIGATIONAL NOTES

Those wishing to pass through Weston Marsh Lock should give British Waterways (01606 723800; enquiries.wbc@britishwaterways.co.uk) advance notice and obtain clearance from the Manchester Ship Canal Company (0151 327 1461; www.shipcanal.co.uk). The Inland Waterways Association, North West Region have compiled advice for small craft using the ship canal – visit www.waterways.org.uk and search for 'Manchester Ship Canal'. For full details, including entry into the Shropshire Union Canal (*see* page 116).

Weston Point Docks
The docks, at the junction of the Weaver Navigation's Weston Canal and the Manchester Ship Canal, are an industrial centre. The docks have been modernised and their facilities expanded to handle ships up to 2500 tonnes. However there is currently no one using this facility. *Northern Star* runs regular calcium chloride cargoes from ICI Runcorn's plant, on Weston Canal, to Ireland via Weston Marsh Lock and the Ship Canal.
Christ Church Situated between Weston Point Docks and the Manchester Ship Canal, this church was built by the Weaver Navigation Commissioners. Known as the island church, its tall spire is a distinctive landmark.

Runcorn
Ches. All services. Runcorn's industrial growth began with the completion of the Bridgewater Canal in the latter part of the 18th C. The old town is to be found down by the docks, where the elegant curved 1092ft single span of the steel road bridge (built 1961), with the railway beside, leaps over the Ship Canal and the Mersey. West of the bridge, by the Ship Canal, is Bridgewater House, built by the Duke as a temporary home to enable him to supervise the construction of the Runcorn end of the canal. The massive flight of ten double locks which connected the canal to the Mersey was finally abandoned in 1966, and filled in, much to the dismay of thousands of industrial archaeologists and canal enthusiasts. Since 1964 Runcorn has been a new town, its rapid growth being carefully planned. It is interesting to note that Runcorn, following local government reorganisation, is now part of Halton (which includes Widnes on the north bank of the Mersey), an echo of the time following the Norman Conquest when it was a dependent manor of the Barony of Halton.
Tourist Information Centre 6 Church Street, Runcorn WA7 1LG (01928 576776; www.halton.gov.uk). *Open Mon–Fri, 08.45–13.00 and 14.00–16.00, and Sat 10.00–12.30.*
Norton Priory Tudor Road, Manor Park, Runcorn WA7 1SX (01928 569895; www.nortonpriory.org.uk). The undercroft was the only part of this 11th-C priory to survive the Reformation: now the abbot's lodgings above have been converted into a viewing area from which you can see, with the aid of a recorded commentary, other points of interest. After 1545 the remains of the priory were sold to Sir Richard Brooke for 1s 9d, and he used the stones to build his Tudor manor house. This was demolished around 1750, and a new Georgian house was built. This was finally knocked down in the 1920s. Enjoy the walled garden and modern sculptures, together with the restored 18th-C summer-house by James Wyatt. Also museum, priory remains, woodland gardens, picnic area, family events, croquet area. There are temporary exhibitions, gift and produce shops. Coffee shop. *Open Apr–Oct, weekdays 12.00–17.00, weekends and B Hols 12.00–18.00; Nov–Mar daily 12.00–16.00. Closed Xmas Eve, Boxing Day and New Year's Day.* Charge for over fives. Inexpensive family day tickets. Regular bus service.
Catalyst Mersey Road, Widnes WA8 0DF (0151 420 1121; www.catalyst.org.uk). Unique, award-winning museum of the chemical industry. Interactive exhibits and hands-on displays. 'Industry in view' is a computer and video based exhibition 100ft above the Mersey, embracing spectacular river views. Reconstructions and original film footage trace the development of the industry from ancient times to the present day. Café with riverside views. Shop selling educational toys, etc and activity guide for home-based experiments! *Open Tue–Fri and B Hol Mon 10.00–17.00, Sat and Sun 11.00–17.00. Closed Xmas, Boxing Day and New Year's Day.* Charge for over fives. Inexpensive family tickets. Any Widnes bus will drop you close to the museum.

Pubs and Restaurants

There are plenty of pubs to choose from in Runcorn.

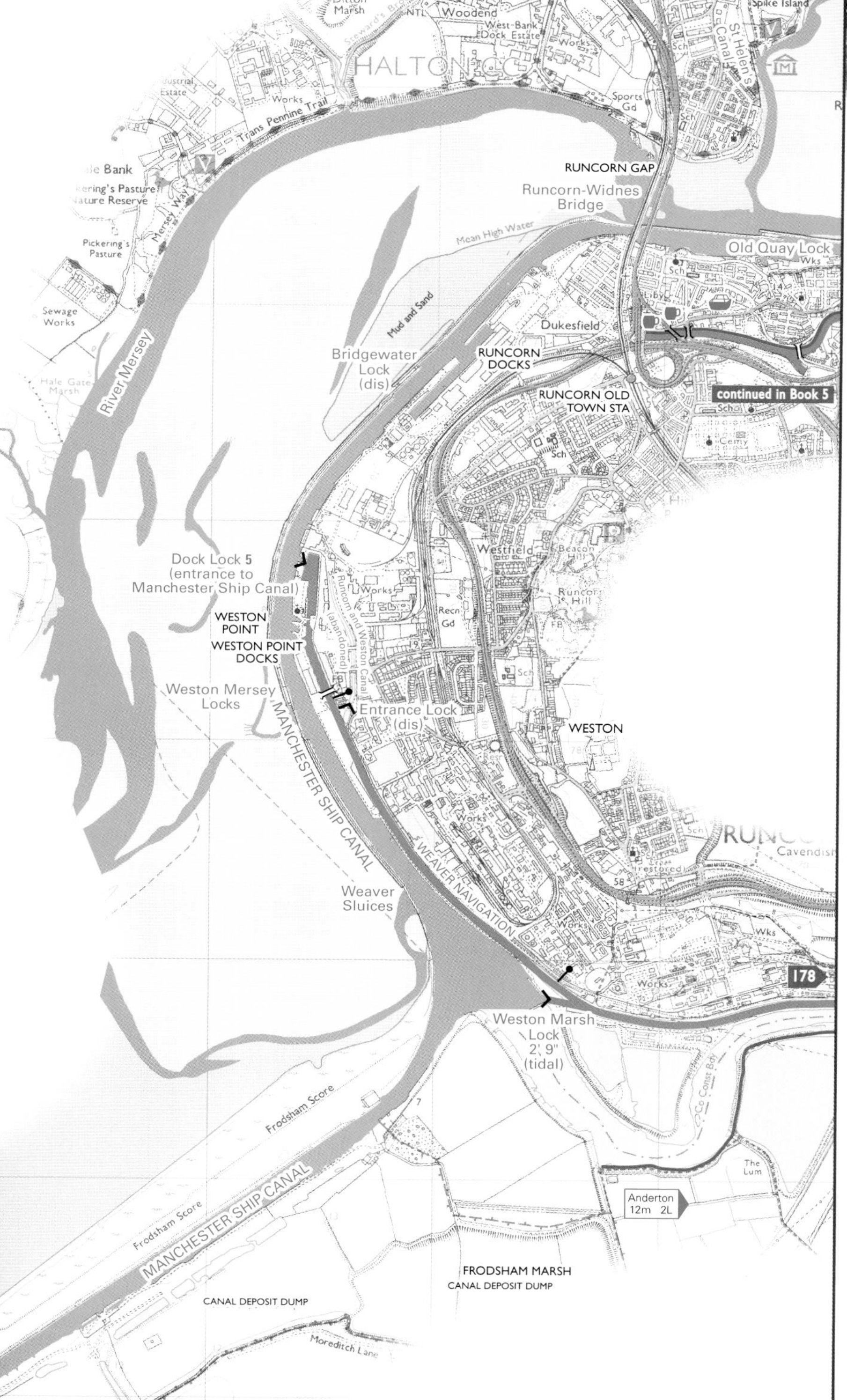
Ditton Marsh
Woodend
West Bank Dock Estate
HALTON
Works
Spike Island
St Helen's Canal
Sports Gd
Trans Pennine Trail
Mersey Way
Pickering's Pasture
Sewage Works
Hale Gate Marsh
River Mersey
RUNCORN GAP
Runcorn-Widnes Bridge
Mean High Water
Old Quay Lock
Wks
Sch
Mud and Sand
Dukesfield
Bridgewater Lock (dis)
RUNCORN DOCKS
RUNCORN OLD TOWN STA
continued in Book 5
Cemy
Westfield
Beacon Hill
Runcorn Hill
Dock Lock 5 (entrance to Manchester Ship Canal)
WESTON POINT
WESTON POINT DOCKS
Runcorn and Weston Canal (abandoned)
Recn Gd
Weston Mersey Locks
Entrance Lock (dis)
WESTON
MANCHESTER SHIP CANAL
WEAVER NAVIGATION
Cavendish
Weaver Sluices
178
Weston Marsh Lock 2' 9" (tidal)
Frodsham Score
Co Const Bdy
The Lum
Anderton 12m 2L
FRODSHAM MARSH
CANAL DEPOSIT DUMP
CANAL DEPOSIT DUMP
Moreditch Lane

INDEX